FROM LISA STREHL
FOR OUR WEDDING 1986

THE BEST OF SHAKER COOKING

THE BEST OF
Shaker Cooking

EDITED BY

AMY BESS WILLIAMS MILLER

AND

PERSIS WELLINGTON FULLER

WITH AN APPRECIATION OF THE
SHAKERS BY

Walter Muir Whitehill

Put your hands to work
and your hearts to God,
and benefits will befall thee.
MOTHER ANN LEE

MACMILLAN PUBLISHING COMPANY
NEW YORK

COLLIER MACMILLAN PUBLISHERS
LONDON

Drawings by Beverly Hallock

Macmillan Publishing Company
866 Third Avenue, New York, N.Y. 10022
Collier Macmillan Canada, Inc.

Library of Congress Cataloging in Publication Data
Main entry under title:
The Best of Shaker Cooking.
Bibliography: p.
Includes index.
1. Cookery, Shaker.   2. Cookery, American.
I. Miller, Amy Bess Williams.   II. Fuller, Persis
Wellington.
TX715.B485634   1985   641.5973   85–13831
ISBN 0–02–584980–8

10 9 8 7 6 5 4 3 2 1

Printed in the United States of America

TO

ELIZABETH TAFT WILLIAMS

·: ACKNOWLEDGMENTS :·

WE ARE deeply grateful to Eldress Gertrude M. Soule of Sabbathday Lake, Maine, for her interest in this book and also for her gentle guidance and assistance to Hancock Shaker Village as it was transformed from a Shaker community to a museum operated for the public.

There have been scores of gifted cooks, present-day "kitchen sisters," whose help at Shaker Kitchen Festivals, dinners and breakfasts for the "World People," and whose contributions to the Good Room shelves have delighted thousands of visitors to Hancock. Several kitchen sisters tested recipes with skill and enthusiasm. Their dedication to good food and high standards has been an inspiration to us and to all cooks. We are indebted also to Mrs. Helen Johnson of the Berkshire County Extension Service and Mr. G. Douglas Bogart of New York for invaluable advice and assistance.

We wish to thank Mrs. Eileen Carmon for completing so efficiently the laborious task of typing the manuscript and Mr. Eugene M. Dodd, Curator of Hancock Shaker Village, for much helpful advice and good suggestions.

We appreciate the visits from many friends of the Shakers who have given us recipes and have shared reminiscences. One person in particular, Haydn Mason, a Pittsfield native, gave us his remembrances of the Hancock Shaker Village as he knew it as a boy.

We are grateful to the many people who have helped put this book into production. All proceeds will go to Shaker Community, Inc., which operates Hancock Shaker Village.

·: CONTENTS :·

C UISINE, of course, is much too fancy a work to be used when thinking of the Shakers. The term Shaker cookery, on the other hand, has a fullness to it, like the thought of bread dough made of stoneground flour as it rises imperceptibly under a towel.

My wife and I, blessed with a persistent interest in the food of early Americans generally, have grown more and more admiring of Shaker cookery ever since we rented a small New Hampshire house not far from Canterbury, where only a few of that village's Believers remained. We've met residents of the Sabbathday Lake Shaker Village in Maine and have tarried in Shakertown, Kentucky, much as outsiders of the nineteenth century were permitted to do. However, the Great Cook Room, as the enormous basement kitchen is called at Hancock Village, is the place where I began to fill in details of a jigsaw picture of Shaker culinary accomplishments.

First it must be made clear that in spite of the celibate lives they led, Shaker men worked closely with women Believers in increasing the efficiency of many kitchen activities. Among their kitchen inventions are a machine for paring apples, a pea sheller, and a dumbwaiter to speed the delivery of food—thus keeping meals hot—from the big kitchen to the upstairs dining room. At Hancock I saw a giant cylindrical oven with shelves that rotate to make possible the simultaneous baking of pies, tarts, and tea cakes. Thirty loaves of bread could be turned out in a single baking, and a system of seven dampers had been devised by male Shakers to make the control of firewood heat as precise as possible.

When sunshine pours in through kitchen windows at Hancock, the light on the warm wooden surfaces and paneled walls makes it hard to think of Shaker cooks as either pietistic or puritanical. The generous space and practical layouts suggest the pleasures of handling food. Today we might call their way of life a commune. They cooked in groups and ate together on the bare tops of beautifully polished trencher tables, using white napkins large enough to spread under their plates as well as over their laps; and the attractiveness of the prepared food—"neatly dished," as the communal etiquette admonished—was all they required as table decoration.

Sometimes cooks and their helpers might leave the kitchens to gather wild food and enjoy the change of scene. "The little band of sisters," one recorded memory tells us, "crossed the fields singing like a flock of young blackbirds on a bright morning. . . . they swing on tangled ropes of grape-vines, gather wild dew-berries and wintergreens. . . . The older sisters now spread their humble feast under a blooming redbud tree. It is more than a feast—songs, mirth, good fellowship! . . . a spotless white cloth is spread on the green turf; great loaves of freshly-baked bread, plump rolls of golden butter, eggs, delicate cakes, and crusty cookies with fruit shrub and creamy milk emerge in abundance from the wide hampers."

During the mid-nineteenth century, a period of overeating, when American menus too often were loaded with preserved meats and fish and excess of starch, Shaker meals were distinguished by vegetables that hadn't been overcooked, along with fresh fruits as they came into season. Shaker manuals warned against boiling out the natural qualities that made roots and greens good to eat as well as good for health.

As the years passed, Shaker cookery began to receive the same kind of admiration that Shaker furniture gets. At Hancock and its sister communities, both food and handcrafts were sold to outsiders, and Shaker labels became symbols of merit. Shaker-designed pottery, kitchen utensils, and a great variety of preserved fruits and vegetables could be bought in markets and also in the communities where they were made.

At Hancock, one of the first buildings that visitors encounter is the Garden House, not far from the often-photographed Round Stone Barn with its turretlike loft and radial stalls for fifty-two cows. Nearby is the colorful geometric pattern of the Herb Garden. Shaker herbs, skillfully used in communal cookery, also were grown for their medicinal value, and the Believers were the first in America to package both seeds and carefully dried herbs.

Instructions for non-Shakers were printed and distributed with the packages of herbs, and recipes appeared from time to time in the periodical called *The Manifesto*. But I'm partial, as are other fans of Shaker simplicity, to many of the "receipts," usually written in longhand, that bear the names of their donors. When chives are on the verge of going to seed in our own garden, we are likely to treat ourselves to "Sister Abigail's Blue Flower Omelet," in which eggs are enhanced first by a delicate aroma, then by the texture of the chive blossoms. With sweet red onions at hand, we turned just the other day to Sister Amelia's method of combining parsley, savory, sage and thyme with minced celery and chicken as a stuffing for a supper of baked onions.

In *The Best of Shaker Cooking*, many of the collected recipes are lifted out of the ordinary by the herbs recommended as seasoning. The recipe for broiled lamb chops ("loin, center cut, or shoulder, cut thick") calls for a paste to be made of oil, pulverized bay leaf, and finely chopped thyme, parsley, marjoram, mint and dry mustard that is spread over the meat. An anonymous Hancock Village cook who had a liking for spices as well as herbs baked her lamb shanks with prunes and apricots and a seasoning of brown sugar, cinnamon, allspice, cloves and chopped fresh mint.

In true provincial cooking, which is what Shaker cooking was to its exponents, all is natural. Most dishes originating in country kitchens require no flourishes, no worldly tricks of the kind that an international chef de cuisine might use as a signature. So it is that Shaker food calls for no knowledge of sophisticated sauces, of risky emulsions of eggs and oils. Like most such regional American dishes, Shaker classics make their own juices in the casseroles in which they braise or roast, and their chemistry and their savor may both be said to be natural.

A case in point is Creamed Sweetbreads with Cider Sauce, an informal combination of meat, vegetables, herbs, country cream and fresh cider that was credited three-quarters of a century ago to a Hancock sister. The sweetbreads require only the removal of membrane and connective tissue after being simmered in acidulated water, and they are blanketed with minced onions, savory and marjoram mixed with butter, cream and cider, and topped with bread crumbs. The result is one of those dishes in which essences blend in the most natural of ways.

The inherent quality of Shaker gastronomy is practical, also. One elder made it clear when to take apples to the cider mill: "Place the apples on the grass on the north or shady side of the barn to mellow," he stipulated. "When at thirty feet distance you catch the fragrant apple aroma, they are ready for the press." In a similar thrifty vein, the famous Shaker Lemon Pie proves how unwilling the sisters were to waste even the skin of a fruit that had to be purchased from afar rather than grown at home. "Slice the lemons as thin as paper, rind and all," the early nineteenth century recipe says. "Place them in a yellow bowl and pour over them 2 cups of sugar. Mix well and let stand for 2 hours or better. . . ." The method for transforming these lemony monacles into a pie for all seasons is given on page 263, and the resulting dessert is likely to stir your guests to applause.

For almost anyone interested in food, the array of recipes in this book must be a delightful prospect. Nothing about Shaker cookery is ersatz. True mastery can't be attained through the use of convenience foods as part of any ingredients, nor can dusty herbs that have been kept for a year or so be a substitute for the fresh cuttings from a window box or a dooryard herb bed. For those who know where the "wild dew-berries" may be gathered, no subterfuge can be countenanced. Shaker cookery is a matter of enjoyable, and delicious, encounters with seasonal ingredients supplied by the natural world. In these times, it is worth jogging the memory to stress the point that really good food is healthy food.

Long ago, Shaker sisters helped to bring art to American cooking. One cosmopolitan visitor in 1886 declared the meal he was served in a Believers' dining room to be "worthy of Delmonico's." Another writer has pointed to the "epicurean touch" of Shaker cooks—"spinach was flavored with rosemary, apple pie with rose water." Even some of today's best professional chefs, who are pleased with their "nouveau" raspberry vinegars, may have unwittingly taken a leaf from the time-darkened pages on which the sisters of Shaker kitchens inscribed many decades earlier their unassuming recipes. Happily for those of you who turn to the pages that follow, there are several raspberry vinegar formulas, one of them perfected a century ago by Eldress Mary Whitcher.

I recommend this as a wonderful book for all who love to cook—it's full of the imaginative ways of people like Eldress Mary.

—EVAN JONES

At Manchester, in England,
This blessed fire began,
And like a flame in stubble,
From house to house it ran:
A few at first receiv'd it,
And did their lusts forsake;
And soon their inward power
Brought on a mighty shake.
—MILLENIAL PRAISES, 1813

THIS inelegant jingle, quoted by the late Edward Deming Andrews at the head of the first chapter of his remarkable study, *The People Called Shakers, A Search for the Perfect Society* (New York, 1953), alludes to the birth on February 29, 1736 of Ann Lees, an unschooled textile worker and cook, who in 1758, at the age of twenty-two, joined the Wardley Society, a group of dissenters led by Quaker tailors living in Bolton-on-the-Moors, a town a dozen miles from Manchester. These religious enthusiasts had fallen under the influence of a radical group of Calvinists from the mountains of the Cevennes, known as "the French Prophets" or "Camisards," who prudently migrated to England after the revocation of the Edict of Nantes in 1685. The Wardley Society, inspired by these "Prophets," took kindly to fasts, trances, prophecies,

heavenly voices, and other "signs." The "mighty shakes" induced by
their spiritual gyrations led to their being called Shaking Quakers, or
Shakers.

Ann Lees in 1762 married a Manchester blacksmith, Abraham Standerin (or Stanley), by whom she had four children. As all four died in infancy, she came to regard their loss as a divine judgment on her "con-
cupiscence" in conceiving them, and before long had concluded that the
cardinal sin was "cohabitation of the sexes." When she carried her pro-
tests into the streets, as some of our neighbors delight in doing today,
she was arrested and imprisoned. While in the Manchester house of cor-
rection, she received "the grand vision of the very transgression of the
first man and woman in the Garden of Eden, the cause wherein all mankind was lost and separated from God"; here, moreover, Christ appeared
to her, delegating her to preach the gospel of the stainless life. Having
been thus miraculously married to the Lord Jesus Christ, she took the
title of "Mother of The New Creation." In accordance with revelations
that a chosen people awaited her in New England, Mother Ann and
eight followers sailed from Liverpool for New York on May 10, 1774.
Although Abraham Standerin was a member of the group, Mother Ann
soon severed her ties with him and was inspired to move up the Hudson
River to a district known as Niskeyuna (now Watervliet) near Albany.
There in the wilderness, she and her followers established the first Shaker
settlement in the New World. There too Mother Ann shortened her
family name from Lees to Lee.

An exuberant revival of New Light Baptists in New Lebanon, New
York; Hancock, Massachusetts; and neighboring towns in the summer of
1779 brought potential converts to Mother Ann Lee at Niskeyuna. The
growing body of Believers attracted the unfavorable attention of the au-
thorities, and, as in England, Mother Ann and some of her followers were
jailed in the summer of 1780. After her release, she traveled through
Massachusetts, Connecticut, and parts of New York State preaching and
exhorting. Although she died at Niskeyuna on September 8, 1784, a year
after her return from this eastward mission, the seed that Mother Ann
Lee had scattered eventually flowered in the establishment of Shaker
communities in Massachusetts at Hancock (1790), Tyringham (1792),
Harvard, and Shirley (1793), and in Connecticut at Enfield (1790–92). In-
directly, her mission led to the establishment of New Hampshire communities at Canterbury (1792) and Enfield (1793), and to those at Alfred
(1793) and Sabbathday Lake (New Gloucester) (1794) in Maine.

After her departure from the visible world, Mother Ann Lee created a church. Her St. Peter was Joseph Meacham, whom she had characterized as "the wisest man that has been born of a woman for six hundred years." "Joseph is my first Bishop," she had stated, "He will have the keys of the Kingdom; he is my Apostle in the Ministry . . . what he does, I do." Father Joseph, as he came to be known among the Believers, promptly designated Lucy Wright as his fellow-leader "in the female line," thus creating a dual order that assumed the equality of the sexes. In the autumn of 1787, Joseph and Lucy concluded that the time had come for all true Shakers to withdraw from the world and for those who were ready, to assemble at New Lebanon, New York. A meeting house had been built there in 1785; various believers in the vicinity offered their houses and lands as the beginning of a venture in Shaker communism. So there came together a company who agreed "to stand as one joint community" to which "they freely gave themselves and services, with all their temporal interest, for the mutual support and benefit of each other, and for other charitable uses, according to the light and revelation of God which they had received." In this community, each member pursued, for the benefit of all, whatever trade or craft he or she had previously practiced for his own profit. Thus, cobblers, blacksmiths, cabinetmakers, tailors, hatmakers, coopers, and the like produced their goods for community use and public sale, while others spun, dyed, and wove, and still others farmed for sustenance and produced garden seeds for sale. Individuals and families flocked in; within a decade the nine other New England and New York communities previously mentioned were established. In 1806, Shaker settlements were founded at Union Village and Watervliet (Beulah), Ohio, and at Pleasant Hill, Kentucky. By 1826, five others had been organized at South Union, Kentucky; West Union (Busro), Indiana; North Union and Whitewater, Ohio; and Sodus Bay, New York.

As the Shaker communities adhered to Mother Ann Lee's prejudice against "cohabitation of the sexes," their membership had to be maintained by external conversion and recruiting rather than by internal combustion. The taste for millennial revelation having diminished in the course of the nineteenth century, the number of converts declined; by the second half of the century, most Shaker communities were shrinking in numbers. In Massachusetts, Tyringham dissolved in 1875, Shirley in 1908, Harvard in 1918; Enfield, Connecticut, gave up in 1917. The seven remaining Shakers at Enfield, New Hampshire, moved to Canterbury in 1923; the survivors of Alfred, Maine, similarly joined forces with those at Sabbathday Lake in 1932. When the Watervliet, New York, community dissolved in 1938, the remaining members moved to New Lebanon; in

1947, the last survivors of New Lebanon crossed the state line to Hancock, Massachusetts, which in its turn dissolved in 1960. Today only the communities at Canterbury, New Hampshire, and Sabbathday Lake, Maine, survive; it seems unlikely that they will outlive their present members.

As vocations to this form of celibate coeducational community life have declined, an avid taste for the products of Shaker craftsmanship has developed in the United States. Museums concerned with the American decorative arts proudly exhibit the elegantly simple products of Shaker cabinetmakers; private collectors pursue them with eagerness. Similarly, persons of no marked religious conviction, with no aversion to the sinful joys of the flesh, are fascinated by the surviving fragments of Shaker life. This is not surprising, for Shaker objects not only came from the age of hand craftsmanship but were made with high standards of excellence and without consideration of profit by men and women to whom time was no object. Joints were tight; drawers and cupboard doors opened effortlessly; nobody ever got a splinter in his finger from a Shaker chair. As designs were of a simple austerity, beauty came from perfection of finish and sensible adaptability to use rather than from superimposed decoration.

With simplicity went a rational decorum of life. Orphan children were brought up and trained in practical arts and crafts so that, if they left the community upon coming of age, they were fitted to make their way in the world. Shakers believed firmly in pure air, well-ventilated bedrooms, and regular bathing. Visitors commented on the neatness and cleanliness of their clothing, no matter what type of work they were engaged in. An English visitor of 1884 to a New England Shaker community observed: "Everything is kept so delicately clean that an air of refinement, not to say luxury, seems to pervade the bedchambers, in spite of their absolute simplicity."

Community life, whether Catholic, Orthodox, Buddhist, or Shaker, tends to engender an innocent gaiety of spirit, an almost childlike delight in simple pleasures. When one's horizon is limited by an enclave, when one's place in a community is fixed, when the days proceed through orderly courses with a set time for everything, small deviations from routine are an exciting novelty that is eagerly enjoyed. The only Shaker eldress that I have had the pleasure of meeting was a brisk, lively, charming elderly lady, thoroughly enjoying the excitement of a visit to the restored village at Hancock. She would have blended imperceptibly into the landscape of the great convent of Las Huelgas at Burgos, although I daresay such a thought would have surprised her had I conveyed it to her.

With the passage of time, the more raucous millennial aspects of early Shakerism had given way to a quiet, simple, New England dignity that helps to explain our 1970 affection for Shaker communities.

When the Harvard, Massachusetts, community dissolved in 1918, Miss Clara Endicott Sears moved one of its buildings to her hillside Fruitlands Museum in the same town and filled it with Shaker artifacts. The Hancock community has a more extensive memorial, for when it dissolved in 1960 a group of sympathetic neighbors organized by Mrs. Lawrence K. Miller of Pittsfield, Massachusetts, created a non-profit organization, Shaker Community, Inc., to buy the Hancock Shaker Village and operate it as a museum open to the public. The only addition has been the fine Shaker meeting house that was moved from Shirley; otherwise, the work of this admirable organization has been the preservation and consolidation of existing buildings and the safeguarding of the singularly beautiful rural landscape in which they stand. This last is of the utmost importance, for Hancock is not far from Pittsfield and is on a convenient highway leading west into New York State. Without the efforts of these friends of history and landscape, the Shaker buildings at Hancock, had they survived, would by now be obscured by an uncorseted suburban sprawl of ranch houses, or the commercial honkytonks that spring up like weeds beside highways. Thanks to Shaker Community, Inc., the Hancock village grows more beautiful every year. The great stone circular barn, which encloses space dramatically as well as practically, is now restored and securely consolidated against New England winters, while the other buildings offer a constantly improving picture of Shaker community life.

Even more recently, in 1968, the remains of the Shaker settlement at Pleasant Hill, Kentucky (founded in 1806, dissolved in 1910), have been opened as a museum by another independent non-profit corporation.

Visiting historic sites seems to make Americans hungry. Perhaps this is an understandable reaction to the clean, standardized mediocrity of victuals offered along superhighways. An escape from the highway into some evocation of the past suggests that food *must* have been better once. Ever since Mrs. Helen Duprey Bullock's *The Art of Williamsburg Cookery* appeared some thirty years ago, there has been a strong tendency to relate cooking and historic preservation, the latest example of which is *The Best of Shaker Cooking*. There is singular appropriateness in this, for Mother Ann Lee was cook in a public infirmary in Manchester at the age of twenty.

Many of the recipes are simple. However, because of the Shakers' extensive use of herbs and spices, their dishes were more exotic than other

American cooking. But, typically American, the primary concern was for simplicity and substance, for several obvious reasons. Those who sat down to table had been working hard. The raw materials were produced on the spot and came to the kitchen without benefit of freezing, travel, or packaging in plastic. In a community, time was no consideration, and the cooking was done over wood or coal, both of which are infinitely superior (gastronomically) to the more painless gas or electricity. When food is carefully produced near its point of origin for hungry people it tastes better.

The Shaker principle was: "Eat hearty and decent, and clear out our plate."

WALTER MUIR WHITEHILL

I N bringing out a new edition of *The Best of Shaker Cooking*, we thought we might devote an additional chapter to one of the most popular and fascinating aspects of Shaker life: cooking with and using Shaker herbs.

At one time there was a certain snobbery about cooking with herbs. It has been said of the late James Beard that he was neither bemused by the "trendy" nor constricted by rigid traditionalism. He believed in using the best of what was available and he taught simple good cooking. His great legacy lives on, as does that, so similar, of the dedicated Shaker Kitchen Sisters.

Whether cooking with herbs is considered fashionable or trendy is a matter for others to debate, we know that it is here to stay. With super-markets, specialty food stores and garden centers offering year-round large selections of dried herbs and, surprisingly, healthy potted and freshly cut herbs, the cook no longer needs a dooryard garden, except for pleasure, in order to produce subtly-flavored dishes. With the medical fraternity in-veighing against salt in the diet, herbs take an important place as a sub-stitute, with no loss of appeal and the advantage of greater variety.

A few years ago Craig Claiborne, renowned bon vivant and cookbook author, went on a low-sodium diet upon the suggestion of his physician. Mr. Claiborne had written, in 1963, *An Herb and Spice Book* (recently reissued in a new edition with the title *Cooking with Herbs and Spices*), so it was not surprising that out of two hundred recipes in his *Gourmet Diet*, published in 1980, ninety-eight called for herbs as seasoning, not for garnish. It is a book to follow for good health whether or not weight is a problem.

Men and women have turned to the kitchen for fun and recreation as well as a matter of necessity. We think the plethora of cookbooks reflects as well as stimulates this renewed interest in good food.

Increasingly, newspaper articles on food preparation, the use of herbs, menu planning for pleasure and practicability and recipes from around the world—all encourage beginners and sustain the seasoned cook. It is not an easy task to write with unjaded palate on a weekly basis.

We have tried to be moderate in our presentation of the Shakers as herbalists. They were not the first to know the importance of herbs or the first to use them in cooking. But as an organization of nineteen large communities in eight states, their influence in the medical and culinary herb field was recognized and duly credited.

In November 1829, the *American Farmer*, a well-known journal of its day, published in Baltimore, reprinted an article from the *New Hampshire Patriot* on farms in that state. The "committee" visited the Shaker farms at Canterbury, examined their gardens and reported that they were the most extensive and "productive of any thing of the kind in this country."

The visiting committee was delighted with the culinary garden at the first family which contained "three acres of perfectly cultivated plants of every variety and all the herbs and roots, useful or necessary for health, all in the most luxuriant state."

However, it was the "botanical garden" which aroused the greatest interest and which the visitors found to be "probably the greatest curiosity in agriculture in the state." There is no mention in the article that similar gardens existed in twenty-three other Shaker villages in nineteen states, but next to the gardens at New Lebanon, New York, the Canterbury gardens, under the direction of Trustee Corbett, were the largest and most productive.

The committee also reported that on this garden of less than an acre "was cultivated two hundred species and genera of roots, plants, herbs and flowers, most of which are of a medicinal nature—cultivated to great perfection." The Shaker responsible for the medicinal herb garden was Elder Thomas Corbett, a skillful manager and horticulturalist who had according to the article made sales in 1828 of one hundred dollars.

The new edition makes it possible to include new recipes discovered in the course of researching our 1976 book *Shaker Herbs*. In the course of that research we found new manuscript material, much of it uncovered for the first time. While it was mainly concerned with medicinal herbs, many day books and some diaries and letters contained recipes using herbs we cook with today.

I hope the readers of this edition will find pleasure in Shaker dishes and share the Shakers' pride in preparing them for others.

IN 1959 a group of thirty people began working with The Shaker Ministry to plan for the preservation and restoration of Hancock Shaker Village. Because there were only three sisters living at the village, which had once contained six "families" and a total membership of about three hundred brethren and sisters, it was decided at this time by the ministry to close the community and dispose of the property.

The village, comprised of eighteen buildings on about one thousand acres of beautiful farm and woodland, is situated in the southeast corner of the small township of Hancock, one of the most beautiful areas in the scenic Berkshire hills of western Massachusetts. It was therefore attractive to many commercial groups, none of whom was interested in the historical aspect of the village. The Shaker Ministry was sympathetic to the group of "new Believers," who were inspired by the Shaker heritage and who resolved to make this village at Hancock a permanent memorial to the movement if it could be acquired for this purpose. This group was greatly honored when the ministry made the decision in favor of its proposal.

Working with Eldress Emma B. King of Canterbury, New Hampshire, head of the society, and Eldress Gertrude M. Soule of Sabbathday Lake, Maine, was a cherished experience for the new group, and no major step was attempted without consultation with these Shaker leaders. Following incorporation of the new organization, Shaker Community, Inc., in 1960, Hancock Shaker Village, a historical museum, was opened to the public the following year. It was dedicated to serve as a living testament to the Shakers and to the contribution they made to the culture of America.

From the beginning it had the wholehearted approval of the Shakers themselves. Eldress Emma stated in reference to the properties of discontinued societies:

The parent ministry has been especially anxious that these lands and buildings be devoted to some use which is charitable or educational and of benefit to the community. . . . It is therefore a satisfaction and a joy to us that the group which will now assume these properties at Hancock will use them for the preservation of the Shaker tradition.

The acquisition of the village was the first successful attempt to save for the future a Shaker settlement. It was also the first step in a unique program of conserving the artifacts and values of an unusually significant way of life and work.

During the ten years following the departure of the last Shakers from Hancock, over 165,000 people have come to the village to study the lovely old buildings on this beautiful farm site, to see at first hand the restoration in progress, and to learn about the remarkable people whose village it had been. The interest of these visitors led to the presentation each August of the "Shaker Kitchen Festival," a week-long program of demonstrations and tastings of typical Shaker foods, and "Dinners for the World People"—the name alluding to the sect's self-imposed isolation.

In the latter part of the nineteenth century the Shakers invited "the people of the world" to their dinner tables, and fond recollections of these occasions have been passed along from one generation to another by word of mouth, by letter, and through an accumulation of recipes from Shaker cooks. Several collections of Shaker recipes have come to us and form a part of this book. They belonged to Mrs. Henry W. Preston, whose mother and grandmother had them from the Watervliet Shakers; Mrs. Frank C. Smith, Jr., and Mrs. Clarence S. Brigham of Worcester, who left us "receipts written down by Shaker cooks" from Harvard and Shirley; and material of a similar nature from Mrs. Oscar P. Tabor of Boscawen, New Hampshire, who often visited with her neighbors, the sisters at Canterbury.

Recipes in manuscript form were made available through many individuals who have come to the village over the past ten years and from the library at the Shaker Museum, Old Chatham, New York, kindness of John S. Williams. In addition several generous friends who wish to remain nameless have turned over family journals with relevant contents. There are also several valuable printed sources: Shaker almanacs dating from 1882 to 1889 with recipes and more recent cookbooks compiled by the existing Shakers at Canterbury and Sabbathday Lake. Many recipes were contributed by the Mt. Lebanon Shakers to *Lebanon Valley Cookery,* originally published in 1889 by Ladies' Guild, Church of Our Savior. We have found these helpful in our research.

In 1953 Caroline B. Piercy of Cleveland, Ohio, published *Not by Bread Alone,* an excellent cookbook which drew much of its material from her mother's old cookbook containing Ohio Shaker recipes as well as recipes from many other communities. William L. Lassiter of Albany, New York, wrote an equally fine *Shaker Receipts* in 1959. Both Mrs. Piercy and Mr. Lassiter have relied as we have on the Shakers' own accounts of food and dietary rules from their monthly publications, *The Shaker, The Shaker and Shakeress,* and *The Manifesto,* which were in continuous publication from 1871 to 1899.

Perhaps the most endearing collection of all is from Mary Whitcher's *Shaker Housekeeper,* the only printed cookbook in early Shaker literature.

Sister Mary, writing from Canterbury, New Hampshire, almost a century ago, wrote the following in her preface:

The Shakers recognize the fact that good food properly cooked and well digested is the basis of good health. The following pages therefore are designed to contribute to that object as far as possible, in the selection and preparation of recipes which are known to be reliable and good, at the same time adapted to the majority of New England homes. The novelty of bills of fare for the dinner of each day of the week is here for the first time introduced. While it is possible that but a small proportion of housekeepers will see fit to follow them exactly, it is, at the same time, hoped that they may suggest something beneficial to them in the preparation of many savory and economical dishes.

Gratefully acknowledging my indebtedness to many friends for the valuable contributions here-in contained and sincerely hoping that this unpretentious book may prove generally acceptable to those who love their homes,

I remain, yours kindly

MARY WHITCHER

Shaker Village, N.H.
March 1, 1882.

Eighty-seven years later we find her work most appealing, and hope that our offering may also help those who share the sweet sisters' love of home.

Amy Bess Miller AND *Persis Fuller*

HANCOCK, MASSACHUSETTS
OCTOBER 1, 1969

THE BEST OF SHAKER COOKING

Note on the Method of Editing

∴

Many of the recipes in this book came to us with ingredients only—obviously the jottings of experienced cooks who formulated their own procedures. We have edited these through testing, keeping whenever possible the Shakers' admirable directness and simplicity. Other recipes, however, have not been edited at all, and are presented in their original form. In many of these "unedited" recipes, the ingredients do not precede the directions. However, we believe you will not have difficulty translating them into usable dishes.

Shaker cooks used rich ingredients in an abundance and variety not always available today. We have not suggested substitutions or economy methods but leave this to the good sense of today's cooks. The Shakers were thrifty and inventive, as seen in many of their dishes. They had to be methodical and careful in order to fulfill their duties. These are admirable traits for us to follow today.

A. B. M. AND P. F.

Quality of Shaker Food

"SHAKER YOUR PLATE" has come down to us as a typical admonition from a people to whom waste was abhorrent and even an affront to God. In a table monitor written for "Our Shaker Home, 1830" and posted in the Visitors' Dining Room two of the eight verses explain:

> We're willing to state—
> Eat hearty and decent,
>   And clear out our plate—
> Be thankful to heaven—
>   For what we receive,
> And not make a mixture
>   or compound to leave
>
> We find of those bounties
>   Which heaven doth give,
> That some live to eat,
>   And, that some eat to live—
> That some think of nothing
>   But pleasing the taste,
> And care very little
>   How much they do waste.

The Shaker sisters were taught to regard their endless labors as a fitting opportunity to serve God. Their sacred commitment and their feeling of equal responsibility with the men in the family in promoting the health and well-being of the large households resulted in food of outstanding quality. If we had to define Shaker food and what makes it different, we would say that it was cooked with a refinement and with a professional skill resulting from the sheer necessity of cooking for large numbers of people and maintaining the high standard which was expected.

The Shakers applied scientific methods in their cooking. For working with vast amounts of food they had to estimate and establish weights and measures and relative amounts. They thought constantly about a balanced diet, and were far ahead of their time in their knowledge of nutrition and food values.

The brethren, under direction of the farm deacons, supplied the best possible produce from the immaculate, well-designed gardens and orchards. Vegetables and fruits were grown in great variety and in quantities sufficient to feed over a hundred people daily. From the large dairies, always shining clean, came buckets of rich milk and cream as well as crocks of golden butter and cheeses superior to any in the neighboring countryside. Bees supplied honey, nuts were harvested from walnut, butternut, and hickory trees on the hillsides, and maples provided vast amounts of the rich syrup. Each Shaker village was almost entirely self-sufficient, and all had splendid herds of fine cattle, hogs and sheep, chickens, ducks, geese and turkeys, supplying all that the family needed for wholesome meals. A visitor records in 1856 that the Shaker community at North Union, Ohio, was most successful in raising high-priced cattle and livestock. "We saw while there," he wrote, "an Angus bull nearly two years old that the herdsman claimed was worth $1500 and some yearling calves that were worth $300 each. . . ."

With such industry on the farm it was logical to avoid waste in the kitchen. The orders for the general organization of the society specifically stated that it be the duty of the deacons and deaconesses to see that suitable food was provided for the family and to assure that the food was cooked with good economy. We could add too that it had to be cooked properly.

Shaker cooking was more than just good plain food. Like Shaker architecture, furniture, and dress, it expressed genuine simplicity, excellence of quality, resourcefulness, and imagination. The sisters did not belong to the "pinch of this or that" school. This is not to say there were not exceptions, for some recipes contained ingredients only when they were exchanged between old friends. But when kitchen deaconesses wrote out the orders, explicit rules were to be followed and perfection was expected.

The kitchen sisters were inspired to follow the words of Mother Ann, their founder, concerning cooking: "See that your victuals are prepared in good order and on time so that when the brethren return from their labors in the fields, they can bless you and eat their food with thankfulness, without murmuring, and thereafter be able to worship in the beauty of holiness."

In their well-equipped nursing houses or infirmaries the Shakers provided well-thought-out diets for the sick and aged. Special meat dishes, fruit wines when indicated, and Shaker tonics and elixirs were a part of the regimen for the elderly. No expense was ever withheld in this area when the need arose. The Shakers solved their old-age problem just as they solved all their problems, by applying the Golden Rule.

A neat little book kept by a nurse has a few rules for food: "Chicken boiled for an invalid or child should always be skinned before cooking —there is a bitter property in the skin which is imparted to the meat in stewing and though not noticeable to the taste, often disagrees with a delicate person. . . ." and in discussing enriched drinks for the elderly this recipe was given: "For one person one glass of the juice of fresh oranges, add one well beaten egg yolk, one tablespoon of nice cream and beat up—a teaspoon of sugar if desired. The drink should be refreshing and cool." In a *Manifesto* for February 1899 an overseer of barns and stock wrote "When overcome by bodily fatigue or exhausted by brain labor no stimulant, so-called, serves so well the purpose of refreshment and rest both bodily and mentally as milk. When heated as hot as one can readily take it, it may be sipped slowly from a tumbler and as it is easily digested one feels very soon its beneficial effect. Few persons realize the stimulating qualities of this simple pure beverage. . . ."

Shaker Kitchens

THE large friendly cookrooms in each Shaker community were precisely arranged in the most efficient way possible to ease the sisters in feeding their large families. Although size alone would classify them as institutional, they somehow escaped the grimness of this category because of the personal concern which characterized the Shaker sisters. There was a careful balance and division of labor in these kitchens, just as in other areas of the villages, and each sister was assigned her particular duties. These were rotated on a regular basis to relieve tedium and hardship, but we know from journals and letters that some were happier in kitchen work than others. All served, however, and all received highly prized instruction and training. When in later years some of the young sisters left the Shakers to marry and live in "the World," they were grateful for the knowledge they had acquired, for it fitted them admirably for house-keeping in their own homes.

The kitchens were organized into a series of specially related rooms. A composite picture of this culinary domain would include a main kitchen, a large separate bake room, a baker's buttery, a serving kitchen and its buttery, with storage rooms for fruits and vegetables leading from it. Then there would be the scullery storeroom and a Good Room (for the very best of all pantry supplies) next to it. The storage of rain water would be conveniently and centrally located, and there was always provision for a cooling system near the larder.

The early Shakers built special-purpose ovens into the walls of their kitchens. Separate ovens for bread and a different one for pies were built near the iron kettles, and flat wrought iron "griddle stoves" were used before the range made its appearance. These built-in kettles of several sizes were called "arch kettles" as they were generally "arched over" with brick on the top side; they were fired by wood from an iron box enclosed by a hinged door at the bottom of the oven. The kettles for soups or for steaming vegetables and puddings were generous, sometimes holding as much as forty to fifty gallons.

In some Shaker kitchens, especially in the South, fireplaces were used for cooking as well as for producing heat, and in some of the northern Shaker kitchens one or two fireplaces were built for use awaiting the completion of the vast bake ovens.

In the 1830s ranges became available, and shortly thereafter, heat indicator dials appeared on oven doors. Such favorites as "The Happy Thought," "The Forest Burner," and "The Glenwood Range" were obtainable commercially, and soon made their way to community kitchens. Heat was regulated by drafts and the amount of wood or coal used. It is not surprising, therefore, that many recipes used by the kitchen sisters had directions for preheating ovens as early as 1840.

Shaker bake ovens were varied and ingenious. One oven found at Canterbury consisted of a series of graduated round shelves all of which revolved. The main bake oven at Hancock, built in 1830, had a series of seven dampers arranged to regulate the heat. Its commodious shelves easily held thirty large loaf pans. The same chimney piece also supported a round pie oven whose three shelves could be used for muffins, rolls, gems, and biscuits if the kitchen sisters were devoting their baking entirely to breads.

"Everything in its place and a place for everything" helped to avoid confusion with so many women working at one time. The spacious cookrooms were colorful and sometimes comfortable, although this was not intentional, as Shakers shunned any luxury, ornamentation, or artfulness. Crisply pleated white curtains covered the lower half of the windows, permitting as much daylight as possible to stream into the rooms. Bright brass and copper basins, sieves and ladles in all sizes were hung from peg boards on the whitewashed walls or were arranged on ample red-stained work tables. Although the Shakers made almost every article they used, they did not manufacture glassware or earthenware, but purchased the best available to them at stores in nearby towns, or ordered from more distant shops. Rich brown and yellowy crockery filled corners or flat wall cupboards, and gray jugs with blue designs and the familiar imprint of the potteries of Bennington, Vermont, and New York State were raised to convenient heights on yellow stools in all work areas. A book of invoices in the library at Hancock Shaker Village covering the period between 1856–1861 supports the fact that the best Sandwich glass was supplied for the "Nurse-shops," for use in the dwellings, and to fill the needs of the herb industry. Glass tumblers were purchased for seventy-five cents a gross for the dining room. Although later recipes were written in a standardized way, earlier ones, especially in manuscript, mention "buttermilk in the blue and white pitcher" or "beat eggs in the yellow bowl with blue stripe." Quantity was in this way established, for the round little jug probably held just two cups, and the yellow bowl was perfect for beating exactly a dozen eggs.

Prints and photographs of the early kitchens show businesslike work stools in front of straight-legged tables. A hanging wall desk with cupboard above and below the writing ledge helped a sister whose duty it was to keep records. An armed rocking chair was placed beside a bright window for an older sister, but primarily the busy kitchen was a professional workroom divided into logical departments to facilitate preparation of the daily meals.

Seasonal activity was streamlined when vast amounts of fruits and vegetables were canned and preserved for winter consumption or for sale to the World. In many communities the canning, drying, and preserving of fruits and vegetables was a lucrative industry. We know for instance that when white sugar became available to the Kentucky Shakers, they recorded that 3,008 jars of peaches had been canned for the market. When a thousand apple trees were producing at New Lebanon,* an elder remarked about the output of cider and applesauce as being "formidable

---

*New Lebanon was used by the New York Shakers until 1861 and Mt. Lebanon thereafter.

in amount." The distribution of produce from Shaker farms was indeed awesome, and they were justly but discreetly proud to have their products sold as far south as New Orleans and "west, beyond Indiana." The high quality of their goods created a great demand for everything the Shakers produced. A wholesale grocer in Albany who placed large orders with the Mt. Lebanon Shakers wrote: "I never have to count boxes, cans or jars or be concerned with quality, taste and conformity, for their products are constantly superior."

The warmth and heart of a great Shaker household could be found in its kitchen. We like this lively hymn by a Shakeress, Hanna Brownson, because to us the inner joy referred to is one of the most endearing qualities of the Shakers. She wrote it as a consequence of a story which claimed that the Shakers put some kind of seed into their cakes which made those who partook of it wish to remain among them:

SPIRITUAL CAKE

As I have been informed of late,
There's something in the Shaker Cake
That does make souls contented here.
I'll now unfold the matter clear,
To all who have got eyes to see,
I will unveil this mystery;
And tell them plainly how to make,
And feast upon the Shaker Cake.

'Tis called in Scripture "living bread,"
Because it quickens from the dead,
It saves the soul from sin and strife,
'Tis therefore called the "bread of life,"
'Tis not much matter what's the name,
For lo! in substance 'tis the same;
Some call it cake with tempting seed,
'Tis that by which the soul is freed.

Though human wisdom cannot scan
How this supports the inner man;
And while the soul is fed thereby,
A carnal nature has to die.
No earthly substance we employ,
But just our inward peace and joy,
Nor is it any natural yeast
That gives us this continual feast.

First, by an honest heart within,
Confessing and forsaking sin,
Gives us a taste of this good cake,
Thus hidden manna we partake.
'Tis seasoned with the seed of grace,
Which strengthens us to run the race;
To quit all vain and earthly ties,
And run that we may win the prize.

And those who do all sin forsake,
May freely feast on this good cake;
We know it is by heaven designed
Both to adorn and feast the mind.
It fills our souls with great delight,
Though 'tis to nature out of sight,
It is a substance we enjoy,
Which death and hell cannot destroy.

When'er enquirers come to see,
This cake is set before them free,
And if they love it, surely, they
Will quit their sins and want to stay.
But if the appetite is low,
The stomach must be cleansed, you know
For while they in the broad way roam,
Their souls will loathe an honey-comb.

And when the system is made clean,
From all that's base or foul within,
They're able to discern the good,
And feast upon this heavenly food.
But if they slight this precious cake,
And our emetics will not take,
We give them up, if they refuse
To serve the master which they choose.

Dining Habits

As the proof of the pudding is in the eating, we are glad to find so many contemporary accounts of the good Shaker food and how it was served. David R. Lamson, who lived for two years with the Hancock Shakers, writing about his experiences in 1848, said, "all conversation in the dining room was strictly forbidden. The sisters who prepared the food also waited on table—and when an individual wished anything which was not before him, he beckoned to a sister who was in waiting and made known to her his wish in a low whisper." Mr. Lamson mentioned one particular evening meal when there was served "oyster soup, succotash, and rice puddings with a very fine selection of breads and preserves" and said that the tables were arranged so that the people sat in groups of four, and platters and serving dishes were adequately filled for this number within easy reach. The food was eaten hastily, the meal not taking much more than fifteen minutes.

In 1858 Hervey Elkins tells his experience of *Fifteen Years in the Senior Order of Shakers:* "In the summer the signal for rising is heard at half past four, in the winter at half past five; meals are punctually served, breakfast an hour and a half after rising, dinner always at high noon and supper at six. These rules are, however, slightly modified upon the Sabbath. They rise and breakfast on this day half an hour later, dine lightly at twelve and sup at four. Every order maintains the same regularity in regards to the meals." Then he goes on to say that at a given signal the large household entered the dining hall, the sisters by one door to the right and the brethren to the left, where they each had their own long table. They arranged themselves "gently" at their respective places at table where they knelt simultaneously "in silent prayer for nearly a minute," rose and seated themselves noiselessly. Eating in silence was apparently in consideration for the staff of sisters working in the kitchen, for it did hasten the meal. When all were satisfied, they rose at the signal of the head elder, fell upon their knees thanking God for His bounty, and quietly filed out of the dining room to their various tasks without stopping or loitering in the halls.

In some Shaker dwellings the central dining room was on the same floor as the kitchens, in others it was on the floor above as at the Hancock Church Family. When this was the case the food was sent up by means of two "sliding shelves" or dumbwaiters, one at each end of the room. These shelves were commodious enough to hold the heavy platters, pots, and tureens and were operated by a system of pulleys and wheels, later mechanized in keeping with the times. When the dining room was above the kitchen a small "water pantry" or auxiliary kitchen was next to the dining room to facilitate service. Some Shaker families provided a separate visitors' dining room, where the table was set with more elaborate glass, china, and silver and where a linen tablecloth would be laid. Bare tables in the family dining hall were sparsely set with milk or cream jugs, salt, pepper, and sugar cruets, with ample individual napkins which could be tucked under the plate and spread upon the lap for protection.

It was not unusual to have a special dining room for the ministry with its own outer door, and a separate room was generally provided for the farm help. Sometimes the ministry ate in the general dining room, but at a separate table. An account appearing in a *Manifesto* (February 1890) discussing Shaker food states: "Before 1823 the tables were set with pewter plates, while the bread was placed on plates made of wood. The supper on Christmas and frequently on the Sabbath was the most sumptuous meal as we served roast fowl, various kinds of pie, cake, preserves, agreeable to the custom of the country in those days. Since the above date [1823] crockery made of porcelain has been more generally used."

In another *Manifesto*, Hester A. Pool, a visitor, describes a visit to Mt. Lebanon—1888.

All are hard workers, leaders and teachers as well as common members. Rising before five o'clock in the morning, each group of men and women repair to their respective duties. Two sisters take charge of the dining room, two of the bake-room and two of the kitchen, the latter a large handsome room fitted with every convenience and exquisite with its well oiled floor and rows of burnished sauce-pans. The Brethren have devised unheard of comforts for the indoor workers and the visitor leaves with the feeling of pity for the housewife who does her cooking in the ordinary way. . . . The food is of the best quality and generous in quantity. Almost no use is made of flesh food and home grown and ground cereals are cooked to perfection. Such vegetables plucked within the hour, and such pies, shortened with sweet cream and filled with fresh fruit or that preserved by their own peculiar process, we mutually confessed to have never tasted before. . . .

Miss Pool referred to a time when vegetarianism was being promoted and there was actually a ban on meat, which lasted ten years (1837–1847). However, it was very hard to enforce this regimen throughout Shakerdom even at Mt. Lebanon, where it originated and had the backing of Elder Frederick W. Evans and Eldress Anna White. There were special tables for those believing in "the bloodless diet," while a smaller number of people followed a "regular diet." In time, according to one report, "the whole family united and found as the years passed that the abundant diet of grains, vegetables, fruits, eggs, and milk products has answered every physiological need as well as satisfying the conscience of the consumer." Although many excellent meatless dishes were created during this period, vegetarianism did not have a lasting influence.

From their own accounts we know that the Shakers were well provided with wholesome, interesting, and bountiful meals. However, this was not always so. In the early history of the society, the people were sometimes reduced to very simple fare, and their provisions were almost wholly the product of their own labors. Instances are recorded when bread and broth formed the greater part of the meal and indeed when even this frugal repast was reduced. Looking back to these lean years an article in *The Manifesto* of February 1890 records:

At times potatoes and bread with a small quantity of bean porridge was all that could be afforded. As the people increased in financial prosperity every other temporal blessing moved along in the same ratio. At this early date a liberal use was made of swine's flesh especially during the winter season. As industrious farmers, they made every acre of land which they tilled produce in abundance and in a very few years they were able to use all that was needed and to bestow much upon the poor. Tea and coffee were freely used and at noon a liberal supply of good cider. It might be quite difficult for us to judge these hardy pioneers by what we may be able to do as they had many advantages that have not fallen to our lot. As we look back and view the road over which they traveled we not only become interested, but we wonder at their power of endurance, as the largest part of them walked upon the earth for nearly a century before they said their last farewell.

The writer goes on to give a complete and accurate account of life in the early days of the Shakers, and we are indeed grateful to this good reporter who concludes:

The chewing and smoking of tobacco were used with the same freedom as the cider and the pork as this was the universal custom of the people; it came with them into the community and remained with them until they perceived more advanced light on the subject. Very little thought was given to the study of hygiene and still less to the food which they ate from day to day. Hot biscuits and butter with meat, potatoes, cabbage, and turnips were sometimes served for breakfast while for dinner they had pork steak or beef, with the vegetables of the season. For supper many preferred bread and milk.

Pies were on the table for breakfast and supper, but rarely for dinner. Cider, which had been used on the table till the present years [1890], was almost wholly abandoned. In these sacrifices there may have been a deprivation to some persons, while at the same time it was a great advantage to the body of Believers as a whole. [Cider referred to was hard cider as fresh cider could not be kept "kind" very long after pressing. It was not pasteurized as is most of our cider today and became a very strong drink.] Our table has not been wanting for variety in good substantial, healthy food, and this prepared in the best and nicest manner. Simple though it may have been when compared with those who abound in wealth, yet we know that it has abundantly supplied all our needs, and for which we thank the Giver of all good gifts. Our table now is set with some kind of meat or eggs, and all the vegetables of the season, and these served in a variety of ways for taste or pleasure. With these come the various sauces and condiments. The apples, cherries, peaches put into pies and always the good puddings and other desserts with nuts and sweetmeats.

The 1890 bill of fare differs very little from the account of earlier meals except for the exclusion of cider, but in the mind of the writer there was apparently a greater refinement in the menu, as well as a greater understanding of nutrition.

Herbs

AN introduction to Shaker food is not complete without an extensive discussion of the Shakers as herbalists. As early as 1800 the Shakers in New Lebanon, New York, and other communities were growing, drying, and harvesting medicinal herbs for the market as one of their chief industries. Shaker cooks used herbs so liberally in cooking that a separate chapter on herbs could easily be the largest of all. Many Shaker recipes call for one or two herbs to flavor or to heal. The Shakers understood the value of herbs as medicine, and the kitchen sisters relied upon them to vary and enrich standard dishes.

The Shakers were the first people in this country to grow herbs on a large scale for the pharmaceutical market. Medicinal plants, chiefly wild herbs, were gathered in enormous quantities; some of these herbs were sold for the purpose of purchasing other medicines, while other medicinal herbs were used by the physicians in the communities. However, as the demand for herbs from the World grew greater, an industry developed, and in all branches of the United Society of Believers, this became one of the most lucrative of Shaker enterprises.

Culinary herbs were grown by the acre, sage being one of the largest crops. Orders were filled for amazing quantities and shipped widely in this country as well as abroad. Hence, this couplet, which appeared on the title page of a Shaker catalogue printed in 1833:

> Why send to Europe's distant shores
> For plants which grow at our own doors?

Wild herbs were gathered to supplement those grown in the Shakers' own gardens. We read in a Hancock journal, "Brothers and sisters spent long mornings gathering roots and plants" and "to Pittsfield, Mass., after sweetflag." Following this entry appears:

Behold, I have given you every herb bearing seed, which is upon the face of the earth . . . to you it shall be for meat.

Genesis, 1:29

Although many country folk gathered herbs in the late eighteenth and early nineteenth centuries to fulfill a part of their daily needs, principally for medicinal purposes, people living in cities had infrequent access to secluded streams, wayside fields, and far-off woods. It was in the successful growing and merchandising of a wide variety of drug, and to a lesser extent, culinary plants that the Shakers built up a truly thriving industry and established themselves as America's first reputable manufacturing druggists in the East and Midwest.

The herb and physic gardens at New Lebanon, New York, prospered from the very first. By the middle 1800s they were producing such quantities that in one season seventy-five tons of medicinal roots and plants were grown, dried, pressed, packed, and shipped to every state in the Union as well as to London, Paris, Australia, and Bombay, India; a fact noted in 1831 by Professor C. S. Raffinesque, a well-known French-American botanist, who commented that "the best medical gardens in the United States are those established by the communities of Shakers or modern Essenes." At this time Canterbury and Enfield, New Hampshire; Harvard and Hancock, Massachusetts; Watervliet, New York; Enfield, Connecticut; New Gloucester (Sabbathday Lake), Maine; Union Village,

Ohio; and other societies were developing their herb industries concurrently with that of the parent order at New Lebanon.

A catalogue issued by the Shakers just prior to the Civil War offered 354 kinds of medicinal plants, barks, roots, seeds, and flowers as well as nearly equal amounts of preparations, including extracts, powders, elixirs and ointments. The Shakers learned an enormous amount of herb lore from their friends the Indians, and many of the wild plants collected by them and later transplanted to their commercial fields were originally Indian materia medica.

The Shakers were renowned as good business people. They considered their societies not "one great community of temporal interest," but several communities or families separately organized, differing in locations, business abilities, industrial pursuits, and the number of members. Yet several families would unite in an industry or a business venture. They would maintain a common store, or distribute their manufactured articles together. A good example of this was their joint efforts in the herb and garden seed business.

In Conclusion

THE Shakers have had a beneficial influence upon our present-day eating habits and further knowledge of their beliefs and practices in this area will be even more helpful in our daily living. They fought adulteration of food products, abhorred waste, and were moderate in their eating habits. While some of their recipes may seem excessively rich and fattening to us today, we must remember that they ate in moderation and thrived on a well-balanced diet. Their intelligent approach to food values and nutrition in general, to good housekeeping practices, to the use of natural foods and the preparation of all dishes with loving care should touch and benefit us as it did so many thousands of the Believers whose legacy of perfection we inherit. They said, "Trifles make perfection, but perfection is no trifle." Mother Ann Lee herself exhorted her children to "Do all your work as though you had a thousand years to live, and as you would if you knew you must die tomorrow," and "Put your hands to work and your hearts to God, and benefits will befall thee."

1685 Revocation of Edict of Nantes, by Louis XIV, followed by escape of Camisards or French Prophets to England.

1706 French Prophets (radical Calvinists) opened meetings near London.

1736 *Manchester, England*—Birth of Ann Lee, February 29. Founder of Shaker Society.

1742 Private baptism of Ann Lee—June 1 in Church of England.

1747 Society of religious dissenters founded by James and Jane Wardley, Quaker tailors living in Bolton-on-the-Moors—a little town twelve miles from Manchester. They were influenced by the French Prophets and held meetings with them.

1758 Ann Lee, twenty-two years old, joined the Wardley Society.

1762 Ann Lee married to Abraham Standerin (or Stanley). Four children born of this marriage died at birth or in infancy. Last child died in October 1766.

1768 Ascendancy of Ann Lee to leadership in the society, gradually replacing Mother Jane Wardley as head of sect sometimes called Shaking Quakers because of a mighty shaking and trembling during religious meetings.

1772 Ann Lee arrested and imprisoned July 14 for disturbing the peace. Sentenced to a month in prison.

1773 Ann Lee rearrested and imprisoned. Received remarkable visions directing her "to seek freedom in the New Land." She is acknowledged as the Shaker leader and spiritual Mother of "The Church of God."

1774   Mother Ann and eight followers sailed for America. Arrived New York City Sunday, August 6, 1774, following a hazardous trip of three months from Liverpool on board the ship *Mariah* (Captain Smith of New York).

1775   Mother Ann severed ties with Abraham Stanley, her husband. Joined members of her party who had moved up the Hudson River to Niskeyuna,[1] later called Watervliet.

1776   At Niskeyuna, New York, entire group now settled in its first Shaker home in the cleared woods about seven miles northwest of Albany. Hardships and fervent converting to the faith followed.

1779–80 Religious revival at New Lebanon, New York, of the New Light Baptists. Leaders visited Mother Ann at Niskeyuna and many were converted to the Shaker faith.

1781–83 Mother Ann toured extensively in Massachusetts, Connecticut, and parts of New York State. This resulted in strengthening the Believers at Hancock, Tyringham, Harvard, and Shirley, Massachusetts; Enfield, Connecticut; and New Lebanon, New York. Communities were eventually established in those towns and the foundation was laid for two in New Hampshire and two in Maine.

1784   Mother Ann Lee, aged forty-eight, died at Niskeyuna September 8, a year after her return from the strenuous eastward mission. Elder James Whittaker succeeded as head of the church.

List of Shaker Societies

ESTABLISHED	DISSOLVED	
1787	1938	Watervliet (Niskeyuna), New York
1787	1947	New (or Mt.) Lebanon, New York
1790	1960	Hancock, Massachusetts
1960		Shaker Community, Inc., established to operate Hancock Shaker Village as a museum open to the public.
1790–92	1917	Enfield, Connecticut
1792	STILL ACTIVE	Canterbury, New Hampshire

[1]Also spelled Niskayuna.

1792	1875	Tyringham, Massachusetts
1793	1932	Alfred, Maine
1793	1923	Enfield, New Hampshire
1793	1918	Harvard, Massachusetts
1793	1908	Shirley, Massachusetts
1794	STILL ACTIVE	Sabbathday Lake (New Gloucester), Maine
1806	1910	(Dayton) Watervliet (Beulah), Ohio
1806	1910	Pleasant Hill, Kentucky
1961		Independent, non-profit, corporation organized to operate Pleasant Hill. Opened to the public in 1968 as a museum.
1807–10	1922	South Union, Kentucky
1810–11	1827	West Union (Busro), Indiana
1822	1889	North Union (Cleveland), Ohio
1824–25	1907	Whitewater, Ohio
1826	1895	Sodus Bay and Groveland, New York

Missions, Branches, "Out Families," and Short-lived Communities

1808	1819	Gorham, Maine—members moved to New Gloucester, Maine.
1817	1825	Savoy, Massachusetts—members moved to New Lebanon, Canaan, and Watervliet, New York.
GROUP MEETINGS 1780		Cheshire, Richmond, and Ashfield, Massachusetts —group meetings in the 1780s were absorbed into the organized communities.
1808		Straight Creek, Ohio—short-lived.
1813	1897	Canaan, New York—Lower Family 1813–1884; Upper Family 1813–1897.
1822	1823	Darby, Ohio
1826	1836	Sodus Bay, Sodus Point, or Port Bay, New York
1846		Philadelphia, Pennsylvania—moved to Watervliet after a few years. Revived temporarily in 1860.
1894		Narcoossee, Florida—branch of New Lebanon, New York, existed several years.
1898		White Oak, Georgia—soon abandoned.

ADVICE TO CHILDREN
on
Behaviour at Table

∵

FIRST, in the morning, when you rise,
Give thanks to GOD, who well supplies
Our various wants, and gives us food,
Wholesome, nutritious, sweet, and good:
Then to some proper place repair,
And wash your hands and face with care;
And ne'er the table once disgrace
With dirty hands or dirty face.
When to your meals you have the call,
Promptly attend, both great and small;
Then kneel and pray, with closed eyes,
That GOD will bless these rich supplies.
When at the table you sit down,
Sit straight and trim, nor laugh nor
frown;
Then let the elder first begin,
And all unite, and follow him.
Of bread, then take a decent piece,
Nor splash about the fat and grease;
But cut your meat both neat and square,
And take of both an equal share.
Also, of bones you'll take your due,
For bones and meat together grew.
If, from some incapacity,
With fat your stomach don't agree,
Or if you cannot pick a bone,
You'll please to let them both alone.
Potatoes, cabbage, turnip, beet,
And every kind of thing you eat,
Must neatly on your plate be laid,
Before you eat with pliant blade:
Nor ever—'tis an awkward matter,
To eat or sip out of the platter.
If bread and butter be your fare,
Or biscuit, and you find there are
Pieces enough, then take your slice,
And spread it over, thin and nice,
On one side, only; then you may
Eat in a decent, comely way.
Yet butter you must never spread
On nut-cake, pie, or diet-bread;
Or bread with milk, or bread with meat,
Butter with these you may not eat.
These things are all the best of food,
And need not butter to be good.
When bread or pie you cut or break,
Touch only what you mean to take;
And have no prints of fingers seen
On that that's left—nay, if they're clean.
Be careful, when you take a sip
Of liquid, don't extend your lip

So far that one may fairly think
That cup and all you mean to drink.
Then clean your knife—don't lick it,
pray;
It is a nasty, shameful way—
But wipe it on a piece of bread,
Which snugly by your plate is laid.
Thus clean your knife, before you pass
It into plum or apple-sauce,
Or butter, which you must cut nice,
Both square and true as polish'd dice.
Cut not a pickle with a blade
Whose side with grease is overlaid;
And always take your equal share
Of coarse as well as luscious fare.
Don't pick your teeth, or ears, or nose,
Nor scratch your head, nor tonk your
toes;
Nor belch nor sniff, nor jest nor pun,
Nor have the least of play or fun.
If you're oblig'd to cough or sneeze,
Your handkerchief you'll quickly seize,
And timely shun the foul disgrace
Of splattering either food or face.
Drink neither water, cider, beer,
With greasy lip or mucus tear;
Nor fill your mouth with food, and then
Drink, lest you blow it out again.
And when you've finish'd your repast,
Clean plate, knife, fork—then, at the
last,
Upon your plate lay knife and fork,
And pile your bones of beef and pork:
But if no plate, you may as well
Lay knife and fork both parallel.
Pick up your crumbs, and, where you
eat,
Keep all things decent, clean, and neat;
Then rise, and kneel in thankfulness
To HIM who does your portion bless;
Then straightly from the table walk,
Nor stop to handle things, nor talk.
If we mean never to offend,
To every gift we must attend,
Respecting meetings, work, or food,
And doing all things as we should.
Thus joy and comfort we shall find,
Love, quietness, and peace of mind;
Pure heavenly Union will increase,
And every evil work will cease.

Soups and Chowders

IN SHAKER KITCHENS large iron kettles were used for making rich, nourishing stews, soups, and chowders, which would bubble all day long in the winter to provide a supper dish. More delicate soups, such as bisques, oyster stews, and fine broths for the ailing would be made in enamel kettles on the range, or on top of an arch, as they did not require such long cooking time.

Shaker discipline permeated every phase of daily life, and every member of a community worked steadily, but without undue pressure. There was great fairness in the planning of strenuous work and, on occasion, outside labor was employed for special help in the fields, in building, and in various industrial enterprises. There was no servant class but the "hired hands" ate and slept apart from "the family"—and it was often noted in *The Manifesto* that, alas, it had been necessary to hire help.

A series of soup recipes is headed "for extra help at dinner" as it was not the regular custom to provide soup with the Shaker noon dinner. This was served as a meal in itself for supper.

CREAM OF ASPARAGUS SOUP

HANCOCK SHAKER VILLAGE

1 pound fresh asparagus
2 cups water
1 small onion, thinly sliced
1½ cups chicken stock
2 tablespoons butter

2 tablespoons flour
2 cups scalded milk
½ cup cream
Salt, pepper

⟨Cut asparagus free of tough ends. Cut 2 inch tips off and reserve. Cut remainder of stalks into small pieces, cover with water, bring to boil, and cook 10 minutes uncovered. Add onion and chicken stock and cook to reduce broth further. Remove from fire and force through sieve. Make thickening by melting butter, adding flour and hot milk. Cook 5 minutes, stirring to keep smooth. Add to sieved pulp. Heat and remove from stove. Add cream and seasonings and tips. SERVES 4.

BAKED BEAN SOUP

HANCOCK SHAKER VILLAGE

It is not surprising to find several very tempting recipes for Baked Bean Soup as this bean pot dish was a staple in all Shaker communities. The soups varied; some recipes called for tomato, some not, and some added fried salt pork as a garnish.

3 cups cold baked beans
6 cups water
2 slices onion
2 stalks celery with leaves
1½ cups stewed and strained tomatoes

1 tablespoon chili sauce
1 teaspoon salt
½ teaspoon pepper
1 teaspoon sugar
2 tablespoons butter
2 tablespoons flour

⟨Put beans, water, onion, and celery in saucepan; bring to boiling point, and then simmer 30 minutes. Rub through a sieve, add tomato, chili sauce, and seasonings. Melt butter, add flour, cook 2 minutes and add to tomato mixture. Cook together and heat through.

Mustard and/or horse-radish was also used by the Hancock Shakers to season Baked Bean Soup. SERVES 6.

BEAN CHOWDER
HANCOCK SHAKER VILLAGE

1 pint dried white beans
½ pound salt pork, diced
2 onions diced
1 quart canned tomatoes with juice

¼ teaspoon pepper
2 teaspoons salt
2 tablespoons molasses or brown
    sugar

⟨[Soak beans overnight or for at least 6 hours in water to cover. Fry the salt pork and onions together until the onions are somewhat soft and the pork is beginning to brown. Bring the beans to a boil, add the fried pork and onions, and then simmer gently. Continue to cook until beans are tender (approximately 30 minutes), adding water as necessary. Add tomatoes and seasonings, including the molasses or brown sugar. Simmer 30 minutes longer. Put part of the beans through a sieve to give a smooth base to the chowder. Dried split peas can be used in a similar way, with or without the tomatoes. SERVES 4–6.

BLACK BEAN SOUP #1
HANCOCK SHAKER VILLAGE

1 quart black beans
2 quarts cold water
3 tablespoons butter
½ cup chopped celery
1 medium onion, chopped
1 pound round of beef

½ pound salt pork
1 teaspoon black pepper
2 teaspoons salt
½ teaspoon dry mustard
Hard-boiled egg slices (optional)
Lemon slices (optional)

⟨[In a large kettle soak beans overnight in water to cover. Drain. Return to kettle and add cold water. Melt butter in saucepan. Cook celery and onion and add to beans. Cube beef and salt pork and add to beans with seasonings. Simmer 3 or 4 hours or until beans are soft. Add more water if necessary.

This makes a thick soup. For a thinner and less hearty soup, strain it. Garnish with sliced egg and lemon. SERVES 6–8.

BLACK BEAN SOUP #2
HANCOCK SHAKER VILLAGE

⟨[Take 1 quart of black beans. Soak them overnight in water to cover. Next day drain and put them in a pot with more water to cover. Add a piece of the round of beef—about 1 pound—and ½ pound of salt pork. Simmer and when beans are reduced to a pulp, strain through a colander and return to the fire putting in 1 cup of finely chopped celery, some chopped red pepper, and some onion. This should be done long before dinner is ready so it can simmer (uncovered) 3 or 4 hours. You may have to add more water. Add salt if need be. The longer the soup simmers the better. SERVES 8.

DELICIOUS BEEF TEA FOR THE INFIRMARY
HANCOCK SHAKER VILLAGE

1 pound lean fresh beef
1 teaspoon salt
A sprig parsley

One or two celery leaves
1 pint cold water

⟨Cut the beef into small pieces and put into a bottle with the salt, parsley, and celery leaves; add a pint of cold water and cork tightly. Put the bottle in a saucepan of lukewarm water and let it come to a boil gradually. Continue to boil for 3 or 4 hours. Uncork, strain, and serve with toasted Diet Bread*[1] or Breakfast Biscuit (a cracker). SERVES 2.

CHICKEN SOUP
HANCOCK SHAKER VILLAGE

¾ cup butter
¾ cup flour
1 cup rich warm milk
1½ quarts hot chicken stock
1 cup warm light cream

1½ cups chopped cooked chicken
1 teaspoon salt
½ teaspoon white pepper
1 teaspoon sugar

⟨Blend butter and flour in soup kettle until well mixed. Cook 3 minutes. Combine milk, 2 cups of the stock, and cream; heat, but do not boil. Add to butter and flour gradually, stirring constantly until thickened.

Add remaining chicken stock, cooked chicken, salt and pepper, and sugar. Heat but do not boil. Makes enough for 18 cups or 12 bowls.

CLAM CHOWDER
SABBATHDAY LAKE SHAKER VILLAGE

⟨Use an 8 quart kettle, put in 2 quarts of diced potatoes and one 16

---

[1]Recipes marked with an asterisk may be found by consulting the Index.

ounce can of minced clams with juice. Cover potatoes and clams with water.

In a frying pan melt a quarter of a pound of butter, add 4 thinly cut medium size onions, and sauté until tender; put this into kettle and add 1 quart of milk and 1 cup of cream or evaporated milk. Season to taste. SERVES 24.

CLAM SOUP #1
SHIRLEY SHAKER VILLAGE

2 cups water
1 quart clams, raw and unshelled
and their liquor
2 teaspoons butter
1 bay leaf
½ teaspoon mace
1 tablespoon finely minced celery

1 tablespoon finely minced onion
1 teaspoon each salt and pepper
2 cups cream
1 teaspoon minced thyme
1 tablespoon minced chives
(optional)

⟨Bring water to a boil, add clams and their liquor and simmer 10 minutes. They must not be overcooked for fear of toughening the clams. Add the rest of the ingredients except cream, thyme, and chives. Cook slowly 20 minutes. Remove clams and chop them, return to broth. Add cream. Add minced thyme and chives, if available, to pot for flavor. Serve at once. SERVES 4.

CLAM SOUP #2
HANCOCK SHAKER VILLAGE

1 quart clams, shucked, cleaned and
picked over
½ cup butter
2 tablespoons flour
4 cups milk

1 slice onion
1½ teaspoons salt
⅛ teaspoon pepper
½ teaspoon nutmeg
1 egg white, beaten stiff

⟨Drain clams from their liquid. Reserve liquor and sieve to have it free of shells. There should be about ¾ of a cup. Put soft part of clams aside. Chop hard part of clams, and add this to the liquor. Bring gradually to a boil, strain through sieve getting as much purée as possible. Cook butter and flour together 3 minutes. Scald milk with onion—remove onion, add milk and stock to roux. Add seasonings and soft part of clams. Bring to a boil. Pour over egg white in a tureen. SERVES 4.

CRANBERRY BEAN SOUP
HANCOCK SHAKER VILLAGE

2 cups cranberry beans[1]
1½ quarts water
1 teaspoon salt
1 teaspoon black pepper
2 tablespoons butter
2 tablespoons olive oil
2 onions, minced
1 clove garlic, minced

1 small carrot, chopped
1 tablespoon minced basil
1 teaspoon minced thyme
1 teaspoon minced summer savory
½ teaspoon dry mustard
1 teaspoon Worcestershire sauce
2 tablespoons dry sherry

⟨[Soak beans overnight or for 8 hours. Drain. Add 1½ quarts water, salt, and pepper. Simmer covered over slow heat. In a fry pan melt butter, add oil, onions, and garlic. Cook slowly 10 minutes, do not burn. Add carrot and herbs. Cook 5 minutes and add mixture to beans. Cover and simmer slowly 3 hours. Remove beans from liquor, purée them, and return pulp to liquor. Add mustard, Worcestershire sauce. Heat again. Add sherry, but do not boil. Serve at once with croutons. SERVES 4.

SALT CODFISH CHOWDER
MT. LEBANON SHAKER VILLAGE

1 pound salt codfish
½ pound salt pork
2 medium onions, diced
6 cups boiled diced potatoes

2 quarts rich milk
8 soda crackers, softened in milk
8 soda crackers, toasted and buttered

⟨[Flake codfish and soak in lukewarm water until the fish is soft and the salt has been removed. Drain and discard water, which will be too salty to use. Dice salt pork, fry until light brown, and reserve. Add the onions and when slightly browned, add potatoes and cover with water. Boil up, but do not overcook as potatoes have already been boiled. Add milk and fish, heat through, and simmer 25 to 30 minutes. Add soda crackers which have been moistened in milk. This is to thicken the stew. Transfer it to a table tureen. Float salt pork on top and toasted buttered crackers broken in pieces, to garnish. SERVES 4–6.

---

[1]These are pink and are also known as succotash beans. There is a good canned source.

CORN CHOWDER
HANCOCK SHAKER VILLAGE

4 tablespoons diced salt pork
1 tablespoon butter
1 medium onion, sliced
3 potatoes, peeled and finely diced
2 cups chicken stock
2 cups corn scraped from the cob *or*

2 cups home canned corn (called home style)
4 cups whole milk
Salt and pepper
1 cup heavy cream
3 tablespoons butter

❲Fry salt pork in butter, remove pieces when crispy and reserve. Add onion to fat and sauté until golden. Add potatoes and stock and cook slowly until soft. Add corn and milk, lower heat, and simmer until corn is tender. Young corn takes 5 minutes. (Dried corn which has been freshened will take longer.) Add salt and pepper. Bring to a boil and remove from heat. Add cream and butter. Stir up well and pour into soup plates or tureen. Float pork on top. SERVES 6.

GREEN CORN SOUP
MARY WHITCHER'S SHAKER HOUSEKEEPER

2 cups freshly grated green (young) corn
2 cups water
1 teaspoon salt
⅛ teaspoon pepper

½ teaspoon sugar
2 tablespoons butter
1 tablespoon flour
2 cups whole milk
1 onion, whole

❲Grate and scrape the corn from the cob; boil in water 5 minutes. Add salt, pepper, and sugar. Melt butter in skillet and blend in flour. Cook 3 minutes. Mix with milk, stir well, and combine the two mixtures. Drop in the whole onion and cook slowly for 10 minutes. Remove onion and serve very hot with crisp buttered crackers. SERVES 6.

CORN SOUP
HANCOCK SHAKER VILLAGE

❲Boil 4 cups of corn, cut from the cob, in 6 cups of water; when the grains are quite tender, mix with them 2 tablespoons of sweet butter rolled in a tablespoon of flour. Let it boil 15 minutes longer. Just before taking up the soup, beat up an egg in a cup of cream and stir it in with ½ teaspoon pepper, 1 teaspoon salt, and 1 teaspoon sugar. SERVES 6.

FISH CHOWDER

FRANCES HALL, HANCOCK SHAKER VILLAGE

2 pounds haddock
4 cups cubed potatoes
¼ pound salt pork or 6 slices bacon
2 onions, chopped fine
1 quart milk

Fish stock (reserved from boiled
 haddock)
1 cup heavy cream
1 tablespoon butter (optional)

([Boil fish until tender in water to cover (about 2 cups). Remove any skin and bones. Reserve any liquid. Move to chowder kettle.

Boil potatoes in water to cover. When cooked, drain and add to fish.

Fry salt pork or bacon, cut in 1 inch cubes. Remove from fat and reserve. Fry onion in fat until tender, add to fish and potatoes. Add 1 quart of milk to fish, potatoes, and onion mixture. Simmer covered 20 minutes and cool.

This dish is best made several hours or a day before serving. Twenty minutes before serving, add reserved stock, if any, bring to a boil, remove from stove. Add cream and salt pork or bacon. A tablespoon of butter can be added too. SERVES 6.

HERB SOUP

HANCOCK SHAKER VILLAGE

2 quarts rich beef stock, clarified
2 teaspoons salt
2 teaspoons sugar
½ teaspoon thyme
½ teaspoon marjoram
⅛ teaspoon ground cumin seed
 (optional, but is nice and spicy)

½ teaspoon celery seeds
6 peppercorns
1 clove garlic, crushed
1 large onion, chopped
¼ cup chopped parsley
2 large ripe tomatoes, skinned and
 chopped

([To clarify beef stock, skim off fat when stock is cool. Simmer stock, with salt, sugar, herbs, and spices for 30 minutes. Add garlic, onion, parsley, and tomatoes. Cook, simmering 15 minutes. SERVES 4.

SHAKER HERB SOUP
SISTER AMELIA'S SHAKER RECEIPTS

1 tablespoon butter
2 tablespoons chopped chives
2 tablespoons minced chervil
2 tablespoons minced sorrel
½ teaspoon finely cut tarragon
1 cup finely cut celery
1 quart chicken broth

Salt and pepper to taste
Suggestion of sugar
6 slices white toast
Dash nutmeg
Grated Cheddar or American
  cheese

⟨[Melt butter in skillet, then add herbs and celery, and simmer for 3 minutes. Add broth and seasonings. Cook gently for 20 minutes. Place slices of toast in tureen and pour soup over them. Add nutmeg and sprinkle with grated cheese. Serve very hot. SERVES 4–6.

INFIRMARY BROTH
MT. LEBANON SHAKER VILLAGE

2 quarts rich chicken or beef broth
1 to 2 pounds veal knuckle
½ teaspoon salt
½ cup cooked rice

4 teaspoons sugar
8 lemon slices
Sprigs of fresh parsley for garnish

⟨[Strain chicken or beef broth so that it is free of sediment and bone. Let it simmer up with veal knuckle for 1 hour to increase its strength and goodness. Strain again. Add salt. In each soup dish put 1 tablespoon of rice, a dash of sugar. Fill with broth. Float slice of lemon and sprig or two of parsley. SERVES 8.

LENTIL SOUP
MT. LEBANON SHAKER VILLAGE

1 cup brown lentils
1½ quarts water
1 teaspoon salt
2 slices bacon
3 tablespoons butter
1 onion, minced
1 clove garlic, minced
2 teaspoons parsley

2 teaspoons winter savory
1 carrot
2 stalks celery with leaves
2 teaspoons horse-radish
1 teaspoon salt
1 teaspoon pepper
1 lemon, cut into 6 slices

⟨Pick lentils over carefully and wash. Soak overnight. In proceeding, drain them. Put into 1½ quarts water with salt and cut-up bacon. Simmer covered 3 hours. Melt butter in fry pan, and fry onion and garlic slowly for 10 minutes. Add herbs and vegetables and cook 10 minutes more. Add this mixture to lentils after they have cooked for the first hour. Drain lentils and vegetables. Purée the mixture, return to liquid. Add horse-radish and seasonings. Mix well. Put slice of lemon in each soup plate. Makes 6 servings.

∴

In the fall of the year there were extensive butchering operations at Shaker villages. The kitchen deaconesses would ask for and get "one leg of beef [saved] for the soup kettle."

OKRA SOUP

MARY WHITCHER'S SHAKER HOUSEKEEPER

This is a hearty stew, translated for today's cook to serve 6.

2 pounds stewing beef or chuck steak	½ pound fresh or 8 ounce package frozen okra
1 pound soup bone	
2 carrots, cut up	2 tablespoons butter
8 tomatoes, cut up	3 tablespoons salt
2 onions, chopped	1 tablespoon pepper

⟨Cover meat with water in a 3 quart soup kettle. Add bone and bring to a boil. Turn heat to low and add all vegetables except okra. Simmer covered for 3 hours. Remove bone, and skim the fat off top. Cut meat into small pieces and return to soup. Add okra, butter, and seasonings and simmer uncovered 30 minutes longer before serving.

OYSTER SOUP

SHAKER ALMANAC, 1882

1 cup butter	2 cups milk
2 teaspoons salt	1 quart water, boiling
1 teaspoon pepper	1 quart shelled oysters and their liquor
8 large soda (or saltine) crackers, rolled fine (This should amount to 1 cup)	

⟨Melt butter, add seasonings and cracker meal. Stir to a paste and add milk, heat, stirring until smooth. Add boiling water and let whole come to a boiling heat. Put in oysters and their liquor. Soup should boil 2 minutes and be removed from the fire to a hot tureen. SERVES 8.

OYSTER CREAM SOUP

HARVARD SHAKER VILLAGE

1 pint shucked oysters and their
 liquor
2 tablespoons butter
2 tablespoons flour

2 cups light cream
1 cup heavy cream, whipped
Salt and pepper to taste

⟨[Poach the oysters in their own liquor over low heat until they are plump. Remove from the liquor and chop as fine as possible. Put to one side. You should have ½ cup oyster liquor; if not, add enough water to make ½ cup.

Melt butter in the top of double boiler over hot water, add flour. Blend and cook 2 minutes. Add the light cream and cook, stirring constantly until mixture is smooth and thick. Add reserved oyster liquor. Combine chopped oysters with whipped cream. Stir this mixture into the hot soup. Season to taste. Serve at once. SERVES 6.

OYSTER SOUP WITH HERBS

MT. LEBANON SHAKER VILLAGE

1 pint oysters out of shell
1 cup finely chopped carrots
½ cup finely chopped onions
1½ cups finely chopped potatoes
2 cups water
3 tablespoons lemon juice
White Sauce #2* (use 2 cups milk)

1 cup heavy cream
1 tablespoon butter
2 tablespoons finely chopped parsley
 or chervil or one of each, or savory
 or marjoram
Powdered cloves or nutmeg

⟨[Drain oysters from their liquid (reserve liquid) and chop. Put to one side. Cook carrots, onions, and potatoes in water until tender. Drain. Discard excess water. This should be a thick puree. Add lemon juice, salt and pepper to taste. Add oysters.

Make white sauce. Cook gently and add reserved oyster liquid. Gradually add this sauce to vegetable and oyster mixture. Add cream and 1 tablespoon butter. Do not boil, but heat through. Add chopped herbs[1] and a dusting of powdered cloves or nutmeg.

----

[1]Herbs given are mild.

OYSTER STEW

MANUSCRIPT FROM SHAKER MUSEUM
OLD CHATHAM, NEW YORK

2 quarts new milk
Salt and pepper
1 quart oysters with liquor, picked
over to remove all shells

½ cup butter
2 large soda crackers, pounded well
1 cup cream

([Put milk on stove, let it heat. Add a little salt and pepper. Add oysters and butter. Bring to a good boil. Add crackers and cream and serve. SERVES 8.

SHAKER PEASE PORRIDGE

NORTH UNION SHAKER VILLAGE, OHIO

2 cups split peas
1 quart beef stock
2 onions, diced
2 carrots, diced
2 stalks celery, cut in inch pieces

1 turnip, diced
1 teaspoon salt
¼ teaspoon pepper
Dash sugar
2 tablespoons butter

([Soak peas overnight in very little water. Simmer covered in beef stock for 2 hours. Add onions, carrots, celery, turnip, and seasonings. Cook slowly another 30 minutes. Pass through a coarse sieve. Add butter just before serving. Serve very hot with well-buttered rye bread croutons. SERVES 4.

PERCH CHOWDER

MANUSCRIPT FROM SHAKER MUSEUM
OLD CHATHAM, NEW YORK

4½ pounds perch
¼ cup good sherry or cider
1 teaspoon dried thyme
2 whole cloves
½ teaspoon salt
½ teaspoon pepper
½ cup thinly sliced onions

⅓ cup well-scraped cut-up celery
stalk
½ cup carrot cubes
1 teaspoon chopped green pepper
3 teaspoons butter
2 cups heavy cream

([From the meat of the fish, fillet at least 1½ pounds of boneless strips and cut into 2 inch lengths. Cover with sherry or cider and let stand 30 minutes. Cut remainder of fish in pieces, put in a kettle with water to cover, add thyme, cloves, salt, and pepper. Simmer 30 minutes. Strain and cook vegetables in the fish broth until tender. In the meanwhile gently simmer the strips of perch in 3 teaspoons of butter 5 to 10 minutes, not longer as they must hold shape. Combine fillets with broth and vegetables. Scald cream and add. SERVES 4.

∴

Many Shaker communities were located near very good fresh water lakes, and there are accounts of fishing excursions in journals and under "Society Items" in *The Manifesto*. One entry relates the pleasure of the outing, but notes there was nothing to show for it. However, when the catch was good there was chowder for supper.

POTATO SOUP
MT. LEBANON SHAKER VILLAGE

⟪Peel, boil, mash, and strain 6 medium-sized potatoes. Chop fine 2 small onions. Bring to a boil 2 tablespoonfuls of either barley or rice in 2 quarts of cold water. When the water and rice mixture boils, add the onions, cook 1 hour. Add mashed potatoes, season to taste. This needs a good lot of pepper. Add a little butter or cream. SERVES 4.

HERB POTATO SOUP #1
HANCOCK SHAKER VILLAGE

8 medium potatoes, peeled	2 teaspoons salt
2 onions, chopped	1 teaspoon pepper
4 tablespoons butter	2 teaspoons sugar
2 tablespoons chopped parsley	2 cups cold milk
1 teaspoon chopped thyme	4 cups scalded milk
1 teaspoon chopped marjoram	2 cups hot potato water
4 tablespoons flour	2 tablespoons chopped parsley

⟪Cook potatoes and onions together in saucepan until potatoes are tender. Drain—save potato water. Put potatoes and onions through ricer. Melt butter in a heavy 6 quart saucepan and add parsley, thyme, and marjoram. Blend in flour, salt, pepper, and sugar. Gradually stir in cold milk. Add scalded milk and potato water. Cook over medium heat; stir constantly until mixture thickens slightly. Stir in potatoes and onions. Heat. Serve in tureen. Sprinkle with parsley. Makes 12 cups.

HERB POTATO SOUP #2

SISTER OLIVE, HANCOCK SHAKER VILLAGE

[Boil 5 or 6 potatoes with a small piece of salt pork and a little celery in water to cover. Pass through a colander. Add 1 quart milk or cream (if milk, also add a little butter) to make the consistency of thick cream. Add a little chopped parsley. Add 2 teaspoons each of chopped marjoram and savory. Let boil 5 minutes.

Cut some dry bread in small cube-like pieces. Fry in hot lard until brown. Drain and place in bottom of soup tureen and pour the soup over. Salt and pepper to please. Chop 2 onions and boil with the soup if liked. SERVES 4.

OLD-FASHIONED POTATO SOUP

MARY WHITCHER'S SHAKER HOUSEKEEPER

4 pounds small potatoes	2 quarts milk
2 tablespoons caraway seeds	2 tablespoons finely chopped
2 teaspoons salt	marjoram
2 quarts water	1 teaspoon paprika
6 small leeks, chopped	6 strips crisp bacon, minced

[Scrub the potatoes thoroughly. Do not peel (the peelings add greatly to the flavor and nourishment while cooking), but place in soup pot whole with caraway seeds, salt, and water. Cook very slowly for half an hour. Remove potatoes, peel and cut fine; put back into pot with liquor in which they were cooked. Add the leeks, tops and all, cut fine. Cook for half an hour and pass through a coarse sieve. Add milk. Heat well. Add marjoram, paprika, and more salt, if necessary. Garnish with minced crisp bacon. Serve with toasted crackers. SERVES 8.

POTATO AND ONION SOUP

SHIRLEY SHAKER VILLAGE

[Take 2 onions, slice thinly, fry until golden brown, in a lump of butter. Clean and cut 3 pared potatoes very small—lay them on top of the onions until they too are brown. Pour over them ½ pint of milk, salt and pepper to taste. Cook slowly until tender about ½ an hour. Boil up (bring to a boil) and remove from stove, stir in 1 cup heavy cream. Sprinkle with finely chopped parsley. SERVES 4.

POTATO STEW
(Also Called Winter Soup)
HANCOCK SHAKER VILLAGE

Potato stew was served for supper in Hancock, and the kitchen sister added "I never seem to make enough." She suggested serving nice rich fruit preserves for dessert or Jam Cake.

1 two inch cube salt pork, diced	1 cup water
2 medium-sized onions, peeled and diced	White Sauce #2*
	1 cup heavy cream
2 medium-sized potatoes, peeled and diced	Salt and pepper
2 medium-sized parsnips, peeled and diced	

❡[In a soup kettle, fry salt pork slowly and remove scraps when they are crisp. Sauté onion in fat until golden brown but not burned. Add diced potatoes and parsnips. Cover with the water and cook slowly until vegetables are tender. Make white sauce. Cook until smooth. When vegetables are very tender add this white sauce. Mix well and simmer to combine all flavors. Have cream at room temperature. Boil up stew and remove from fire. Add cream and salt and pepper just before pouring into tureen. Float pieces of crisp salt pork on top. SERVES 4–6.

TOMATO BISQUE
FRANCES HALL, HANCOCK SHAKER VILLAGE, 1907

2 cups strained cooked tomatoes	1 teaspoon salt
1 teaspoon butter	1 teaspoon sugar
1 teaspoon flour	1 quart hot milk
⅓ teaspoon baking soda	½ cup heavy cream

❡[Purée tomatoes. Melt butter, add flour. Cook 2 minutes. Add to tomato purée and add soda, salt, and sugar. Simmer 15 minutes. Heat milk and combine with tomato mixture. When hot remove from stove and then add ½ cup cream. Very delicate. SERVES 4.

TOMATO SOUP

SISTER OLIVE, HANCOCK SHAKER VILLAGE

½ teaspoon baking soda
1 quart peeled very ripe tomatoes
½ gallon (2 quarts) whole milk
1 teaspoon salt
1 teaspoon pepper

1 teaspoon mace
1 teaspoon sugar
2 tablespoons butter
8 saltines, finely crushed

⁅Add soda to tomatoes, mash and stew until they are completely cooked. Boil milk. Add tomatoes and stir well. Let all boil together, including seasonings, for 5 minutes. Add butter and just before serving thicken with finely crushed crackers. SERVES 10.

ELDRESS CLYMENA'S TOMATO SOUP

NORTH UNION SHAKER VILLAGE, OHIO

24 medium-sized ripe tomatoes
2 stalks celery, chopped
2 tablespoons minced green pepper
2 bay leaves
2 large basil leaves, freshly chopped
1 teaspoon salt

1 teaspoon sugar
Dash cayenne
1 tablespoon minced parsley
1 teaspoon onion juice
1 teaspoon lemon juice
½ cup whipped cream, lightly salted

⁅Do not skin tomatoes; cut in quarters and place in heavy pot with celery, green peppers, bay leaves, and basil. Cover tightly and simmer 20 minutes without adding any water. Pass through a sieve; add seasonings, parsley, onion juice, and lemon juice and allow soup to come to a boil. Pour into hot soup bowls and top with lightly salted whipped cream. SERVES 6.

FORCEMEAT BALLS FOR SOUP

HANCOCK SHAKER VILLAGE

⁅Chop ⅔ cup raw beef, veal or chicken very fine or grind. Add flour enough to make it stick together in balls about the size of a walnut. Roll in flour and fry in butter until golden brown. Add to soup just before serving. Use beef and/or veal meat for Black Bean Soup,* veal or chicken for Chicken Soup,* beef for beef broth or consommé.

VEGETABLE BARLEY SOUP

HANCOCK SHAKER VILLAGE

A good-sized (soup) marrow bone
 (2–3 pounds), cracked
1 pound chuck beef, cubed
2 tablespoons butter
2½ quarts water
1½ teaspoons salt
1½ teaspoons sugar
¼ teaspoon pepper
2 tablespoons minced parsley

¼ cup barley
1 cup diced carrots
2 cups cooked skinless tomatoes
¼ cup finely chopped onions
½ cup finely chopped celery
1 cup peas
1 cup cubed potatoes
½ cup chopped cabbage

⟨[Put soup bone in large kettle. Brown beef lightly in butter, add to kettle. Add water, salt, sugar, pepper, and parsley. Bring to boil, cover, and simmer 1 hour. Skim surface occasionally. Add barley and simmer 1 hour longer. Add carrots, tomatoes, onions, and celery. All vegetables should be chopped fine. Cover. Simmer 45 minutes. Add remaining ingredients. Simmer 15 minutes longer. SERVES 6–8.

SPRING VEGETABLE SOUP

SISTER AMELIA'S SHAKER RECEIPTS

1 tablespoon butter
2 leeks, sliced
3 stalks celery, sliced
3 sprigs fresh parsley, chopped
2 parsley roots, chopped
¼ cup chopped green pepper
1 cup shredded lettuce
2 quarts chicken broth

3 medium-size potatoes, sliced
1 carrot, sliced
1 teaspoon salt
1 teaspoon pepper
1 teaspoon sugar
All vegetables should be in very fine
 pieces

⟨[Melt butter and add leeks, celery, and parsley sprigs and roots, being careful not to brown. Blanch the green pepper and lettuce in boiling water for 1 minute. Drain. Heat broth and pour over all vegetables including potatoes and carrot. Add seasonings and cook slowly for 20 minutes. Serve very hot with toasted buttered crackers. SERVES 4–6.

EGG BALLS FOR SOUP
HANCOCK SHAKER VILLAGE

([Boil 4 eggs until hard, put into cold water. Peel eggs and mash yolks with yolk of 1 raw egg and 1 teaspoon of flour. Add pepper, salt, and very finely chopped parsley. Make into balls and cook in rapidly boiling water 2 minutes. Serve with Chicken Soup* and different vegetable soups.

Fish and Shellfish

·: FISH AND SHELLFISH :·

ALL SHAKER COMMUNITIES had fine fresh water ponds or lakes on their vast acreages. At the Canterbury Society, seven of the series of eight ponds are still in existence. While artesian wells now supply water for the family, the ponds are in good order and undoubtedly still full of fish as in the past. A sister reminiscing recently recalled the pleasure of fishing as an outing. She said, "Sister Rebecca Hathaway would take some of us girls to fish. We always caught a lot and Sister Rebecca would clean them. We would build a fire and cook them beside the pond." Sometimes a larger catch was taken home to share with other sisters.

An elder writing from Mt. Lebanon, December 1889 (in *The Manifesto*), comments: "After we made our second fish pond, a new idea floated to us. . . . We are making a cranberry bed of about ⅓ of an acre, having a splendid opportunity to flood it from the pond." And from North Union, Ohio, we read:

> Last evening a number of the brethren went fishing in Lake Erie. Toward noon today they brought home their catch, except the small ones which they always cast into their mill-pond on the way home. They had enough fish for all three families [200 persons]. There were several muskies, a fine haul of white fish, a number of pike along with a lot of catfish and yet other kinds. They are all splendid eating. This evening we had a good supper of boiled catfish with herb sauce, fried potatoes, boiled greens, pickled peppers, hot bread, and lemon pie and tea.

Fresh water fish was augmented by salt water fish from the seaports of New England and New York State. Oysters, clams, lobster, sea bass, and pollock, among other fish, were on the bill of fare frequently and not considered luxurious or even hard to get as is often the case today.

Mary Whitcher wrote:

Fish can be a delicious dish and it is a wholesome food when properly prepared, but only too often this delicate food is ruined in cooking, for very special care must be taken in neither over-cooking nor under-cooking fish. Chervil, tarragon and mushrooms combined with lemon juice all make excellent flavorings for sauces with fish. The heads, backbones and tails of fish should be cooked with a dash of marjoram and thyme for half an hour and the liquid used in making sauces for fish or to use in chowders. Green onions and parsley stewed in butter and combined with two cups of fish broth and poured over two slightly beaten eggs make a delectable sauce for boiled or baked fish.

Mary Whitcher is justly renowned as a good cook and housekeeper.

Oysters

THE Shakers used oysters plentifully during the fall and winter months.
In one issue of *The Manifesto* there were six recipes for oysters (November 1880).

This bivalve, which might seem a luxury to others, was valued by the Shakers as a nutritious and healthful food. There are accounts of the brothers going to the Lee (Massachusetts) railroad station from Hancock, Massachusetts, to pick up a barrel twice a month during the oyster season, while the New Lebanon Shakers bought theirs in Albany. The oysters were kept covered with cold water and fed corn meal and were plump and tasty when needed for soups, stews, and pies, or to fry and to pickle.

SHAKER FISH AND EGGS
MARY WHITCHER'S SHAKER HOUSEKEEPER

Shaker Fish and Eggs was a favorite in many Shaker communities. We found six or seven recipes for this dish, all differing to some degree. The recipe below is almost identical to one which Eldress Prudence Stickney of the Sabbathday Lake Shakers in Maine gave to the Boston *Herald* on March 22, 1939, for which she received a prize.

2 cups rich milk or light cream
1 tablespoon butter
3 medium-sized boiled potatoes, sliced
1 cup boiled and finely chopped codfish
6 hard-cooked eggs
¼ teaspoon salt
⅛ teaspoon pepper

❡Scald milk and add butter. In a 2 quart buttered baking dish place a layer of sliced boiled potatoes, sprinkle with boiled codfish, then a layer of sliced hard-cooked eggs. Repeat and add seasonings and cover with heated milk. Simmer in a slow (300° F.) oven for 25 minutes. Garnish top with minced hard-cooked eggs. SERVES 6.

SHAKER BAKED FISH WITH HERB DRESSING

MARY WHITCHER'S SHAKER HOUSEKEEPER

1 whole fish (2 pounds), cleaned
6 soda crackers, crushed
1 teaspoon salt
1 teaspoon pepper
1 teaspoon sugar
1 tablespoon minced parsley
1 tablespoon minced thyme
1 tablespoon powdered cloves
1 tablespoon butter
Fish broth to moisten
4 strips salt pork
Salt and pepper
Corn meal for dredging

❡Scrape fish well and wash; remove head and tail and simmer in water to cover to make broth. Make a dressing of crushed crackers, salt, pepper, sugar, minced herbs and butter. Moisten with fish broth. Stuff fish and fasten with skewers. Place in buttered baking dish and cut a few shallow slashes across fish. Lay on thin strips of salt pork and dredge with salt, pepper, and corn meal. Bake in slow oven (300° F.) for 1 hour. Serve on hot platter surrounded with tomato sauce and wedges of lemon or horse-radish sauce. SERVES 4.

SHAKER BOILED FISH

NORTH UNION SHAKER VILLAGE, OHIO

1 quart water
½ cup cider
½ teaspoon crushed peppercorns
1 stalk celery, chopped
1 large onion, sliced
2 carrots, sliced
3 pounds whitefish or fresh mackerel
2 eggs, beaten
1 tablespoon butter
1 tablespoon flour
½ cup heavy cream
Salt, pepper, and sugar to taste

([Boil water, add cider, peppercorns, celery, onion, and carrots. When broth is flavored, add fish and cook gently until tender but not soft, about 20 minutes.

Place fish where it can be kept hot while making sauce. Beat eggs, strain broth and pour hot over eggs, stirring to make smooth. In a separate pan melt butter, add flour, and cook gently. When flour has really cooked, add egg and broth mixture, stirring well all the while. Cook over low heat to mix well. Remove from fire and stir in cream. Season to taste. Pour over fish. SERVES 6.

FISH OR CLAM FRITTERS
SHIRLEY SHAKER VILLAGE

2 eggs
⅓ cup milk
1⅓ cups flour
2 teaspoons baking powder
2 cups cleaned, well drained, and
    chopped clams or oysters
        or

2 cups chopped but not mashed
    white raw fish—haddock, cod
    (not salt cod), or halibut
½ teaspoon salt
½ teaspoon pepper
1 teaspoon thyme or marjoram
Deep fat for frying

([Beat eggs until light, add milk, and flour which has been mixed and sifted with baking powder. Add clams or fish and season. Drop by spoonfuls in deep fat and fry. Drain and serve with a sauce, such as Caper,* Tartar,* or Tomato Sauce.* SERVES 4.

DRESSED FISH FROM OUR BOSTON COUSINS
SHIRLEY SHAKER VILLAGE, 1848

([Take any fish that has been boiled, break it in small pieces, about 4 cups. Slice 3 or 4 cold boiled potatoes and 3 hard-boiled eggs. Put it all into a saucepan with a small quantity of White Sauce #2*—sufficient to moisten the fish. Add 1 cup of little crushed capers, a teaspoon or so of elderberry wine vinegar, the juice of half a lemon, chopped parsley, salt, and pepper. When all is together and well blended, heat it through. Lift it out onto an oven dish, cover with bread crumbs, sprinkle with melted butter and brown in the oven at 300° F.

A nice way to use leftover fish. SERVES 6.

FISH HASH
(Left-over White Fish, Potatoes, and Beets)
WATERVLIET SHAKER VILLAGE, NEW YORK

This recipe uses left-over fresh white fish (not salt cod), equal amounts of chopped cooked potatoes or mashed potatoes, half the above amount of chopped cooked beets. Add salt and pepper, melted butter, and cream. Put in a spider with hot pork fat, cover and brown slowly.

2 cups cooked flaked white fish	1 teaspoon pepper
2 cups chopped cooked potatoes	½ cup melted butter
or	1 cup chopped cooked beets
2 cups mashed cooked potatoes	½ cup heavy cream
1 teaspoon salt	Hot pork fat

⟨Mix fish and potatoes together well. Add salt, pepper, and butter. Fold in beets and cream. Put hot pork fat in a spider. Heat, add hash. Cover and brown slowly, turning once. Leave cover off to dry out hash. SERVES 4.

FISH PIE
HANCOCK SHAKER VILLAGE

4 tablespoons butter	1 tablespoon chopped parsley
2 medium onions, sliced thin and chopped	3 cups flaked cooked white fish
2 tablespoons chopped celery	1 eight inch uncooked pastry shell*
Salt and pepper to taste	1 cup fine bread crumbs
½ teaspoon marjoram	2 cups heavy cream

⟨Melt butter in saucepan, add onions and celery and sauté until soft and golden but not brown. Season with salt and pepper, marjoram, and parsley. Let this blend, then remove from fire and combine with cooked fish. Pour this mixture into pie shell. Sprinkle over with bread crumbs. Pour in cream. In an oven preheated to 350° F. bake for 10 minutes, then reduce to 325° F. for another 20 minutes. Watch to prevent burning. SERVES 4.

FRICASSEE OF CLAMS
A MAINE SHAKER RECEIPT

⟨[Clean 2 cups of clams—free of shell. Chop hard portion finely and reserve soft part. Melt 2 tablespoons butter, add 2 tablespoons flour. Simmer 2 minutes slowly. Add ½ cup heavy cream gradually, stirring constantly. Add chopped clams. Put through a sieve. Add soft part of clams. Cook 1 minute. Season with salt and pepper. Add yolk of 1 egg slightly beaten. Heat thoroughly, stirring. Serve over toast. SERVES 4.

SCALLOPED CLAMS
HANCOCK SHAKER VILLAGE

2 cups bread crumbs
2 cups drained chopped clams,
  reserve liquor
Salt and pepper
1 tablespoon minced parsley

1 tablespoon minced onion
¼ cup heavy cream
½ cup clam liquor
2 tablespoons butter

⟨[Place one-third of the bread crumbs and half of the chopped clams in a buttered 8 inch baking dish. Sprinkle with some of the salt, pepper, parsley, and onion. Add another layer of crumbs, the rest of the clams, and seasonings. Cover with the cream and clam juice. Finish with the rest of the crumbs and dot with butter. Bake 20 minutes in a hot 400° F. oven. SERVES 6.

CLAM PIE
MT. LEBANON SHAKER VILLAGE

2 tablespoons salt pork, cut in small
  pieces
1 tablespoon butter
1 onion, minced
3 potatoes, peeled and cubed

Salt and pepper
1 cup chopped drained clams
4 tablespoons heavy cream
Pastry* for 8 inch piecrust

⟨[Fry salt pork in butter. Add onions and fry until very light brown. Add potatoes, salt, and pepper. Cover pan and cook slowly until potatoes are done, with just enough water to keep from scorching. Add clams and put mixture in a buttered 8 inch pie dish. Add cream and top with rich piecrust. Bake at 350° F. until golden brown. SERVES 4.

CLAM PIE
SHIRLEY SHAKER VILLAGE

1 pastry shell* for 8 inch pie plate
1 pint shelled clams
¼ cup clam liquor
½ cup cracker crumbs
1 teaspoon lemon juice
1 egg, beaten

1 cup rich milk
1 teaspoon salt
⅛ teaspoon pepper
⅛ teaspoon dry mustard
1 tablespoon melted butter
1 upper crust* for 8 inch pie plate

⟦Line an 8 inch pie plate with pastry. Wash clams, reserve juice, and chop them fine. Blend together the cracker crumbs, lemon juice, the beaten egg, milk, salt and pepper, mustard, and melted butter. Add clams and clam juice. Mix well. Pour into pastry shell. Cover with upper crust and make slits for steam to escape. Bake in moderate 350° F. oven for 1 hour. SERVES 4–6.

BAKED COD OR HADDOCK
A NEW HAMPSHIRE RECEIPT

⟦Cut a 4 pound fish in slices as for frying, after removing bones. Pack a layer of fish in a baking pan for the oven and over it put slices of salt pork, cut thin. Pour in 1 cup of water. Sprinkle over with a little flour and pepper. Bake 30 minutes at 300° F. browning the pork well on top. Pour a cupful of heavy cream over the fish a few minutes before taking from the oven.

The cook should not be discouraged by the simplicity of this recipe. It makes a delicious dish.

CODFISH SHAKER STYLE, WITH DROPPED EGGS
WATERVLIET SHAKER VILLAGE, NEW YORK

⟦Flake 1 pound of uncooked salt codfish. Cover with boiling water, and let stand on the back part of the range for 15 minutes. (On a modern stove simmer 15 minutes.) Do not boil as this toughens fish. Drain and cover again with fresh boiling water. Let it stand again away from stove, and drain. Beat up the fish with a fork.

Melt 2 tablespoons of butter in a saucepan and then add an equal amount of flour. Mix well and cook 2 minutes. Add 1 cup of boiling milk. Stir continuously until it has thickened. Add 2 teaspoons of pepper and the codfish. Mix and pour into a shallow baking dish. Drop a number of eggs (about 6) over the top of the codfish, taking care not to break yolks. Dust lightly with salt and pepper. Surround eggs with 1 cup heavy cream. Place in the oven a few minutes until the whites are set and the cream is light gold. SERVES 4–6.

CREAMED CODFISH IN POTATO RING
MT. LEBANON SHAKER VILLAGE

6 cups shredded salted codfish
3 cups butter
3 cups flour
3 cups milk, warmed
1 cup heavy cream
1 teaspoon pepper

1 teaspoon sugar
½ teaspoon nutmeg
6 large potatoes, diced
3 tablespoons butter
½ cup milk
4 hard-boiled eggs, sliced

⟨Cover salted codfish with water and soak overnight on drainboard. Drain, cover wth fresh water, and cook slowly. Let it simmer covered on back of stove 4 to 6 hours. If fresh codfish is used, soaking and simmering are not necessary. Boil gently 20 minutes. Melt butter, add flour, and cook 5 minutes. Add warm milk, stirring until smooth. Add cream and remove from heat. Add codfish to white sauce. Add seasonings and heat.

Proceed with potatoes as for mashed potatoes. Cook potatoes in water, drain, mash; add butter and milk and whip. When potatoes are a good consistency, select a large round platter, make a neat ring of the potatoes, fill center with codfish, garnish with eggs. SERVES 6–8.

COLD COD SALAD
WATERVLIET SHAKER VILLAGE, NEW YORK

1½–2 pounds cod (head off and without bones)
4 cups fish stock
Lettuce
4 tablespoons fresh grated horse-radish
4 tablespoons mayonnaise

Chopped chives
Lemon juice
3 large boiled potatoes, peeled, diced, and salted
1 cup sliced gherkin pickles
2 fresh tomatoes, peeled

⟨Poach the fish in the stock about 20 minutes, covered. Drain well, chill, and cut into small slices. Arrange on a bed of lettuce on a serving platter.

Add horse-radish to mayonnaise and cover fish. Sprinkle with chopped chives. Decorate dish in circle with diced potatoes, sliced gherkins, and sliced tomatoes. Pass extra mayonnaise flavored with lemon juice.

If cod is not available, haddock or halibut may be used, but do not overcook. They need about the same cooking time. No longer. SERVES 4.

CODFISH BALLS, BACON, MILK GRAVY, AND HONEYED APPLE RINGS*
HARVARD SHAKER VILLAGE

2 cups shredded codfish	Dash sugar
2 cups diced raw potatoes	Dash nutmeg
1 tablespoon butter	*No salt* because of natural salt in cod
1 egg, beaten	Lard or drippings for frying
Dash pepper	

⟨[Cook the raw codfish in boiling water with raw potatoes until potatoes are done. Drain well and mash together. Beat until smooth. Then add butter, the beaten egg, and seasonings. Omit salt. Mix well. Have lard or drippings boiling. Drop in fish mixture by the spoonful and fry to a golden brown. Do not soak the fish before boiling (with the potatoes) and do not mold into cakes. This method makes them fluffier. Serve with oven-broiled salt pork or bacon and Milk Gravy. SERVES 4.

MILK GRAVY

3 tablespoons bacon fat, strained	2 cups hot milk
3 tablespoons flour	1 cup heavy cream

⟨[Have bacon fat hot, not boiling. Add flour and simmer 2 to 3 minutes. Add hot milk gradually. Cook to smooth consistency. Remove from fire and add cream. Makes 3½ cups.

COD FISH SOUFFLÉ
WATERVLIET SHAKER VILLAGE, NEW YORK

1 cup flaked salt codfish	2 tablespoons butter
3 cups sliced raw potatoes	⅛ teaspoon pepper
2 tablespoons milk	2 eggs, separated

⟨[Simmer fish and potatoes together in a large amount of water until potatoes are tender. Drain well and mash. Add milk, butter, pepper, and

2 beaten egg yolks. Mix well, then fold in 2 stiffly beaten egg whites. Pour into greased 1 quart baking dish and bake in moderate 375° F. oven for about 20 minutes. SERVES 4.

Serve with sour cream, chives, and fried salt pork, mixed together as sauce, or:

Chopped hard-boiled egg and sour cream and chives sauce, or:

Parsley Sauce: Melt together 1 tablespoon butter and 1 tablespoon flour. Add 2 tablespoons finely chopped parsley; simmer 2 minutes. Add ½ cup heavy cream, salt, and pepper.

For Codfish Balls: Follow above recipe, substituting 1 beaten egg for the 2 separated eggs. Beat ingredients well, shape into balls, and fry in hot deep fat until brown. SERVES 4.

FILLETS OF SOLE COOKED IN CREAM
HANCOCK SHAKER VILLAGE

6 fillets of sole or flounder	1 teaspoon pepper
1 cup cider	1½ tablespoons butter
1 cup water	1½ tablespoons flour
1 tablespoon lemon juice	1 cup heavy cream, sweet or sour
3 tablespoons butter	2 tablespoons grated cheese
1 teaspoon salt	2 tablespoons finely chopped parsley

❡Simmer the fillets in 1 cup cider and 1 cup water to which lemon juice has been added. Add the butter, salt, and pepper, and cook 10 minutes. Drain, reserve liquid, and put in a buttered 2 quart baking dish. Melt butter in a saucepan and add flour. Mix and simmer together 3 minutes. Add the reserved liquid, cook 5 minutes, then add the heavy cream, which can be either sweet or sour. Pour this sauce over the sole and bake until well browned, approximately 20 minutes in a 350° F. oven. Garnish with very fine grated cheese and parsley mixed together. SERVES 4.

HALIBUT IN HEAVY CREAM
HARVARD SHAKER VILLAGE

3 pounds halibut in one piece	½ cup water
2 teaspoons flour	½ cup cider
Salt and pepper	1½ cups heavy cream
6 teaspoons butter	

❡Rub halibut with flour seasoned with salt and pepper. Butter 2 quart baking dish, put fish in center and use remaining butter to cover top of fish. Pour water and cider around it. Cover baking dish and cook for 20 minutes in moderate oven (325° F.), basting when necessary as fish must not become dry. Add 1 cup heavy cream and cook another 15 to 20 minutes, increasing heat to 350° F. Baste when necessary. Serve fish surrounded by very small new boiled potatoes. Strain sauce in which fish has cooked, add enough of the remaining cream to make a thick sauce. If not thick enough add beaten yolks of 2 eggs, pour over fish on platter. SERVES 4–6.

FRESH HALIBUT ON TOAST
THE MANIFESTO
NORTH UNION SHAKER VILLAGE, OHIO

2 cups flaked halibut
2 tablespoons butter
2 tablespoons flour
1 cup milk, heated

1 cup light cream
8 rounds toast, buttered
1 hard-boiled egg, chopped
Salt and pepper to taste

⟪Cover fish with cold water and bring to a boil slowly and drain, or cooked fish may be used. Blend butter and flour and simmer 1 minute. Add heated milk slowly. Add cream, stir. When smooth add fish. Cook until thickened. Serve on toast. Garnish with chopped egg. Season. SERVES 4.

LOBSTER CROQUETTES
THE MANIFESTO
A MAINE RECEIPT

⟪Chop the meat of 1 two pound lobster fine, add pepper, salt, and mace. Mix with this ¼ cup of bread crumbs, and 2 tablespoons of melted butter. Form into balls, roll them in beaten egg, then in cracker crumbs. Fry in butter or lard in skillet. SERVES 2.

LOBSTER NEWBURG
FRANCES HALL, HANCOCK SHAKER VILLAGE, 1900

½ cup butter
½ cup flour
1 tablespoon cornstarch
2½ cups milk
1 cup light cream
3 eggs, slightly beaten
2 pounds cooked lobster meat

⅛ tablespoon nutmeg
½ tablespoon paprika
½ tablespoon salt
⅛ tablespoon white pepper
1 tablespoon lemon juice
¾ cup sherry (optional)

《Melt ¼ cup butter in saucepan. Add flour and cornstarch blended together and simmer 2 minutes. Add 1 cup milk gradually to butter and flour, stirring constantly. Add the remaining 1½ cups milk and the cream. Cook over medium heat, stirring frequently, until mixture thickens and sauce is smooth. Add beaten eggs. Meanwhile lightly sauté lobster meat in the remaining ¼ cup butter. Add nutmeg, paprika, salt and pepper, lemon juice, lobster, and sherry to the milk and cream mixture. Makes about 10 servings.

BAKED MACKEREL
HARVARD SHAKER VILLAGE, 1855

《Clean the fish, weighing about 3 pounds, put into a deep dish, and cover with ½ cup cider and ½ cup cider vinegar. Add 1 large onion cut in slices, a dozen peppercorns, and 1 teaspoon sugar. Leave in a slow oven, 300° F., for 4 hours. Dill (fresh, chopped) is a good addition to the onion. SERVES 4.

SAUTÉED OYSTERS
HANCOCK SHAKER VILLAGE

《Allow 8 plump oysters per serving. Shuck and drain oysters, season with salt and pepper. Prepare very fine cracker crumbs, fine as flour. Roll oysters in cracker crumbs. Fry in hot butter until brown on both sides (not too dark). Serve hot on crisp buttered toast and put nicely fried bacon on platter, too.

Serve a nice lot of fried apple rings, too.

CREAMED OYSTERS
(Served on Corn Bread, Toast, or Fried Bread)
HANCOCK SHAKER VILLAGE

1 quart plump oysters, drained	4 tablespoons butter
2 cups reserved oyster liquid and light cream	4 tablespoons flour
	2 egg yolks, beaten

《Shell and drain oysters, reserving as much liquid as possible. To oyster liquid add enough top milk or light cream to make 2 cups. Melt 4 tablespoons butter and stir in 4 tablespoons flour. Boil slowly to cook flour, stirring constantly. Cool and add oyster liquid and cream. Stir until very smooth and thick. Add oysters. Cook 2 minutes. Beat 2 egg yolks and add while Creamed Oysters are still hot, but do not bring to boil. Add more cream if consistency is too thick. SERVES 8.

Split corn bread and cut into 3 inch squares. Toast lightly under broiler, and then top with Creamed Oysters.
Or:

Trim crusts from homemade bread, cut in 1 inch thick slices. Melt some butter in large thick spider, fry two pieces of bread at a time. Drain, keep warm in oven. Serve cut in triangles as a trimming to dish of Creamed Oysters.

SCALLOPED OYSTERS
MANUSCRIPT FROM MT. LEBANON SHAKER VILLAGE

4 cups grated bread	Pepper
1 quart shelled oysters	2 cups butter
Mace	3 tablespoons sherry

⟨Grate the bread, wash and scald the oysters, drain quite dry, reserving liquid. Put a thin layer of bread upon the bottom and sides of a 2 quart baking dish, then alternate a layer of oysters and bread and season well with mace and pepper. The butter is added in small pieces with each layer of oysters and upon the top. Two layers of oysters is enough in order to cook all well. Add the liquor hot, then a top layer of crumbs.

We use the English sherry, but wine is left to individual preference. SERVES 8.

OYSTERS AND SAUSAGE
SHIRLEY SHAKER VILLAGE

1½ cups white flour	1 cup drained chopped oysters
3 teaspoons baking powder	6 tablespoons oyster liquor
½ teaspoon salt	8 pork sausages
1 tablespoon butter	

⟨Sift flour, baking powder, and salt together. Cut in butter as for pastry. To this mixture add oysters and their liquor, blend together, and spread in a buttered, shallow baking pan. On top arrange sausages, which have been cooked 10 minutes in boiling water. Bake 30 minutes in a 350° F. oven. Turn sausages once to brown. SERVES 4.

OYSTER PATTIES

MT. LEBANON SHAKER VILLAGE

1 tablespoon butter
1 tablespoon flour
2 cups hot rich milk
2 teaspoons salt
2 teaspoons chopped parsley

3 teaspoons lemon juice
½ teaspoon cayenne
½ teaspoon celery salt
2 cups shelled oysters
4 Puff Pastries*

⟨Melt butter, add flour, and simmer. Add hot milk, stir constantly to make sauce, and add salt, parsley, lemon juice, cayenne, and celery salt. Add oysters and stir gently until they puff up. Have 4 hot Paste Patties to fill with mixture or pour over hot toast. SERVES 4.

OYSTER-VEAL PATTIES

HANCOCK SHAKER VILLAGE

⟨Chop 2 cups of shucked oysters with 1 cup of chopped cooked veal or chicken. Add ½ cup fine bread crumbs, salt and pepper. Pound all together and make into small cakes. Dip in beaten egg, then into flour, and fry them dry. Serve with or without sauce. See Index for sauces for fish, such as Egg Sauce, Dill Sauce, Sour Cream Sauce, and Cucumber Sauce. Makes 8 cakes. SERVES 4.

FRIED OYSTER PATTIES

WATERVLIET SHAKER VILLAGE, NEW YORK

Puff pastry*
2 cups chopped shucked oysters
4 hard-boiled eggs, chopped
2 tablespoons minced parsley
½ teaspoon salt

½ teaspoon pepper
½ cup heavy cream
1 egg yolk, beaten
Hot lard

⟨Make some good puff paste rolled rather thin and cut into small round pieces 2 inches across. Combine chopped raw oysters, hard-boiled eggs, and minced parsley. Add salt, pepper, and heavy cream enough to moisten. Put a good spoonful on each piece of paste, fold and moisten the edges

with a little cream, then press them together. Brush each with beaten
egg yolk and fry brown in hot fat in a skillet. Makes 12 patties.

OYSTER PIE

MT. LEBANON SHAKER VILLAGE

1 cup finely chopped carrots
½ cup finely chopped onions
1 cup finely chopped potatoes
1 teaspoon salt
½ teaspoon pepper
2 cups shelled oysters or clams and
  their liquid

⅓ cup heavy cream
3 egg yolks, beaten
½ teaspoon powdered cloves or
  nutmeg
1 tablespoon chopped parsley
Pastry* for 8 inch pie

❮This recipe includes almost the same ingredients as the Oyster Soup
with herbs. Clams can be substituted for the oysters.

Cook carrots, onions, potatoes, in water to cover. Drain. Add salt and
pepper. Add oysters or clams and their liquid. Combine cream with
beaten egg yolks, gradually stir this into the vegetable and oyster or
clam mixture. Add powdered cloves or nutmeg and chopped parsley.
Turn above mixture into 8 inch pie plate and cover with rich pie pastry.
Bake at 350° F. for 40 minutes. SERVES 6.

OYSTER AND HAM PIE

THE MANIFESTO

Best pie pastry (two 9 inch crusts)
3 cups ground cooked ham
2 tablespoons prepared mustard
2 cups shelled and drained oysters
2 tablespoons finely chopped onion

½ teaspoon salt
½ teaspoon pepper
2 tablespoons butter
1 cup heavy cream

❮Line a shallow 9 inch pie plate with your best pie pastry. Spread ham,
which has been mixed with prepared mustard, over bottom crust. Put in a
layer of oysters, sprinkle with chopped onion. Sprinkle with salt and pepper, dot with butter; pour heavy cream over all, cover with pastry, prick
well. Bake in hot oven (400° F.) until brown, about 30 minutes. Serve
hot or cold. SERVES 6.

Three cups chopped hard-boiled eggs may be substituted for ham.

SWORDFISH BOSTON STYLE
SHIRLEY SHAKER VILLAGE

1 three pound slice swordfish, cut
    1½ inches thick
¼ pound butter (room temperature)
¾ cup fine bread crumbs

2 tablespoons finely chopped onion
Salt and pepper to taste
Lemon wedges

([Preheat broiler. Coat one side of the slice of fish with half the butter. Pat on one-half the bread crumbs and 1 tablespoon onion, flavor with salt and pepper. Broil 5 minutes, turn, repeat on other side. More butter may be needed here to prevent fish from drying out. Serve with lemon wedges. WILL SERVE 5–6.

CURRIED SWORDFISH—HANCOCK STYLE
HANCOCK SHAKER VILLAGE

2 slices swordfish (4 x 8 inches in size
    and 1½ inches thick weighing 3
    pounds in all or more)
3 cups boiling water
1 teaspoon salt
½ teaspoon black pepper
1 bay leaf

1 tablespoon lemon juice
3 tablespoons butter
1 tablespoon chopped onion
2 tablespoons flour
1 teaspoon curry powder
¼ cup light cream
Paprika

([Place swordfish slices in large frying pan and cover with boiling water. Add salt, pepper, bay leaf, and lemon juice. Simmer uncovered over low heat for 15 minutes, until just tender. With a wide spatula lift fish out of stock and place on ovenproof platter or in a shallow casserole, and keep warm.

Strain stock. Measure out 1½ cups. Melt butter in saucepan, sauté onion in it until it is limp. Blend in flour. Gradually pour in the strained stock and cook until thickened. Blend in curry powder and cream. Pour sauce over fish slices, sprinkle with paprika, slip under preheated broiler for 5 minutes to brown lightly. Cut in serving portions. SHOULD SERVE 5–6.

TURBOT IN CREAM
MARY WHITCHER'S SHAKER HOUSEKEEPER

2 pounds bass
2 cups light cream
1 bunch parsley
1 onion
3 stalks celery

2 tablespoons flour
2 tablespoons milk
4 tablespoons butter
Bread crumbs
Grated cheese

❲Boil bass in salt water; flake it, removing all skin and bones. Scald the cream with parsley, onion, and celery. Discard vegetables and thicken the cream with flour moistened with milk. Stir until smooth and add butter. Butter a deep baking dish and put in a layer of fish and a layer of sauce. Repeat until dish is two-thirds filled. Cover top with a layer of fine bread crumbs and dust with grated cheese. Bake 30 minutes in medium 350° F. oven. SERVES 6.

Poultry

·: POULTRY :·

"THE WORLD," as the Shakers called those outside the Society, came to the villages in great numbers; some from curiosity, some from genuine interest, and some with a view of joining them. Visitors were treated with great hospitality and it is from these many accounts that we have records of the generous and interesting meals which made a trip to Shaker villages an important event.

Shaker farms raised quantities of chickens. Guests might forget the complete menu, but they would say "the chicken was wonderful." A Shaker journal from Harvard, Massachusetts, records in 1843, "A load of the *World* from Boston here awhile today and took dinner" and again in 1845, "We receive intelligence that there is company a-coming here to dine tomorrow." A farmer's wife living near Shirley wrote relatives in Worcester that she was required every week by the sisters for help in preparing chickens for almost forty visitors from Boston, and she said "it is yellow and rich with little herb dumplings in the gravy." Probably it was a fricassee. For leftovers, we find this among Shirley papers:

Second Day Chicken (Mould)
Return nice pieces of cooked chicken to saucepan with a little of the stock and 1 ounce of gelatin, which has been soaked in lukewarm water. Season to taste, adding some mace and chopped parsley if liked. Simmer for 10 minutes or so. Then place in mould. This is a nice cold breakfast dish or a change from the ordinary boiled fowl.

Chicken fat was used as a butter substitute in many Shaker recipes. It was also used to make a very delicate soap. It was used for shortening in veal and lamb dishes and was excellent in pastry, gingerbread, cookies, and steamed puddings.

To Render Chicken[1]

CUT solid uncooked fat in small pieces or put through a food grinder (do not use a blender). Melt in a double boiler over warm water (not boiling) as the fat should melt but not cook. Fat can also be melted in a shallow pan in a warm 250° F. oven or in a heavy skillet over low heat.

Pour off melted fat. If bits of meat or gristle still cling to fat, add boiling water and let stand until cool; lift cake of fat from solids and store in refrigerator. These fats should be used soon as they become rancid if stored too long.

In substituting lard or a vegetable fat for butter in a recipe, use about one fourth less, as butter is not a solid fat, but contains some liquid. Also add salt to taste.

SHAKER CHICKEN FRICASSEE
HANCOCK SHAKER VILLAGE

1 young hen (roasting chicken), 3–4 pounds	1 teaspoon tarragon
Seasoned flour	⅓ cup chopped parsley
3 tablespoons clear fat	1 small onion, chopped
3 cups boiling water	1 teaspoon each salt and pepper
1 bay leaf	4 tablespoons butter
5 peppercorns, ground	4 tablespoons flour
1 teaspoon summer savory	2 egg yolks
	1 cup heavy cream, heated

[Cut up the chicken into four pieces; wash and dry it. Roll in seasoned flour and brown to a golden color in the fat in a deep pot. When richly golden, add boiling water to cover, bay leaf, pepper, herbs, parsley, and onion. Cover the pot and simmer until chicken is tender, 1 to 1½ hours. Add salt and pepper. More salt may be used if needed. Remove chicken from the stock and keep it warm. There should be 3 cups of stock; if not, add heated chicken broth or hot water with butter in it to make 3 cups.

In a saucepan, melt 4 tablespoons butter, stir in the flour, and cook lightly, but do not permit it to color. Stir it constantly, then pour over it

---

[1] Or other fats—beef, pork, or goose, but not lamb because of its tallow content.

gradually 1 cup of the hot stock. Simmer a moment, then add rest of stock, stirring constantly. Simmer 10 minutes.

In a bowl beat egg yolks well and pour the hot cream over them gradually, stirring constantly. Add to the chicken and gravy in the pot and very slowly reheat, but do not permit to boil, as the egg-cream mixture might curdle.

This sauce and indeed the entire dish should be golden and rich in taste. SERVES 4.

.·.

The trolley line ended in West Pittsfield a mile short of the Hancock Shaker community. Such was the fame of the Shaker Chicken Fricassee, however, that old-timers declared it was worth every step through the summer dust or the frigid blasts of the fall weather.

NEW HAMPSHIRE WAY OF COOKING CHICKEN

MANUSCRIPT FROM SHAKER MUSEUM
OLD CHATHAM, NEW YORK

2 chickens, 3 pounds each, quartered	4 tablespoons butter
4 cups water	4 tablespoons flour
1 teaspoon each salt and pepper	1 cup sweet heavy cream
1 tablespoon chicken fat	Shortcake* or Cream Biscuits*

⟮Put chickens in large kettle, cover with water and season. Cook uncovered. When tender and the water is nearly boiled out, remove pieces, discard skin and bones, and reserve liquid. Use 1 tablespoon of chicken fat, add to it the butter and flour, cook 2 minutes. Add 2 cups chicken liquid and cream and cook until gravy is thick and smooth.

Have ready a nice Shortcake or the Cream Biscuits. Split and butter and lay on a platter. Lay the chicken on this and pour the gravy over the whole. People come miles for this. SERVES 8.

SHAKER FRIED CHICKEN

ELDRESS CLYMENA MINER
NORTH UNION SHAKER VILLAGE, OHIO

2 spring chickens, quartered (broilers, fryers, 2½ pounds each, cut up)	¼ cup flour
	Salt and pepper
3 tablespoons soft butter	2 tablespoons butter
1 tablespoon fresh minced parsley	2 tablespoons lard
1 teaspoon minced fresh marjoram or ¼ teaspoon dried marjoram	1 cup light cream

([Select chickens weighing 2½ pounds or a little over; smaller ones lack flavor and cook up waxy. Wash well and quarter. Rub thoroughly with soft butter and sprinkle generously with parsley and marjoram. Let stand for 1 hour at room temperature. Then roll in flour to which salt and pepper have been added. Heat heavy skillet, add butter and lard combined. Cook chicken on all sides until golden brown. Pour cream over it and let simmer, covered, for 20 minutes. SERVES 6.

CHICKEN IN HEAVY CREAM
(A Rich Dish)
HANCOCK SHAKER VILLAGE

1 small chicken, young and tender
2 tablespoons sweet butter
1 tablespoon flour
1 medium-size onion
4 whole cloves
1 teaspoon salt

½ teaspoon white pepper
2 tablespoons tarragon sprigs (do not chop since sprigs must eventually be removed)
1½ to 2 cups hot water
1 cup heavy cream

([Sauté chicken in melted butter but do not brown. Sprinkle with flour and cook covered in skillet for 5 minutes. Each piece of chicken must be coated with butter and flour—no lumps. Add onion with cloves stuck in it, salt, pepper, and sprigs of tarragon. Pour hot water over all, barely to cover, and cook covered until chicken is tender, 20 to 30 minutes. Remove chicken to a hot platter in oven. Remove tarragon from stock in skillet and add 1 cup heavy cream. Reduce liquid to 1 cup. Pour hot over chicken. SERVES 4.

CHICKEN AND OYSTER PIE
HANCOCK SHAKER VILLAGE

3 cups cubed cooked chicken
2 cups chopped shucked raw oysters
2 tablespoons butter, melted
½ teaspoon salt
¼ teaspoon pepper

2 cups very rich cream sauce flavored with a little dry mustard (optional)
1 eight inch crust of your best piecrust

([Combine the chicken and oysters. Place in a buttered 8 inch pie dish. Add the butter, salt, and pepper.

Make 1 cup thick rich cream sauce and pour over chicken and oysters.

Cover dish with piecrust and bake in a moderate 375° F. oven for 35 to 40 minutes. SERVES 5–6.

SISTER CLYMENA'S CHICKEN PIE
WITH MUSHROOM SAUCE

ELDRESS CLYMENA MINER
NORTH UNION SHAKER VILLAGE, OHIO

2 small chickens, about 3 pounds each	4 sprigs parsley, minced
2 cups water	4 sprigs chervil, minced
3 eggs	Salt and pepper to taste
2 cups heavy cream	½ teaspoon sugar
½ small onion, chopped	2 pastry crusts* for 12 inch pie plate

⟦Cut chickens in quarters; boil with water to cover for 30 minutes. Remove meat from bones, but leave in large pieces; remove skin. Beat eggs well. Add cream, onion, herbs, and seasonings. Add enough of the hot chicken liquor to cream and eggs to cover chicken. Butter well a baking dish or deep pie dish (the village uses 12 inch pie plates). Line the bottom and sides with a rich pastry. Fill with chicken mixture and pour over cream, egg, and broth mixture. Cover with top crust, allowing small vents for steam. Bake in hot 425° F. oven for half an hour to 45 minutes —watch. Serve at once with Mushroom Sauce. SERVES 4–6.

MUSHROOM SAUCE

2 pounds mushrooms, chopped fine	Salt
1 cup butter	Pepper
1 onion, chopped	½ teaspoon sugar
½ cup flour	½ cup heavy cream
1 cup warm milk	

⟦Clean and chop mushrooms, removing tough stems. Melt butter and sauté mushrooms and onion until tender. Add flour. Stir on low heat until smooth. Add warm milk and simmer covered until mixture is very smooth. Add seasonings, heat up and remove from stove. Stir in cream, cook until liquid is somewhat reduced and serve in sauceboat. Makes 4–5 cups.

CHICKEN POT PIE

SISTER AMELIA'S SHAKER RECEIPTS

1 double recipe for biscuit dough*
1 cooked chicken, boned and without skin
6 small raw potatoes, peeled and sliced very fine
2 cups raw shelled peas

Salt and pepper
4 sprigs marjoram, minced
4 sprigs parsley, minced
3 cups light cream
2 eggs, beaten

❴Line the sides but not the bottom of a 3 quart baking dish with your best biscuit crust (one-half recipe). Place in bottom a layer of cooked chicken, which has had bones and skin removed. Cover with a layer of raw sliced potatoes and sprinkle with raw peas, salt, and pepper. Lay a few very thin strips of half the remaining dough across and sprinkle with herbs. Repeat layers until pan is three-quarters filled. Season light cream, add well-beaten eggs, and pour over layers. Put on a thick top crust, using one full recipe if necessary, allowing a steam vent. Bake in a moderate (350° F.) oven for 45 minutes to 1 hour. SERVES 6.

CHICKEN GELATIN

SISTER LISSET, NORTH UNION SHAKER VILLAGE, OHIO

2 tablespoons gelatin
¼ cup cold water
2 cups chicken stock
½ teaspoon salt

⅛ teaspoon paprika
3 hard-cooked eggs
1 tablespoon minced parsley
3 cups sliced cooked chicken

❴Pour gelatin on cold water and let stand 5 minutes. Heat chicken stock and dissolve gelatin in it. Add salt if necessary and paprika. Pour ½ cup gelatin into a flat pan. Let harden. Slice eggs and arrange on set gelatin; sprinkle with minced parsley. Add ⅛ cup gelatin mixture (just enough to hold eggs and parsley). Let harden. Then add chicken to remaining stock. Pour into mold on top of other layers. Let chill until set and turn out onto a platter. SERVES 6.

Can be served with a homemade mayonnaise sauce of not too thick texture (thinned with cream), or a sour cream sauce with capers.

CHICKEN PUDDING
FRANCES HALL, HANCOCK SHAKER VILLAGE

1 chicken, 3½–4 pounds	Salt and pepper
½ cup chopped onions	Nutmeg
½ cup chopped celery	2 tablespoons butter
½ cup chopped peeled cored apples	2 tablespoons flour
3 tablespoons butter	1 cup cream
½ cup cider	1 cup very dry bread crumbs

⟮Cook chicken in covered pot with water to cover. When tender, remove bones and skin and set aside meat. Fry onions, celery, and apples in butter until tender and golden, not brown. Add cider and seasonings and cook until vegetables are mushy. If there seems to be an excess of liquid, simmer gently until mixture is fairly thick. Remove to a buttered 4 quart baking dish and combine with cooked chicken cut in pieces. To this mixture add a white sauce made with 2 tablespoons butter, 2 tablespoons flour, and 1 cup cream. Blend well; top with bread crumbs. Bake at 325 to 350° F. for 30 minutes. SERVES 4–6.

BROTHER RICARDO'S[1] FAVORITE CHICKEN PUDDING
HANCOCK SHAKER VILLAGE

1 fowl, 5–6 pounds	Dressing
2½ quarts water	Sauce
1 teaspoon salt	1 cup dried bread crumbs
1 large onion, peeled and cut up	¼ cup butter, melted

⟮Place cut-up fowl in a kettle which has a lid. Add water, salt, and onion. Cover and simmer slowly until meat is ready to leave bones, 2 to 3 hours. The time of cooking will depend upon the age of fowl. Remove kettle from heat and let fowl cool right in the broth. While the bird is cooling make the Dressing and the Sauce below. When fowl is cool enough to handle, remove from broth and reserve 1 cup of fat for the sauce. Remove skin and bones from chicken, reserving skin for sauce.

Grease one large (10x15) baking pan or two small ones. Put a layer

---

[1]Brother Ricardo Belden was the last surviving brother at Hancock and was well known to many for his talents in repairing clocks and sewing machines.

of dressing (see below) in the bottom of the pan. Cover with half the sauce (see below), then a layer of the chicken, and cover with rest of the dressing and sauce. Stir crumbs in the melted butter until well coated, sprinkle over top of chicken mixture in pan. Bake about 30 minutes in 400° F. oven until top is nicely browned and all is bubbling hot. This will serve a dozen people well.

DRESSING

Giblets from the fowl, cooked
Salt
1½ one pound loaves stale bread
½ cup butter
1 medium onion, peeled and diced

2 medium stalks celery, diced
1 teaspoon sage
1 teaspoon salt
Pinch pepper
¾–1 cup hot chicken broth

⟮Cook giblets until tender in salted water, drain and put through food grinder. Cut crusts from bread and discard. Cut bread into ¾ inch cubes. Melt butter in a large frying pan. Add onion and celery and sauté about 5 minutes; then add bread cubes. Add ground giblets, sage, salt, and pepper. Mix well, then moisten with broth. The exact amount of broth is difficult to give, since bread varies in consistency, but do not use too much or the dressing will be heavy. Bake with chicken as directed. Yields about 4 cups dressing.

SAUCE

1 cup flour
1 cup chicken fat
4 cups chicken broth
1 cup milk

1 teaspoon salt
4 eggs, slightly beaten
Cooked skin from chicken, ground

⟮Add 1 cup flour to 1 cup chicken fat. Heat the 4 cups broth with the milk and stir into the fat and flour mixture. Cook over low heat, stirring constantly, until sauce thickens. Add salt. Remove from fire and stir hot sauce into beaten eggs very slowly so sauce will not curdle. Return to heat and cook 5 minutes, stirring constantly. Remove from stove and add ground chicken skin. Bake with chicken as directed. Makes 6–8 cups.

CHICKEN AND RICE PUDDING
HARVARD SHAKER VILLAGE

1½ tablespoons butter
2 cups milk
2 eggs
2 cups cooked rice

½ teaspoon each pepper, celery salt,
nutmeg, mustard
2 cups 1 inch pieces cooked chicken

([Stir the butter, the milk, and the eggs into cooked rice. Mix well, adding seasonings.

Put a layer of rice mixture into a baking dish; cover with chicken, then a layer of rice. Just the 3 layers. Bake in a moderate 350° F. oven until well browned, about 40 minutes. SERVES 4.

CHICKEN SCALLOP
HANCOCK SHAKER VILLAGE

4 cups cut up cold roast chicken
1 cup White Sauce #2*
2 cups thinly sliced leftover dressing

2 tablespoons butter
2 tablespoons chicken stock

([In a buttered 2 quart baking dish combine chicken and white sauce. Top with dressing left over from roast chicken. Dot with butter and dribble chicken stock over it. Cook in 350° F. oven for 20 to 30 minutes. SERVES 4–6.

CHICKEN SHORTCAKE
HANCOCK SHAKER VILLAGE

1 large chicken, boiled in water to cover
2 cups chicken stock
2 tablespoons flour
1 pound mushrooms, cleaned and chopped

2 tablespoons butter, melted
Salt and pepper
1 recipe Corn Bread* seasoned with some dried poultry seasoning (thyme, sage, etc.)

([Remove the skin and bones from the cooked chicken. Cut meat into small pieces. Make a sauce using 2 cups of the chicken stock, thickened with flour. Sauté chopped mushrooms in butter. Add chicken and mushrooms to the sauce. Season to taste.

Cut corn bread into 4 inch squares, split and butter. Cover the lower halves with some of the chicken mixture. Lay the top crusts on these and cover with more of the chicken mixture. SERVES 4–6.

CHICKEN IN CIDER AND CREAM
HANCOCK SHAKER VILLAGE

1 chicken, about 4 pounds, quartered
5 tablespoons butter, heated
½ cup cider
1 tablespoon grated lemon rind

1 cup heavy cream
1 teaspoon each salt and fresh pepper

《[Cook chicken in hot butter until brown all over. Cover the pan and continue cooking over low heat until tender, 30 to 40 minutes. Add cider and lemon rind and spoon this liquid over the chicken. If chicken seems to be drying out, add cider before chicken is fully cooked to the tender point. Remove chicken to warm serving platter. Quickly add cream and seasonings to frying pan, stir around to mix with pan juices. Pour this hot sauce over chicken on platter. SERVES 4 OR 5.

CHICKEN AND SPINACH PUDDING WITH BREAD LID
HANCOCK SHAKER VILLAGE

4 cups diced cooked chicken
3 cups chopped cooked spinach, flavored with rosemary (See Spinach with Rosemary*)
1 cup ½ inch cubes cheese (preferably rich American cheddar)
3 tablespoons butter

1 teaspoon salt
1 teaspoon pepper
1 teaspoon dry mustard
1 teaspoon scraped raw onion
3 tablespoons flour
2 cups rich milk
Bread lid

《[In a greased 3 quart baking dish mix chicken and spinach; cover with half of the cubed cheese; poke the little pieces into the mixture. In a pan melt butter, add all seasonings, onion, and flour, blend. Add milk and cook, stirring for 4 to 5 minutes. Add remaining cheese to this and cover mixture in dish. Let this stand while arranging bread lid.

A round lid for a round baking dish can be cut from a round loaf of bread.[1] The lid should be almost an inch thick. Score in serving pieces to make cutting easy. If a square or oblong baking dish is used, cut bread in squares to fit top. Toast day-old bread on one side. Put toasted side down; butter upper side thickly. Bake in 350° F. oven for 20 minutes, or just long enough to melt cheese, heat mixture through, and brown crusty lid. SERVES 8.

[1]If round loaf is not available, shape square slices to fit dish.

CHICKEN AND VEGETABLE PUDDING
HANCOCK SHAKER VILLAGE

2 cups small cubes cooked chicken
½ cup peeled and seeded tomatoes
½ cup chopped cooked onion
1 teaspoon salt
1 teaspoon chopped rosemary

½ teaspoon pepper
2 hard-boiled eggs, chopped
1½ cups chicken stock
5 eggs, well beaten

⟨[Combine first seven ingredients. Mix stock and beaten eggs together. Put dry mixture in a 2 quart baking dish. Pour over it stock and egg combination. Put dish in a pan of water in oven. Cook at 300 to 325° F. for 1 hour. SERVES 6.

CHICKEN CUTLETS WITH CHOPPED MUSHROOM SAUCE
HANCOCK SHAKER VILLAGE

½ cup butter
½ cup flour
½ cup milk
1 teaspoon chopped onion
2 teaspoons chopped parsley

Salt, pepper, nutmeg to taste
4 cups finely minced cooked chicken
Very fine bread crumbs
1 egg, beaten
Lard and butter, half and half

⟨[Combine ½ cup butter and ½ cup flour, cook slowly 5 minutes. Add milk, onion, parsley, and seasonings; cook until quite thick. Add chicken. Mix well and put on a platter to cool. Handle quickly. Shape into small cutlets. Roll in bread crumbs, then in beaten egg, then again in bread crumbs. Fry to a golden brown in hot fat, half lard and half butter. Makes 10 little cutlets. Serve with Mushroom Sauce.

MUSHROOM SAUCE

4 cups chopped mushrooms
2 tablespoons chopped onions
4 tablespoons butter

2 tablespoons thick homemade
  catsup*
1 teaspoon Herb Vinegar*
2 tablespoons heavy cream

⟨[Combine mushrooms, onions, and butter and sauté well until mushrooms and onions are both very tender and dark. Add catsup and Herb Vinegar and continue cooking another 10 minutes, slowly. It should bubble. Remove from heat and add cream. Stir briskly. Do not reheat. Pour around the cutlets or serve in sauceboat. Makes about 4 cups.

CHICKEN LOAF OR MOLD

MT. LEBANON SHAKER VILLAGE

1⅓ cups scalded milk
5 tablespoons butter
2 cups soft bread crumbs
2 cups chopped cooked white meat
  chicken

2 eggs, well beaten
1 tablespoon chopped parsley
1 tablespoon chopped tarragon
1 tablespoon very finely grated onion

⟪Melt butter in hot milk, combine with other ingredients in order given, and mix well. Pour into greased 8 inch loaf pan. Bake 30 to 35 minutes in moderate 350° F. oven with pan set in another pan of water. Unmold and serve with following sauce. SERVES 8.

SAUCE FOR CHICKEN MOLD

3 tablespoons butter
3 tablespoons flour
¼ teaspoon salt

1 cup milk
½ cup cider
½ cup sour cream

⟪Melt butter; add flour and salt. Stir until well blended. Pour in milk gradually while stirring constantly. Bring to boiling point; boil 2 minutes. Cool slightly, add cider, and cook 1 minute. Remove from stove and stir in the sour cream. Do not reheat.

Pour this sauce around the loaf or serve in sauceboat separately. Makes about 2 cups.

CHICKEN CAKES

SHIRLEY SHAKER VILLAGE

2 eggs slightly beaten
½ cup cream
¼ teaspoon each salt and pepper
1 cup finely minced cooked chicken
Milk (optional)
Bread crumbs, rolled fine

Shortening for frying
2 tablespoons butter
2 tablespoons flour
1 cup cream
½ cup finely chopped celery
Parsley

⟪Add 1 egg, cream, salt, and pepper to the minced chicken. Make into small flat cakes. Dip in the remaining egg mixed with a little milk if desired. Roll cakes in bread crumbs. Fry in shortening on both sides until well browned. Make white sauce by melting butter, adding flour. Cook 3 minutes. Stir briskly, add celery, and pour around cakes when ready to serve. Garnish with parsley. SERVES 4.

Variation: Omit celery and add 1 tablespoon washed capers, 1 tablespoon sour cream, and 1 tablespoon chopped tarragon to the white sauce.

CHICKEN LIVERS
SHIRLEY SHAKER VILLAGE

⟨When a sufficiency of chicken livers has accumulated, put a piece of butter in a large frying pan, add livers cut in two, salt, pepper. Add 2 tablespoons of catsup* and some brandy. Cook a few minutes over a quick fire. Stir but do not break up. Remove from fire and stir in some heavy cream. Have a nice piece of hot toast ready, pile on livers, and sprinkle with parsley. This supplies a good quantity of iron for the system.

ELDRESS CLYMENA'S
DRESSING FOR STUFFING A CHICKEN
NORTH UNION SHAKER VILLAGE, OHIO

3 teaspoons butter	1 teaspoon thyme
2 medium onions, minced	1 teaspoon salt
3 cups dried bread crumbs	1 teaspoon pepper
½ cup chopped celery leaves	10 chestnuts, blanched and shelled
1 tablespoon chopped summer savory	½ cup hot water
1 teaspoon minced fresh basil	3 tablespoons butter

⟨Melt butter. Sauté onion but do not brown; add to bread crumbs. Add celery leaves, all herbs, salt, and pepper. Slit each nut ½ inch on each side, put chestnuts in deep saucepan. Add hot water. Shake over heat 5 minutes. Peel. Chop very fine. Add to dressing. Heat water and add butter and mix well into dressing. Stuff chicken and truss well. Rub the skin with soft butter and dust with salt.

This is sufficient for a 4–5 pound chicken.

SAGE STUFFING

HANCOCK SHAKER VILLAGE

4 cups dry bread crumbs
½ cup melted butter
1 egg, beaten
½ teaspoon salt
¼ teaspoon pepper
1 teaspoon brown sugar
1 tablespoon minced onion
1 tablespoon finely cut fresh sage
   or

1 teaspoon dried ground sage
   or
2 tablespoons minced fresh mixed herbs, such as a combination of thyme, sweet basil, marjoram, rosemary—any one herb or several. Don't use too many, as flavors should come through separately
1 teaspoon each cloves, nutmeg, and ginger

⟪Mix bread crumbs and melted butter together. Add beaten egg, seasonings, onion, and herbs. When all ingredients have been well mixed determine if a more moist dressing is desired. If so add some hot liquid —this can be stock or water. Makes 4 cups.

BROILED CHICKEN WITH CREAM OF TARRAGON SAUCE

HANCOCK SHAKER VILLAGE

3–4 pound broiler
Salt and pepper
Lard
½ cup water
3 tablespoons butter
3 tablespoons flour
1½ cups strained chicken stock
¼ teaspoon pepper
½ teaspoon salt

½ teaspoon brown sugar
1 tablespoon butter
1 egg yolk mixed with ½ cup cream
½ cup finely chopped fresh tarragon leaves
   or
2 teaspoons dried tarragon leaves
1 tablespoon Herb Vinegar* or lemon juice

⟪Prepare chicken, cut in serving pieces. Rub each piece all over with salt, pepper, and lard or clear drippings. Put ½ cup water in pan and broil flesh side up. Turn. Check on dryness, oil skin, and watch as chicken should broil to a light brown, but not burn. Make the sauce as the chicken cooks:

Melt 3 tablespoons butter. Add flour. Stir well and cook lightly 5 minutes. Add chicken stock, cook until smooth. Add seasonings. Add very slowly the 1 tablespoon butter. Let the sauce blend. Gradually heat almost to the boil. Remove from fire and add egg and cream mixture, stir rapidly. Add tarragon leaves and herb vinegar and beat to make smooth. Chicken should be hot on a hot platter—cover with the sauce. SERVES 4.

CHICKEN AND CORN
HANCOCK SHAKER VILLAGE

½ cup butter
2–2½ pound broiler-fryers, quartered
1½ cups chopped onions
2 tablespoons flour
2 teaspoons salt
1 tablespoon chopped fresh tarragon
        or

1 tablespoon chopped fresh basil
1 cup chicken stock or 1 cup cider with 1 tablespoon butter melted in it
4 cups corn, scraped from cob
2 cups sour cream

❮Melt butter in large skillet, brown chicken pieces on all sides and remove to a baking dish. In butter which remains in skillet sauté onions until they are soft. Add flour, cook 2 minutes, and then add salt, tarragon, and stock. Bring to a boil, stirring to keep smooth. Add corn and sour cream. Heat through, but do not boil as sour cream might separate. Pour over and around chicken in baking dish. If this mixture seems too thick, thin out with sweet cream. Cover and cook in moderate 350° F. oven about 25 to 30 minutes or until chicken is tender. SERVES 8.

BOILED TURKEY
HARVARD SHAKER VILLAGE

❮Have a 10 pound turkey nicely cleaned and let it lie in salt and cold water a few minutes. Fill with a dressing of bread, butter, salt, pepper, and parsley or see Sage Dressing.* Dressing is optional. Sew or skewer and tie legs together. Tie up in cheesecloth. Place on trivet in a large kettle, with salted water to cover fowl halfway. Cover and cook slowly. Turn occasionally. A 10 pound turkey will boil in about 3 hours and it should be kept boiling all the time, but not too fast or it will boil to pieces.

Serve with Oyster Sauce* or Drawn Butter,* hard-boiled egg and parsley sauce, or rich cream caper and herb sauce.

TURKEY CAKES

SISTER OLIVE, HANCOCK SHAKER VILLAGE

1 cup finely chopped cold cooked
   turkey
¼ teaspoon salt
¼ teaspoon pepper

1 egg, beaten
1 tablespoon flour
1 tablespoon heavy cream
3 tablespoons melted butter

❴In a bowl mix together turkey, seasonings, and beaten egg. Sprinkle in flour. Mix and add cream. Form into small cakes and fry in hot butter. Arrange on a hot platter and pour around them the following sauce. SERVES 2.

SAUCE

½ cup butter
½ cup flour
½ cup milk, warmed

⅓ cup chopped cooked celery
1 teaspoon chopped chives
3 tablespoons heavy cream

❴Make a white sauce of the butter and flour and cook 5 minutes. Add warm milk and cook until smooth. Add celery and chives. Let heat up and remove from fire. Stir in cream; pour around cakes. Makes about 2 cups.

Meat

THE SHAKERS provided delicious and nourishing food in great variety. Unlike some sects whose theories embraced abstaining from all but the smallest measure of food that would sustain life, the Shakers believed in building up a strong body in order to work the better for "the glory of God."

Elder Henry C. Blinn writing in *The Manifesto* said, "If the food that we eat to sustain life has anything to do with the ruling of our mind or body, and a large class of intelligent people, today, entertain that thought, it becomes highly important, especially for those of the Christian faith, to examine the subject with great care."

The Shaker sisters were ingenious in contriving countless ways of adding variety to their meals. Chicken or a joint of venison, rabbits, and an occasional wild turkey, in the pioneer days, brought relief from the monotonous diet of salt meat. Apart from the ten year ban on meat, which was not successfully enforced, meat formed an important part of the diet at breakfast and dinner. In the early days surplus stock was butchered in the fall and converted into a variety of fresh meats and eaten as soon as possible due to the lack of adequate refrigeration. Meats were stored in the cold cellars of the dwellings, and in the barns were barrels of corned beef in brine and rows of crocks full of herb-ladened sausages. Huge tubs of lard delicately scented with bay leaf or thyme sat side by side with vats of assorted meat scraps, which would be turned into loaves of scrapple or head cheese, stews and jellied or pressed meat dishes. Great hams were hung in the smokehouses and the carcasses of beef and mutton were kept as long as possible on ice cakes covered with sawdust and piled in the north side of the barn out-sheds.

At Hancock and West Pittsfield the Shakers raised the English Berkshire hog and were well known for their excellent hams.

FRENCH BEEFSTEAK
SHAKER ALMANAC, 1882

⟨Cut the steaks ⅔ to an inch thick from a fillet of beef. Dip into melted fresh butter—lay them on a heated gridiron and broil over hot coals. When nearly done sprinkle with salt and pepper. Have ready some parsley chopped fine and mixed with softened butter. Beat them together to a cream and pour into the middle of the dish. Dip each steak into the butter, turning them around on the platter. If liked, squeeze a few drops of lemon over and serve very hot.

BEEF STEW WITH DUMPLINGS
MARY WHITCHER'S SHAKER HOUSEKEEPER

4 pounds beef for stew, cut in 2 inch squares	2 pounds small potatoes, peeled
Flour for dredging	5 good-sized onions
Salt and pepper	1 pint peeled and cubed carrots
3 tablespoons butter	1 pint peeled and halved turnips
2 quarts boiling water	3 stalks celery, chopped

⟨Dredge meat in flour seasoned with salt and pepper. Melt butter in iron pot and sear meat. Add boiling water and simmer 3 hours. Add potatoes, onions, carrots, turnips, and celery. Add more flour for thickening if necessary, and simmer 30 minutes. Potatoes help to thicken the stew, but may be omitted if dumplings are used. Have dumpling mixture ready and drop into stew by spoonfuls. Cover tightly and cook 12 minutes more. SERVES 6–8.

DUMPLINGS

2 cups flour	2 eggs
6 teaspoons baking powder	About ¾ cup milk
1 teaspoon salt	1 quart beef stock if dumplings are not to be cooked in stew liquid
1 tablespoon chopped parsley	
or	
1 tablespoon mixed chopped herbs, such as marjoram and chervil or thyme and chives	

⟨Sift flour with baking powder and salt. Add parsley and/or other herbs. Break eggs into cup and fill with milk; beat well and mix into dry ingredients. Heat stock in a 12 inch skillet and bring to a boil. Dip spoon into stock, then fill it with batter and drop into stock. Do not cook too many at a time; dumplings must not touch. Cover tightly and cook 2 minutes. Turn dumplings and cook 2 minutes longer. Serve very hot with gravy. SERVES 6.

BEEF STEW WITH HERBS
NORTH UNION SHAKER VILLAGE, OHIO

Lump of suet, approximately 4
  ounces
1 pound boneless chuck beef, cut in
  chunks
1 tablespoon flour
1 teaspoon salt
¼ teaspoon pepper

1 large onion, sliced
½ cup cider
½ cup water
¼ teaspoon minced marjoram
½ teaspoon minced thyme
2 carrots, diced
2 turnips, diced

⟮Cut suet fine and try it out in an iron pot. Remove cracklins (bits of browned fat). Roll meat in flour, salt, and pepper and brown well in the hot fat. Add onion and simmer with meat for 10 minutes. Add cider and water; cover pot tightly and let cook very slowly for 2 hours. Add a few drops of liquid from time to time, if needed. Last half hour add minced herbs, diced carrots and turnips. Taste to see if seasoned satisfactorily. Simmer until vegetables are tender. SERVES 2.

HERBED BEEF STEW FROM THE COLD ROAST
SHIRLEY SHAKER VILLAGE

Bones of the roast
About 1½ pounds meat without fat
2 cups boiling water
5 tablespoons liquid fat (lard or oil)
1 large onion
2 tablespoons minced carrots
2 tablespoons minced celery

1 tablespoon butter
1½ tablespoons flour
2 level teaspoons salt
¼ teaspoon pepper
2 cups minced raw potatoes
1 teaspoon each, chopped thyme,
  marjoram, and mint

⟮In a stew pan combine bones of roast, meat cut into small pieces, and 1 cup of the boiling water. Simmer gently 5 minutes. In a fry pan heat fat, add onions, carrots, celery, and fry gently until they are soft. Add to meat and bones. In same frying pan melt butter and add the flour, salt, pepper, and second cup of boiling water. Cook 3 minutes. Add potatoes and simmer 5 minutes. Add herbs. Simmer 5 minutes and add to bones, meat, and other vegetables. Remove bones. Cook 10 minutes. SERVES 4–6.

CORNED BEEF AND CABBAGE

HANCOCK SHAKER VILLAGE

4 pounds corned beef	6 carrots
1 tablespoon brown sugar	6 onions studded with cloves
6 potatoes, peeled	Salt
6 turnips	1 medium cabbage, quartered

⟨[Soak choice brisket of corned beef in cold water for an hour. Drain and cover with fresh cold water and bring to a boil. Skim well. Put pot on low heat, add tablespoon of brown sugar, and let meat simmer partially covered very gently for 4 hours; 30 minutes before meat is done, boil in a separate pot, the peeled potatoes, turnips, carrots, and onions, salted lightly. In still another pot cook the cut cabbage 15 minutes. Lift the brisket onto a large, well-heated platter and surround with the cooked vegetables. Serve with fresh horse-radish or mustard or Shaker Horse-radish Sauce* and Shaker Made Mustard.* Sauce with this should be tart because vegetables are sweet. SERVES 4–6.

PRESSED CORNED BEEF

MARY WHITCHER'S SHAKER HOUSEKEEPER

⟨[The thin part of the ribs, the brisket, and the flank are the best parts to press. Wash the meat and if it is very salty, cover with boiling water, let it come to a boil, and skim; then cover and simmer 6 hours, unless the piece weighs more than 10 or 12 pounds; in which case allow 15 minutes for every additional pound. No matter how small the piece, it will require 6 hours to cook. When done, take from the fire and let it stand 1 hour in the water in which it was boiled; then take out the bones, place the meat on a platter or cake pan, put a tin sheet on top of it; and on the sheet a weight. Set in a cool place. In the morning trim the edges; use the trimmings for hash. If the beef is boiled rapidly, it will be dry and stringy, but if it is allowed only to bubble it will be tender and juicy. This is true of all kinds of meat. Ten pounds of meat serves about 15.

Serve with your favorite sauce. Horse-radish goes especially well with this dish.

CHIPPED BEEF PIE WITH MUSHROOMS

HANCOCK SHAKER VILLAGE

½ cup melted butter
4 cups fresh bread crumbs
2 tablespoons grated onion
½ teaspoon salt
¼ teaspoon pepper
¼ teaspoon powdered dried thyme
½ cup butter

½ cup flour
2 cups rich milk
2 cups shredded chipped beef
1 cup chopped mushrooms, sautéed
½ cup heavy cream
1 cup buttered bread crumbs

(To prepare bread crumb piecrust, combine melted butter, bread crumbs, onion, salt, pepper, and thyme. Mix well. Press mixture onto bottom and sides of 2 quart baking dish. Bake in preheated oven at 425° F. for 25 minutes.

Make a cream sauce by melting ½ cup butter, adding flour and milk. Bring to a boil stirring constantly to keep smooth. Add shredded chipped beef and sautéed chopped mushrooms. Cook 5 minutes, add heavy cream, pour into crust in baking dish. Top with buttered crumbs. Bake for 20 minutes at 350° F. or until golden brown. SERVES 8–10.

POT ROAST OF BEEF WITH CRANBERRY SAUCE*

FRANCES HALL, HANCOCK SHAKER VILLAGE

5 pounds chuck beef, boned and
rolled (or bottom round roast)
4 tablespoons fat
2 cups strained Cranberry Sauce*
3 cloves

1 onion, chopped
1 cup water
Salt and pepper
4–6 tablespoons flour
4 tablespoons butter

(Put meat in heavy kettle on top of stove. Sear in fat and brown on all sides. Add Cranberry Sauce (if thicker sauce is desired use sauce made of whole fruit and not strained), cloves, onion, water, salt and pepper to taste. Combine flour and butter and add to pot. Simmer covered 3 hours or until tender. Pour off liquid, cook down until it thickens. If not rich enough add a little extra butter. SERVES 8–10.

SHAKER FLANK STEAK
HANCOCK SHAKER VILLAGE

3 pounds round beef, cut 1½ inches
   thick
2 tablespoons flour
2 tablespoons butter
1 teaspoon salt
¼ teaspoon pepper

1 stalk celery, chopped
1 carrot, chopped fine
½ green pepper, chopped fine
2 medium onions, chopped fine
Juice ½ lemon
½ cup catsup

《Cut or score both sides of the meat diagonally and dust with flour. Sauté in heated butter until well browned on both sides. Season with salt and pepper, then add all the chopped vegetables. Last of all, add lemon juice and catsup. Cover tightly and simmer very gently for 1 to 1½ hours, or until the steak is tender when tested with a fork. The vegetables cook down to a rich sauce to be served with the meat. SERVES 6.

SOUR CREAM STEAK
SHIRLEY SHAKER VILLAGE

3 pounds top round of beef, cut 1½
   inches thick
3 tablespoons flour
2 teaspoons salt
Suet for frying
    or

2 tablespoons butter
4 medium onions, sliced thin
1 cup boiling water
1–1½ cups sour cream

《Trim meat, cut into serving pieces, or leave in one piece and carve after cooking. Pound flour and salt into meat. Thorough pounding will help make it more tender and shorten baking time. Brown well in fat in hot frying pan, on both sides. Brown onions and put on top of meat. Transfer to a baking pan. Add 1 cup of boiling water to sour cream. Mix well and cover meat with it. Bake 2½ hours in moderate 350° F. oven or until meat is very tender. SERVES 4–6.

MEAT LOAF WITH HERBS
MT. LEBANON SHAKER VILLAGE

3 pounds beef (bottom round),
   chopped fine or ground
½ pound salt pork, chopped fine
   or ground
1 onion, minced fine
1 tablespoon butter

½ tablespoon minced marjoram
½ tablespoon minced savory
½ tablespoon minced chives
½ teaspoon each salt and pepper
½ teaspoon sugar
4 slices bread soaked in 1 cup milk

《Knead together all ingredients. Form into a loaf and put in a 9 inch oiled loaf pan. Bake 1½ hours in 350° F. oven. Baste at 10 minute intervals with the following mixture:

1 tablespoon bacon drippings   1 tablespoon vinegar
1 tablespoon olive oil   1 tablespoon tomato catsup

Remove to platter, pour around a tomato or brown sauce. SERVES 6.

HAM BAKED IN CIDER
MARY WHITCHER'S SHAKER HOUSEKEEPER

11 pound ham   2 tablespoons brown sugar
24 whole cloves   2 small onions
1 cup boiling water   1 tablespoon lemon juice
4 cups apple cider   1 tablespoon flour, browned[1]

《Scrub ham thoroughly and soak overnight in cold water. If the ham has been precooked, it will be ready for baking. If not, put in cold water and bring to a rapid boil; reduce heat and simmer covered for 3 hours. Let cool in liquid. Remove rind and trim fat; score and stud with cloves. Combine boiling water, cider, brown sugar, and onions and boil 10 minutes. Strain and pour over ham in roaster and bake 1 hour in moderate 350° F. oven, basting every 15 minutes. Remove ham from roaster and strain liquid; add lemon juice and thicken with browned flour.[1] Serve this as a sauce with the ham, or serve Cider Sauce.* SERVES 12.

HAM CROQUETTES WITH RAISIN SAUCE
HANCOCK SHAKER VILLAGE

2 cups ground ham   1 teaspoon sugar
1 tablespoon minced onion   1 cup White Sauce #2*
½ teaspoon pepper   1 cup fine bread crumbs or cracker
1 tablespoon vinegar   crumbs
1 teaspoon minced thyme or sage   1 egg and 2 tablespoons water,
1 teaspoon minced rosemary   mixed
1 tablespoon minced parsley   Deep fat for frying

《Combine ham, onion, pepper, vinegar, herbs, parsley, sugar, and 1 cup of White Sauce. Blend well, chill thoroughly. Shape into croquettes. Roll croquettes in crumbs, dip in egg and water mixture to coat all sides; roll again in crumbs. Fry in deep hot fat about 6 minutes until well browned. Drain on absorbent paper. Serve with Raisin Sauce* or Egg and Mustard Sauce.* SERVES 6.

---

[1]*Browned Flour:* Place 1 tablespoon flour in small skillet oven low heat. Stir constantly until browned.

HAM FRITTERS WITH HOT TARTAR SAUCE

MT. LEBANON SHAKER VILLAGE

([To Basic Fritter Recipe* for batter add sufficient ground or finely chopped ham to make a very thick mass. Drop by spoonfuls into hot lard. Turn once and serve when golden.

Sauce: Heat thoroughly 2 cups White Sauce #2.* Remove from heat and stir in 1 cup Hot Tartar Sauce.* Do not reheat.

HAM LOAF

HANCOCK SHAKER VILLAGE

2 pounds ground smoked ham
1 pound lean pork or veal
½ teaspoon salt
¼ teaspoon pepper
1 tablespoon very finely chopped
   (almost mashed) onions

1 cup bread or cracker crumbs
2 eggs, beaten
1½ cups tomato juice with 1
   teaspoon sugar dissolved in it
8 whole cloves (for the top)

([Mix all ingredients except cloves and ¼ cup of the tomato juice. Shape into a loaf. Pour rest of tomato juice over top. Stick with cloves. Use 8 inch loaf pan. If loaf pan is set inside another pan of water, it will make a moister loaf. Cook at 350° F. for 2 hours. SERVES 8.

Variation: Mix together all of the ingredients except whole cloves and put in top of double boiler, covered. Steam over boiling water 3 hours, or until mixture holds its shape. Unmold on platter and serve with the following sauce.

SAUCE

1 cup White Sauce #2*
½ cup onion purée
1½ teaspoons prepared mustard

1 teaspoon horse-radish
1 teaspoon brown sugar
½ cup chopped raisins

([Heat white sauce. Add puréed onion and remaining ingredients. Serve very hot. If it needs thinning, thin with cider. Makes 2 cups.

HAM AND POTATO HASH WITH HOT EGG SAUCE
HANCOCK SHAKER VILLAGE

2 tablespoons butter
½ cup finely chopped celery
½ cup finely chopped onion
2 tablespoons flour
1 cup chicken stock
1 cup ground cooked ham

1 cup finely diced cooked potato
Salt and pepper
Dry mustard
2 tablespoons clear bacon grease
   or drippings

([Melt butter, add celery and onion, and sauté until soft; sprinkle with flour. Add chicken stock and mix well. Let thicken, stirring all the time. Add ham and potatoes and seasonings; mix well to blend. In another skillet melt bacon drippings and heat. Fry ham and potato mixture on one side until brown, turn, brown other side. Slip onto a heated platter. Encircle with Hot Egg Sauce, given below. SERVES 4.

HOT EGG SAUCE

3 tablespoons butter
3 tablespoons flour
1 cup milk
½ cup heavy cream
2 hard-boiled eggs, chopped

1 tablespoon chopped parsley
½ teaspoon salt
½ teaspoon pepper
½ teaspoon dry mustard

([Melt butter, add flour, and simmer 5 minutes. Add milk and bring to a boil, stirring constantly. Add cream and remove from heat. Stir vigorously. Add eggs and remaining ingredients and return to heat to blend. Makes 2 cups.

HAM STEAK IN CREAM SAUCE
MT. LEBANON SHAKER VILLAGE

([The ham slice should be cut to serve 4 and should be at least 1½ inches thick (2 pounds).

Poach ham slowly over low heat in cider to cover. This can be cooked in the oven at 300° F. or on top of stove, covered.

When ham is tender, in about 30 minutes, remove to baking dish and cover with the following sauce.

CREAM SAUCE

4 tablespoons chopped onions
4 tablespoons butter
4 tablespoons flour
½ cup dry (hard) cider—plus cider
  from poached ham up to ½ cup

1 teaspoon cinnamon
1 teaspoon nutmeg
Some pepper
½ cup heavy cream

❡ Sauté onions in butter. Add flour and cook slowly, being careful not to brown, approximately 2 minutes. Add cider and stock from ham. Add seasonings and lastly the cream. This should cover the ham, but if not, add more liquid—cider and cream.

Return to oven or top of stove until it bubbles. Remove and serve. SERVES 4.

∴

"Food experts claim liver is a real blood-builder and that it furnishes quick energy. We try to serve it to our sick and aged at least once a week. Pork, poultry, and game liver are equally healthy, but are best made into dressing, sausage loaves and fillings."

LIVER BAKED WITH ONIONS AND HERBS
THE MANIFESTO

1 large onion, sliced
2 tablespoons melted butter
¼ cup hot water
6 slices liver (calf, veal, or beef),
  cut ½ inch thick
2 tablespoons flour, seasoned with

salt and pepper
1 tablespoon chopped parsley
2 teaspoons thyme
2 tablespoons thick chili sauce
1 tablespoon brown sugar
2 tablespoons butter

❡ Place onion in oven pan, pour over it butter and water. Cover and bake in moderate 350° F. oven 30 minutes. Dredge liver in flour; arrange over onions, sprinkle with parsley and thyme and dot with chili sauce, sugar, and butter. Bake covered for 30 minutes at 350° F. and uncovered until liver is browned. SERVES 6.

HOW TO COOK SALT PORK

This recipe comes from a kitchen notebook and also appeared in a *Manifesto* and Mary Whitcher's *Shaker Housekeeper*.

"At certain seasons it is hard to procure fresh meat, and salt pork becomes a steady diet for weeks at a time. Therefore, it is well to know how to cook it in sundry ways and avoid monotony of diet. If only a little thought and care are given to the matter, salt pork can be made a palatable dish. The proper way to fry it is to boil it first for 10 minutes. When cold, remove rind and cut in neat slices ¼ inch thick. Roll in corn meal and fry to a golden crisp. Or broil it over the live coals of the stove, which gives it a delicious flavor. Yet another tasty mode makes it a most satisfactory dish; fry the strips partly and then dip them into a batter of eggs and flour and fry in a well-buttered skillet. Or, cut the bacon in thick slices and bake them with your beans. Again, place thin slices on the succotash and brown in the oven. Vary your vegetables as much as possible; also your sauces, relishes and salads as well as your desserts and this will help to relieve the monotony of a salt pork diet."

ROAST PORK
HANCOCK SHAKER VILLAGE

4 pound loin of pork
1 clove garlic, sliced
Salt and pepper
4 tablespoons melted butter
1 cup sweet cider

1 cup applesauce
2 apples, pared and sliced thin
½–¾ cup brown sugar
½ cup heavy cream

❡Tie roast if needed to hold shape. Pierce here and there and insert bits of garlic in the holes. Rub with salt and pepper. Place fat side up in an open roasting pan. Sear in a very hot oven (450° F.) for 30 minutes, basting now and then with a mixture of fat in the pan, butter, and cider. After 30 minutes reduce heat to moderate (350° F.) and roast meat for another hour, basting often with drippings. Remove from oven and pour off about three-quarters of the fat in the pan. Spread roast with applesauce and arrange apple slices sprinkled with brown sugar around the roast in the pan. Return to the oven and roast about 1 hour longer, basting frequently. Add cream to pan gravy before serving. Serve gravy separately.

If cider is not available, apple juice or dry white wine can be substituted. SERVES 4.

ROAST OF PORK
NORTH UNION SHAKER VILLAGE, OHIO

5 or 6 pounds loin of pork
Juice ½ lemon
1 teaspoon ground ginger
1 teaspoon salt

½ teaspoon pepper
1 teaspoon flour
Small peeled potatoes
3 tablespoons flour

⟮Trim off some of the fat, for too much fat spoils the flavor of any meat and makes pork indigestible. Place roast in baking pan and pour the lemon juice over it. Dust with ginger; sprinkle with salt and pepper, and dredge with flour. Bake in a moderate 350° F. oven for 3 to 3½ hours. For the last half hour, surround with small peeled potatoes. These will absorb some of the fat. Make a brown gravy from pan leavings.

Remove enough pan gravy to make 2 cups (otherwise augment with hot beef boullion). Mix 3 tablespoons flour with ½ cup pan juice and beat to make smooth. Heat gravy in saucepan and gradually add flour, stirring to keep smooth. Add salt and pepper to taste. SERVES 8.

The Shakers thought ginger aided digestion, and it was added often to pork and other hearty dishes.

ROAST OF PORK WITH HERBS
HANCOCK SHAKER VILLAGE

1 loin of pork, 8–10 pounds
2 tablespoons butter
1 teaspoon each salt and pepper
1 tablespoon sugar
½ cup flour
2 cups beef broth
1 cup cider

1 clove minced garlic
1 teaspoon crushed rosemary
1 teaspoon chopped basil
1 teaspoon nutmeg
1 teaspoon ginger
1 cup heavy cream

⟮Rub meat with butter, salt and pepper, sugar, and sprinkle with flour. Put in moderate 350° F. oven and cook 30 minutes. Then baste with mixture made by cooking broth, cider, herbs, and spices together for 5 minutes. Cook 3 to 3½ hours longer.

Add cream to pan gravy and serve hot, but do not boil as this would curdle cream.

Serve Shaker Applesauce* with this or Spiced Grapes.* SERVES 8–10.

PORK CHOPS WITH MUSTARD
MT. LEBANON SHAKER VILLAGE

4 thick pork chops (rib or loin)	Salt and pepper
2 tablespoons butter	½ cup heavy cream
½ cup cider	2 tablespoons finely chopped
1 teaspoon mustard	parsley or chives

◖In a large skillet fry the chops very slowly in the butter until brown on both sides. This should take 30 to 40 minutes, keeping the pan covered. Add cider and cook 10 minutes longer if necessary. This depends on the thickness of the chops. Chops should be tender. Pork needs slow, long cooking.

Remove chops to heated platter and keep warm. Add seasonings and cream to liquid in fry pan; heat up. Pour over chops, garnish with parsley or chives, and serve at once. SERVES 4.

PORK CHOPS COOKED WITH SOUR CREAM
MARY WHITCHER'S SHAKER HOUSEKEEPER

6 thick pork chops (center or loin cut)	2 cups rich chicken stock, seasoned with salt and pepper
2 tablespoons prepared mustard	8 small onions, chopped
½ cup flour	1–1½ cups thick sour cream
4 tablespoons butter, melted	

◖Before frying, rub each thick pork chop with prepared mustard. Then roll chops in flour. In deep skillet fry in butter until brown. Add chicken stock and onions and simmer covered on low heat 1 hour.

Pour off liquid. To this add 1 cup and possibly another ½ cup of thick sour cream if more sauce is wanted. Mix well. Do not let sauce boil after adding cream. Sour cream should be at room temperature when added to hot pan liquid. Place chops on serving platter; pour hot sauce over all. SERVES 6.

As a suggestion serve with Corn Fritters.*

PORK PIE
SHIRLEY SHAKER VILLAGE

3 thin slices ham
6 strips lean bacon
1 pound fresh pork, diced
2 cups diced raw potatoes
1 cup finely chopped onions
3 hard-boiled eggs, sliced
1 cup chicken broth
1 tablespoon flour

½ teaspoon salt
1 teaspoon pepper
1 teaspoon sugar
1 teaspoon thyme
1 teaspoon sage
½ cup heavy cream
Pastry* for 8 inch pie dish

⟨In a deep pie dish (8 inches across and 4 inches deep), arrange alternately the ham, bacon, and pork. In another layer arrange potatoes, onions, and hard-boiled eggs. Moisten both layers with chicken broth and sprinkle with flour, seasonings, and herbs. Lastly add cream and cover with pastry. Bake in a moderate 350° F. oven for 2 hours. SERVES 4.

PORK STEAKS WITH WINTER CABBAGE
SHIRLEY SHAKER VILLAGE

1 small winter cabbage
Salt and pepper
1 cup heavy cream
4 lean pork steaks (center cut or
   loin chops)
2 tablespoons butter
½ teaspoon salt

½ teaspoon pepper
½ cup winter cider (hard)
½ teaspoon sage
½ cup heavy cream
2 tablespoons butter
Fine bread crumbs

⟨Remove tough portion of cabbage. Slice cabbage fine and boil for 10 minutes in salted water to cover. Drain thoroughly. Add salt, pepper, and cream. Simmer covered for 20 minutes.

Trim chops of most of fat. Sauté in butter until they are brown and cooked through, about 25 to 30 minutes. Remove chops and season with salt and pepper. Stir cider into pan juices; add sage and simmer 2 minutes. Stir this mixture into creamed cabbage.

Butter a baking dish; put cabbage in dish and nestle pork well into the cabbage. Cover with heavy cream. Dot with butter and sprinkle with fine bread crumbs. Bake uncovered at 350° F. for 20 minutes or until top is golden and bubbly. SERVES 4.

LIMA BEANS AND PORK CHOPS
A NEW HAMPSHIRE SHAKER MANUSCRIPT

2 cups green lima beans
2 teaspoons salt
1 teaspoon pepper
2 tablespoons sugar
1 teaspoon dry mustard
1 tablespoon finely chopped parsley

2 tablespoons finely chopped onion
6 pork chops, cut 1 inch thick
2 tablespoons butter
2 cups fine bread crumbs, toasted
1 cup sour cream

⁅Cook lima beans until almost tender. Pour into a large flat baking dish with ½ cup of water beans were cooked in. Add salt, pepper, sugar, mustard, parsley, and chopped onion. Mix well.

Brown chops in butter. Place on top of the beans.

Mix bread crumbs with sour cream. Spread over chops. Cover dish. Bake 50 minutes at 350° F. Check and uncover the last 10 to 20 minutes to brown. SERVES 6.

PORK STEAKS
(Double Pork Chops)
HANCOCK SHAKER VILLAGE

4 pork chops (center cut or loin),
    cut 1½ inches thick
Butter
Salt and pepper
1 teaspoon ginger
1 tablespoon brown sugar

2 tablespoons butter
2 tablespoons chopped onion
½ cup chopped peeled apples
½ cup cider
½ cup heavy cream

⁅In a skillet fry chops in butter until brown on both sides. Add salt and pepper, ginger, and brown sugar. Remove to an oven pan. In same skillet melt butter, add onions, and cook until really soft. Add apples and cider and cook down until it is all soft like applesauce. When this state is reached, add cream and pour over chops. Bake chops an hour at 350° F. or until tender. If more moisture is needed add more cider. SERVES 4.

HOMEMADE SAUSAGE MEAT
PLEASANT HILL SHAKER VILLAGE

5 pounds fat pork meat
15 pounds lean pork
½ cup salt
½ tablespoon red pepper

1½ tablespoons black pepper
2½ tablespoons ground sage
1 tablespoon sugar

⟨[Run meat through meat chopper twice and mix thoroughly. Add seasonings and mix very thoroughly. Cover tightly and refrigerate well. Stir well each time before using. Use within 2 weeks. Yields 20 pounds.

SAUSAGE MEAT #1
NORTH UNION SHAKER VILLAGE, OHIO

5 pounds lean pork tenderloin,
  no bones
5 pounds fat pork
4 tablespoons ground sage

1 tablespoon black pepper
1½ tablespoons salt
1 teaspoon ground allspice
1 teaspoon ground cloves

⟨[Put pork through grinder; add remaining ingredients. Mix thoroughly. The consistency should be fine. Roll into a cylinder and wrap in muslin or cheesecloth—this is to keep sausage in shape. Refrigerate. When ready to use, cut into cakes and fry in butter. Yields 10 pounds.

SAUSAGE MEAT #2
ENFIELD SHAKER VILLAGE, CONNECTICUT

6 pounds lean pork
3 pounds fat pork
12 teaspoons powdered sage
6 teaspoons black pepper
6 teaspoons salt

2 teaspoons powdered mace
2 teaspoons powdered cloves
1 whole grated nutmeg
Melted lard

⟨[Chop the meat fine, or grind. Mix the seasonings with the meat well, and pack down in stone jars, pouring a layer of melted lard on top. This is to keep nicely. When you want to use, take enough for a meal, replacing lard layer, form into small cakes and fry. The fat in the sausage meat is sufficient to fry them; do not use any other grease in the pan. Yields 9 pounds.

BAKED STUFFED APPLES WITH SAUSAGE
HANCOCK SHAKER VILLAGE

⟨Wash, pare, and core 1 apple per serving. Apples should be fairly large if they are to provide main dish, smaller if used to garnish a roast turkey or capon.

Fill cavity with pork sausage, using, if possible, Homemade Sausage Meat.*

Bake in a moderate 350° F. oven about 1 hour, or until apples are tender and sausage thoroughly cooked.

SAUSAGE COOKED IN CIDER
WATERVLIET SHAKER VILLAGE, NEW YORK

1 pound link sausage
¼ cup water
Butter
1 small onion, finely chopped

2 teaspoons finely chopped parsley
1 tablespoon flour
1 cup cider

⟨Use thick link sausages. Prick them all over. Put in a frying pan with water. Cover and cook 5 minutes. Uncover, turn sausages to brown evenly. Remove when brown to a serving dish and keep warm.

Use fat in pan and add butter to make 3 tablespoons. Add onion and fry until golden. Add parsley and flour; blend, and then add cider. Stir well and have liquid come to a boil. Stir to keep smooth and return sausages to the pan. Simmer a few minutes. Place sausages on serving plate; pour sauce over them. SERVES 4.

Serve with Honeyed Apple Rings.*

SAUSAGE HASH
HARVARD SHAKER VILLAGE

3 cold boiled medium potatoes
2 cooked link sausages
½ teaspoon salt

⅛ teaspoon pepper
¼ teaspoon sugar
1 teaspoon butter

⟨Chop potatoes coarsely. Chop sausage a bit finer. Season potatoes with salt, pepper, sugar, and add sausage. Melt butter in a frying pan. Add mixture, spread lightly, but do not stir. Cover pan and cook over low heat to brown hash slowly. Cook ½ hour. Turn out on a hot platter. SERVES 2.

SAUSAGE LOAF

1½ pounds sausage meat in bulk
½ cup milk
1½ cups fine bread or cracker
   crumbs
1 tablespoon finely chopped onion

2 tablespoons tomato catsup,*
   homemade if possible
2 tablespoons Horse-radish Sauce,*
   homemade if possible
½ teaspoon dry mustard
1 egg

⟮If sausage meat is not well seasoned, add ½ teaspoon each of salt and pepper and 1½ tablespoons ground sage. If you taste the raw sausage meat, taste only, and do not swallow, as pork not raised on one's own farm should be cooked well before eating. Once cooked, pork is as safe as any other meat purchased from a reputable dealer.

Mix ingredients in order listed. Mix well and mold into a loaf. Place on a rack in a shallow pan, not a loaf pan. Bake uncovered in a moderate 350° F. oven for 1 hour. Serve with Tomato Sauce* made the Shaker way. SERVES 4–5.

∴

Sheep were raised in great numbers on Shaker farms to provide wool for cloth and knitted garments and to supply meat. The carding, spinning, and weaving were done by the sisters and the cloth used for brethren's and sisters' clothing was woven on orders from the tailors in the clothiers' shops. Weavers' records list thousands of yards of cloth for dresses, shirts, coats, cloaks, trousers, jackets, bed blankets, and horse blankets for each community.

It is not surprising, therefore, that with such a need for wool, mutton was plentiful, and in the spring young lambs were slaughtered to keep the flocks manageable in size. Lamb could be eaten soon after the animal was killed and dressed. Mutton was hung from two to three weeks and stored in the village ice houses. It was very plentiful.

Today lamb is more likely to be a yearling before it is killed and may weigh up to 8 pounds a leg. Some of this heavy meat is comparable to mutton. Good mutton from sheep 3 years old or more, without its fat, is ranked with the flesh of beef in nutritive value and digestibility and when available is hard to beat.

BREADED MUTTON OR HEAVY LAMB CHOPS

MT. LEBANON SHAKER VILLAGE

⟨[Wipe and trim chops, and sprinkle with salt and pepper. Dip in fine bread crumbs, beaten egg, and again in crumbs. Fry in deep fat from 5 to 8 minutes and drain. (Never fry but four at a time and allow fat to reheat between times.) Then put all the chops back in skillet with some fat on low heat and allow chops to continue to cook so that surface of chops may not be too brown while the inside is still underdone.

Serve with Spicy Tomato Sauce.*

Variation: Chops or cutlets may be steamed first and then fried. Serve with Caper Sauce* or Mint Sauce for Lamb.* This preparation was used by the Harvard (Massachusetts) Shakers.

LAMB STEAKS

THE MANIFESTO

1 bay leaf
1 teaspoon finely chopped thyme
1 teaspoon finely chopped parsley
1 teaspoon finely chopped sweet
    marjoram
1 teaspoon finely chopped mint

4 lamb chops (loin, center cut, or
    shoulder), cut thick
1 teaspoon each salt and pepper
Olive oil
1 teaspoon dry mustard

⟨[Pulverize bay leaf. Mix with finely chopped herbs about an hour before cooking meat. Salt and pepper chops and broil on both sides. Mix olive oil with herbs and dry mustard to make a paste. When chops are very hot, spread each one with a mixture of olive oil and herbs. Serve at once. SERVES 4.

MUTTON CHOPS

MT. LEBANON SHAKER VILLAGE

⟨[Cut chops at least 1½ inches thick. Brown in butter on both sides in frying pan. Add chicken broth to depth of ½ inch. Simmer 15 minutes, or until tender. Remove to warm platter and cover with following sauce.

LEEK SAUCE

⟨Simmer 3 leeks cut up fine in 2 cups chicken broth. Reduce to ½ cup. Add this to 1 cup White Sauce #4.* Add 1 teaspoon each salt and pepper. Cook until very thick; add ½ cup sour cream. Serve at once. Yields 2 cups sauce.

MINTED LAMB SHANKS
HANCOCK SHAKER VILLAGE

4 lamb shanks	1 tablespoon brown sugar
Salt and pepper	½ teaspoon cinnamon
Flour	½ teaspoon allspice
1 cup water	¼ teaspoon cloves
½ cup pitted cooked prunes	3 tablespoons vinegar
½ cup cooked apricots	¼ teaspoon salt
1 tablespoon chopped parsley	1 tablespoon chopped mint

⟨Season meat with salt and pepper, dredge with flour, and place in large (4 quart) greased baking dish. Cover and bake in moderate 350° F. oven until meat is tender, 1¾ to 2 hours. Combine remaining ingredients, heat to boiling, and simmer about 5 minutes. Draw most of fat from cooked shanks, add fruit mixture to meat, cover and bake at 400° F. for 30 minutes. SERVES 4.

ROAST OF LAMB WITH GINGER AND CIDER
HANCOCK SHAKER VILLAGE

⟨Rub a 5 pound roast of lamb with butter and ginger, salt and pepper, and sprinkle with flour. Put in hot oven to brown, 450° F., then reduce to 325° F. and baste with following mixture, which has simmered 5 minutes. Do not cook more than 3 hours altogether. SERVES 4–6.

Sauce:

½ cup beef broth	1 onion, minced
½ cup dry cider	1 teaspoon sugar
2 tablespoons minced mint and/or rosemary	1 teaspoon ginger

LOIN OF MUTTON
MT. LEBANON SHAKER VILLAGE

⟨[Remove the leg from the carcass. Broil the joint very slowly until a quarter done, about 1 hour, basting with butter and ginger. Take it out and sprinkle with herbs—dill, rosemary; basil is especially good—and bread crumbs; then put in 350° F. oven and bake until done, approximately 1 hour, basting all the while.

Serve with Egg Sauce.*

BRAISED LEG OF MUTTON OR HEAVY LAMB
MT. LEBANON SHAKER VILLAGE

¼ cup butter, melted
1 small onion, sliced
1 small carrot, sliced
1 bay leaf
1 teaspoon thyme
1 teaspoon parsley

3 cups hot water
1 teaspoon ginger
1½ teaspoons salt
12 peppercorns
5–7 pound boned leg of lamb

⟨[In melted butter cook onion and carrot, add remaining ingredients. Simmer until tender and pour over meat, which has been wiped, stuffed, sewed, and placed in deep pan. Cover closely. Cook slowly (325° F.) 3 hours. Uncover for last half hour. Remove meat to hot platter and pour over the gravy. Stuffing and gravy are given below. SERVES 8.

STUFFING

½ cup bread or cracker crumbs
½ cup melted butter
¼ teaspoon salt
⅛ teaspoon pepper

1 tablespoon brown sugar
1 teaspoon powdered allspice
¼ cup boiling water

Mix all ingredients and stuff leg. Yields 1½ cups.

GRAVY

1 cup butter
2 cups Browned Flour*
½ cup brown sugar
Juice 2 lemons
1 teaspoon allspice
1 teaspoon nutmeg

1 cup mint jelly
Pan juices
2 tablespoons butter, melted
1 cup finely chopped onion
½ cup finely chopped celery
Salt and pepper

([Melt butter, add flour and sugar, cook 2 minutes; add lemon juice, spices, mint jelly, and any pan juices. In 2 tablespoons butter cook onion and celery until soft, add salt and pepper. Add to flour mixture. If gravy is too thick, add hot water and butter, half and half. Stir to make smooth. Yields 5–6 cups.

LAMB PIE WITH DILL
HANCOCK SHAKER VILLAGE

3 pounds breast of lamb
Salt and pepper to taste
1 large carrot, sliced
1 medium onion, diced
½ cup diced celery
1–2 tablespoons flour, depending
   on thickness of sauce desired

1 tablespoon vinegar
1 teaspoon sugar
½ cup heavy cream
2 egg yolks
¾ cup chopped fresh dillweed, or
   more to taste
Piecrust* for 9 inch pie dish

([Trim meat of excess fat. Cut meat into 2 inch cubes. Sprinkle with salt and pepper. Place in deep kettle with carrot, onion, celery, and water to cover. Simmer covered over low heat 1 to 1¼ hours or until meat is tender. Skim off fat if necessary and stir occasionally.

Drain off liquid into a saucepan and reduce to 1½ cups. Mix flour with a little water and stir into liquid. Cook until smooth and thickened, stirring constantly. Stir in vinegar and sugar.

Beat together the cream and egg yolks. Stir into sauce.

Pour sauce over meat. Sprinkle with dill. Remove lamb with liquid to deep 9 inch pie dish. Cover with your best pastry. Cook at 350° F. for 45 minutes. SERVES 5 to 6.

Variation: Can also be served without piecrust on a large platter surrounded with parsley or plain dumplings.

Dillweed is foliage of dill plant. If dried powdered dill is substituted use ½ cup.

LAMB STEW, OVEN BAKED
HANCOCK SHAKER VILLAGE

3 pounds shoulder of lamb, boned and cut into 1 inch pieces
⅓ cup flour
2 teaspoons salt
½ teaspoon pepper
1 teaspoon brown sugar
½ cup butter
1 large onion, chopped fine
1 cup finely chopped celery

2 cups peeled, seeded, and chopped tomatoes
2 cups chicken stock
2 small onions
2 cups chopped carrots
1 cup heavy cream with 2 egg yolks beaten up in it
1 cup cooked peas
2 tablespoons chopped parsley

⟮Dredge lamb in flour seasoned with salt, pepper, and brown sugar. In a skillet sauté meat in butter until it is browned on all sides; add onion, celery, and tomatoes and sauté 10 minutes. Remove to a greased oven baking dish. Add chicken stock, onions, and carrots. Cover, bake in 350° F. oven 1½ hours. Liquid should be reduced considerably. Add cream and peas. Serve sprinkled with parsley. SERVES 6–8.

LAMB STEW
MT. LEBANON SHAKER VILLAGE

3 pounds lean shoulder of lamb (free of bone), cut in 2 inch pieces
Flour
Salt and pepper
Dry mustard
4 tablespoons butter or chicken fat*
4 tablespoons grated onion

3 cups boiling water to cover lamb, use more if necessary
1 cup cider
3 large onions, sliced
2 carrots, diced small
3 teaspoons celery seeds
3 tablespoons catsup*
3 tablespoons chopped parsley

⟮Use a cast iron kettle or deep skillet. Dredge lamb in flour seasoned with salt, pepper, and dry mustard. Melt butter or fat, add grated onion, and meat, cook over medium heat until well browned. Stir in water and cider, cover and simmer 30 minutes. Add onions, carrots, celery seeds, more salt if needed. Remove cover and simmer another hour. Check liquid; add water, or chicken broth or cider if necessary, but there should not be an excess of liquid. The meat should cook until tender. It should absorb liquid and be moist. Add catsup and chopped parsley 5 minutes before removing from heat. SERVES 8.

Suggestion: Boil new potatoes in their jackets. Break open with a fork; add butter, sprinkle with chopped chives, and surround stew on platter.

SWEETBREADS

MT. LEBANON SHAKER VILLAGE

2 pairs sweetbreads	½ cup heavy cream
Juice 1 lemon	Salt and pepper
3 tablespoons butter	Nutmeg
2 tablespoons flour	4 pieces thinly sliced ham
1 cup hot chicken stock	4 slices toast
2 egg yolks	

❴[Gently cook the sweetbreads in water with lemon juice, about 15 minutes. Drain and cool. Remove all connecting and covering tissue. Make a cream sauce of melted butter, adding flour. Cook 2 minutes; remove from stove. Add warm chicken stock and cook until it thickens. Add to sweetbreads, which have been cut into bite-size pieces. Heat well.

Add beaten egg yolks to cream. Add this mixture to sweetbreads. Season with salt, pepper, and nutmeg; do not boil.

To serve, arrange a thick slice of ham, which has been sautéed in butter just enough to heat through, on a piece of toast. Cover with sweetbreads. Finely chopped chives can be added as a garnish. SERVES 4.

CREAMED SWEETBREADS WITH CIDER SAUCE

FRANCES HALL, HANCOCK SHAKER VILLAGE, 1910

❴[Gently cook a pair of sweetbreads in salted water or with lemon juice until tender and white about 25 minutes. (Sweetbreads can be soaked for 30 minutes before cooking, if you like. It is not necessary.) Cool and remove membrane or connective tissue. Combine with the following sauce. Top with seasoned bread crumbs. Serve when just bubbly. SERVES 4.

CIDER SAUCE

4 tablespoons butter	½ cup heavy cream
4 tablespoons finely chopped onions	4 tablespoons very fine bread crumbs
4 tablespoons flour	2 tablespoons melted butter
1 cup sweet cider	1 tablespoon mixed chopped herbs
1 teaspoon salt	(marjoram, savory, parsley)
1 teaspoon pepper	

⟨[Melt butter and sauté onions without browning until they are very soft. Add flour, cook 2 minutes; add cider. Sauce should be smooth and thick. Add salt and pepper. Drain sweetbreads. Break up into small pieces. Combine with sauce. Add cream, mix well. Put in an ovenproof dish and sprinkle top with bread crumbs which have been sautéed in melted butter with 1 tablespoon mixed chopped herbs.

SWEETBREAD OR CHICKEN OR LAMB CROQUETTES
HARVARD SHAKER VILLAGE

2 tablespoons butter
3 tablespoons flour
1 cup boiling milk
½ teaspoon each salt and white
  pepper
2 eggs, lightly beaten
2 cups cut-up cooked
  sweetbreads

Flour
1 egg
2 teaspoons milk
Deep fat for frying
1 tablespoon heavy cream
1 egg yolk
chopped chives

⟨[Melt butter, add flour, and cook gently 3 minutes. Add milk and cook until thick. Add salt and pepper. Add eggs, cook 1 minute, and add sweetbreads, or chicken, or cooked lamb.

Cook 5 minutes, stirring all the time. Spread mixture on buttered platter and cool. Shape croquettes into desired shape. Roll in flour, then into 1 egg beaten with 2 teaspoons milk. Cook in hot deep fat until golden brown.

Serve with White Sauce #4* made with cream and yolk of egg and add chopped chives to flavor. SERVES 4–6.

TONGUE SAUTÉE
SHIRLEY SHAKER VILLAGE

⟨[Cut cold, cooked tongue into thin slices. Allow 3 or 4 slices per serving. Dip each slice in flour, then in beaten egg, and then in very, very fine bread crumbs.

Sauté in melted, hot butter until delicately brown on both sides.

Serve with Dill Sour Cream Sauce,* Horse-radish Sauce,* or Hot Tartar Sauce.*

FRESH BEEF TONGUE WITH SPICY SAUCE
SHIRLEY SHAKER VILLAGE

1 fresh beef tongue	8 peppercorns
2 onions	2 teaspoons salt
1 large carrot	6 small ginger cookies
4 sprigs parsley	½ cup raw cranberries
1 stalk celery	1 tablespoon brown sugar
½ bay leaf	½ lemon, sliced and quartered

❨Scrub tongue and place in large kettle with onions, carrot, parsley, celery, bay leaf, peppercorns, and salt. Cover with boiling water, bring to a boil. Skim and simmer, covered, for 3 to 4 hours or until tender. Reserve the tongue liquid in case some is needed for the sauce. Remove the skin and root ends. Strain following sauce over tongue when ready to serve. SERVES 8.

SAUCE

Soak gingersnaps in enough water to cover, add cranberries, brown sugar, and lemon and simmer. Cook until soft, about 15 minutes. Mash cranberries, gingersnaps, and lemon. Check seasoning. If more liquid is needed, use tongue liquor. Makes 2 cups.

VEAL IN RICH CREAM SAUCE
HANCOCK SHAKER VILLAGE

❨The Shakers' very large herds provided an ample amount of veal. It was considered very easy to digest and the sisters prepared veal broth for invalids as they did chicken broth. The following dish is like Shaker Chicken Fricassee* and was served almost as often at Hancock.

4 pounds stewing veal, cut in 2 inch pieces	2 tablespoons thyme
	1 tablespoon salt
8 small onions, studded with cloves	½ teaspoon white pepper
2 stalks celery	

❨Cover veal with cold water, add onions, celery, thyme, and seasonings. Cover and boil on top of stove until tender, about 45 minutes. Remove from broth, keep warm while making Cream Sauce.

CREAM SAUCE

4 tablespoons butter
4 tablespoons chopped onion
4 tablespoons flour
Strained broth from veal

Heavy cream
4 egg yolks beaten with juice
  3 lemons
1 teaspoon nutmeg

([Melt butter in saucepan, add onions and sauté until soft. Add flour and cook 5 minutes slowly, stirring carefully to keep smooth. Measure strained broth. If there are not 2 cups, add cream to make this amount of liquid. Stir into sauce and let it come to a boil. Remove from heat and very gradually stir in egg yolks which have been beaten with lemon juice. Add nutmeg. SERVES 8. Serve with mashed potatoes.

BOILED SMOKED TONGUE WITH ONION SAUCE

MT. LEBANON SHAKER VILLAGE

1 smoked beef tongue
2 onions, sliced
1 bay leaf
½ teaspoon thyme

4 whole cloves
10 peppercorns
1 cup vinegar
1 cup brown sugar

([Wash tongue, cover with cold water and boil 10 minutes. Skim, add onions, vinegar, and sugar. Cover and simmer gently for about 4 hours or until it is tender. Remove skin and roots. Place on a hot platter and serve with Onion Sauce. SERVES 8.

ONION SAUCE

3 medium onions
2 teaspoons butter
1½ teaspoons flour
1¾ cups beef stock
¼ cup chopped celery

¼ bay leaf
Salt and pepper
2 tablespoons capers
1 teaspoon vinegar

([Peel and slice onions, fry in butter until quite brown. Add flour, blend thoroughly, and let brown a little too. Pour in stock, add celery, bay leaf, salt, and pepper. Simmer gently for 30 minutes until onions and celery are mushy. Put all through a sieve to obtain a purée with the stock. Put back on heat, cook 10 minutes. Add capers and vinegar and serve hot. Yields 2 cups.

VEAL CHOPS

MANUSCRIPT FROM SHAKER MUSEUM
OLD CHATHAM, NEW YORK

4 tablespoons butter and 2
   tablespoons chicken fat
4 veal chops about 1 inch thick
4 tablespoons chopped onion
4 tablespoons flour

1 cup cider
1 cup cream
Salt and pepper
1 tablespoon chopped parsley

⁅In 2 tablespoons of butter and 2 tablespoons of chicken fat, fry chops until they are golden on both sides. Remove to ovenproof baking dish and keep warm. Add remaining butter to fat in skillet and cook chopped onions. When soft, add flour. Cook 1 minute, stirring. Add cider and cook until sauce is thick and smooth. Add cream and seasonings. Pour sauce over chops in oven and cook until tender. This make take 25 minutes at 350° F., or more, depending on tenderness of meat. Garnish with parsley. SERVES 4.

VEAL CUTLETS BAKED

HARVARD SHAKER VILLAGE

2 pounds veal cutlets
1 cup butter
2 tablespoons flour
½ teaspoon salt
¼ teaspoon pepper
1 cup sour cream

½ teaspoon each savory and
   marjoram
1 tablespoon very finely chopped
   onion
Chopped parsley
Lemon slices, cut thin

⁅Cut veal in pieces 2 inches square and brown quickly in hot butter. Put into ovenproof dish which has a cover. Make a smooth paste of flour and seasonings, mixed with a little water. Stir in sour cream. Mix with the herbs. Cook in a saucepan until slightly thickened. Add chopped onions. Pour over meat, cover, and bake in a slow 300° F. oven for 1 hour. Check at this point and add whole milk or sour cream if dish seems to need more gravy.

When serving, sprinkle with chopped parsley and garnish with lemon slices. SERVES 4–5.

VEAL CUTLETS IN SOUR CREAM

HARVARD SHAKER VILLAGE

4 veal cutlets
2 tablespoons flour
Salt and pepper
4 tablespoons butter or chicken fat
1 cup chopped onions
1 cup sour cream

Some top milk
1 cup drained cooked tomatoes
     or
½ cup tomato paste
Chopped chives

❡Pound veal to make it thin, roll in seasoned flour. Sauté in butter or fat until golden brown; add onions and cook until onions are tender. Gradually add sour cream thinned out with milk. The meat should cook slowly until tender. Add tomatoes or tomato paste about 10 minutes before removing from fire. This is all done in skillet on top of stove and will take about 30 minutes. Sprinkle with chives. SERVES 4.

SISTER LETTIE'S VEAL LOAF

NORTH UNION SHAKER VILLAGE, OHIO

6 hard crackers, ground fine
3 eggs
1 cup rich milk
3 pounds ground veal
2 teaspoons salt
¼ teaspoon pepper

1 teaspoon celery seeds
2 tablespoons soft butter
Flour
½ cup heavy cream
½ cup finely chopped mushrooms
1 tablespoon dry sherry

❡Roll the crackers to fine crumbs. Beat eggs and add milk. Mix veal, salt, pepper, and celery seeds together thoroughly with cracker crumbs and egg-milk mixture. Shape into long roll. Place in roaster and dot with butter. Bake at 325° F. for an hour, basting frequently. Make gravy by browning some flour in iron skillet, then blend with loaf juices in bottom of pan. Add cream to make gravy, add finely chopped mushrooms and simmer until they are soft. Add some sherry to flavor. SERVES 4–6.

Meatless Dishes

THE PERSON RESPONSIBLE for introducing vegetarianism to the Shaker Society was English-born Frederick William Evans, who joined the Shakers at Mt. Lebanon as a young man. We think his intense conviction regarding the healthful effects of a diet which excluded animal flesh is responsible for many interesting and delicious recipes for cooking vegetables and breads and other meatless dishes.

Elder Evans was regarded by those in "the World" as one of the most forceful Shaker leaders and on his successful lecture trip in 1887 to Scotland, England, and Ireland, he was acclaimed as the official spokesman for the sect. His friend and traveling companion, J. M. Peebles, writing about this mission, spoke of the many well-attended private meetings and public gatherings, although "both the Jubilee [Queen Victoria's Fiftieth] and 'the season' were against us in London."

Elder Evans was gracefully entertained in London and Manchester, England, by flourishing vegetarian societies and in the spacious dining rooms of these groups he was served many interesting dishes made of fresh and choice vegetables, fruits, and nuts and bread, which he said "was such as a Christian could conscientiously eat." After these dinners the elder gave a very able address on vegetarianism and the principles and practices of Shakerism, advising that in the formation of Shaker Societies in England (whence it was founded) animal flesh be utterly ignored.

Being a rigid vegetarian did not, however, prevent Elder Evans from building up a fine, large herd of Holsteins with splendid examples of grade-A Ayrshires and Jerseys also in the beautiful, well-ventilated barns at Mt. Lebanon, or in maintaining spacious poultry yards—for as he told visitors, "Poultry keeping pays."

The "bloodless diet" did not discourage visitors, apparently, as one who went to Mt. Lebanon in 1887 wrote:

The table, almost entirely vegetarian, is perfect. Food is fresh, abundant, exquisitely cooked, and served with care and intelligence. Cereals, with the exception of superfine flour, are cleansed and crushed in their own mills and used in a variety of ways. There is a large dairy, and tons of fruit, deliciously prepared, are ranged in storerooms for the winter's consumption. Woman's work is simplified by curious machinery invented and made by some of their leaders. All work, but none overwork.

APPLE OMELET

WATERVLIET SHAKER VILLAGE, NEW YORK

This is a very delicate dish.

6 large tart apples
1 tablespoon butter
1 cup sugar

Cinnamon and other spices to taste, such as nutmeg and mace
4 eggs

([Peel the apples. Cover with water and cook to a very soft mush; beat out all the lumps.

Add the butter and sugar and the spices. Let the mixture cool.

Beat the eggs and add to apple mixture.

Bake in a shallow, buttered dish or in two pie tins for 15 to 20 minutes at 300° F. until delicately brown.

Serve with roast pork.

SERVES 4.

This omelet can be served as a dessert with Cider Sauce.*

CREAMED ASPARAGUS AND EGG FOR SUPPER

MT. LEBANON SHAKER VILLAGE

Use tips from 2 pounds of fresh asparagus. Steam in small amount of water. Drain. Make a rich sauce:

3 tablespoons butter
3 tablespoons flour
2 cups milk
Salt and pepper

Nutmeg
1 cup heavy cream
4 hot hard-boiled eggs

[Melt butter, add flour and milk and cook 10 minutes. Add seasonings and cream and remove from heat. Peel hot eggs. Slice and arrange on platter. Add asparagus tips to sauce and pour over eggs. Surround with toast. SERVES 4–6.

Suggestion: Cut remaining asparagus in 1 inch pieces. Cook in water to cover 15 minutes. Drain. Add 2½ cups White Sauce #4* and ½ cup grated American cheese. Serve on toast. SERVES 4–6.

ASPARAGUS CUSTARD
HANCOCK SHAKER VILLAGE

[Cook just the tips of 2 pounds of asparagus in steamer 5 minutes or less, as they must be tender and not overcooked.

Put in a pudding dish and cover with a 4 egg custard,* omitting sugar and adding salt, pepper, nutmeg, and cloves to taste.

Bake at 325° F. for 20 to 30 minutes.

SERVES 4–6.

See suggestion above for serving the rest of the asparagus.

SHAKER BAKED BEANS
SISTER JOSEPHINE, CANTERBURY SHAKER VILLAGE

4 cups navy beans	1 cup butter
2½ cups hot water	1 teaspoon salt
1 onion	2 teaspoons dry mustard
½ cup molasses	½ cup tomato catsup*

[Soak the beans overnight. Drain and cook in fresh hot water until tender, about 30 minutes. Peel onion and place in bottom of bean pot. Drain beans and save liquid. Pour beans into bean pot. Add molasses, butter, salt, dry mustard, and catsup to bean liquid and pour over beans. Cover pot and cook in very slow 250° F. oven for about 3 hours. Add more water or cider whenever necessary. Remove cover for last half hour and brown well. SERVES 10–12.

This excellent recipe was used during the Shaker ban on pork. Several older Shaker "receipts" for this dish call for "medium slices of salt pork laid in the bottom of the bean pot which gradually work their way to the top and flavor the entire contents of the pot as they rise to the surface." When salt pork was used, the butter was omitted. The bean pots were made at Bennington, Vermont, and are worthy reminders of pioneer days.

SISTER ABIGAIL'S BLUE FLOWER OMELET
(Blue Flower of the Chive)
NORTH UNION SHAKER VILLAGE, OHIO

4 eggs
4 tablespoons milk or water
½ teaspoon salt
⅛ teaspoon pepper

1 tablespoon minced parsley
1 teaspoon minced chives
2 tablespoons best butter
12 chive blooms

❲This delicious omelet can be made only when the chives are in full bloom.

Take the eggs and beat them just enough to blend whites and yolks well. Add milk or water, seasoning, minced parsley, and chives. Melt butter in a heavy iron skillet; pour in the mixture. When the edges of omelet begin to set, reduce the heat. With a broad pancake spatula stir uncooked eggs to the bottom of skillet until all ingredients are cooked. (This gives the omelet a golden color when folded over.) Then sprinkle the washed blooms over the omelet and fold. Serve immediately on hot platter. The blue blossoms add a delicious flavor to the dish. SERVES 4.

BUTTERNUT PUDDING
(Nice Dish for Visitors)
MT. LEBANON SHAKER VILLAGE

2 cups chopped butternuts
  (walnuts may be used)
1 cup grated dry bread
½ teaspoon baking powder
1 egg

1 small onion, chopped fine
1 cup butter, melted
½ teaspoon salt
1 cup heavy cream

❲Combine butternuts with bread crumbs. Add baking powder and mix well. Add egg. Cook onion in butter, add salt. Beat cream and fold into nut-crumb-egg mixture. Bake in small pie tins in 350° F. oven for 30 minutes. SERVES 4.

CHEESE DISH HANCOCK
HANCOCK SHAKER VILLAGE

❲Scrape or thinly pare some country cheese—Cheddar or Cheshire type—into a cup until it is three-fourths full. Fill up with boiling water to the rim of the cup and cover with saucer. Stand in warm place for 10 minutes. Pour off water, pour the cheese, which will be like a thick cream, upon hot toast. Sprinkle with salt and pepper and serve. If the cheese is packed fairly compactly, this amount will be enough for 2 slices of toast. SERVES 1.

CHEESE CROQUETTES
HANCOCK SHAKER VILLAGE

3 tablespoons butter
⅓ cup flour
1 cup milk
½ teaspoon salt
¼ teaspoon pepper
2 egg yolks
2 tablespoons heavy cream

2 cups small pieces soft mild
   cheese (American Cheddar "store
   cheese" or Cheshire)
Bread crumbs
1 egg, beaten
Deep fat for frying

❈[Melt butter, add flour, cook 2 minutes and add milk while stirring. Season. Bring to boiling point and add yolks beaten with cream. Add cheese and cook at low heat only long enough to melt cheese. Remove from fire, spread on plate, and cool. Shape, dip in crumbs, beaten egg, and crumbs. Fry in deep fat and drain. SERVES 4.

CHEESE CUSTARD WITH BREAD SAUCE*
SHIRLEY SHAKER VILLAGE

4 eggs
1 cup milk
2½ tablespoons melted butter
3 tablespoons grated cheese,
   Cheddar or Cheshire

½ teaspoon salt
¼ teaspoon pepper
1 teaspoon ground thyme
1 teaspoon raw scraped onion

❈[Beat eggs slightly and add remaining ingredients. Turn into buttered molds. Set in pan of hot water and bake for about 40 minutes in a 325° F. oven until brown. Remove from molds to hot platter and pour around Bread Sauce.* SERVES 4.

CHEESE FRITTERS
MT. LEBANON SHAKER VILLAGE

1 cup grated cheese, Cheddar
   or Cheshire
1¼ cups flour
1 teaspoon baking powder

2 teaspoons salt
½ teaspoon paprika or pepper
2 eggs, separated
Lard for frying

❲Grate cheese, add dry ingredients sifted together. Add yolks of eggs beaten until thick and mix well. Fold in stiffly beaten whites of eggs. Drop by spoonfuls into a frying pan of fresh hot lard. Cook until golden brown. Drain on paper. SERVES 4.

CHEESE OMELET

SISTER MARY, ENFIELD SHAKER VILLAGE, CONNECTICUT

Called "Cheese Pudding" at Hancock and in *The Manifesto*.

6 slices bread, well buttered
¼ teaspoon prepared mustard
1 pound Yankee Cheese (Cheddar type)

4 eggs, 2 cups milk (beaten together)
½ teaspoon salt
¼ teaspoon pepper

❲Butter a 2 quart baking dish; cover the bottom with medium thick slices of bread well buttered and lightly spread with prepared mustard. Then cover lavishly with thin slices of cheese. Repeat the layers. Pour the well-beaten eggs and milk over this and season. Bake for 20 minutes in a moderate 350° F. oven. Serve very hot. SERVES 4.

CHEESE PUDDING

THE MANIFESTO, SEPTEMBER 1880

"This is a supper dish and costs 12 cents."

2 quarts boiling water
2 tablespoons salt
2 cups yellow corn meal

½ cup grated cheese, Cheddar or Cheshire
Extra ½ cup grated cheese

❲Into 2 quarts of boiling water containing 2 tablespoons of salt, stir 2 cups yellow Indian Meal and ½ cup grated cheese ("cost 4 cents"). Boil it for 20 minutes, stirring it occasionally to prevent burning, then put it in a greased baking pan; sprinkle over the top ½ cup of grated cheese, and brown in a hot 400° F. oven. Serve hot. If any remains, slice it cold and fry brown in good hot butter. SERVES 4–6.

．．

Groves of nut trees were an important part of all Shaker villages. Black and English walnuts, hickory nut, butternut, and chestnut trees were all important crops, for food, and for wood to make into furniture by the skillful Shaker brethren.

CHESTNUT CROQUETTES
HARVARD SHAKER VILLAGE

1 cup mashed cooked chestnuts
2 tablespoons thick cream
2 egg yolks
1 teaspoon sugar
½ teaspoon salt

¼ teaspoon vanilla
Bread crumbs
1 egg and 1 tablespoon water, beaten
Deep fat for frying

⟨Make slits in chestnut shells. Cover nuts with water in a saucepan. Bring to a boil and remove. Shells will be easy to peel off. Mash enough chestnuts to yield 1 cup.

Mix ingredients in order given except for bread crumbs and egg-water mixture. Shape in balls, dip in fine sifted bread crumbs, egg beaten with 1 tablespoon water, and crumbs again. Fry in deep fat and drain. SERVES 4.

CHESTNUTS AND MUSHROOMS
HANCOCK SHAKER VILLAGE

2 pounds chestnuts
1 pound mushrooms, sliced
3 tablespoons butter
3 tablespoons flour
3 cups milk

1 teaspoon salt
1 teaspoon pepper
1 cup heavy cream
½ cup grated cheese, Cheddar or Cheshire

⟨Make two cross cuts on flat side of each chestnut. Put in saucepan with boiling water to cover. Boil 15 to 20 minutes. Peel and remove inner skins. Slice and put in greased ovenproof dish. Cover with mushrooms. Mix lightly. Make a white sauce by melting butter and cooking flour in it for 2 minutes. Add milk and seasonings, stirring constantly until it thickens. Cook over low heat and add cream. Pour sauce over chestnuts and mushrooms. Sprinkle with cheese. Bake in moderate 350° F. oven for 20 to 25 minutes. SERVES 6–8.

Variation: Garnish with parsley, and serve with corn bread or hot baked potatoes.

CHESTNUT AND RICE PATTIES
MT. LEBANON SHAKER VILLAGE

1 cup boiled, peeled, and chopped
  chestnuts
½ cup toasted bread crumbs
2 cups boiled rice
2 eggs
1 teaspoon chopped parsley

2 tablespoons rich milk
1 egg, beaten with 1 tablespoon
  water
Flour
Deep fat for frying

❡Mix all ingredients well except egg-water mixture and flour and shape into patties. Dip into beaten egg and dust with flour and fry to a rich brown. Fat for frying should be lard, beef drippings, or vegetable oils. A combination of ⅔ lard and ⅓ beef suet (tried out and clarified) is better than lard alone. Butter alone burns too quickly and is not successful except in a skillet, watched carefully.

This is a very palatable dish. It can be served with White Sauce #4. SERVES 4–6.

ESCALLOPED EGGS
SHIRLEY SHAKER VILLAGE

2 tablespoons butter
2 tablespoons flour
1 tablespoon parsley
1½ cups heavy cream

4 tablespoons grated Cheddar
  cheese
4 hard-boiled eggs
2 tablespoons bread crumbs

❡Make a sauce by melting butter and adding flour. Simmer. Add parsley, cream, and cheese; blend well, and cook 5 minutes. Cover bottom of pie dish with half of sauce, arrange quartered hard-boiled eggs—cover with remaining sauce. Sprinkle with bread crumbs and bake for 5 minutes in fairly quick 400° F. oven. SERVES 4.

WHITE SCRAMBLED EGGS
SHIRLEY SHAKER VILLAGE

2 tablespoons melted butter
2 tablespoons heavy cream
1 teaspoon salt
1 teaspoon white pepper

4 egg whites, beaten
Toast
4 egg yolks, poached and put
  through ricer

❨Combine melted butter and cream with seasonings. Add beaten egg whites and scramble. Mound upon toast and sprinkle with riced egg yolks. SERVES 4.

RICE CROQUETTES, WHITE, BROWN, OR WILD
WATERVLIET SHAKER VILLAGE, NEW YORK

1 cup rice, white, brown, or wild
3 cups rich chicken broth
4 egg yolks, beaten
2 teaspoons onion juice or scraped
   onion pulp
1 teaspoon each finely chopped
   parsley and chives

2 tablespoons chopped nuts
   (optional)
Salt and pepper
2 eggs, beaten
1 tablespoon milk
1 cup sieved dry bread crumbs
Hot fat

❨Wash rice. Cook in chicken broth uncovered for about 30 minutes, or until rice is tender and all liquid has been absorbed. Stir in beaten egg yolks, onion juice, parsley, chives, nuts, and seasonings. Mix well. Cool and chill.

Form rice mixture into croquettes, dip in mixture of beaten egg and milk, roll in very fine, sieved, dry bread crumbs. Chill the croquettes until ready to serve. Fry 3 croquettes at a time in hot fat in a deep skillet for about 2 minutes or until golden. Drain on absorbent paper. Serve with or without a sauce. Caper,* Spicy Tomato,* or Herb Sauce* goes well with this. SERVES 6.

EGG CUSTARD RING FILLED WITH ROSEMARY SPINACH*
WATERVLIET SHAKER VILLAGE, NEW YORK

6 eggs
1 teaspoon salt
½ teaspoon pepper

½ teaspoon nutmeg
2½ cups light cream

❨Beat eggs slightly, add seasonings. Heat cream, but do not let it boil. Slowly pour it over the eggs, stirring. Butter a ring mold and strain custard into it. Set mold in pan of hot water. Bake in a moderately slow 325° F. oven until firm—45 minutes to 1 hour. When knife comes out clean, custard is done. During baking care must be taken that water surrounding mold does not come to a boil or custard will whey.

Remove from oven. Turn ring out onto a large platter and fill center with Spinach with Rosemary.* SERVES 4.

VEGETABLE-CUSTARD RING WITH CHEESE SAUCE

HANCOCK SHAKER VILLAGE

2 tablespoons butter
1½ cups scalded milk
3 eggs, slightly beaten
1½ cups raw spinach run through food chopper (If spinach juice is used, reduce milk by this much liquid. In other words use 1½ cups of solid drained vegetable and no more than 1½ cups of liquid)
1 teaspoon salt

([Heat butter with milk and eggs, add spinach and salt. Pour into a ring mold. Set pan of custard mixture in larger pan of hot water. Bake like a custard in a moderate 350° F. oven for 45 minutes to 1 hour. Unmold and serve with Cheese Sauce in center. SERVES 4–6.

CHEESE SAUCE

2 tablespoons butter
2 tablespoons flour
2 cups milk—less if you wish thicker sauce
½ cup small pieces cheese—or more if richer sauce is wished
½ teaspoon each salt and pepper
1 teaspoon dry mustard

([Melt butter, add flour, blend well. Add milk and stir constantly until smooth. Add cheese, salt, pepper, and mustard. Cook until cheese is well melted and the sauce is smooth and even. Yields 2 cups.

∴

Good Tip: Best way to poach an egg—before breaking, immerse in boiling water for a minute, then poach. You will find it will set beautifully and be a perfect shape.

∴

Gentle Manners, 1823—Shaker book on etiquette
   "Learn to eat an egg from the shell. It is easily done."

Vegetables

THE SHAKERS WERE primarily agriculturists, raising not only their grain, vegetables, sugar (maple and honey), fruits, and meats, but also all their dairy products. They became skilled horticulturalists too, developing with frequency new and better species of vegetables. They raised seed for the World market and were able to supply the demand and variety of vegetable seeds required.

Tomatoes were introduced into the family at New Lebanon in 1823 as "a fruit which becomes a prominent and beneficial article of food. . . . We preserve hundreds of gallons for winter use." The daily cooking of vegetables was closely supervised and kettles were used for steaming in preference to boiling for "the long boiling of any vegetable in water extracts the salts which are so beneficial." A sister from Shirley notes in her journal "have you ever tried to eat a raw tomato with sugar instead of salt? Very good. . . ." and "when frying onion always add a little water and sugar to the pan after they start to cook. They will be much softer and more digestible. Add seasonings while frying."

Shaker seed catalogues list an enviable variety of vegetable seeds— endive, leek, four kinds of onions, six kinds of squash, eight varieties of beans and as many peas, four or five kinds of white and yellow sweet corn, six choices of carrots and beets, melons from the largest watermelon to the tiny citrons for preserving; cabbages, red, green, and "fancy blue," were listed, as well as many sorts of sprouts, kohlrabi, collards, other greens, and mustard. Sweet and white potatoes were part of a vast assortment of root vegetables.

In one Shaker farm journal we read: "Do not be content with one planting; peas, beans, cucumbers, lettuce, spinach, corn and tomatoes and potatoes should be planted for a constant succession of crops and can be planted as late as the second week in August and yield before the frost sets in." In July 1899 a stalwart Shaker vegetarian notes: "The large variety of vegetables will more than compensate us for all the trouble they have been and will be and make us the more thankful that we are vegetarians, really, if we are not strictly so."

GREEN BEAN CASSEROLE
SHAKER FESTIVAL
AUBURN, KENTUCKY

3 tablespoons butter, melted	½ medium-sized onion, grated
2 tablespoons flour	1 cup sour cream
1 teaspoon salt	1½ pounds fresh green beans
¼ teaspoon pepper	½ pound grated Cheddar cheese
1 teaspoon sugar	½ cup bread crumbs

⟪Combine 2 tablespoons butter and flour and cook gently; remove from heat; stir in seasonings, onions, and cream, fold in beans. Place in shallow 2 quart casserole. Cover with cheese; then with crumbs, mixed with 1 tablespoon butter. Bake in moderate 350° F. oven for 30 minutes. SERVES 8.

GREEN STRING BEANS WITH DILLWEED
HANCOCK SHAKER VILLAGE

Dill was grown in most Shaker villages. It was used for pickling and flavoring. The seed was sold in bags to the pickling industry and the feathery leaves were dried, crushed, and, known as dillweed, were used for seasoning.

This is a delicious dish using cooked fresh green beans with a rich cream sauce flavored with dill.

4 cups cooked green beans	1 tablespoon powdered dillweed
1 cup White Sauce #4*	1 teaspoon grated raw onion
½ teaspoon salt	½ cup heavy cream
¼ teaspoon pepper	

⟪Mix ingredients as given, heat well, and blend thoroughly, adding cream as mixture comes off the heat. SERVES 4–6.

DILLED GREEN BEAN SALAD

FRANCES HALL, HANCOCK SHAKER VILLAGE

1½ pounds green beans
Salt

Dressing:
1 cup olive oil
4 tablespoons tarragon—or other
  herb—vinegar

½ bunch watercress or small leaves
  of young lettuce

1 tablespoon chopped chives
2 tablespoons chopped dillweed
Salt, pepper, sugar to taste

⟨The beans should be young. If small use whole, otherwise cut them before cooking. Cook covered in salted, boiling water until tender but not mushy, about 15 minutes. Drain well and cool. Meanwhile mix dressing ingredients and let stand awhile before mixing with the beans. Shake the dressing well, and then mix the beans with the dressing and chill. Before serving, drain off excess moisture and mix with watercress or small leaves of young lettuce. SERVES 4.

STRING BEAN SALAD

NORTH UNION SHAKER VILLAGE, OHIO

2 cups cooked string beans
2 cups shredded lettuce
2 cups minced green onions,
  including tops
2 sprigs minced summer savory

6 nasturtium leaves
12 nasturtium pods
Salt and pepper to taste
Any favorite dressing (amount
  depends on choice)

⟨Mix the cold, cooked green beans with the shredded lettuce. Mince green onion over beans. Add the minced summer savory and nasturtium leaves and pods. Season with salt and pepper and toss with dressing. SERVES 4.

LIMA BEANS AND SOUR CREAM

HANCOCK SHAKER VILLAGE

4 cups cooked lima beans
4 tablespoons sour cream
½ teaspoon salt
¼ teaspoon pepper

1 tablespoon grated raw onion
4 tablespoons bread crumbs
2 tablespoons melted butter

⟨Combine cooked beans with sour cream, salt, pepper, and onion and set to one side for 15 minutes. Put in a greased baking dish and top with bread crumbs mixed with melted butter. Bake in oven set at 350° F. for 25 minutes or until heated through. SERVES 4.

MIXED BEAN SALAD
HANCOCK SHAKER VILLAGE

1 cup white beans, cooked and chilled

1 cup small lima beans, cooked and chilled

1 cup French-style string beans, cooked and chilled

1 small onion, chopped very fine and chilled

¼ cup chopped parsley and basil mixed

½ cup chopped black olives

3 tablespoons olive oil

1 teaspoon lemon juice

1 teaspoon salt

1 teaspoon pepper

Lettuce

⟅Mix all the beans, onion, parsley, and olives together well. Add olive oil, lemon juice, salt, and pepper. Marinate.

When ready to serve arrange on salad platter, surround with nice pieces of lettuce. Mask with mayonnaise and garnish with tomatoes and sprinkle sieved hard-boiled egg over mayonnaise—or omit mayonnaise and garnish with cucumber slices and tomatoes, quartered. SERVES 6.

SLICED BEETS
MT. LEBANON SHAKER VILLAGE

⟅Wash and boil 1 quart small beets until nice and tender, being careful not to cut the skin. When done, pour cold water over them. Rub off the skins and sliver up in very small pieces. Add pepper and salt, a little piece of butter, half a teacup of vinegar, and powdered caraway to season. Stir all together and set on low heat in a covered earthen dish until wanted for dinner. SERVES 4.

BEETS IN HONEY SAUCE
HANCOCK SHAKER VILLAGE

3 cups small whole cooked beets

2 tablespoons sour cream

1 tablespoon cornstarch

1 teaspoon salt

2 tablespoons cider

¼ cup honey

1 tablespoon butter

1 tablespoon powdered caraway (optional)

¶Mix beets and sour cream and put to one side. In a saucepan combine cornstarch, salt, cider, and blend to a smooth consistency. Stir in honey and butter, cook over low heat stirring constantly. Add caraway; cook until thick and smooth, remove from heat. Stir in beets and sour cream; cover; let stand 10 minutes to blend flavors. Return to low heat and stir. SERVES 4.

GINGER BEETS

HANCOCK SHAKER VILLAGE

2 cups sugar
6 tablespoons cornstarch
3 teaspoons ginger
6 cups small cooked beets
1 cup cider
     or

½ cup vinegar and ½ cup cider
1 tablespoon butter
½ teaspoon salt
1 cup seedless raisins

¶Combine sugar, cornstarch, and ginger; if there is some liquid from the cooked beets, perhaps a cup, add this with the vinegar and cider. If there is no liquid because the beets have been steamed, use an additional cup of cider. Bring to a boil, cook stirring constantly until thick and clear. Add butter, salt, and raisins, and lastly, beets. Heat thoroughly and serve. SERVES 8.

SISTER LETTIE'S BEET SALAD

NORTH UNION SHAKER VILLAGE, OHIO

2 tablespoons sugar
1 teaspoon salt
1 teaspoon mustard
½ cup vinegar
6 cooked beets, sliced

4 hard-cooked eggs
4 small onions
Lettuce
2 green peppers

¶Make a dressing by combining sugar, salt, mustard, and vinegar. Heat and pour over sliced beets. When cool add the whole hard-cooked eggs and let stand overnight. Arrange sliced beets in center of dish and surround with rings of sliced onions and garnish with slices of the pickled eggs. Dress with lettuce and slices of green pepper. Pour some of the dressing over the salad and serve. SERVES 6.

TURNIPETTS

THE MANIFESTO, SEPTEMBER 1879

❲"The true way to cook a beet is to bake, not boil it. Thus treated and sliced either in vinegar or in butter, it is much sweeter than when boiled and said to be more nutritious. I save the vinegar in which my beets were pickled for dinner, the next day boil a few small young turnips and slice them up in the same vinegar. I added a little fresh vinegar, pepper and salt, and no one at the table knew that they were not eating white beets, until I called their attention to the fact."

RAW CABBAGE

THE MANIFESTO, AUGUST 1880

"A nice way to prepare raw cabbage is as follows:

"Select a fine, good head; chop finely in a bowl what you think will be needed [4 cups of cabbage], and to every quart add ½ teacupful [½ cup] of *thick* sweet cream; 2 tablespoonfuls of strong vinegar or lemon juice, 1 cupful of white sugar and mix thoroughly."

CUT CABBAGE IN CREAM

MT. LEBANON SHAKER VILLAGE

❲One medium-sized head of cabbage, sliced fine. Put in a close-covered porcelain dish with 3 to 4 cups water. Cook covered half an hour. Pour off the water, add a little thickened milk or cream, season to taste. Cook 15 minutes more over a moderate heat, and it is ready for the table.

COOKED CREAMED CABBAGE

THE MANIFESTO, AUGUST 1880

❲Cut cabbage fine as for raw; put into a kettle and add water to cover. Cook until tender; drain; then add ½ cup of *thick sweet cream;* ½ cup vinegar mixed with 1 tablespoon of flour; season with pepper and salt to suit the taste; let it boil up and serve.

∴

"A small piece of charcoal put into the pot with boiling cabbage removes the smell. . . ."

CABBAGE AND SOUR CREAM
HARVARD SHAKER VILLAGE

1 medium-sized cabbage	2 tablespoons flour
Salt	1 cup sour cream
2 tablespoons chopped onions	2 teaspoons vinegar
2 tablespoons butter	Pepper to taste

([Boil a medium-sized cabbage until just tender in boiling salted water, about 10 minutes. Drain. Chop.

Cook onion in butter until tender, add flour. Cook 2 minutes. Stir in sour cream, vinegar, salt and pepper. Cook sauce on low heat until thick, stirring constantly. When cooked, mix with cabbage. Serve at once. SERVES 6.

GREEN AND RED CABBAGE
HANCOCK SHAKER VILLAGE

½ head red cabbage	1 teaspoon salt
½ head green cabbage	¼ cup boiling water
2 tablespoons finely chopped onion	4 tablespoons brown sugar
3 tablespoons butter	4 tablespoons vinegar
2 tart apples	1 teaspoon chopped chives or basil

([Remove outer leaves from cabbage. Shred, rinse in cold water, drain but do not dry. Sauté onion for 3 minutes in butter. Combine cabbage and onion. Cook covered 10 minutes. Peel and core apples, cut into fine pieces. Add to cabbage and onion mixture. Add salt and boiling water. Mix well. Simmer covered for 30 minutes or until cabbage is tender. Add brown sugar and vinegar. Simmer 10 minutes longer. Add chopped chives or basil. SERVES 4–6.

SCALLOPED CABBAGE
WATERVLIET SHAKER VILLAGE, NEW YORK

3 cups cooked shredded cabbage	1 cup soft bread crumbs
2 cups White Sauce #2*	½ cup grated American Cheddar
Salt and pepper	cheese

([Mix cooked shredded cabbage and white sauce, seasoned well, together.

Put a layer of this mixture in a greased baking dish. Add a layer of crumbs and repeat process until all material is used.

Sprinkle with cheese. Bake in a moderately hot 375° F. oven about 20 minutes or until brown and bubbly. SERVES 4–6.

CABBAGE IN CARAWAY CREAM #1

HANCOCK SHAKER VILLAGE

2 teaspoons butter
1 small head firm white cabbage,
　coarsely shredded
1 teaspoon salt
1 clove garlic, minced

1 tablespoon caraway seeds
1 teaspoon sugar
1½ tablespoons vinegar
½ cup sour cream

⟨[Heat butter in skillet. Add cabbage, salt, and garlic and stir well. Cover tightly and steam 10 minutes.

Add caraway seeds, sugar, and vinegar. Mix well. Stir in sour cream and serve immediately. SERVES 4.

CABBAGE IN CARAWAY CREAM #2

HANCOCK SHAKER VILLAGE

1 small head firm white cabbage,
　coarsely shredded
½ cup water
2 tablespoons butter
2 tablespoons (white) flour
1 cup rich milk

1 teaspoon salt
1 teaspoon sugar
1 teaspoon curry powder
1 tablespoon caraway seeds
1½ tablespoons vinegar
½ cup sour cream

⟨[Cook by steaming cabbage in water. Make white cream sauce by melting butter, adding flour, and cooking together, stirring, for 4 minutes. Add milk, salt, and sugar. Cook at low heat and keep sauce smooth. Add curry powder, caraway seeds, and cabbage. Cook 20 minutes until cabbage is quite tender. Add vinegar and at the very last before serving add sour cream and incorporate well. This mixture is spicy and should be as smooth as velvet. SERVES 5–6.

CABBAGE PIE

HARVARD SHAKER VILLAGE

Heart of a small firm cabbage
Salt
2 tablespoons butter
1 medium onion, sliced finely
1 teaspoon caraway seeds

½ teaspoon each salt and pepper
½ teaspoon sugar
Pastry* for two 8 inch piecrusts
2 hard-boiled eggs
¾ cup sour or sweet cream

⟨[Blanch cabbage 2 to 3 minutes in boiling salted water. Drain thoroughly. Shred finely and reserve. Melt butter in a large pan. Cook onion slowly until soft, but not brown. Add caraway seeds. Add cabbage and continue cooking, stirring frequently. Season with salt, pepper, and sugar. Roll out pastry. Line a deep 8 inch pie plate with half the pastry. Spread in cabbage mixture. Make a pattern on top with slices of hard-boiled eggs. Top with cream. Cover with rest of pastry. Press edges down. Bake in 325° F. oven about 35 minutes or until crust is golden. SERVES 4.

CABBAGE SALAD
SHAKER ALMANAC, 1882

1 head cabbage	1 teaspoon mustard mixed in a
1½ cups cider vinegar	little boiling water
2 teaspoons white sugar	Salt and pepper to taste
3 tablespoons thick sour cream	3 egg yolks

([Shave a hard white cabbage into small white strips. Mix all the remaining ingredients but the eggs together, and boil. Then stir in the eggs rapidly. Add the cabbage and stir well. Make enough for 2 days as it keeps perfectly and is an excellent relish for all kinds of meats. Yields 6–8 cups.

BAKED CARROTS
ENFIELD SHAKER VILLAGE, CONNECTICUT

3 cups grated carrots	½ teaspoon pepper
3 tablespoons butter	1 teaspoon ginger
1 teaspoon salt	1 tablespoon brown sugar

([Put grated carrots in an earthenware casserole. Add butter, salt, pepper, ginger, and brown sugar. Cover and bake in a moderate 350° F. oven for half an hour. SERVES 6.

CARROTS IN CIDER #1
ENFIELD SHAKER VILLAGE, CONNECTICUT

3 cups sliced carrots (1 inch rounds)	Salt and pepper
4 cups cider	1 tablespoon butter

([Cook carrots in cider on top of stove 20 minutes, slowly, or until liquid is thick and syrup-like. Add salt, pepper, and butter. SERVES 6.

CARROTS IN CIDER #2
ENFIELD SHAKER VILLAGE, CONNECTICUT

3 cups sliced carrots
3 tablespoons butter
1 cup cider (maybe more)

½ teaspoon salt
¼ teaspoon pepper

❪[Slice carrots fairly thin, add water, cider, and seasonings. Cook slowly in covered pan until carrots are tender. Add butter. Remove cover for last 2 minutes of cooking. SERVES 4–5.

CARROT HASH
ENFIELD SHAKER VILLAGE, CONNECTICUT

2 cups sausage meat
2 medium onions, sliced thin
2 tablespoons butter
1½ cups small pieces liver

1½ cups finely diced carrots
1 cup chopped potatoes (optional)
½ teaspoon salt
¼ teaspoon pepper

❪[Cook sausage meat in heavy skillet. Remove from pan and cook onions in same fat until golden. Strain fat, put back 2 tablespoons, and add butter. With cover on skillet, slowly cook liver and carrots together (potatoes, too, if desired). When carrots are soft return sausage and onions to pan with seasonings. Cook until brown and becoming crusty. SERVES 6.

CARROT PUDDING
HANCOCK SHAKER VILLAGE

2 cups hot mashed potatoes
2 cups hot mashed cooked carrots
1 egg, beaten
½ cup very small cubes Cheshire
   cheese
2 tablespoons grated onion

2 tablespoons melted butter
2 tablespoons sour cream
½ teaspoon salt
¼ teaspoon pepper
Butter (optional)

❪[Combine potatoes and carrots, add egg, and blend well so that over-all color is pink. Combine remaining ingredients, except butter, and add to vegetables. Put in an ovenproof baking dish and bake at 350° F. until thoroughly heated and golden on top. Dot top with butter if desired. SERVES 4–6.

CARROT PURÉE
ENFIELD SHAKER VILLAGE, CONNECTICUT

2–3 cups White Sauce #3*
1 cup thin sweet cream
Salt, pepper, and onion juice to
    taste

Chopped chives
2 cups grated carrots

([Make white sauce and add cream, seasonings and chopped chives. Stir until it boils. To this add carrots and cook slowly for 10 minutes. SERVES 4.

SISTER MARY'S ZESTY CARROTS
HANCOCK SHAKER VILLAGE

6 carrots
Salt
2 tablespoons grated onion
2 tablespoons horse-radish
½ cup mayonnaise

1 teaspoon salt
¼ teaspoon pepper
¼ cup water
¼ cup buttered bread crumbs

([Clean and cut carrots into thin strips. Cook until tender in salted water; place in 6x10 inch baking dish. Mix together grated onion, horse-radish, mayonnaise, salt, pepper, and water. Pour over carrots. Sprinkle with ¼ cup buttered crumbs. Bake about 15 minutes in moderately hot 375° F. oven. SERVES 4–6.

GLAZED CARROTS
ENFIELD SHAKER VILLAGE, CONNECTICUT

3 cups sliced carrots (1 inch rounds)
Salt
½ cup honey

½ cup catsup*
½ cup butter
Pepper to taste

([Cook carrots in slightly salted water until barely tender. Transfer to oven casserole. Mix well with honey, catsup, butter. Add salt and pepper to taste. Cook slowly in medium 350° F. oven for 20 to 30 minutes. SERVES 4.

CARROTS COOKED IN HONEY
ENFIELD SHAKER VILLAGE, CONNECTICUT

3 cups ¼ inch thick carrot rounds
3 tablespoons butter
½ cup chicken broth

½ cup honey
½ teaspoon salt
¼ teaspoon pepper

⟨Cook carrots in butter and chicken broth 5 minutes with cover on saucepan. Remove lid, add honey and seasonings and cook until carrots are tender, about 15 minutes. SERVES 4–5.

CELERY SALAD
ENFIELD SHAKER VILLAGE, CONNECTICUT

3 cups cut-up celery
½ cup salad oil
¼ cup tarragon vinegar
½ teaspoon salt
½ teaspoon sugar
¼ teaspoon pepper

1 teaspoon finely chopped fresh tarragon
1 teaspoon finely chopped fresh chives
1 tablespoon drained capers
Lettuce leaves

⟨Cook celery in 2 quarts boiling water until soft. Drain into bowl, add oil, vinegar, and seasonings while celery is still warm. Chill. Add tarragon, chives, and capers. Mix well. Arrange on lettuce leaves. SERVES 6.

SHAKER DRIED CORN
MT. LEBANON SHAKER VILLAGE

1 cup dried corn
2 cups boiling water
2 teaspoons sugar

½ teaspoon salt
2 tablespoons butter
½ cup heavy cream

⟨Place corn in heavy bowl and cover with boiling water. Cover and have it stand at least an hour. At the end of this period, stir in sugar, salt, and butter. Cook uncovered in the top of a double boiler over simmering water, for about 30 minutes. Stir in cream and cook 5 minutes. SERVES 4.

∴

Behavior at Table: "Corn by the common usage is eaten from the cob, but the exhibition is not interesting."—*Gentle Manners.*

JOHN PERSIP'S CORN FRITTERS

HANCOCK SHAKER VILLAGE

3 eggs
1½ cups milk
3 cups Shaker Convenience Mix #3
   (special pancake mix)* or 3 cups
   prepared pancake mix

2 cups cream-style corn
2 cups drained crushed pineapple
Deep fat for frying

⟨Blend eggs and milk, add pancake mix, and stir until smooth. Fold in corn and pineapple. Drop batter by spoonfuls into hot fat ½ inch deep. Cook about 3 minutes on each side. Drain on paper toweling. Serve hot with butter and maple syrup. Makes 12 to 15 servings. Fritters may be kept hot or reheated in slow oven.

CORN FRITTERS TWO WAYS

HANCOCK SHAKER VILLAGE

12 ears tender green corn, grated
   or scraped
1 teaspoon salt
1 teaspoon pepper

1 teaspoon sugar
1 egg beaten into 2 heaping
   teaspoons flour
Lard or butter

⟨Mix thoroughly. Make into small cakes, fry in hot lard or butter. Depending on size of cakes, SERVES 6–8.

6 ears tender corn, grated
2 eggs
1 tablespoon butter

Salt, pepper, and sugar to taste
1 teaspoon flour
Fat

⟨Mix all ingredients. Beat. Make into cakes. Fry in hot fat on a griddle. SERVES 4–6.

CORN CROQUETTES, RICE CROQUETTES,
OR SWEET POTATO CROQUETTES

WATERVLIET SHAKER VILLAGE, NEW YORK

2 tablespoons butter
3 tablespoons flour
1 cup boiling milk
½ teaspoon each salt and white
   pepper
2 eggs, lightly beaten

2 cups cooked corn, rice, or chopped
   well-drained cooked sweet potatoes
Flour
1 egg beaten with 2 teaspoons milk
Fine bread crumbs
Deep fat for frying

¶[Melt butter, add flour, and cook gently 3 minutes. Add milk, cook until thick. Add eggs. Cook 1 minute, then add heavy material—corn, rice, or sweet potatoes. Season. Cook 5 minutes stirring all the time. Spread mixture on buttered platter and cool. Shape croquettes into desired shape. Roll in flour, then into 1 egg beaten with 2 teaspoons milk. Drain, dip into very fine bread crumbs. Cook in hot deep fat until they are golden brown. SERVES 4.

Serve corn and rice croquettes with mushroom sauce or tomato or cheese sauce or with White Sauce #4* made with cream and add chopped chives and egg yolk. Serve sweet potato croquettes with raisin sauce flavored with orange.

CORN OYSTERS
SHIRLEY SHAKER VILLAGE

2 egg yolks, beaten	¼ teaspoon pepper
2 cups grated fresh corn	¼ cup flour
½ teaspoon salt	3 egg whites, stiffly beaten

¶[Add the beaten egg yolks to the grated corn and add salt and pepper. Mix in flour and fold in the stiffly beaten egg whites. Drop onto a well-greased skillet in globs the size of an oyster. Brown on both sides and serve at once. Makes 12. A very nice side dish with cold meat.

Recipes for corn oysters came from several villages and were all similar.

GREEN CORN PATTIES
SHAKER ALMANAC, 1882

2 cups grated green (young) corn	1 egg, beaten
1 cup flour	Pepper and salt to taste
1 cup butter, melted	Butter

¶[Beat into corn the flour, butter, and egg. Add seasonings and beat well to make the mixture light. Fry cakes in butter. SERVES 4.

GREEN CORN PUDDING
SISTER AMELIA'S SHAKER RECEIPTS

2 cups grated green (young) corn	⅛ teaspoon pepper
3 eggs	2 cups rich milk
¼ cup sugar	½ cup buttered bread crumbs
Dash nutmeg	2 tablespoons butter
½ teaspoon salt	

❨Grate uncooked kernels from fresh corn. Put in buttered baking dish. Beat eggs well; add sugar, nutmeg, salt, pepper, and milk and blend. Sprinkle top with buttered bread crumbs and dot with butter. Place in a dish of boiling water and bake in slow 250° F. oven for 1 hour. SERVES 6.

SWEET CORN PUDDING
SISTER ABIGAIL GROSSMAN
THE MANIFESTO

4 cups grated sweet corn
6 eggs, beaten
1 teaspoon nutmeg
1 teaspoon salt

2 tablespoons sugar
4 cups milk
2 tablespoons melted butter

❨In a mixing bowl combine corn, eggs, seasonings. Stir in milk. Pour into a greased baking dish and dot with butter. Bake in a slow 300° F. oven 1 hour or until set. SERVES 8–9.

If wanted, buttered bread crumbs can be sprinkled on pudding before dotting with butter.

BOILED CUCUMBERS
SHIRLEY SHAKER VILLAGE

❨Cut cucumbers into quarters and peel. Boil in lightly salted water to cover in a saucepan large enough to lay cucumbers flat. Boil until tender, about 10 minutes. Drain. Serve with toasted bread crumbs mixed with melted butter, salt, and pepper. Two cucumbers would serve 2–4.

COOKED CUCUMBERS
HANCOCK SHAKER VILLAGE

At Hancock cucumbers were cooked by frying them in butter until transparent, adding salt and pepper and chopped chives—or by cooking them in salted water, draining and adding cream, sweet or sour, salt, and pepper.

3 cucumbers
2 tablespoons butter
½ teaspoon salt

¼ teaspoon pepper
Chopped parsley

❨Peel cucumbers and cut in slices ½ inch thick. Cook in butter slowly until tender, about 15 minutes. Add seasonings and parsley. SERVES 4–5.

CUCUMBERS COOKED WITH MINT
HANCOCK SHAKER VILLAGE

3 medium cucumbers
4 tablespoons butter
2 tablespoons flour
Salt
Pepper

1 egg yolk
¼ cup heavy cream
2 tablespoons finely chopped
fresh mint

⟨[Peel cucumbers and slice 1 inch thick. Barely cover with water and bring to a boil. Drain and reserve stock. Melt butter in saucepan, add flour, cook 1 minute. Stir until smooth and gradually add 1 cup of cucumber liquor. Stir and bring to a boil. Add cucumbers, salt, and pepper and cook until they are tender, about 15 minutes. Mix egg yolk and cream; turn off heat and add to the cucumbers. Add mint. Blend carefully. SERVES 4–6.

CREAMED CUCUMBERS
ENFIELD SHAKER VILLAGE, CONNECTICUT

⟨[Cook 4 pared, sliced cucumbers in salted water 5 minutes. Drain very well. Put in a casserole with 3 or 4 tablespoons of butter. Cook until tender, about 15 minutes. Drain. Add ½ cup heavy cream and serve. Should not be too liquid. Garnish with chopped chives or parsley. SERVES 4–6.

CUCUMBERS IN SOUR CREAM
MT. LEBANON SHAKER VILLAGE

⟨[Soak 6 peeled, thin-sliced cucumbers in cold water until crisp. Drain well and add to them 3 white onions sliced paper thin. Sprinkle with salt and pepper and pour over them ½ cup or more of vinegar. Place in cold place ½ hour. Drain well. When ready to serve pour over them 1 cup or more of sour cream. Stir well and sprinkle well with chopped dill. Serve at once. Do not let it stand. SERVES 6.

STEWED CUCUMBERS
MT. LEBANON SHAKER VILLAGE

⟨[Pare 8 or 10 large cucumbers and cut them into large slices. Flour them well and fry them gently in butter. Put them in a saucepan with

1 cup chicken stock—season with cayenne, salt, and catsup. Let them simmer for an hour and serve hot. Nice with fish. SERVES 6–8.

PLEASANT HILL BAKED EGGPLANT
SHAKERTOWN, PLEASANT HILL

1 large eggplant	2 cups stewed mushrooms
Salt	Worcestershire sauce (to season)
½ medium onion	Pepper
2 tablespoons butter	1½ cups cracker crumbs
3 tablespoons chopped parsley	2 tablespoons butter

([Cut eggplant top lengthwise, scrape out inside, leaving ¼ inch around sides and bottom of shell. Take eggplant meat and parboil in salt water until it is tender. Drain thoroughly. Sauté the onion in the butter and add chopped parsley. Mix eggplant and onion-parsley mixture with stewed mushrooms. Season with Worcestershire sauce, salt, and pepper. Add 1 cup cracker crumbs. Place in eggplant shell. Sprinkle top with remaining crumbs and dot with butter. Bake at 375° F. for 30 to 35 minutes. SERVES 4.

VEGETABLE FRITTERS
HANCOCK SHAKER VILLAGE

Basic Fritter Recipe*	Deep fat for frying
Peeled or pared vegetable pieces	

([Drop peeled or pared vegetable pieces into batter, fry in deep fat. Drain. Add more milk if thinner batter is called for.

Serve asparagus fritters with cheese sauce or chopped egg sauce; cauliflower fritters with cheese sauce; and tomato fritters with cheese sauce.

LEEKS TO COOK LIKE ASPARAGUS
ENFIELD SHAKER VILLAGE, CONNECTICUT

([Leeks are generally looked upon as a species of onion and as such are commonly employed in the same manner, though milder in flavor. Boil in separate waters two or three times, changing water each time, until tender, about 20 minutes. Serve on toast like asparagus and cover with a rich white sauce made with cream. (Use White Sauce #2,* but substitute cream for milk.) A flavor of cheese may be added.

BRAISED LETTUCE
HANCOCK SHAKER VILLAGE

4 small heads crisp lettuce   Celery salt
¼ cup minced onion   4 poached eggs
4 tablespoons butter   Paprika
Heavy cream

⟮[Shred lettuce. Cook onion in butter for 5 minutes over low heat. Add lettuce and cook 10 minutes stirring frequently. There should be about 4 cups of the lettuce-onion mixture.

Add enough cream to moisten lettuce and simmer until tender. Season lightly with celery salt. Cook away all moisture. Arrange on hot vegetable dish and place 4 trimmed poached eggs on top. Dust with paprika. Sorrel or spinach may be substituted for lettuce. For a vegetable to accompany meat or fish, omit eggs. SERVES 4.

MUSHROOMS IN SHERRY BUTTER
HARVARD SHAKER VILLAGE

2 cups finely sliced mushrooms   ¼ teaspoon pepper
2 tablespoons butter   1 tablespoon dry sherry wine
½ teaspoon salt   1 tablespoon finely chopped dill

⟮[Put mushrooms in very hot butter. Season with salt and pepper and cook briskly for 2 to 3 minutes. Then add sherry and dill. Blend and serve with toast. Nice with chicken. SERVES 2.

∵

"From our own experience and the observations of others, we can fully indorse the testimony of the St. Louis miller of the healthful properties of the above esculent. Lung and liver complaints are certainly benefitted, often cured, by a free consumption of onions, either cooked or raw. Colds yield to them like magic. Don't be afraid of them. Taken at night, all offense will be wanting by morning and the good effect will amply compensate for the trifling annoyance. Taken regularly, they greatly promote the health of the lungs and the digestive organs. An extract made by boiling down the juice of onions to a syrup, and taken as a medicine, answers the purpose very well, but fried, roasted, or boiled onions are better. Onions are very cheap medicine, within everybody's reach; they are not by any means 'bad to take' as the costly nostrums a neglect of their use may necessitate."—*The Manifesto*, 1881.

The Shakers also put sliced raw onions in a sickroom to draw the bacteria. The onions were of course discarded at frequent intervals. —*Journal of an Observer.*

AGREEABLE ONIONS

ENFIELD SHAKER VILLAGE, CONNECTICUT

3 cups sliced, cooked, drained young onions
1 cup heavy cream
2 tablespoons butter

2 tablespoons flour
½ teaspoon pepper
1 teaspoon salt

⟨[Put young onions in boiling water. Boil ½ hour or until tender. Drain. Mash and chop with a hand chopper. Pour over a good amount of cream, add a good piece of butter rubbed in flour. Season with pepper and salt and simmer a few minutes. Mix well. It should not be too liquid. Cook off original liquid before adding cream. Simmer 10 minutes. SERVES 4.

BOILED ONIONS

ENFIELD SHAKER VILLAGE, CONNECTICUT

⟨[Boil 1½ pounds peeled button onions in water to cover. When they are tender (approximately 20–25 minutes) put into following sauce:

2 strips bacon
2 tablespoons butter
4 tablespoons flour

1 cup chicken broth
½ cup thick cream

⟨[Fry bacon until crisp. Remove from pan leaving bacon fat. To this add butter and flour. Simmer to cook flour. Add chicken broth and cook until nice consistency. When very hot, add onions and remove from fire. Add cream. Stir gently and serve. Sprinkle with crumbled bacon. SERVES 4.

ONIONS WITH CREAM

ENFIELD SHAKER VILLAGE, CONNECTICUT

This dish is nice because it's just onions and cream, well seasoned.

8 large onions, peeled
2 cups boiling water
1 teaspoon pepper

½ teaspoon dry mustard
1 teaspoon sugar
2 cups heavy cream

⟨[Slice peeled onions fairly thin. Put in large saucepan on top of stove, pour boiling water over them, and let stew for about 20 minutes. Drain. Mix pepper, mustard, and sugar together and add to cream. Pour over onions and cook on low heat until onions have absorbed most of cream. Dish should be pale, not yellow. SERVES 4–6.

ONION CAKES WITH CHIVES

MT. LEBANON SHAKER VILLAGE

1 cup chopped onions
2 cups boiling water
1 egg yolk, beaten thick
½ cup plus 2 tablespoons flour

½ teaspoon baking powder
½ teaspoon salt
1 tablespoon chopped fresh chives
1 egg white, beaten stiff

⟨[Cover chopped onions with boiling water and let stand 5 minutes. Drain well. To onions add beaten egg yolk and dry ingredients, which have been sifted together. Add chives and let mixture sit 15 minutes. Fold in stiffly beaten egg white.

Drop from a tablespoon into hot fat. Cook until a delicate brown. SERVES 4–6.

ENFIELD ONIONS WITH GRAPES AND BRUSSELS SPROUTS

ENFIELD SHAKER VILLAGE, CONNECTICUT

1½ pounds small white onions
Salt and pepper
3 cups small Brussels sprouts
3 tablespoons butter, melted
3 tablespoons flour

1 cup rich milk, heated
½ cup heavy cream
1 cup seeded and peeled green
grapes
1 tablespoon sweet butter

⟨[Peel onions and cook in a covered saucepan in a small amount of

water for 18 minutes or until tender. Drain well and season onions with
salt and pepper.

Trim 3 cups of small Brussels sprouts (about a pound). Soak in salted
water (30 minutes). Drain and cook in fresh water just to cover, for
about 15 minutes covered, or just until tender.

Make thick cream sauce. Cook together melted butter and flour, stirring
constantly over medium heat—3 minutes. Add heated milk. Add heavy
cream and green grapes. Bring this sauce to a boil and add sweet butter.
Stir gently to keep it smooth. Add salt and pepper to taste.

Combine well-drained onions and Brussels sprouts. Add sauce and
heat. SERVES 6.

ONION PIE
SHIRLEY SHAKER VILLAGE

4 cups thinly sliced onions
3 tablespoons butter
Pepper and salt
Nutmeg

4–6 ounces pastry*
2 eggs
½ cup sour cream mixed with 2
    tablespoons sweet cream

⟮Sauté onions slowly in butter until soft but not brown. Season highly
with pepper, salt, and nutmeg. Line a deep pie pan with pastry. Beat
the eggs lightly, fold into the onions. Add onions to pastry-lined tin.
Top with sour cream mixture. Bake in 325° F. oven for 30 minutes or
until top is golden brown. SERVES 6.

SCALLOPED ONIONS
NORTH UNION SHAKER VILLAGE, OHIO

6 medium onions
4 tablespoons butter
⅓ cup bread crumbs
½ teaspoon salt

⅛ teaspoon pepper
2 tablespoons heavy cream
Grated Cheddar cheese
Paprika

⟮Peel and slice onions. Melt butter and sauté onions in butter until
tender. Place in buttered baking dish, sprinkle with crumbs, salt, and
pepper, and the cream. Dust on grated cheese and a sprinkling of paprika.
Bake until crumbs are brown. SERVES 4.

A SIDE DISH OF ONIONS
HANCOCK SHAKER VILLAGE

2 pounds small white onions, boiled
  and drained
½ cup butter
3 tablespoons brown sugar

1 tablespoon dry mustard
¼ teaspoon pepper
1½ teaspoons salt
⅓ cup chopped parsley

⟮Place onions in a buttered quart-sized shallow ovenproof dish. Combine butter, sugar, mustard, pepper, and salt, and pour over onions. Bake 20 to 40 minutes in 325° F. oven or until well heated through. Sprinkle with parsley before serving. SERVES 8.

SMOTHERED ONIONS #1
MT. LEBANON SHAKER VILLAGE

4 tablespoons butter
4 tablespoons flour
1 cup chicken stock
4 cups sliced onions

½ cup water
¼ cup cider
½ cup rich heavy cream
Salt, pepper, nutmeg to taste

⟮Melt butter and add flour. Cook together on low heat 2 minutes. Add chicken stock and stir to make a smooth sauce. Cook onions in water slowly, covered, and when they are tender and water has been cooked away, add to cream sauce. Add cider and cook stirring for 15 minutes. Add cream and seasonings and remove from fire.

This version of smothered onions should be served with chicken, veal, ham. SERVES 4.

SMOTHERED ONIONS #2
MT. LEBANON SHAKER VILLAGE

4 cups sliced onions
4 tablespoons butter
4 tablespoons flour
1 cup beef bouillon

¼ cup vinegar
Salt and pepper
Nutmeg

⟮Stew onions in butter until they are tender and transparent. Do not brown. Add flour and stir well. Add bouillon and cook slowly. Taste. The vinegar is added for sharpness only—use judgment. Add seasonings. Cook until onions thicken. SERVES 4.

This version should be served with beef and lamb.

STEWED ONIONS
WATERVLIET SHAKER VILLAGE, NEW YORK

❲Choose small onions. Peel them, flour them, and fry in a little butter until lightly brown. Cover with a weak gravy (chicken broth), season and stew slowly 2 hours. Serve them upside down with the sauce over them. In peeling be careful not to cut the top or bottom too closely, else the onion will not keep whole.

STUFFED ONIONS
HARVARD SHAKER VILLAGE

6 large onions
1½ cups minced cold meat
1 cup cooked chopped spinach
½ cup bread crumbs

½ cup grated Cheddar cheese
½ cup heavy cream or chicken broth
Salt and pepper to taste

❲Parboil onions—take out center of onion. Mix meat, spinach, bread crumbs and cheese. Moisten with cream—season. Place filled onions in an ovenproof dish with water or broth to come up ¼ inch. Bake at 375° F. for 35 minutes or until golden. SERVES 4–6.

SISTER AMELIA'S STUFFED ONIONS
NORTH UNION SHAKER VILLAGE, OHIO

6 large sweet onions
1 cup finely chopped veal or chicken
1 cup minced celery
1 teaspoon salt

⅛ teaspoon pepper
2 tablespoons heavy cream
Stock
1 tablespoon butter

❲Skin onions and boil whole in saucepan for 10 minutes. Core out centers for stuffing. Make dressing of finely chopped veal or chicken, celery, seasoning, and cream; stuff in onions. Place in buttered baking dish, moisten with stock and dot with butter. Bake in medium 350° F. oven for 20 minutes. (This is a good way to use up soup meat; additional seasoning and herbs should be added to soup meats when so utilized because some flavor may have cooked out.) SERVES 6.

PARSNIPS

THE MANIFESTO

Parsnips are sown from seed in the spring with other garden vegetables but are not harvested until the late fall or following spring. They are considered sweeter if permitted to freeze in the ground, for they need to be frostbitten to develop their full flavor. They are one of the first harbingers of spring on the farm or in the markets and their thin delicate sweetness is welcome after winter and canned vegetables.

8 medium parsnips (about 4 cups small pieces)	1 tablespoon flour
Salt	1 cup sweet cream
1 tablespoon butter	Pepper

《Wash and scrape parsnips. Cut into small pieces and cook in boiling salted water until tender, about 30 minutes. Drain well. Melt butter and add flour, simmer and add cream. Stir to keep sauce smooth. When thickened add parsnips and heat thoroughly, adding salt and pepper to taste. SERVES 4–6.

Other suggestions for parsnips: Cook in salted water, rice or mash, add butter and cream, and serve in place of potatoes.

Fry cooked parsnips in butter until golden brown on all sides.

Dip in batter and fry as a fritter.

Sauté cooked parsnips, cut in short finger lengths, in butter in a skillet. Add brown sugar, seasonings—makes fine candied parsnips—really delicious.

PARSNIP CAKES

FRANCES HALL, HANCOCK SHAKER VILLAGE

2 cups mashed cooked parsnips	2 egg yolks
1 tablespoon butter	Cracker crumbs
1 tablespoon flour	½–1 cup butter
1 teaspoon salt	

《Mix parsnips, 1 tablespoon butter, flour, salt, and egg yolks together well; shape into flat cakes. Dip into powdered cracker crumbs and sauté in butter until brown. SERVES 4.

SCALLOPED PARSNIPS
MT. LEBANON SHAKER VILLAGE

4 cups parsnips   1 cup grated Cheddar cheese
Salt   1 cup White Sauce #2*
2 cups cracker crumbs

([Dice parsnips and boil in salted water until tender, but not too soft, about 15 to 20 minutes. Put in a greased 1 quart baking dish in layers alternating with cracker crumbs and grated cheese. Make 1 cup of White Sauce and pour this over the dish. Bake in moderate 350° F. oven until brown. SERVES 4–6.

"The more simply potatoes are cooked, the easier they are digested. A steaming dishful of white, mealy potatoes is appetizing, but when they are soggy or half done, it is usually from improper cooking. They should be done, and have the water turned off ten minutes before they are taken up. Slide the cover off a little way, so that the steam may escape.

"Potatoes should never be fried in fat of any kind. Sliced fine, when cold, and heated in a little milk or cream, with seasoning, they are much better than when saturated in grease. They are good at breakfast and dinner but at the tea meal should only be served as baked with a pat of butter for they may be considered heavy in the evening."—Elder Frederick W. Evans, Mt. Lebanon Shaker Village.

PEAS AND NEW POTATOES IN CREAM
MT. LEBANON SHAKER VILLAGE

2 quarts tiny new potatoes, brushed   2 cups shelled peas
  but not peeled   1 cup thick cream
½ pound lean salt pork, chopped   Butter
2 tablespoons chopped onion   Salt and pepper to taste

([In a saucepan large enough to accommodate potatoes, boil with water to cover. Cook 20 minutes. Drain. In a separate pan fry salt pork, add onions. Fry until soft. Add peas and cream, cover and cook until peas are done but not mushy. Combine with potatoes, which have been broken open with a fork and buttered. Do not peel. Season lightly to taste. SERVES 6–8.

POTATOES WITH BREAD SAUCE
ELDER FREDERICK W. EVANS, MT. LEBANON SHAKER VILLAGE

❲Slice 8 parboiled waxy potatoes. Butter an ovenproof dish lightly and put in bottom a thinnish layer of bread sauce (this sauce is merely toasted bread crumbs rolled out not too fine), dot with butter. On this put a layer of sliced potatoes and so on repeating until dish is full, seasoning each layer with salt, pepper, nutmeg. Let the top layer be of bread sauce. Cover this with browned buttered bread crumbs. Over all pour 1½ cups of very heavy cream. Cook for ½ hour in a 350° F. oven. SERVES 8.

WHITE POTATOES IN CASSEROLE
MT. LEBANON SHAKER VILLAGE

6 to 8 large raw potatoes, peeled and grated, about 6 cups
⅓ cup grated onion
3 eggs, beaten

1 cup hot cream
6 tablespoons melted butter
2 teaspoons salt
1 teaspoon white pepper

❲Mix all ingredients well. Put in well-buttered shallow pan, 2 inches deep. Bake in moderate 350° F. oven for about 1 hour and 15 minutes. Top should be golden brown. This can be cooked in a frying pan and turned once when bottom is brown. If cooked in skillet, melt 2 extra tablespoons butter to grease pan before putting in the hash. SERVES 6–8.

SHAKER CREAMED POTATOES
SISTER JENNIE WELLS, HANCOCK SHAKER VILLAGE

¼ pound butter
3 cups light cream
10 large cold boiled potatoes, sliced thick

1 teaspoon salt
¼ teaspoon pepper

❲Put butter in iron skillet. Melt but do not brown. Add light cream and heat very gently. Drop the sliced potatoes into the cream mixture. Season with salt and pepper. Simmer very slowly until all milk is absorbed. Turn very carefully only once. This takes about an hour. Serve piping hot. Very delicious. SERVES 8.

SWEET OR WHITE POTATO CROQUETTES
MT. LEBANON SHAKER VILLAGE

❲Peel 1 pound of potatoes and boil in water until soft. Drain well and put through a sieve. Dry them out over heat. Add 1 tablespoon butter, salt, pepper, and nutmeg to taste, 1 whole egg yolk and 1 whole egg. Beat until purée is very smooth and cool. Coat in crumbs or flour and fry in hot fat by the tablespoonful. SERVES 4.

POTATOES AND EGGS
ELDER FREDERICK W. EVANS, MT. LEBANON SHAKER VILLAGE

Served for the brethren's breakfast, after the brothers came back from the fields for a six o'clock breakfast.

❲Fill a buttered 2 quart ovenproof dish with 6 large cooked potatoes sliced the long way, which have been sautéed gently in about 6 table-spoons butter. (When sautéeing, turn over repeatedly to avoid burning.) Sprinkle potatoes with ½ cup grated Cheddar cheese.

On top of cheese and potatoes, break 6 whole eggs. Keep them well arranged on top of potatoes. Keep egg yolk and white together. Sprinkle well with salt and pepper. Cover eggs (bring to within ½ inch of top of dish) with fresh heavy cream. Bake 10 minutes in oven at 375° F. Serve from dish. SERVES 6.

POTATO PANCAKES
SHIRLEY SHAKER VILLAGE

2 cups grated raw potatoes
2 eggs, well beaten
1½ teaspoons salt
½ teaspoon baking powder
1 tablespoon flour
2 tablespoons grated onion
Bacon or chicken fat

❲Drain potatoes and add all but fat. Mix well. In a large skillet heat fat and drop mixture in by the spoonful. Form smallish thin cakes. Cook over fairly high heat. When brown turn to cook other side. Serve very hot—with meat or chicken. SERVES 6.

POTATO CAKES
SHAKER ALMANAC, 1882

⟨Roast 6 potatoes in the oven. When done, skin and pound in a mortar with a good piece of butter, warmed in a little milk. Chop a shallot and a little parsley very finely, mix well with the potatoes, add pepper and salt. Shape into cakes; egg and bread them, crumb them, and fry a light brown. SERVES 4.

POTATO PIE
THE MANIFESTO, 1897

⟨Potatoe pie may be made by lining pie tins with ordinary piecrust* and filling with mashed potatoes seasoned with a little fried onion and summer savory. Dot with butter and put on an upper crust, or not, according to choice. Bake from 20 to 30 minutes at 350° F. Serve hot. SERVES 4.

POTATO PIE WITH BUTTERED CRUMB TOP
ENFIELD SHAKER VILLAGE, NEW HAMPSHIRE

3 cups mashed potatoes	1 cup cubed Cheddar cheese
1 cup thick cream	1 tablespoon grated raw onion
1 teaspoon salt	1 cup buttered bread crumbs
½ teaspoon pepper	

⟨This is a nice way to use up mashed potatoes. Beat them with cream to make them fluffy. Season; put in ovenproof baking dish and push little pieces of cheese within the potatoes. Mix onions and buttered bread crumbs together and let this form the crust of the pie. Cook in moderate 350° F. oven for 20 minutes or to heat through. SERVES 4.

POTATOES AND ROSEMARY
HANCOCK SHAKER VILLAGE

4 cups mashed cooked potatoes	1 teaspoon salt
2 egg yolks	1 scant tablespoon powdered
2 tablespoons butter	rosemary
½ cup heavy cream	½ teaspoon pepper

❨The potatoes should be freshly cooked and mashed. Beat in the egg yolks, butter, cream, and seasonings. The mixture should be of a fairly soft consistency. Cooking will thicken it. SERVES 4.

HOT POTATO SALAD
SHIRLEY SHAKER VILLAGE

6 potatoes
2 tablespoons chicken fat
2 tablespoons grated raw onion
2 tablespoons flour
1 cup vinegar (tarragon, or other herb vinegar)
1 teaspoon salt

1 teaspoon celery seeds
½ teaspoon dry mustard
½ teaspoon pepper
1 tablespoon chopped sweet pickle
Some sprigs parsley and tarragon
2 chopped hard-boiled eggs

❨Cook potatoes in their skins and while they are boiling make dressing as follows:

Melt chicken fat, add onion, and cook. Add flour, simmer 3 minutes, add vinegar, and cook 2 minutes, stirring to keep smooth. Combine salt, celery seeds, mustard, pepper, and pickle, add to other mixture. When potatoes have cooked, remove from the pan, peel and slice thinly. Work quickly so that potatoes are still hot when dressing is added. Mix in the dressing with two forks, so as not to break up potatoes. Decorate with herbs and chopped eggs. SERVES 4.

PURÉE OF VEGETABLES
HARVARD SHAKER VILLAGE

❨Boil in some stock with a bundle of sweet herbs, salt, pepper, and spices to taste, any combination you like of such vegetables as: carrots and white potatoes; carrots, leeks, and white potatoes; white turnips and white potatoes; corn and summer squash; or a choice of carrots, turnips, potatoes, parsnips, leeks, onions, and peas. When thoroughly done, pass the whole through a sieve. Mix in a saucepan with a little piece of butter and some flour, adding the purée little by little. For each 4 cups purée stir in the yolks of 2 eggs mixed with a little cream and well beaten. Serve with snippets (2 inch squares or smaller) of fried bread. SERVES 4–6.

STEWED POTATOES #1

WATERVLIET SHAKER VILLAGE, NEW YORK

8 potatoes   Salt and pepper
1 quart milk   4 tablespoons butter

⟨Put peeled raw diced potatoes, milk, salt, and pepper in top of double boiler. Bring water in lower half to boil and reduce heat so water merely simmers. Cook potatoes this way for 1 hour. Check and cook longer until they are tender. (This depends on age of potatoes.) Add butter and cook another 10 minutes. SERVES 4–6.

STEWED POTATOES #2

NEW LEBANON SHAKER VILLAGE

New Lebanon Shakers used oven-baked potatoes.

⟨Take 6 potatoes that have been slightly cooked in salted water with their skins on and then baked 1 hour at 300° F. Peel and cut them in slices. Put them into a saucepan with milk or cream to cover. Let boil gently 5 or 6 minutes. Add a good piece of butter, and salt and pepper to taste.

Potatoes bought in today's markets need only be baked 1 hour. Precooking is not necessary. These directions refer to winter potatoes which have been stored.

Let potatoes cook long enough to absorb all the cream or milk. This will thicken them without using flour. SERVES 4–6.

SOUR CREAM POTATOES

ENFIELD SHAKER VILLAGE, NEW HAMPSHIRE

⟨Season 4 large hot cooked sliced potatoes with salt and pepper. Pour over them and mix well 1 cup sour cream. Heat thoroughly but do not bring to a boil. Sprinkle with particles of fried salt pork before serving. SERVES 4.

CREAMED RADISHES
WATERVLIET SHAKER VILLAGE, NEW YORK

⟨[Slice nice firm spring radishes thinly, do not peel, and simmer in water to cover. When tender, but not mushy, drain and strain stock. For 4 cups of sliced radishes make following sauce:

2 tablespoons butter	1 cup radish liquid, or if not 1 cup,
2 tablespoons flour	add milk to make 1 cup
½ teaspoon salt	½ cup heavy cream
¼ teaspoon pepper	Chopped parsley

⟨[Melt butter, add flour, salt, and pepper. Cook 2 minutes, add liquid and/or milk. Simmer and stir to make a smooth sauce. Add radishes, heat well. Remove from fire and add heavy cream. Sprinkle with parsley when serving. SERVES 4–6.

This dish should be pink in color.

SAGE CAKES
FRANCES HALL, HANCOCK SHAKER VILLAGE

Serve with fried sausages and Honeyed Apple Rings.

4 tablespoons flour	1 tablespoon chopped sage leaves
¼ teaspoon salt	or
½ teaspoon sugar	2 teaspoons dried powdered sage
6 tablespoons water	1 egg white
1 egg yolk	Deep fat for frying

⟨[Sift flour, salt, and sugar into a bowl. Mix to a smooth paste with water, add egg yolk, and set aside to rest for at least 30 minutes. Add sage leaves. Rest a while longer. When ready to use, fold in stiffly beaten white of egg. Mix well, but gently. Fry cakes, which are really more like fritters, in deep hot fat, or vegetable oil, by the teaspoon, until golden brown. Drain. SERVES 4. Serve with Honeyed Apple Rings (see next page).

HONEYED APPLE RINGS

2 cups honey	1 teaspoon salt
1 cup vinegar	2 quarts apples, cored but not
1 teaspoon cinnamon	peeled, cut in rings ½ inch thick

⟪Heat the honey, vinegar, cinnamon, and salt together in a deep skillet and cook apple rings, a few at a time, in the syrup until they become transparent. Pour the syrup that remains in the pan, after all the fruit is cooked, over the apples.

A nice-looking platter can be made by arranging the fried sausages in the middle with apple rings next and Sage Cakes on the very outside. SERVES 4–6.

SPINACH WITH ROSEMARY
HANCOCK SHAKER VILLAGE

2 pounds spinach	1 tablespoon chopped green onion
1 teaspoon minced fresh rosemary	2 tablespoons butter
1 teaspoon chopped parsley	Salt and pepper to taste

⟪Wash the spinach three or four times to rid it of grit and sand. Chop rather fine and place in heavy pot. Add rosemary, parsley, onion, and butter and cover well; let simmer in its own juice until tender (about 15 minutes). Remove cover and add salt and pepper. Serve very hot. SERVES 4.

CHOPPED SPINACH RING
FILLED WITH CREAMED RADISHES*
HANCOCK SHAKER VILLAGE

⟪Use ½ pound spinach per person. Boil, drain well, and chop fine. Press out all juice and pack into a greased ring mold, pressing down firmly. (Prepare ahead.) Place mold in a pan of hot water, cover and heat through in a moderate 350° F. oven. Unmold on a large platter, fill center with Creamed Radishes (or creamed mushrooms).

SHAKER SQUASH
MT. LEBANON SHAKER VILLAGE

4 pounds Hubbard squash, cut up   ½ teaspoon pepper
4 cups hot water   3 tablespoons butter
½ teaspoon salt   ½ cup maple syrup

❰Steam the squash in the hot water. Remove from shell when tender. Drain if necessary and discard seeds. Pass through sieve and season with salt, pepper, butter, and maple syrup. Beat well and heat before serving. SERVES 6.

Variation: Put a whole Hubbard squash in a slow 300° F. oven and bake for 2½ hours. Remove. It will now cut easily. Remove seeds and fiber. Divide into serving portions, place in pan and dust well with salt, pepper, and brown sugar and dot heavily with butter. Set under broiler to brown. Any remaining squash can be used for pies or puddings in place of pumpkin.

∴

Many varieties of winter squash were grown, some not on the city markets now, but worth looking for in country farm markets. As well as Hubbard or blue squash, there are marrow and turban. Turban and Hubbard are drier than marrow. Marrow and turban have a thin shell, which may be pared off before cooking. In selecting winter squash see that it is heavy in proportion to its size. People living in the city can buy winter squash in the late fall at country roadside stands for use later on. It keeps well.

YELLOW VELVET (Squash)
HARVARD SHAKER VILLAGE

❰Equal parts cooked summer squash and cooked corn scraped from the cob, or whole kernel corn, chopped. Cook each separately and combine. Add butter, salt, pepper, and thick cream to taste. This is a delicate dish and does not need any other seasonings.

STEWED TOMATOES

THE MANIFESTO, SEPTEMBER 1880

"Stew tomatoes in water to cover in a porcelain stewpan, having first removed the skins and pits of the tomatoes. Allow to boil briskly partially covered for 20 minutes. Then remove to back of stove to simmer slowly until required. Season liberally with butter, salt, and pepper. They will be cooked to a creamy consistency and will not need flour or cracker crumbs, which to our taste are no improvement. Cook slowly at least 2 hours. Watch heat as tomatoes burn suddenly."

BAKED TOMATOES

THE MANIFESTO, SEPTEMBER 1880

([Select large ones; remove part of the inside, but do not skin. Make a stuffing of any kind of cold, cooked meat chopped fine, bread crumbs, green corn, minced onion or parsley, a well-beaten egg, butter, salt, and pepper. Fill the tomato with this dressing; put a piece of butter on the top of each, in dish with some water or cider in it, and bake in a 300° F. oven three-quarters of an hour.

BAKED TOMATOES AND CORN

THE MANIFESTO, SEPTEMBER 1880

([Line a deep 1 quart ovenproof dish with slices of tomatoes, then cover with green corn scraped from the cob; season with butter, salt, and pepper. Then add another layer of tomatoes, corn, butter, and seasonings, until the dish is full; add 1 pint of good rich meat or chicken broth; sprinkle top with bread crumbs and dots of butter and bake 1 hour at 300° F.

If canned corn must be used see that it is cream style. SERVES 4–6.

BROILED TOMATOES

THE MANIFESTO, SEPTEMBER 1880

([Cut small tomatoes in halves and place upon a wire gridiron (broiler pan) cut surface down; when the surface is somewhat cooked, turn tomatoes with the skin toward the fire and finish cooking, about 5 more minutes; serve hot with butter, salt, and pepper upon each half. These make a nice garnish for broiled steak.

TOMATO DUMPLINGS
MT. LEBANON SHAKER VILLAGE

([Proceed as for an apple dumpling. Remove seeds with care from tomato fruit. Skin it. We have eaten this raw vegetable, or fruit as some call it, without anything but salt, pepper, sugar, and vinegar—also fried and creamed, but to our mind, of all the modes of cooking it, the dumpling produces the finest dish and is served with a splendid sauce. Be sure that the tomato sits well in its dough envelope and that the steaming is timed right.

4 medium-sized tomatoes
Pastry* for two 9 inch crusts
½ cup sugar

2 tablespoons heavy cream
½ cup hot cider

([Select nice fruit and peel. Remove seeds. Roll pastry thin and cut into squares large enough to wrap around tomatoes. Mix together sugar and cream. Place each tomato in middle of pastry square and sprinkle with sugar-cream mixture. Bring corners of pastry square together and wet edges so they will cling together around the fruit. Prick pastry with fork. Place in baking dish and bake 15 minutes in hot (450° F.) oven. Baste with cider. Reduce heat to 350° F., bake 15 additional minutes, then baste again and bake 15 more minutes. SERVES 4. Serve with Tomato Sauce.*

TOMATO CUSTARD
MARY WHITCHER'S SHAKER HOUSEKEEPER

4 pounds ripe tomatoes
4 eggs, beaten
1 cup milk

½ cup sugar
½ teaspoon salt
⅛ teaspoon nutmeg

([Stew tomatoes in own juice, and pass through sieve. Cool and add to beaten eggs, milk, and seasonings. Place in buttered custard cups in larger pan of hot water. Bake in moderate 350° F. oven 25 to 30 minutes. Do not let water boil. Reduce heat if necessary. SERVES 6.

FRIED TOMATOES
THE MANIFESTO, SEPTEMBER, 1880

⟨Dip thin slices of ripe tomatoes into flour, salt, and pepper, and fry in boiling butter or lard until nicely browned.

TOMATO PIE
MARY WHITCHER'S SHAKER HOUSEKEEPER

⟨Peel and slice up tomatoes and sprinkle over them a little salt; let them stand a few minutes, then pour off the juice and add sugar to taste, half a cupful of cream beaten with 1 egg, and nutmeg. Cover bottom of 8 inch pie plate with pastry shell. Put tomato mixture in pastry shell and cover with a pastry top. Bake in moderate 350° F. oven for half an hour. This makes an excellent and much approved pie. SERVES 4.

∵

A Shaker sister said, "We have tomatoes for every meal—fried for breakfast, stewed for dinner, soup for supper."—Hancock Shaker Village.

TOMATO PUDDING
HANCOCK SHAKER VILLAGE

4 cups canned tomatoes cooked
  down to 2 cups
1 cup light brown sugar
1 tablespoon grated onion
½ teaspoon salt

¼ teaspoon pepper
1 cup bread crumbs
½ cup melted butter
1 pastry* lid for 8 inch pie plate

⟨Combine first 5 ingredients and bring to a boil. Simmer to thicken.
In an 8 inch pie dish put bread crumbs, cover with butter, top with tomato mixture, and cover with pastry crust. Bake in 350° F. oven for 30 minutes. Watch to see that bottom doesn't burn (use tip of knife to lift up crust). Tomatoes burn easily. SERVES 4–6.

A DELICATE TOMATO SALAD
THE MANIFESTO, SEPTEMBER, 1880

⟨For salads we prefer skinning tomato with a sharp knife without immersing in hot water. Cut in slices, and squeeze a bit of lemon juice over them. Very wholesome and refreshing.

HANCOCK TOMATO PUDDING
HANCOCK SHAKER VILLAGE

6 tablespoons butter
1 cup chopped onions
4 cups chopped skinned fresh
   tomatoes
Salt and pepper to taste

¼ cup brown sugar
2 tablespoons chopped fresh basil
2 tablespoons chopped fresh parsley
1½ cups small bread cubes
1 cup fresh buttered bread crumbs

❲Melt 2 tablespoons butter in large saucepan and cook the onion until very tender. Add tomatoes and stew them until they are reduced by half. Add to them the salt, pepper, sugar, basil, and parsley. Pour the bread cubes into a 1 quart baking dish. Melt remaining butter and pour it over the bread. Spoon the tomato mixture over all, sprinkle buttered bread crumbs on top. Cover closely with aluminum foil or a lid. Bake 30 minutes at 350° F. SERVES 4–6.

TOMATO TOAST
THE MANIFESTO, SEPTEMBER, 1880

❲Take 1 dozen large, ripe tomatoes, pare and slice them, put in a stew pan over a moderate fire. Add salt and pepper to taste. Toast 2 slices of bread, butter the toast, lay it in the bottom of a deep dish and pour the tomatoes over it. SERVES 6.

ALABASTER (Turnips)
MT. LEBANON SHAKER VILLAGE

2 pounds white turnips, peeled and
   diced
2 pounds white potatoes, peeled and
   diced

1 teaspoon salt
½ teaspoon white pepper
1 cup heavy cream

❲Cook turnips in water to cover, drain and mash. Cook potatoes in water to cover, drain and mash. Combine and add seasonings and cream. Beat to make nice and smooth. Should be all white. Don't use butter or black pepper. Use cream and white pepper. SERVES 8.

TURNIPS IN WHITE SAUCE
MT. LEBANON SHAKER VILLAGE

⟨[When a scoop is not handy, cut some finely grained white turnips into quarters and then pare to resemble plums or pears, but of a small size. Arrange evenly in a broad stew pan and cover with good veal broth or a nice chicken broth. Add a little salt and a morsel of sugar and boil them rather quickly to be tender, but keeping unbroken. Lift them out, draining well. Pour over them a thick white sauce made this way:

A cup of cream and a teaspoon of arrowroot mixed may be added to the broth in which the turnips have been cooked; when it boils add a good-sized tablespoon of butter and serve very hot. Use white pepper to flavor.

Or this cream sauce may also be used:

Combine 1 cup of butter, 1 cup of flour and cook well together. Add 1 cup of rich new milk and beat smooth. To make proper consistency, as sauce will be thick, thin with liquid from turnips. At the end add some rich cream, and when hot, but not boiling, cover the turnips and serve. SERVES 6.

Breads, Biscuits, Muffins, and Hotcakes

THE SHAKERS STAUNCHLY battled against adulterated products. As early as 1871 their official monthly magazine, *The Shaker,* carried articles in which they claimed that millers were separating and discarding the "live germ of the grain" in order to produce a lighter flour. They protested that "what had for countless ages been the staff of life had now become but a weak crutch."

In a day when many of their neighbors followed an unvaried diet heavy with meats, starches, and sweets, the Shakers maintained the good health of the communities by relying upon natural foods such as pure milk, whole grain, fruits, vegetables, greens, and herbs. They said, "Bread is the one food one can eat thrice daily and not tire of." Indeed, the range of recipes found in the many regions in which the Shakers lived guarantees a delightful variety for daily consumption. The origin of many of the recipes can be traced through the names which are a nostalgic reminder of other homes left behind them when families joined the Shakers: Marshfield (Massachusetts) Cakes; Pemigewasset (New Hampshire) Rolls; Rutland (Vermont) Buttermilk Loaf; Chester (Vermont) Muffins; Brunswick (Maine) Crumb; Lebanon (Ohio) Spiced Rolls; "My Grandmother's Jumbles from Dedham" (Massachusetts).

Breads, muffins, and hot cakes among other dishes were accompanied by sweet butter, fruit butters, syrups, and preserves at breakfast, which was a hearty meal. Biscuits, rolls, and gems (muffins) appeared again at noon dinner. Supper, although simple, was a treat with the sisters providing a generous choice of fruit and nut breads, coffee cakes, Sally Lunn, Indian loaves, and scones. There would be a colorful array of jams and jellies and big dishes of fruit preserves and sauces.

In a little copybook we found the following account written in a childish hand, but with great care:

> The longer bread bakes the sweeter and more wholesome it is. A good baker can always tell when bread is well baked by the sweet odor which comes from it on opening the oven door, or if, by taking

it in your hand and putting it to your ear, you do not detect any hissing, then your bread is thoroughly baked.

The young sister was learning and she may also have written:

Bring in from the cold pantry a quart of liquid yeast left over from yesterday's baking. Mix with half a cup of salt, a cup of sugar, a cup of butter and enough warm milk to fill a gallon crock. Set near the fire to keep warm while you sift the flour into the dough-tray, a peck and a half of the best wheaten flour. Make a well in the center of the flour and pour in the yeast mixture. Knead until it no longer sticks to your hands. Add flour if necessary. Cover with clean cloth and put lid on dough-tray. Place near a low fire for the night.

The sisters appointed to the kitchens arose at four on summer mornings and five o'clock in the winter and went at once to fire up the ovens. Bread which had been set the night before to rise was baked early for that day's supper, but it was not to be consumed any sooner, for tempting as it smelled, it was considered injurious until it ripened. This meant letting it cool for several hours in an airy dry place, which in a Shaker kitchen or pantry was a bread safe, either a boxlike receptacle with four screened sides hanging from hooks in the ceiling beams, or a four-shelf cupboard raised a foot from the floor with a screened door to admit air.

The seductive aroma of bread baking drew many a visitor to the big kitchens hoping to buy the large golden loaves, sugared doughnuts, and dainty muffins. The sisters might hesitate to part with what seemed like a generous supply of the "daily loaf" if they were planning a bread pudding for the family supper. They were quick to explain that puddings, stuffings, and "lids for meat pie" must never be made with bread past its prime. "Stale bread" to them was extra bread kept a day and then dried in the oven. They rolled it to a coarse powder and used it in preference to cracker crumbs, which were neither as tasty nor nutritious.

Eldress Nancy E. Moore of the South Union Kentucky Shaker colony kept a diary during the Civil War or, as she called it, "this unnatural war." This unique journal, edited by Mary Julia Neal, tells of the hectic arrival of soldiers from both armies demanding food, cloth, horses, and forage or shelter for the night. The Shakers remained neutral and fed with generosity great influxes of tired, sometimes sick soldiers. The diary reads:

The sisters are still engaged baking bread for the soldiers. . . . Just as the family were retiring to rest at nine o'clock an order came from the

Officers to the sisters for six hundred pounds of bread. The sisters without murmuring set to work to fill the order. . . . The victuals were placed [on tables] under the sugar trees for the soldiers' breakfast. They marched up from the camping ground to the Center and North families in nice order, and depend on it there was a long line of them. We had for their breakfast good fresh coffee, fresh loaf and biscuit, boiled beef and fried ham, sweet and Irish potatoes, canned peaches and fresh strawberries, butter and cornbread. . . . There is a call from the military department . . . to furnish bread for the soldiers in Russelville. We agreed to try it for one week, and furnish 25 loaves of bread per day. . . .

They were paid 3 cents a pound for the bread. And another time:

For supper they [the military] had biscuit and loaf, fried ribs, sausage and Middling of pork; sweetened and well creamed sassafras tea, and as much milk as they would drink; we opened a three gallon jar of green peaches which they consumed and the very best of sweet potatoes that they could eat and onions. For breakfast they had biscuits, loaf, fried pork, eggs, sausage, onions, pickles—sassafras and sage tea, as much milk as they desired, stewed apples and butter and corn bread.

Is it any wonder the Shakers were renowned for their patience and hospitality?

Sister Lisset of the North Union Village, Ohio community left behind her many recipes and helpful household hints. Perhaps her truest words were: "No cook is really good without a lively imagination and the will to use it."

Many of the recipes in this book are for breads and sweetmeats (preserves, jams, jellies, sponges, creams, puddings, pies, cakes, and such). These represent in a way the structure of most Shaker meals. There were always plates of a variety of breads at each meal, and the long tables were laden three times a day with preserves, jams, and jellies—and, particularly at supper, with generous amounts of puddings, sponges (porous puddings of gelatin, egg white, etc.), jellies, creams, cakes, and cookies.

Baking of Bread

NOTHING smells quite so good as bread baking, especially in one's own oven. There are some fundamental rules to follow and they are listed here in order of procedure:

DOUGH is mixed;
Dough is kneaded;
Dough is kept warm at all times;
Dough rises, in warm place;
Dough is punched down;
Dough rises again;
Dough is shaped in loaves;
Dough rises in loaf pans;
Dough is baked.

The exact size of one's bread pan is not too critical. If too large a pan is used the bread will conform to the shape of the pan; if too small a pan is used the bread will rise high above edges making a deep loaf.

When no mention of size is made the standard pan 9x5x3 inches or 8½x4½x2½ inches should be used. Round tins are a matter of preference and differ in size.

When baking time is up, remove one loaf from pan and tap the bottom side of loaf. If there is a hollow sound, bread is done. If no such sound, return bread to oven and bake 5 minutes longer and then test again.

To cool bread remove from oven. Place on wire racks away from drafts to prevent crust from cracking.

Oven Heats

PREHEAT the oven unless your oven heats so rapidly that preheating is not necessary. Do not crowd the oven, free circulation of air is essential for baking.

250° F.	Very slow
300° F.	Slow
325° F.	Moderately slow
350° F.	Moderate
375° F.	Moderately hot
400° F.	Hot
450–500° F.	Very hot

Quick Breads

INCLUDED in *Household Hints* from some of the communities are little notes relative to "emergency loaves—for they are quickly made." These were made without kneading and the cook was cautioned not to let the mixture rise above the tops of the pans or the bread would fall during the baking. The texture of these breads was not as fine as the old-fashioned breads, but it was possible to make a great variety of them.

Like yeast breads, quick breads depend on bubbles of carbon dioxide gas for their lightness. Yeast breads rise more slowly because the yeast manufactures the bubbles as they increase. With quick breads the bubbles start forming in the mixing bowl as soon as liquid is combined with baking powder and/or baking soda and acid, such as molasses, sour milk or sour cream, or buttermilk. These bubbles expand and form tiny air pockets, which make doughs and batters light.

Yeast breads are beaten, stirred, and kneaded and involve much handling, all a part of the rising process.

Quick breads are handled as little as possible and are delightfully tender. Mary Whitcher, in her *Shaker Housekeeper,* gives directions for making baking powder. They are repeated here on the theory that even the best-stocked shelves often have a bare spot.

In a warm and dry room mix ½ pound (1 cup) pulverized tartaric acid (cream of tartar), ¾ pound (1½ cups) of pure bicarbonate of soda, ¾ pound (1½ cups) pure pulverized potato farina (potato flour, cornstarch). Pass mixture through a sieve and cover securely in dry cans. More useful today would be these measurements:

2 cups cream of tartar   1 cup bicarbonate of soda
1½ cups pure potato farina
Makes 3 cups of baking powder.

HOMEMADE BREAD

SABBATHDAY LAKE SHAKER VILLAGE

½ ounce yeast
½ cup warm water
⅓ cup sugar
⅓ cup shortening

2 tablespoons salt
2 cups hot scalded milk
1½ cups cold water
10–12 cups all purpose flour

⟪Soften yeast in warm water. Using a 4 quart mixing bowl, combine sugar, shortening, salt, and hot milk. Stir well to melt shortening. Cool to lukewarm by adding cold water. Add yeast, mix well, and add flour gradually, to form a stiff dough. Knead about 5 or 10 minutes, cover, let rise in warm place. Let dough double its size, about 2 hours. Knead again, let rise about 1 hour.

Now divide dough into 3 parts, mold into balls, and place in bread pan 9x3x3 inches. Cover with cloth. Let rise in warm place until tops of loaves are well above edge of pan, about 1½ hours.

Bake at 425° F. for 10 minutes, then reducing heat to 400° F. After 10 minutes reduce heat to 375° F. Bake an hour. Makes 3 one pound loaves.

BELIEVERS' BREAD

HANCOCK SHAKER VILLAGE

2 cups milk
¼ cup granulated sugar
4 teaspoons salt
4 tablespoons butter
2 cups lukewarm water

2 cakes yeast or 2 envelopes active
    dry yeast
¼ cup warm water
10 to 12 cups sifted all purpose flour
Melted butter

⟪Scald milk, add sugar, salt, butter, and half the water, just lukewarm. Stir until sugar is dissolved and butter melted. Cool to lukewarm.

Soften yeast in remaining 1¼ cups warm water and add to milk mixture.

Add flour a cupful at a time, mixing thoroughly each time with a knife until the dough comes away from the bowl and can be turned out on a floured board and kneaded. Knead 8 to 10 minutes. Shape dough into round ball, put in greased bowl and brush top with melted butter. Cover and let rise in warm place (80°–85°) away from drafts until double in bulk. This will take from 2 to 2½ hours. Knead down again, cover, and let rise again, until double in bulk, about 1 hour.

Turn dough out onto a floured board and knead well again. Cut into 4 equal portions. Round up each piece. Cover with a clean towel and let rise 10 to 15 minutes on board. Shape each ball into loaf form and place smooth side up in 4 greased pans. Brush lightly with melted butter. Cover with clean cloth and place in warm place (80°–85°). Let rise until double in bulk about 1½ hours. Preheat oven to 400° F. Bake at 400° F. for first 10 minutes and then at 350° F. for 35 minutes. Brush with melted butter. Remove from pans and let cool on rack.

Makes 4 one pound loaves. Takes about 7 hours—maybe less, to make.

This recipe can also be used to make rolls. To make rolls, shape as desired. Place in lightly greased 8 inch round layer cake pan or on lightly greased cooky sheet. Cover and let rise in warm place until doubled in size—about 35 minutes. Bake in 400° F. oven for 15 to 20 minutes.

Variation: For whole wheat bread use ½ whole wheat flour and ½ white flour. For graham bread use ½ graham flour and ½ white flour.

WHITE BREAD WITH EGG
HANCOCK SHAKER VILLAGE

1 cup milk	2 packages active dry yeast
2 tablespoons sugar	½ cup warm water
2 teaspoons salt	2 eggs
2 tablespoons lard or shortening	5½ to 6 cups sifted flour

⟪Scald milk; stir in sugar, salt, and lard. Cool to lukewarm.

Sprinkle yeast on warm water and dissolve. Add yeast, eggs and 2¾ cups of flour to milk mixture. Beat with spoon until smooth and runny.

Add enough remaining flour a little at a time to make a dough that leaves the side of the bowl. Turn onto lightly floured board and cover. Let rest in warm spot 10 minutes.

Knead until smooth and elastic 8 to 10 minutes. Round into ball and place in lightly greased bowl. Grease top of dough. Cover and let rise, again in a warm place, until doubled, from 1 to 1½ hours.

Punch down, cover, and let rise until almost doubled, about 30 minutes.

Turn onto bread board and divide in half; shape into loaves and place in 2 greased 9x5x3 inch loaf pans. Cover and let rise in warm place until dough reaches top of pan, fills corners, and top is rounded above pan.

Bake in hot 400° F. oven for 30 to 40 minutes until golden brown. Cool on wire racks away from drafts. Makes 2 loaves.

SHAKER DAILY LOAF

NORTH UNION SHAKER VILLAGE, OHIO

1 package active dry yeast or 1 cake
   compressed yeast
¼ cup warm water
1¾ cups milk
3 tablespoons butter

2 tablespoons sugar
2 teaspoons salt
6–6½ cups sifted all purpose flour
Butter

⟪[Dissolve yeast in warm water in large mixing bowl. Scald milk; stir in butter, sugar, and salt. Cool to lukewarm; add to yeast. Add 3 cups flour; beat until smooth. Add enough additional flour to make a soft dough. Turn out onto lightly floured board. Knead until smooth and elastic, about 10 minutes. Place in buttered bowl, grease top with soft butter, and let rise to double its bulk. Knead lightly this time and shape into loaves in 2 pans. Again brush with butter and let dough rise to twice its bulk in warm place. Bake at 400° F. about 30 minutes. Makes 2 loaves.

SHAKER BROWN BREAD

SISTER LAURA, CANTERBURY SHAKER VILLAGE

1 cup rye flour
1 cup corn meal
1 cup graham flour
1 teaspoon salt
¾ teaspoon baking soda

3¾ cups sour milk
¾ cup molasses
2 tablespoons butter, melted
1 cup chopped raisins

⟪[Sift the dry ingredients together and mix well. Combine in a bowl the sour milk, molasses, and melted butter. Combine the two mixtures and stir thoroughly, adding the chopped raisins, lightly floured. Pour into 2 buttered molds. Fill only two-thirds full. Steam for 2 hours by putting molds in an uncovered pan with 1 inch of water in it on top of stove and then bake for ½ hour in moderate 350° F. oven. Yields 2 loaves.

∴

In a *Manifesto* we read: "Nothing is superior to brown bread for bone and tooth building. Baked beans, too, have a considerable supply of these lime salts and should be on every one's table hot or cold twice a week."

BROWN BREAD

MARY WHITCHER, THE MANIFESTO

"During the fall and winter brown bread from one of our own receipts was baked twice weekly, 12 to 20 loaves at a time. The only time I recall its being baked during the summer was during haying time when dinner pails were filled for the brothers and other help to take away with them."

1 cup unsifted whole wheat flour
1 cup unsifted rye flour
1 cup corn meal
1½ teaspoons baking soda

1½ teaspoons salt
¾ cup molasses
2 cups sour cream
1 cup chopped seeded raisins

❨Combine the dry ingredients. Stir in molasses, sour cream, and raisins. Fill a greased 2 quart mold, or tin can, two-thirds full. Cover closely. Set mold or can on a rack in a large kettle. Pour in boiling water to half the depth of the mold. Cover kettle tightly and steam 3½ hours. Keep water boiling all the time. Serve hot. Yields 1 loaf.

YEAST CHEESE BREAD (Quickly Made)

HANCOCK SHAKER VILLAGE

4 cakes yeast
3 cups lukewarm water
¼ cup sugar
1 tablespoon salt
4 large eggs
10 cups all purpose flour
4 cups grated Cheddar cheese

⅓ cup caraway seeds (optional)
or
⅓ cup celery seeds mixed with dried
  onion (also optional) [Personally
  we like it with cheese only]
Melted butter

❨In a large bowl dissolve yeast in water. Stir in the sugar, salt, eggs, and 5 cups of the flour. Beat thoroughly for 2 or 3 minutes or until dough is really smooth. Add cheese and seeds and remainder of flour. Beat until completely blended. Cover with a clean cloth and let rise until double in bulk. This will take 30 minutes and bowl should be in a warm spot. Stir down with a large wooden spoon and pour into 3 greased loaf pans. Cover and let rise again until batter reaches top of the pan. Bake in a 375° F. oven for 1 hour. Turn out on rack, brush with melted butter, and cool. Makes 3 large loaves.

CHEESE BREAD
HANCOCK SHAKER VILLAGE

2 cups sifted flour
3 teaspoons baking powder
¾ teaspoon salt
1½ teaspoons sugar
1 cup grated Cheshire cheese

½ cup chopped onion
1 egg, beaten by hand with fork
¾ cup milk
2 tablespoons melted butter

⟨[Sift together dry ingredients, add cheese and onion. Combine egg and milk and butter. Add to dry ingredients. Stir to blend well, do not beat. Turn into a greased 8 inch bread pan. Let stand 20 minutes. In a preheated 350° F. moderate oven bake for 1 hour. Makes 1 loaf.

CORN BREAD
(Or for Meat Pie Topping)
TYRINGHAM SHAKER VILLAGE

1½ cups yellow corn meal
½ cup sifted flour
1 tablespoon baking powder
1 teaspoon salt

1 tablespoon sugar
1 egg
¼ cup melted butter
1 cup milk

⟨[Sift together dry ingredients into a large bowl. In a smaller bowl beat egg, add butter and milk, and add to dry ingredients. Stir only to blend. Put in greased 8 inch square baking pan. Bake in hot 425° F. oven for 20 to 25 minutes or until golden on top.

This corn bread can also be used to top a meat pie.

∴

A note said, "Our meat pie with corn bread lid much admired by the Ministry."

AUGUST CORN BREAD
WATERVLIET SHAKER VILLAGE, NEW YORK

¾ cup yellow corn meal
3 teaspoons baking powder
1 tablespoon sugar
½ cup flour
1 teaspoon salt

2 eggs
1½ cups milk
1 cup fresh corn grated from cob
3 tablespoons melted butter

⟨[Blend together in a mixing bowl corn meal, baking powder, sugar, flour,

and salt. Beat eggs, add to milk, corn, and butter. Combine dry ingredients with liquid mixture. Pour mixture into buttered muffin tins
or a square 9 inch tin. Bake in moderate 350° F. oven for about 40
minutes or until bread is set. Serve hot with lots of butter. Yields 9
servings from square pan or 8 muffins.

BUTTERMILK CORN BREAD

ANONYMOUS
MANUSCRIPT FROM A KENTUCKY SHAKER

2 cups white corn meal

1 teaspoon salt

½ teaspoon baking soda

1 teaspoon baking powder

1¼ cups buttermilk

2 tablespoons melted butter or lard

2 eggs, beaten

⟮Sift together corn meal, salt, soda, and baking powder. Stir in buttermilk
and butter and mix well. Add eggs and beat until smooth. Grease a 9
inch square pan with lard and heat it before filling it with the batter.
Bake in a very hot 450° F. oven for 20 minutes. SERVES 8.

SHAKER CORN STICKS

PLEASANT HILL SHAKER VILLAGE

½ teaspoon salt

½ teaspoon baking soda

3 teaspoons sugar

½ teaspoon baking powder

1 cup plus 2 tablespoons corn meal

1 egg, well beaten

½ cup buttermilk

⟮Sift together dry ingredients, add egg and buttermilk. Mix well. Bake
in heated iron corn stick pans at 450° F. until brown. Makes 22 small
corn sticks.

RICE-CORN BREAD

HANCOCK SHAKER VILLAGE

1 cup very soft cooked rice, rubbed
   smooth

2 eggs, beaten

2 tablespoons melted butter

1 cup white corn meal

1 cup milk

1 teaspoon salt

1 teaspoon sugar

⟮Rice should be soft. Add eggs, butter, and beat. Add corn meal, milk,
salt, and sugar and beat thoroughly. Bake in shallow greased 9 inch pan
for 20 minutes in moderate 350° F. oven. Bread should be the consistency of pound cake. SERVES 9.

SOFT CORN BREAD
HANCOCK SHAKER VILLAGE

¾ cup corn meal	1 teaspoon baking powder
¼ cup sifted flour	1½ cups plus 1 tablespoon milk
½ tablespoon sugar	1 egg, lightly beaten
½ teaspoon salt	2 tablespoons butter, melted

⟨Combine dry ingredients. Stir in 1 cup plus 1 tablespoon milk. Stir in egg. Put butter in 9 inch baking pan in oven; when butter is hot pour batter into pan. Pour remaining ½ cup milk over top and do not stir it in. Bake in preheated oven at 400° F. for 30 minutes. SERVES 8–9.

CRANBERRY BREAD
HANCOCK SHAKER VILLAGE

2 cups flour	Juice and grated rind 1 orange
½ teaspoon salt	1 egg, beaten
½ teaspoon baking soda	2 tablespoons melted shortening
1 cup sugar	1 cup cranberries
1½ teaspoons baking powder	½ cup broken nut meats

⟨Sift dry ingredients together into large bowl. Put juice and grated rind of orange in measuring cup, add enough boiling water to make ¾ cup and add to dry mixture. Add egg and melted shortening and mix just enough to moisten flour mixture. Add cranberries and nut meats. Bake in greased loaf pan 45 to 50 minutes at 325° F. Store 24 hours before cutting. Yields 1 loaf.

SISTER OLIVE WHEELER'S DIET BREAD
MT. LEBANON SHAKER VILLAGE

"The weight of 6 eggs in sugar—the weight of 4 eggs in flour. The whites and the yolks should be beaten thoroughly and separately. The eggs and sugar should be well beaten together, but after the flour is put in it should not be stired a moment longer than is necessary to mix it."

Note: This bread was not for those trying to lose weight. It was made for its nutritive value and probably almost exclusively for elderly Shakers since it omitted yeast which did not always agree with everyone. Eggs provide the rising agent. We have left Sister Olive's recipe as we found it in manuscript form and add our own version which we have followed in testing.

10 eggs   1 cup flour
1½ cups sugar   ½ teaspoon salt

⟨[Separate the eggs. Beat the yolks until lemon color, then slowly beat in the sugar. Beat the egg whites until stiff and fold them into the sugar-yolk mixture. Sift flour and salt together and add to first mixture, stirring only to mix well. Bake in ungreased bread pan in a slow oven 45 minutes

GRAHAM BREAD
MARY WHITCHER'S SHAKER HOUSEKEEPER

4 cups graham flour   2 teaspoons salt
⅔ cup white flour   ½ cup molasses
2 teaspoons baking soda   2 tablespoons butter or lard, melted
¼ cup sugar   2½ cups sweet milk[1]

⟨[Sift flours, soda, sugar, and salt together. Add molasses, melted butter, and milk. Beat well as air and soda are only rising agents. Put into greased bread tins and bake 1 hour in moderately hot 375° F. oven.

Variation: One cup raisins may be added.

GRAHAM-BUTTERMILK BREAD
MARY WHITCHER'S SHAKER HOUSEKEEPER

2 cups graham flour   3 tablespoons melted butter
½ cup corn meal   ½ cup maple syrup
1 teaspoon baking soda   2 cups buttermilk
1 teaspoon salt

⟨[Combine dry ingredients. Mix butter, maple syrup, and buttermilk together. Stir into dry ingredients. Mix well quickly. Fill a buttered loaf pan. Bake in a 350° F. oven about 45 minutes. Test by inserting a straw in the middle of the loaf. Bread is done if straw comes out clean. Yields 1 loaf.

Variation: Chopped raisins or nuts may be added to taste. If buttermilk is not available, use whole milk, omit soda, and add 1 tablespoon of baking powder to dry ingredients.

---

[1] "Sweet milk" was Mary Whitcher's term for whole, fresh milk. There was lots of skimmed milk left after cheese making, and also lots of sour milk was used.

HERB BREAD #1

HANCOCK SHAKER VILLAGE

2 cups milk
¼ cup sugar
¼ teaspoon salt
2 envelopes active dry yeast
2 eggs, well beaten
1 teaspoon powdered nutmeg or cloves

2 teaspoons crumbled dried sage leaves
4 teaspoons caraway seeds
1 teaspoon dried rosemary
1 teaspoon dried dill
7½ to 8 cups presifted flour
¼ cup melted butter

⟨Scald milk. Stir in sugar and salt, cool to lukewarm. Add yeast. Stir well until completely dissolved. Add eggs, nutmeg, herbs, and 4 cups of the flour. Beat until smooth. Add butter and enough of remaining flour to make a soft dough that is easy to handle. Turn onto lightly floured board. Knead until smooth and elastic. Place dough in greased bowl —cover—let rise for about 2 hours or until doubled in bulk. Grease 2 loaf pans. Punch dough down. Divide in half. Fill each pan, cover, let rise again, 1 hour or until doubled. Preheat oven to 425° F. Bake for 15 minutes. Reduce heat to 375° F. Bake 35 minutes. A nice addition is 2 teaspoons of celery seeds. Yields 2 loaves.

HERB BREAD #2

HANCOCK SHAKER VILLAGE

3 cakes yeast
3 cups warm water
¼ cup sugar or honey
5 teaspoons salt
½ teaspoon each dried savory and marjoram

¼ teaspoon dried thyme or sage
1 teaspoon minced dried parsley
9 or 10 cups all purpose flour
5 tablespoons melted butter

⟨Dissolve yeast in water, add sugar or honey, and stir well. Add salt, herbs, and parsley to flour. Add half this mixture to yeast mixture. Beat hard with a spoon until dough is smooth. Add remaining flour and blend well. Pour melted butter over dough and knead in the bowl for a few minutes, 2 or 3, no more. The dough will absorb the butter. Cover bowl and let dough double in a warm place—this will take about 45 minutes. Punch down, turn onto lightly floured board and knead slightly. Shape into 2 loaves and place in buttered loaf pans. Cover and let rise again until dough reaches rim of pans, about 30 minutes. Bake at 400° F. for 30 minutes or until done. Yields 2 loaves.

CARAWAY BREAD
HANCOCK SHAKER VILLAGE

¼ cup butter
¾ cup sugar
1 egg, well beaten
1⅔ cups flour
1 tablespoon baking powder

¾ cup milk
1 tablespoon caraway seeds
¾ teaspoon vanilla
¼ teaspoon salt

([Cream butter, add sugar gradually, and well-beaten egg. Mix and sift flour and baking powder and add alternately with milk to first mixture. Add caraway seeds, vanilla, and salt. Mix well. Put in a buttered and floured pan, sprinkle with sugar and extra caraway seeds. Bake in moderate 350° F. oven 35 minutes. Remove from pan. Cut in squares and serve hot with butter. Makes 1 loaf.

HANCOCK DILL BREAD
HANCOCK SHAKER VILLAGE

2 cups mashed potatoes
2 cups boiling water
2 envelopes active dry yeast
½ cup warm water
¼ cup plus 1 teaspoon sugar
¼ cup melted butter

1 tablespoon salt
1 tablespoon powdered dry dill
8 cups sifted flour (about)
Melted shortening
Crushed dillweed and dill seed
 (optional)

([Combine potatoes and boiling water. Mix until smooth and cool to lukewarm. Soften yeast in warm water with 1 teaspoon sugar for 10 minutes. Beat ¼ cup sugar, ¼ cup butter, salt, and dill into potato mixture. Gradually add about 4 cups of the flour. Beat thoroughly. Stir in the yeast. Work in remaining flour, enough to make a dough that won't stick to hands. Turn out onto floured board. Knead until smooth and elastic. Cover; let rise for about 2 hours or until double in bulk. Punch dough down, cover, let rise again for about 1½ hours or until double in bulk. Grease 3 bread pans; divide dough into them. Brush with melted shortening. Bake in preheated 375° F. oven for 45 minutes. Remove from oven and brush again with shortening and if desired sprinkle with crushed dillweed and dill seed, mixed half and half.

Dillweed is foliage of the plant while dill seed is the ripened seed of the flower. Makes 3 loaves.

DILL BREAD

HANCOCK SHAKER VILLAGE

1 package active dry yeast
¼ cup warm water
1 cup lukewarm creamed cottage
    cheese
2 tablespoons sugar
1 tablespoon butter

1 tablespoon finely chopped onion
2 teaspoons dill seed
1 teaspoon salt
¼ teaspoon baking soda
1 egg
2¼ to 2½ cups flour

([Dissolve yeast in warm water. In a large bowl combine cottage cheese, sugar, butter, onion, dill seed, salt, soda, and the egg. Stir. Add yeast mixture and stir gradually. Add and stir in the flour to make a stiff dough. Beat well. The mixture must be smooth. Cover bowl with a warm cloth and let rise in a warm place, outside of drafts, for 50 to 60 minutes or until dough has doubled in bulk. Punch down and turn into a well-buttered 1½ quart round casserole, if a round loaf is wanted, or use well-buttered regular bread loaf tin. Let bread rise again 30 to 40 minutes. Bake in moderate 350° F. oven for 40 to 50 minutes. Makes 1 round loaf or 2 small oblong loaves.

SAFFRON BREAD

HANCOCK SHAKER VILLAGE

2 teaspoons saffron
½ cup boiling water
1½ cups scalded milk
1 cup butter
1 cup sugar
2 cakes yeast
2 large eggs
1 teaspoon salt

½ teaspoon nutmeg
1 teaspoon cinnamon
6 cups flour
2 cups currants or raisins
½ cup cut up candied lemon peel
    or
Grated rind 3 large lemons

([Steep the saffron in the boiling water for 5 minutes. Drain and reserve the liquid. Pour the hot scalded milk over butter and sugar and stir to melt butter. Let cool to lukewarm; stir in yeast and let it dissolve. Add saffron liquid and eggs. Blend well. Add dry ingredients, reserving some of the flour to dust the fruits with. Stir in floured fruits last. The dough should be fairly stiff; if it isn't add more flour. Knead the dough, then place in a buttered bowl. Cover, let it rise. Knead down and shape into 2 loaves. Put in buttered tins. Let rise again until doubled. Bake in a

350° F. oven for 45 minutes to 1 hour or until browned and done. Makes 2 loaves.

This same recipe can be used to make Saffron Buns: Shape dough into small buns instead of 2 loaves. Place on greased baking sheet. Let rise 30 minutes or until doubled in bulk. Bake in preheated 350° F. oven for 25 to 30 minutes. Makes about 24, depending on size of buns.

INDIAN BREAD
HANCOCK SHAKER VILLAGE

1½ cups sifted flour
1 cup corn meal
½ teaspoon baking soda
½ teaspoon baking powder
¼ teaspoon salt

1 egg, beaten
½ cup molasses
1⅔ cups milk
2 tablespoons shortening, melted

([Sift dry ingredients together. Add egg. Add molasses and milk. Beat until smooth. Lastly add shortening. Turn into a greased 9 inch square baking tin. Cook in a hot 450° F. oven for 20 minutes. SERVES 10.

A nice variation is to add 1 cup blueberries. In this case bake in round cake tin and cut in pie-shaped pieces.

LEMON BREAD
HANCOCK SHAKER VILLAGE

⅓ cup shortening
1⅓ cups sugar
2 eggs
1½ cups sifted flour
1½ teaspoons baking powder

¼ teaspoon salt
½ cup milk
½ cup chopped nuts (optional—
    makes it more like cake)
Grated rind and juice 1 lemon

([Beat together shortening and 1 cup of the sugar until light and fluffy. Add eggs one at a time, beating well after each one. Sift dry ingredients together and add alternately with milk to the sugar mixture, beating well after each addition. Add nuts and lemon rind. Turn batter into greased 8½ inch bread pan. Bake in preheated 350° F. oven 50 to 60 minutes. Blend remaining sugar and lemon juice. Pour over bread as soon as it comes from oven. Makes 1 loaf.

MAPLE TOAST

HANCOCK SHAKER VILLAGE

([Dip slices of bread in maple syrup and simmer in melted butter until crisp and golden outside, sweet and tender inside. Do not let butter brown.

OATMEAL BREAD

MARY WHITCHER'S SHAKER HOUSEKEEPER

2 cups boiling water
2 cups rolled oats
1 tablespoon softened butter
½ cup molasses
½ teaspoon salt

1 cake yeast
½ cup lukewarm water
5 cups sifted white flour
   (approximately)

([Add boiling water to rolled oats and let stand 1 hour. Then add butter, molasses, and salt. Dissolve yeast in lukewarm water and add to the rolled oats mixture with enough flour to make a stiff dough. Turn out on floured board. Knead 4 to 5 minutes. Place in a greased bowl, brush with melted butter. Cover and let rise overnight in warm place. In the morning knead lightly and shape into 2 loaves. Let rise until double in bulk and bake in 425° F. oven for 10 minutes and at 375° F. for 40 minutes. Makes 2 loaves.

POTATO BREAD

MT. LEBANON SHAKER VILLAGE

2 cups scalded milk
1 cup hot mashed potatoes
1 cake yeast
¼ cup warm water
2½ cups flour
1 egg, well beaten
⅜ cup butter

⅜ cup lard
1 cup sugar
2 teaspoons salt
2¾ cups flour
2 tablespoons brown sugar mixed
   with 1 teaspoon ground cinnamon

([When milk is lukewarm add potatoes, and yeast cake, which has been dissolved in warm water, and 2½ cups flour. Mix well. Cover and let rise until light. Punch down and add egg, butter, lard, sugar, salt, and remaining flour. Turn into a buttered loaf pan. Cover and let rise. Brush melted butter over top. Sprinkle with brown sugar mixed with cinnamon. Bake 35 minutes at 350° F. Makes 1 loaf.

SISTER JENNIE'S POTATO BREAD
NORTH UNION SHAKER VILLAGE, OHIO

2 eggs
½ cup sugar
¼ teaspoon salt
1 cup mashed boiled
   potatoes

½ cake yeast
¼ cup warm water
4 to 5 cups bread flour
½ cup butter
1 cup warm water

⟨Beat eggs and add ¼ cup sugar. Add salt and mashed potatoes, which have passed through a sieve. Add yeast which has been dissolved in warm water. Stir in enough flour to make a stiff dough. Dough should pull away from sides of bowl. Sometimes more flour is needed than stated in ingredients. Place in a buttered dish and let rise for 2 hours. Then cream butter and the remaining sugar together. Work this into the dough and let rise very slowly for 6 hours. Then work in warm water and shape into loaf. Place in buttered bread pan. Let rise again until very light, and bake in a hot 450° F. oven for 15 minutes. Lower heat to 350° F. and bake until well browned, about 45 minutes. Makes 1 loaf.

PRUNE BREAD
ENFIELD SHAKER VILLAGE, CONNECTICUT

1 cup dried uncooked prunes
3 cups sifted all purpose flour
4 teaspoons baking powder
½ teaspoon baking soda
1½ teaspoons salt

2 tablespoons white sugar
6 tablespoons butter
2 tablespoons grated orange rind
2 eggs, beaten
1 cup milk

⟨Rinse prunes, drain and dry. If they are very dry, boil 5 minutes. Remove pits and put through food chopper or chop finely by hand. Sift together flour, baking powder, soda, salt, and sugar. Cut in shortening with a pastry blender. Add prunes and orange rind and stir well. Combine eggs and milk and add to other ingredients. Mix well. Pour into a greased loaf pan and bake in moderate 350° F. oven for 1 hour or until done. Makes 1 loaf.

PRUNE LOAF

SHIRLEY SHAKER VILLAGE

1 cup white sugar
2 tablespoons melted butter
1 egg, beaten
1 cup cut up cooked prunes
½ cup prune juice
1 cup sour milk or buttermilk

1 cup fine whole wheat flour
2 cups all purpose white flour
1 teaspoon baking soda
¼ teaspoon baking powder
½ teaspoon salt

❲Cream together sugar, butter. Beat in egg. Add prunes, prune juice, and milk. Sift together all the dry ingredients and add to the first mixture. Beat together thoroughly. Use 2 buttered loaf pans 9x5 inches. Bake in 350° F. oven about 1 hour. Makes 2 loaves.

PUMPKIN LOAVES

HANCOCK SHAKER VILLAGE

2 cups granulated sugar
1 cup melted butter
3 eggs
2 cups cooked and strained pumpkin
2 cups sifted all purpose flour
½ teaspoon salt

½ teaspoon double acting baking powder
1 teaspoon baking soda
1 teaspoon ground cloves
1 teaspoon ground cinnamon
1 teaspoon ground nutmeg
3 loaf pans

❲In bowl beat sugar and melted butter to blend. Beat in eggs, one at a time, and continue beating until light and fluffy. Then beat in pumpkin. In a separate bowl sift together sifted flour, salt, baking powder, baking soda, and all of the spices. Beat this mixture into pumpkin mixture. Divide batter between 3 greased loaf pans (7½x3½x2¼ inches). Bake 60 minutes at 325° F. or until straw tester comes out clean when inserted in middle of loaf. Cool in pans 10 minutes. Remove and place on wire racks and continue to cool. Makes 3 loaves.

SALLY LUNN

MARY WHITCHER'S SHAKER HOUSEKEEPER

2 tablespoons butter
2 tablespoons sugar
1 teaspoon salt
1 cup scalded milk

½ yeast cake
¼ cup lukewarm water
3 eggs
1–1½ cups flour (about)

([Put butter, sugar, and salt in a bowl, pour over scalded milk and when lukewarm, add yeast cake dissolved in lukewarm water, well-beaten eggs, and enough flour to make stiff batter. Cover and let rise until very light and soft to touch. Fill a buttered baking tin half full, cover, again let rise for 2 hours. Bake in hot 400° F. oven 30 minutes. Makes 1 loaf.

SISTER ABIGAIL'S SALT RISING BREAD
NORTH UNION SHAKER VILLAGE, OHIO

3 cups scalded milk	2 tablespoons sugar
½ cup coarse corn meal	5 tablespoons butter
1¾ teaspoons salt	5 cups flour, sifted (about)

([Scald 1 cup milk and pour over corn meal. Let stand in a warm place until bubbles rise to the surface (about 6 to 7 hours). Then heat remaining 2 cups milk just lukewarm and add to it salt, sugar, and shortening and dissolve thoroughly. Now add the corn meal mixture and set bowl in a dish of lukewarm water until bubbles rise throughout mixture. Then work in sifted flour. Knead until sponge dough is very elastic. Place in a greased bowl and let rise in a warm place 2 hours. Divide into 3 parts and work into loaves. Place in pans and let rise to double the bulk. Place loaves in moderately hot 375° F. oven for 15 minutes. Lower heat to 350° F. Bake 30 minutes longer. Makes 3 loaves.

A very old recipe. Salt rising bread depends on yeast spores in the air to start fermentation. It is not as light as yeast bread but is moist and crumbly.

SHAKER WHEATEN BREAD
ELDRESS CLYMENA MINER
NORTH UNION SHAKER VILLAGE, OHIO

1 cup milk	1 cup warm water
1 tablespoon salt	1 cake yeast
4 tablespoons honey or maple syrup	1 cup white flour, sifted
3 tablespoons butter	4 cups whole wheat flour

([Scald milk and add salt, sweetening, and butter and ¾ cup warm water and stir well. Let cool to lukewarm. In the remaining ¼ cup warm water dissolve yeast and add to other liquid mixture. Add flours gradually and knead into a smooth ball. Proceed as with Shaker Daily Loaf.* Bake in moderate 350° F. oven for 50 to 60 minutes. Yields 1 very substantial loaf of extremely wholesome bread, or 2 medium-sized loaves.

CONVENIENCE MIXES

Some Shaker cooks made their own convenience mixture to use for muffins, biscuits, pancakes, etc. When eggs, milk, and sour cream were added it became standard batter. This was not typically Shaker; our grandmothers did the same thing. It takes experience to tell *exactly* how much liquid or eggs to add to make a good consistency.

SHAKER CONVENIENCE MIX #1
(Short-step Mixture)
MT. LEBANON SHAKER VILLAGE

12 cups sifted flour	6 teaspoons salt
6 tablespoon baking powder	3 cups shortening

〔Sift dry ingredients together two or three times. Cut in shortening. Mix well until like grain—coarse corn meal. Place mixture in glass jars, or crockery bowl—cover lightly and keep cool in refrigerator. The above will make about 4 quart jars. Should be used within 3 or 4 weeks.

Biscuits:

To 2 cups basic mix add ½ to ¾ cup milk—or sour cream. Make a soft dough, roll out on floured board—knead lightly. Roll out and cut ½ inch thick biscuits of any desired size or shape. Bake on ungreased baking sheet at 450° F. for 12 to 15 minutes or until delicately brown.

Muffins:

To 2 cups basic mix, add 1 well-beaten egg, 2 tablespoons sugar, ¾ cup milk. Blend lightly. Fill greased muffin pans two-thirds full and bake in hot 425° F. oven for 20 minutes.

Variation: For richer muffins 2 teaspoons melted butter may be added after the milk.

SHAKER CONVENIENCE MIX #2
NORTH UNION SHAKER VILLAGE, OHIO

In a clean gallon glass jar with a snug-fitting cover keep the following

mixture to have on hand as a basis for biscuits and muffins with variations. Keep refrigerated but use up in 3 to 4 weeks.

5 pounds (10 cups) flour	2 cups butter
½ cup baking powder	1 tablespoon mace
3 tablespoons salt	

❡[Mix dry ingredients together in a large bowl. Cut in butter until fine,
with consistency of coarse meal. Add mace. Put in jar and cover lightly.

Biscuits:

Measure 4 cups of mix into a bowl. Add a cup of rich milk and stir
until a soft dough is formed. Knead on lightly floured board about 10
times. Roll ½ inch thick. Cut with floured cutter. Bake on ungreased
baking sheet in a hot 450° F. oven for 12 to 15 minutes, until lightly
browned.

Plain Muffins:

Measure 4 cups of the mix into a bowl. Add ¼ cup sugar, 2 well-
beaten eggs, and 1½ cups rich milk. Add 2 tablespoons of sour cream.
Mix until dry ingredients absorb liquids. Fill muffin pans almost to rim.
Bake in hot oven 425° F. 20 minutes. Makes 2 dozen muffins.

Variation: Add 1 cup chopped raisins and 1 teaspoon cinnamon to
above.

Blueberry Muffins:

Use plain muffin recipe but increase sugar from ¼ cup to ⅔ cup. Add
1 cup blueberries. When cooked, brush with melted butter and sprinkle
with sugar.

Jam or Marmalade Muffins:

Fill pans one-third full of plain muffin dough, drop in a teaspoon of
jam or marmalade then add more dough to fill pans two-thirds to three-
quarters full. Dust with 2 tablespoons sugar and 1 teaspoon cinnamon
mixed together.

Shortcake:

Use 6 cups mix, ¾ cup sugar, 2 beaten eggs, and ⅔ cup rich milk or
light cream. Knead as in biscuits, pat into rounds to fit buttered 8 inch
cake pans. Brush tops with melted butter. Bake in hot 425° F. oven for
10 to 15 minutes or until golden. Put one circle on a serving plate, spread-
ing with butter and sweetened fruit. Place other circle on top, cover with
whipped cream and more fruit.

SHAKER CONVENIENCE MIX #3

HANCOCK SHAKER VILLAGE

9 cups sifted white flour   ⅓ cup baking powder
1 tablespoon salt   1½–2 cups shortening

❲Combine dry ingredients in a large bowl. Cut in the shortening as for pastry. When thoroughly blended store in a cannister or glass jar in the refrigerator. It should keep 2 months, but check to be on the safe side.

Biscuits:

Use 2 cups mix, 1 large egg, and ½ cup milk, cream, or sour cream. Make as usual and bake at 400° F. for 12 to 15 minutes.

Muffins:

Use 3 cups mix, ¼ cup sugar, 1 cup milk, and 1 egg. Mix as for muffins and spoon into buttered muffin pans. Bake at 425° F. for 20 minutes. To the above muffin recipe can be added 1 cup blueberries and ¼ cup additional sugar. Blend well.

Cranberry Muffins:

Add 1 cup chopped fresh cranberries, and 1⅓ cups sugar. Blend well into batter. Remember always to stir—*never beat*—the batter.

Jam Muffins:

Follow basic muffin recipe. After muffins have been baking 10 minutes, add 1 teaspoon of any jam, jelly, or marmalade by dropping into center of muffin. Finish baking.

Pancakes:

Use 1½ cups of mix, 1 tablespoon sugar, ½ cup milk, 2 large eggs. Mix and bake as usual.

Variation: Add to the pancakes above ½ cup blueberries or 1 cup peeled, cored, and chopped apples.

CREAM BISCUITS #1

NORTH UNION SHAKER VILLAGE, OHIO

2 cups bread flour, sifted   1 cup heavy cream
3 teaspoons baking powder

❲Sift flour and baking powder together. Whip cream until stiff. Mix lightly with flour, using fork. Turn onto lightly floured board and knead for 1 minute. Pat dough to ½ inch thickness and cut with biscuit cutter. Bake in hot 450° F. oven for 12 minutes. Makes 12–16 biscuits, depending on size.

∵

Sister Lisset says in her biscuit hints: "If you do not wish to light your oven on a hot day, bake your biscuits on a hot griddle. Grease lightly and place biscuits a good inch apart. Brown on one side for 5 minutes, turn and brown on other side. Very good biscuits! Almost endless variety of biscuits can be made from any standard recipe by adding grated cheese, minced fruit, berries or spices." Sister Miriam's Sour Cream Biscuits* can be made this way, too.

CREAM BISCUITS #2
CANTERBURY SHAKER VILLAGE

2 cups sifted flour
1 tablespoon baking powder
½ teaspoon salt

1 cup heavy cream, whipped
½ cup maple sugar or brown sugar (or less), lightly packed

⟨Combine sifted flour, baking powder, and salt. Mix thoroughly. Sift. Pour in whipped cream and fold in thoroughly. Turn dough out on a floured board and knead 10 times. Pat or roll to ½ inch thickness. Cut with floured cutter and put on ungreased baking sheet. Sprinkle with maple or brown sugar. Bake at 425° F. for 10 to 12 minutes until golden.

BAKING POWDER BISCUITS
HANCOCK SHAKER VILLAGE

1 cup white flour
2 teaspoons baking powder
1 teaspoon salt
1 teaspoon sugar
2 tablespoons lard or other shortening[1]

Rich milk
or
Cream to moisten
or
Sour Cream[2]

⟨Combine flour, baking powder, salt, and sugar. Cut in lard. Add milk and pat out ½ inch thick on a floured board. Cut into rounds. Bake on buttered cooky sheet 15 minutes in 400° F. oven. Makes 8–10 small biscuits.

---

[1] Chicken fat can be used in place of lard, but measure scant. Such national brands as Crisco, Spry, and those put out by the large chain grocery stores can also be used.
[2] If sour cream only is available use Sour Cream Biscuits recipe.*

ROSEMARY BISCUITS

HANCOCK SHAKER VILLAGE

2 cups sifted flour
1 tablespoon baking powder
1 teaspoon salt
1 tablespoon sugar
½ cup butter
¾ cup milk

1 egg
2 teaspoons dried rosemary
or
3 teaspoons crumbled fresh
rosemary

([Sift dry ingredients together. Cut in the butter. Combine milk and egg and rosemary. Stir into dry mixture. Mix well, but lightly. Roll out dough on a floured bread board, cut into rounds. Place on an ungreased cooky sheet. Bake in a 450° F. oven for 12 to 15 minutes or until done. Makes 12–16, depending on size.

SISTER OLIVE WHEELER'S SODA BISCUITS

NEW LEBANON SHAKER VILLAGE, 1844

(["Two quarts flour, 1 pint of milk, 4 teaspoons of cream of tartar, stirred in the flour. Two teaspoons soda dissolved in the milk and baked immediately."

Today's cook would make these as follows:

1 teaspoon cream of tartar
2 cups flour
½ teaspoon salt

½ teaspoon baking soda
½ cup milk

([Mix cream of tartar, flour, and salt. Dissolve soda in milk. Mix, pat thin, cut into squares and bake on greased cooky sheet in a hot oven (400° F.) 10 minutes. Makes 12–16 biscuits.

SISTER LETTIE'S BUTTERMILK BISCUITS

NORTH UNION SHAKER VILLAGE, OHIO

2 cups flour, sifted
½ teaspoon salt
3 level teaspoons baking powder

½ teaspoon soda
3 tablespoons butter
¾ cup buttermilk

([Sift flour, salt, baking powder, and soda together. Cut in butter with two knives. Add buttermilk and knead lightly. Roll to ¾ inch thickness and cut shape with small cutter. Dab top with melted butter and bake 12 minutes in hot 450° F. oven. These are light and delicious. Make plenty! Makes 12–16, depending on size.

SISTER MIRIAM'S SOUR CREAM BISCUITS
CANTERBURY SHAKER VILLAGE

2 cups bread flour, sifted
3 teaspoons baking powder
1 teaspoon sugar

½ teaspoon salt
2 tablespoons butter
1 cup sour cream

❡Sift dry ingredients together. Cut in butter and add sour cream. Mix lightly with a fork and turn onto a floured board. Pat dough to desired thickness and cut with round tin cutter. Bake at 400° F. 12 to 15 minutes on greased cooky sheet. These biscuits are rich and can also be used for fruit shortcakes if made 1 inch thick and buttered after cooking. Makes 12–16, depending on size.

Variation: Sprinkle scraped maple sugar over tops of sour cream (or other) biscuits just before removing from oven so it can melt.

ROSE GERANIUM ROLLS
HANCOCK SHAKER VILLAGE

1½ cups milk, scalded
1 cup sugar
2 envelopes active dry yeast
4 eggs, lightly beaten

1 teaspoon salt
6 cups sifted flour
1 cup melted butter
Several scented rose geranium leaves

❡Pour milk over sugar in large bowl. Cool to lukewarm. Add yeast to milk mixture. Add eggs and salt. Let stand 5 minutes, then stir to blend. Stir in 3 cups of the flour; mix well. Gradually work in enough remaining flour to make a soft dough. Cover, let rise for about 1½ hours, or until double in bulk. Punch down. (If not baking at once, cover dough and refrigerate. Actually this dough will keep in refrigerator 3 to 4 days.)

About 2 hours before baking, grease muffin cups, form dough into small balls and bury a fragment of a small geranium leaf in the very center of the ball. Place balls in muffin cups. brush top generously with melted butter, cover, let rise for 2 hours. Preheat oven to 400° F. Bake in preheated oven for 20 minutes. Makes 3 dozen.

Rose Geranium belongs to the sweet-scented leaved Geranium family, not to be confused with large-flowering garden types. A few of the scented varieties also bear handsome flowers, but the majority, while free flowering, produce tiny blossoms and are grown for scent not flowers.

WHOLE WHEAT GERM BISCUITS

HANCOCK SHAKER VILLAGE

1 cup toasted wheat germ
½ cup flour
2 teaspoons baking powder
1 teaspoon salt

1 teaspoon sugar
2 tablespoons butter
¼ cup ice water

❡Mix together ½ cup toasted wheat germ and remaining dry ingredients. Cut in butter, add water, and blend well. Roll out or pat dough ½ inch thick. Cut in rounds and place on greased cooky sheet. Sprinkle one-half of them with remaining wheat germ, top with another round to make a sandwich. Press firmly together. Bake in 350° F. oven about 15 minutes until brown. Makes 10–12, depending on size.

BUTTERMILK ROLLS

HANCOCK SHAKER VILLAGE

1 envelope active dry yeast
¼ cup warm water
1½ cups lukewarm buttermilk
3 tablespoons sugar

½ cup melted shortening
4½ cups sifted flour
½ teaspoon baking soda
1 teaspoon salt

❡In mixing bowl soften yeast in water. Add buttermilk, sugar, and shortening. In another bowl sift together dry ingredients. Stir into buttermilk mixture. Beat until smooth. Let stand 10 minutes. Roll out dough. Shape into rolls; arrange on greased cooky sheet, cover, let rise for about 30 minutes. In preheated 400° F. oven bake 15 to 20 minutes. Makes about 2 dozen.

SCONES

HANCOCK SHAKER VILLAGE

2 cups flour
2 teaspoons sugar
3 teaspoons baking powder
1 teaspoon salt

4 tablespoons fat (butter)
⅓ cup light cream
2 eggs, beaten—reserve a little
   unbeaten white

❡Mix and sift dry ingredients. Work in the fat quickly with a fork or dough blender. Add cream mixed with beaten eggs (there will be a little less white of egg—see above) all at once and stir lightly to make a soft dough. Turn out on slightly floured board, knead lightly for a very few seconds, roll to ½ inch thickness. Cut, dipping cutter in flour after each using. These scones should be diamond shape, each side about 2 inches. If such a cutter is not available, the scone should be cut free hand. Brush each scone with the reserved egg white and sprinkle with sugar. Bake in a hot 400° F. oven for 12 to 15 minutes. Yields a dozen or more, depending on size.

SHORTCAKES
HANCOCK SHAKER VILLAGE

To use for tea with butter and jam or with fruit and whipped cream for fruit shortcake.

2 cups flour   ½ cup brown sugar
¾ cup unsalted butter, or wash
  butter to remove salt

⟨Mix ingredients. Roll out ½ inch thick. Mark and cut into squares. Put on cooky sheet.

Cook in moderate 350° F. oven for 15 minutes or until a light golden color. These are really shortcakes and should not be baked too long as there is little moisture in them and no raising agent. Makes 12–16, depending on size.

SQUASH CAKES OR PUMPKIN CAKES #1
CANTERBURY SHAKER VILLAGE

¼ cake yeast   1 tablespoon butter
¼ cup lukewarm water   1 cup milk, scalded
1 egg, well beaten   1 cup mashed well-drained boiled
½ cup sugar   winter squash
¼ teaspoon salt   1 cup sifted flour

⟨Soften yeast in lukewarm water. Add egg, sugar, salt, butter, and milk to the squash. Cool to lukewarm. Add softened yeast and flour. Cover and let rise in warm place overnight.

Shape into biscuits and let rise about 20 minutes. Bake on greased cooky sheet in moderate 350° F. oven 12 to 15 minutes. Makes 1½ dozen cakes.

Variation: For pumpkin cakes—1 cup mashed cooked pumpkin instead of the squash; ½ cup molasses or maple syrup may be used instead of sugar; use ¾ cup milk instead of 1 cup.

SQUASH CAKES OR PUMPKIN CAKES #2

CANTERBURY SHAKER VILLAGE

1½ cups sifted flour	⅓ cup melted shortening
3 teaspoons baking powder	1 cup boiled, well-drained mashed
2 tablespoons sugar	winter squash
1 teaspoon salt	¾ cup milk
1 teaspoon cinnamon	

⟨[Sift dry ingredients into a mixing bowl. Stir in shortening and squash. Mix well. Add milk. Mix lightly with a fork. Turn dough onto floured board. Knead with floured fingers—quickly. Pat dough out to a thickness of ½ inch. Cut into rounds with biscuit cutter. Bake on a greased cooky sheet 18 to 22 minutes in hot 450° F. oven. Yields 2 dozen.

Variation: Pumpkin can be used in place of winter squash.

SQUASH CAKES OR PUMPKIN CAKES #3

HANCOCK SHAKER VILLAGE

½ cup well-drained steamed winter squash	½ cup scalded milk
¼ cup sugar	¼ yeast cake
½ teaspoon salt	¼ cup lukewarm water
¼ cup butter	2½ cups flour

⟨[Add squash, sugar, salt, and butter to milk. When lukewarm, add yeast cake, which has been dissolved in water, and flour. Cover and let rise overnight. In morning shape into biscuits, let rise, and bake on buttered tin sheet in hot 400° F. oven 25 minutes. Yields about 2 dozen.

Variation: Pumpkin may be used in place of squash.

BEST CRACKERS

OLIVE WHEELER, NEW LEBANON SHAKER VILLAGE, 1844

1 cup flour	½ cup butter
1 teaspoon baking powder	3 tablespoons milk
¼ teaspoon salt	

⟨[Mix and sift dry ingredients and work in the butter using pastry mixer. Add milk. Dough will be stiff. Toss on floured board, pat and roll ¼ inch thick. Shape with round or square cutter dipped in flour. Arrange on greased baking sheet. Bake 10 minutes in hot 400° F. oven. Split while hot. Return to oven and bake until golden color. These crackers will keep well without crumbling. Makes 12–24, depending on size.

ICE WATER CRACKERS
HANCOCK SHAKER VILLAGE

❴Using commercial crackers (Westminster, Massachusetts, soda crackers), split crackers and put on shallow pan, barely covered with ice water, for 5 minutes.

Remove carefully with slotted spatula and drain very well without pressing. Don't break.

Place crackers on a buttered cooky sheet. Brush with melted butter. Bake in a very hot 450° F. oven. for 15 to 20 minutes, until they have puffed and are golden brown.

If Westminsters are not used, substitute a thick saltine cracker.

HERB DUMPLINGS AND PARSLEY DUMPLINGS
MARY WHITCHER'S SHAKER HOUSEKEEPER

2 cups flour, sifted
4 teaspoons baking powder
1 teaspoon salt
2 eggs
¾ cup milk (about)
2 tablespoons melted butter
2 cups chicken or beef stock or water
  (stock is better)

1 tablespoon chopped fresh parsley
  or
1 tablespoon mixed chopped fresh herbs (tarragon, basil, thyme, rosemary—mixed or singly) If using dried herbs, reduce by half

❴Sift flour with baking powder and salt. Break eggs into cup and fill with milk; add butter. Beat well and mix into dry ingredients. Add parsley or herbs and mix well. Heat stock in a 12 inch skillet and bring to a boil. Dip spoon into stock, then into dough, and drop into stock. Do not cook too many at a time; dumplings must not touch. Cover tightly and cook 2 minutes. Turn dumplings and cook 2 minutes longer. Serve very hot.

This is Sister Mary Whitcher's basic recipe for dumplings to be made plain or with herbs or with a sweet flavoring and served with a sauce for dessert.

If they are to be used for dessert, omit herbs, flavor with vanilla and sugar, and cook in water. Serve with sweet dessert sauce. See Dumplings Cooked in Maple Syrup.*

CORN MEAL FRITTERS

HANCOCK SHAKER VILLAGE

1 cup corn meal	1 egg, beaten
1 cup flour	1 cup milk (about)
2 teaspoons baking powder	Deep fat for frying
¾ teaspoon salt	

⟨[Mix dry ingredients together. Stir in beaten egg and enough milk to make a stiff batter. Drop by spoonfuls into deep hot fat and fry until brown. Drain on brown paper. Serve hot with maple syrup. SERVES 4.

GRAHAM GEMS

MARY WHITCHER'S SHAKER HOUSEKEEPER

1 tablespoon sugar	1½ cups graham flour
1 teaspoon baking soda	1 cup sour milk
½ teaspoon salt	1 egg, well beaten

⟨[Mix and sift dry ingredients. Add sour milk. Stir well. Beat in well-beaten egg. Bake in hot buttered gem (muffin) pans in a hot 400° F. oven 25 minutes. Makes 10–12, depending on size.

SISTER LOTTIE'S SHAKER GEMS

CANTERBURY SHAKER VILLAGE

"North Union Shaker Village Household Hint: 'Serve gems on Sabbath morning with plenty of butter and maple syrup.' The Shaker communities which made maple syrup usually opened a two-gallon jug of this luscious commodity each Sabbath for breakfast."

¾ cup bread flour, sifted	1 egg, beaten
¼ cup bran	¾ cup warm milk
½ teaspoon salt	2 tablespoons molasses
1 teaspoon baking powder	

⟨[Sift dry ingredients together. Add beaten egg blended with milk and molasses. Beat batter until light and foamy and pour into very hot buttered gem pans. Bake in a quick hot 425° F. oven for 15 minutes. These are light and crusty. Makes 10 small gems.

CHERRY MUFFINS
SHIRLEY SHAKER VILLAGE

2 cups sifted flour
3 teaspoons baking powder
6 tablespoons white sugar
½ teaspoon salt

1 egg, well beaten
1 cup milk
3 tablespoons melted butter
¾ cup drained chopped cherries

⟨[Sift flour into mixing bowl with baking powder, sugar, and salt. Combine egg, milk, and butter. Add to dry ingredients. Add cherries, stirring only until blended. Fill greased muffin pans ⅔ full. Bake at 425° F. for 20 to 30 minutes. Makes 12 medium-sized muffins.

HOMINY MUFFINS
SHAKER ALMANAC, 1882

2 cups boiled hominy grits
3 cups sour milk
½ cup melted butter
2 teaspoons salt
2 tablespoons sugar

3 eggs, well beaten
1 teaspoon baking soda dissolved in
  a little hot water
2 cups flour, sifted

⟨[Beat hominy until smooth. Stir in sour milk, butter, salt, and sugar. Add beaten eggs and soda. Beat and add sifted flour gradually, mixing all ingredients well. Bake in muffin tin in a hot 400° F. oven for 25 minutes. Makes about 2 dozen.

SISTER HATTIE'S HUCKLEBERRY MUFFINS
WATERVLIET SHAKER VILLAGE, NEW YORK

2 cups flour, sifted
¼ teaspoon salt
4 teaspoons baking powder
5 tablespoons sugar

1 egg, beaten
1 cup milk
3 tablespoons butter, melted
1 cup huckleberries

⟨[Sift the dry ingredients together and mix well. Add egg to milk and melted butter and combine with dry ingredients. Dust berries lightly with flour and fold into batter. Drop by the spoonful into well-buttered muffin tins, but do not fill more than one-third full, for if the muffins are thin the berries are not so apt to settle to the bottom, and the muffins will not be soggy. Bake 25 to 30 minutes in a moderate 350°F. oven. Makes 1 dozen.

SOUR CREAM MUFFINS

HANCOCK SHAKER VILLAGE

1½ cups flour
½ teaspoon salt
½ teaspoon baking powder
⅓ teaspoon baking soda
1 teaspoon nutmeg

1 tablespoon sugar
2 eggs, beaten
¾ cup sour cream
3 tablespoons melted shortening

⟮Sift dry ingredients together, add alternately the eggs and the sour cream. Add the shortening. Mix lightly but completely. Pour into buttered muffin tins and sprinkle with sugar. Bake in 450° F. oven 15 to 20 minutes or until browned.

Shakers used brown sugar or shaved maple sugar to sprinkle on top.

If muffins have to wait, turn on their sides in muffin tins to prevent steaming. Makes about 10 medium-sized muffins.

SOUR MILK GOLDEN CAKE

TYRINGHAM SHAKER VILLAGE

1 teaspoon baking soda
1½ cups sour milk
½ cup sugar
½ teaspoon salt

2 tablespoons butter
1 egg
1 cup yellow corn meal
1 cup white flour

⟮Dissolve soda in the sour milk. Mix the sugar, salt, and butter together. Add the egg. Beat well. Add the corn meal and flour alternately with sour milk. Cook in greased square 9 inch cake tin or greased muffin pans, at 425° F. to 450° F. for about 30 minutes. Makes 1 dozen.

CHEESE CRUMPETS

HANCOCK SHAKER VILLAGE

2 cups Shaker Convenience Mix #1*
¾ cup grated Cheddar cheese (taste
   for salt)

1 cup rich heavy cream or 1 cup sour
   cream
½ cup melted butter and olive oil
   mixed (half and half—¼ cup each)

⟮Mix Shaker Convenience Mix, grated cheese, and cream, stirring well and beating lightly. Add to the melted butter and oil. Mix well. Pour into generously greased muffin tins.

Bake in preheated 450° F. oven for 12 minutes. Makes 12–16.

HANCOCK CORN MEAL WAFERS

HANCOCK SHAKER VILLAGE

¾ cup boiling water
1 teaspoon salt
⅔ cup yellow or white corn meal

1 teaspoon sugar
2 tablespoons butter
Celery seeds or poppy seeds, or grated
    Cheddar cheese or dried herbs

❊In a mixing bowl pour boiling salted water over corn meal, sugar, and butter. Stir well to mix. Drop by teaspoonfuls onto buttered baking sheets, leaving plenty of room for batter to spread. Sprinkle with seeds or cheese or dried herbs.

Bake in 425° F. oven about 10 minutes or until light brown—golden. Let stand to crisp. Remove with large spatula and cool. Makes 1 dozen wafers.

CORN MEAL BATTER CAKES #1

MT. LEBANON SHAKER VILLAGE

1½ cups yellow or white corn meal
1 tablespoon flour
¾ teaspoon salt
2 teaspoons baking powder

1½ cups milk
1 tablespoon melted shortening
2 eggs, well beaten

❊Sift together dry ingredients, add milk, and shortening. Add well-beaten eggs and fry on a lightly greased hot griddle.

The Shakers served these for supper with melted butter and shaved maple sugar. Makes 6–8.

CORN MEAL BATTER CAKES #2

HARVARD SHAKER VILLAGE

2 cups corn meal
2½ cups sour milk, hot
1 teaspoon soda
½ cup flour

1½ teaspoons salt
2 tablespoons melted butter
1 egg, beaten

❊Add the corn meal to hot milk and boil 5 minutes. Turn into bowl. Mix dry ingredients together and add. Add melted butter and egg and mix well. Drop by the spoonful on a hot greased griddle. Turn once and brown. Serve with hot syrup. Makes 9–10 cakes.

RICE BATTER CAKES
HARVARD SHAKER VILLAGE

([Combine 1 lightly beaten egg, 1 cup sour milk, with enough baking soda stirred in to make it foam. Then mash thoroughly 2 cups cold boiled rice. Add to egg mixture with enough flour to make the cake turn well. Have the griddle hot and well greased.

A modern cook would proceed this way to make an excellent dish using leftover rice:

½ cup sifted flour
¼ cup sugar
2 cups cold cooked rice, mashed
1 egg, well beaten

1 cup sour milk
1 teaspoon baking soda
2 tablespoons melted butter

([Mix flour and sugar. Work in rice. Add well-beaten egg. Heat sour milk, add soda, and combine with rice mixture. Mix well. Drop by spoonfuls on hot, greased griddle. Brown, turn once, brown. Serve with melted currant jelly, a syrup, or as a meat accompaniment instead of potato. Makes 9–10 cakes.

OLD-FASHIONED BUCKWHEAT CAKES
HANCOCK SHAKER VILLAGE

We found several recipes for buckwheat cakes, which are griddle cakes using buckwheat flour, and have chosen this one, which gives a choice of using bread crumbs or corn meal. Remember bread crumbs should be rolled to the same consistency as corn meal.

½ cup bread crumbs or ½ cup fine
  corn meal
½ teaspoon salt
2½ cups scalded milk
½ cake yeast

2 cups buckwheat flour
2 tablespoons molasses
2 tablespoons melted butter
¼ teaspoon baking soda
¼ cup lukewarm water

([Add bread crumbs or corn meal and salt to scalded milk. Cool. When lukewarm, add yeast cake, stirring until dissolved. Add buckwheat flour, stir until smooth and set in a warm place overnight. In the morning add molasses, butter, soda mixed with water, and beat until smooth.

Bake on a hot greased griddle using about ¼ cup of batter for each cake. Brown on one side, turn only once.

When using corn meal allow a longer time for frying than for wheat cakes. Makes about 10 cakes.

∵

There is little difference between pancakes and griddle cakes—one being fried in a pan, the other on a griddle. Griddle cakes are crisper because the griddle is usually cast iron.

HUCKLEBERRY GRIDDLE CAKES

FRANCES HALL, HANCOCK SHAKER VILLAGE, 1901

Sour milk is best for making Huckleberry Griddle Cakes although they can be made of sweet milk and baking powder. If possible, make the batter of sour milk and flour the evening before and let it stand overnight, adding the soda, eggs, salt, and berries in the morning.

2 cups sour milk
2 cups flour
½ teaspoon salt
1 teaspoon soda

2 eggs, separated
2 cups huckleberries
Flour

⟪Mix sour milk and flour, let stand overnight. Next morning combine salt, soda, and egg yolks. Beat. Add to flour mixture. Beat egg whites until stiff. Add berries drenched with flour to whites and fold into first mixture. Fry on well-greased griddle. Yields 10–12 cakes.

INDIAN GRIDDLE CAKES

WATERVLIET SHAKER VILLAGE, OHIO

1 cup yellow corn meal
1 cup white flour
½ teaspoon salt
½ teaspoon sugar
1 teaspoon baking powder

½ teaspoon baking soda
2 eggs, separated
2 tablespoons melted butter
2 cups buttermilk

⟪Sift corn meal, flour, salt, sugar, baking powder, and soda together. Add slightly beaten egg yolks and melted butter to buttermilk and beat the two mixtures together. Fold in the stiffly beaten egg whites. Bake on a hot griddle. A soapstone griddle greased with a ham rind makes the tastiest griddle cakes. Fry to a rich brown. Corn meal requires longer frying than wheat cakes. Makes 8 generous cakes.

BUTTER ORANGE FLUFF FOR WAFFLES OR PANCAKES
HARVARD SHAKER VILLAGE

¼ pound butter
½ cup brown sugar

1 teaspoon grated orange rind

([Cream butter until light and fluffy. Add brown sugar gradually, beating the mixture to a light fluffy mass. Stir in grated rind.

Serve with waffles or pancakes. Makes about 1 cup.

POTATO GRIDDLE CAKES
WATERVLIET SHAKER VILLAGE, NEW YORK

6 potatoes
3 eggs
5 tablespoons flour

3 tablespoons cream
2 teaspoons salt

([Grate raw potatoes, add remaining ingredients, and mix well. Fry cakes in a greased pan or on a hot greased griddle until light brown on both sides. A nice variation is to use 2 teaspoons of caraway seeds or dillweed to flavor. Makes 9–10 cakes.

PUMPKIN GRIDDLE CAKES
FRANCES HALL, HANCOCK SHAKER VILLAGE

½ cup yellow corn meal
1 cup boiling water
¼ cup well-drained pumpkin pulp
⅞ cup milk, scalded and cooled
1 cup flour

2 teaspoons baking powder
¾ teaspoon salt
1½ teaspoons sugar
1 teaspoon allspice
1 egg, beaten

([Combine corn meal and water and let stand 5 minutes. Add pumpkin and cooled milk and stir until smooth. Sift rest of dry ingredients together and add to first mixture. Beat egg and stir in. Mix all well together. Drop batter by tablespoonfuls onto well-greased hot griddle. Bake until bubbles form all over, turn and bake other side until golden and crisp. Serve with maple syrup. Makes 9–10 cakes.

SHIRLEY GRIDDLE CAKES

SHIRLEY SHAKER VILLAGE

2 cups hominy grits
Salt
2 cups water
2 eggs, beaten

1 teaspoon salt
1 cup flour
2 cups milk

❨[Cook hominy in salted water until tender. Drain if any water remains. Cool. Add remaining ingredients. Drop by the spoonful onto hot buttered griddle. Brown to a golden color on both sides. Serve in place of potatoes. Makes 15 cakes.

GRIDDLE CAKE SYRUP

❨[An excellent spread for griddle cakes is made with 2 cups of maple syrup which has been boiled for 10 minutes, to which a tablespoon or so of the best butter is added. Remove from fire, stir smooth, and serve very hot. Yields about 2 cups syrup.

PANCAKES

HARVARD SHAKER VILLAGE

1½ cups scalded milk
2 tablespoons butter
1½ cups fine stale bread crumbs
2 eggs, well beaten

½ cup flour
½ teaspoon salt
4 teaspoons baking powder

❨[Add milk and butter to crumbs and soak until crumbs are soft. Add well-beaten eggs to flour, salt, and baking powder, which has been mixed and sifted. Cook same as other griddle cakes. Serve with hot maple syrup and melted butter. Makes 9–10 cakes.

A nice variation is to add brandy to taste to the hot maple syrup and butter. This is called Mystery Syrup, for the amount of brandy is a mystery; let your conscience be your guide.

APPLE PANCAKES
HANCOCK SHAKER VILLAGE

2 cups sifted flour
1 teaspoon baking powder
  (for buttermilk pancakes,
  substitute baking soda here)
½ teaspoon salt
1 teaspoon sugar
2 eggs, lightly beaten

1½ cups rich milk
  (for buttermilk pancakes,
  substitute buttermilk here)
2 tablespoons melted butter
½–1 cup peeled, finely chopped
  apple

⟨Sift flour with other dry ingredients in mixing bowl. Add eggs and milk and beat to make smooth. Add butter and apples. Stir well. Grease a hot griddle for the first batch. Generally greasing is not necessary after that if recipe contains 2 tablespoons or more of fat. Griddle is at proper heat if when tested with drops of water, they do a lively dance. Serve with Mystery Syrup. Yields 10–12 cakes.

After pancakes have browned sprinkle with cinnamon and sugar or pass cream flavored with cinnamon, or flavored with rose water.

Variation: For blueberry pancakes add ⅔ to 1 cup of berries. Serve with melted butter or maple syrup.

SOUR CREAM BLUEBERRY PANCAKES
HANCOCK SHAKER VILLAGE

1 cup sifted flour
3 teaspoons baking powder
¼ teaspoon salt
2 tablespoons sugar
1 egg

1 cup milk
¼ cup sour cream
2 tablespoons melted butter
½ cup blueberries

⟨Sift dry ingredients together. Beat together egg, milk, and sour cream and pour over dry mixture. Beat until batter is smooth. Stir in butter and fold in blueberries. Cook on greased griddle until edges bubble, turn once only. Serve with Berry Mountain Blueberry Syrup

BERRY MOUNTAIN BLUEBERRY SYRUP
HANCOCK SHAKER VILLAGE

Simmer together for 10 minutes:

2 cups blueberries
½ cup sugar

½ cup water
Thin slice lemon

⟪Cook longer if berries are very juicy. Should make a nice syrup. Makes 2½ cups.

POPOVERS
HANCOCK SHAKER VILLAGE

There are several popover recipes used by the Shakers. These are from *The Manifesto* and from Mary Whitcher's *Shaker Housekeeper*. All of them are traditional in contents and directions, using a preheated oven for baking. The following recipe was used at Hancock and is a very successful method which starts with a cold oven.

2 eggs
1 cup milk

1 cup flour
½ teaspoon salt

⟪Break eggs into a bowl, add milk, flour, and salt. Mix with spoon until eggs are well blended. Disregard lumps. Fill 6 well-greased (use oil, not butter) custard cups three-quarters full. Set in muffin tin for easy handling.

Place in cold oven, set it at 450° F., and bake ½ hour. Remove, puncture each popover (prick with point of knife or toothpick), return to oven for 10 minutes. Makes 6 popovers. Double recipe for 12.

SHAKER PUFFS OR HANCOCK PUFFS
WATERVLIET SHAKER VILLAGE, NEW YORK, TO
HANCOCK SHAKER VILLAGE VIA SISTER MARY DAHM

4 eggs, separated
2 cups milk

¼ cup butter, melted
1 cup flour

⟪Separate the eggs and beat yolks until thick. To the egg yolks, add milk and melted butter. Stir the liquid mixture into the flour. Mix well. Beat by hand.

Beat the egg whites until they are dry, fold into the flour mixture and stir through very lightly. Bake in moderate 350° F. oven in buttered cups not more than one-half filled for 25 minutes. SERVES 6–8.

CORN PUFFS

HANCOCK SHAKER VILLAGE

½ cup corn meal　　　　　　　½ teaspoon salt
½ cup boiling water　　　　　　2 egg whites

⟨[Mix together corn meal, boiling water, and salt. Fold in stiffly beaten whites. Drop by teaspoonfuls on a greased baking sheet. Bake in a moderate 350° F. oven for about 30 minutes until puffed up and delicately browned. Serve hot with lots of butter. SERVES 4.

Sweetmeats

∴

SWEETMEATS in the form of cakes, cookies, pies and puddings, candies and confections, creams, dreams, floats, jams, jellies, and preserves made up a substantial part of every meal. It was considered beneficial to eat the natural sugars for they produced heat and energy. In addition, light suppers were more satisfying when a generous selection of preserves, puddings, jams, and cake could be offered. Pies, which were more hearty, were reserved for breakfast and the noonday dinner.

Many people will associate anything maple with Shaker sweetmeats since so many Shaker recipes call for maple syrup or maple sugar to sweeten and flavor. These were important commodities before sugar was available, and the large maple groves furnished an abundance of it. Enfield, New Hampshire, reported in *The Manifesto* for April 1890, "Our Society have tapped 3,757 maple trees and now it remains to be seen how kind the fates will be in giving us the flow of sap necessary for the sugar making."

Thirty-two gallons of sap boiled down made 1 gallon of syrup and to make dry maple sugar the syrup had to be further concentrated. It was a long process. The sugar was made by boiling standard syrup until it reached the necessary temperature and then stirring or beating it until it reached the required thick, dry consistency. Under ordinary conditions a half gallon of maple syrup in a good-sized kettle could be converted into sugar within 40 minutes. Great care had to be taken so that the fire under the kettle was hot enough to keep the thick liquid boiling but not hot enough to cause the boiling liquid to spill out on the stove top and set a fire or so hot that it would scorch the syrup-sugar.

All the Shaker communities with maple groves were busy when sugaring time came around in the middle of March. It was of two or three weeks in duration and the sap houses would bustle all day and sometimes into the night with strenuous activity. A sister described the hard work of cleaning out the pails after they were emptied and before they were attached again to the trees by the brothers. The brothers spoke of the exhausting "tapping pace" set by other men in the village. Many country people regarded sugar making as the most delightful of all farm work and the Shakers shared this opinion. The great reward was the "sugaring off" party when all the syrup was boiled and in tin containers and jugs, and the wooden buckets were filled with hard sugar in shades ranging all the way from pale gold to the color of dark molasses. This last was not considered by some to be suitable for anything but to use in flavoring baked beans, boiled cider applesauce, or dark gingerbread. It tasted just the same.

The "sugaring off," as it was known, was a delicious maple-sugar product, never made commercially but called "sugar on snow" or "maple wax." Hot syrup just before the hard sugar stage was ladled out on packed pans or banks of new-fallen snow. The thick syrup when poured out in trailing spoonfuls was a delicious concoction, fragrant and flavorsome, chewy and ice cold. There was nothing quite like it in the way of a sweet, and the hard-working Shaker sisters and brothers looked forward to this part of their hard work with understandable anticipation.

Cakes and Cookies

Cake Making and Baking

PREHEAT THE OVEN unless your oven heats so rapidly that preheating is not necessary. Do not crowd the oven, free circulation of air is essential for roasting or baking.

250° F.	Very slow
300° F.	Slow
325° F.	Moderately slow
350° F.	Moderate
375° F.	Moderately hot
400° F.	Hot
450–500° F.	Very hot

WEIGHTS AND MEASURES:

3 teaspoons	1 tablespoon
2 tablespoons	1 liquid ounce
4 tablespoons	¼ cup
1 cup	8 liquid ounces
1 pint	2 cups
1 quart	4 cups
1 pound butter	2 cups
1 pound sugar	2 cups
1 pound flour	4 cups

The mixing and baking of cake requires almost more care and judgment than any other branch of cookery. However, all cooks should work at perfecting the art of cake making, and by following a few basic rules success and great pleasure for all will be ensured.

Cakes can be divided into two categories: without butter and with butter.

Without Butter—Example: Sponge-type cakes in which either no shortening is used or shortening in liquid form is carefully folded into a spongy batter. Separate yolks from whites of eggs. Beat yolks until thick and lemon-colored, using an eggbeater; add sugar gradually and continue beating; then add flavoring. Beat whites until stiff and dry, when they will fly from the beater, add to the first mixture. Mix and sift flour with salt and dry seasonings if any and cut and fold in at the last. Don't beat mixture after addition of flour as much of the work already done of enclosing a large amount of air to make cake light and sponge-like will be undone by breaking the air bubbles. These rules apply to a mixture where baking powder is not employed.

With Butter—Example: Cup and pound cakes in which sugar is blended into butter or shortening until light and fluffy before the other ingredients are added. This creaming should be done in an earthen bowl if possible, and a wooden cake spoon with slits lightens the labor. (Today's cooks may use an electric mixer, but it is not necessary.) When butter is used the sugar will blend in more readily if butter is at room temperature. Measure dry ingredients and mix and sift baking powder and spices if used with flour. Count out number of eggs required, breaking each separately so that there may be no loss should a stale egg chance to be found, separating yolks from whites if rule so specifies. Measure butter, then liquid. Having everything in readiness, add eggs to creamed mixture, then liquid and flour alternately.

A cake can be made fine-grained only by long beating, although light and delicate with a small amount of beating. Never stir cake after the final beating, remembering that beating motion should always be the last used.

In every case follow recipe carefully.

Note: It will be observed that recipes do not call for preheated ovens. Shaker ovens were always in use and therefore heated. Ovens today should be heated to degree indicated as cooking heat before material is set in oven.

Fruit Cakes

FRUIT when added to cake is usually floured to prevent its settling to the bottom. This is not necessary if it is added directly after the sugar, which is desirable in all dark cakes. If a light fruit cake is made, fruit added in this way discolors the loaf. Citron is first cut in thin slices, then in strips, floured, and put in between layers of cake mixtures. Raisins are seeded and cut rather than chopped. To seed raisins wet tips of fingers in a cup of water. Break skins with fingers or cut with vegetable knife, remove seeds and put in cup of water. Dry raisins before dredging with flour to avoid pasty mess. Washed currants put up in packages are free from stems and need only picking over and rolling in flour. Currants are handled the same way as raisins, unless bought in bulk. In this case they will need to be cleaned by rolling in flour. Wash in cold water, drain, and dry well. Roll in flour again before using.

Christmas Cake

SHAKER families differed in their preparations for Christmas, which was observed primarily as a religious day with each village celebrating it in its own way. The following account of Christmas with the North Union Shakers, published by the Shaker Historical Society, Shaker Heights, Ohio, contains many traditions followed in other villages:

Although austerity was the hallmark of the Shakers, it did not prevent them from celebrating Christmas in the joyful manner of their English forebears. Lacking personal funds and worldly goods, the Shakers built their Christmas celebration on sacred music, specially prepared foods, and useful gifts made with their own hands.

Several weeks before Christmas, one or more groups of young people would secretly organize and request the hymnist to write some new sacred music appropriate to the season. Once the song was written, the group or groups would practice in secret. If there was more than one group, each would have its own new hymns and guard them carefully from the other. Part of the excitement of Christmas was in maintaining an air of mystery concerning the music.

While the young people were secretly occupied with their music, there was great activity in the kitchens. Thanksgiving was not celebrated on the Ohio frontier, but the North Union Shakers, remembering their New England origins and the harvest feast, made great culinary preparations for Christmas. The apples were carefully sorted and the best placed in a barrel to be eaten on the holiday. Special cakes and pies were baked.

The elders and eldresses bought bolts of cloth in Cleveland and distributed them among the women of the Shaker families. Soon the women were busy cutting and sewing the cloth to make wearing apparel for the children.

The elders, in a special message to all of the members of the colony, warned the members to reconcile any differences among them in order that nothing might interfere with the Christmas spirit and the Biblical admonition of "Peace on Earth, Goodwill Among Men."

At 7:30 P.M. on Christmas Eve a bell sounded and all the Shakers retired to their quarters. One of their number in each building read the story of the washing of the disciples' feet from the Book of John. They then washed each other's feet. The members of the singing groups then departed surreptitiously to a shop some distance from the dwelling house for a final practice. By prior arrangement with the elder in charge of the shop, a fire had been built and the singers were admitted to the shop upon giving a secret signal. The final rehearsal was completed before nine o'clock. The singers departed and the village was cloaked in silence.

At four-thirty on Christmas morning, the singers awoke, hurried to the kitchen for a light repast, and then set out for the family dwellings in horse-drawn sleighs. At each building they sang their specially prepared Christmas songs and hastened on to each house where members of the three North Union families lived. Their rounds completed, the singers and all other members of the colony gathered at the sisters' dwelling houses at 10:00 A.M. for a union meeting. The men and boys sat on one side and the women and girls on the other side of the room. They reminisced together of Christmases past, sang religious songs, and ate nuts and popcorn. At eleven o'clock a light lunch was brought to the sisters' dwelling houses. After lunch all of the members went to the meeting house, which stood at the northeast corner of the present day intersection of Lee Road and Shaker Blvd. There, a service similar to the usual Sunday church program was held. In addition, special Christmas hymns were sung and there was reading from the Scriptures. At the conclusion of the church service the barrel of selected apples was opened and the contents distributed, along with the special gifts which had been carefully made.

Then came the great feast when the finest delicacies of the Shaker kitchens were spread upon the holiday festive board. When the meal was finished a big basket was passed around the room and each person placed an offering of clothing or some other useful gift in it for the poor people. These gifts were then distributed to needy persons in Cleveland or on nearby farms. The day closed with singing and the Shakers were once again ready to "put their hands to work and their hearts to God."

APPLE CAKE
SHIRLEY SHAKER VILLAGE

⅓ cup butter
¾ cup sugar
1 egg
1⅓ cups flour
¼ teaspoon salt
2 teaspoons baking powder

½ cup milk
1 teaspoon vanilla
3 apples, peeled and chopped
¼ cup currants or raisins
Powdered sugar
Ground cinnamon

⟨Cream butter and add half the sugar gradually, beating well. Beat egg with remaining sugar, add to first mixture. Sift in flour, salt, and baking powder alternately with the milk. Flavor with vanilla. Add apples and currants or raisins. Beat well to mix and turn into well-buttered 9 inch cake tin, square or round. Sprinkle with powdered sugar and cinnamon, and bake in moderate 350° F. oven for 30 minutes. Makes 1 cake.

SHAKER DRIED APPLE (OR APRICOT) CAKE
NORTH UNION SHAKER VILLAGE, OHIO

1 cup dried apples (or apricots)
1 cup molasses
⅔ cup sour cream
1 cup sugar
1 egg

1¾ cups flour, sifted
2 teaspoons baking soda
1 teaspoon cinnamon
½ teaspoon cloves
½ teaspoon salt

⟨Soak dried apples in water overnight. In the morning cut fine and simmer in molasses for 20 minutes. Cool. Combine cream, sugar, and egg and beat until smooth. Combine dry ingredients and sift several times. Blend both mixtures and beat until smooth. Add fruit and molasses. Turn into buttered bread pan and bake in moderate 350° F. oven for 1 hour. This is a very tasty dessert; the dried apples take on a citron flavor. Makes 1 cake.

CARAMEL CAKE
FRANCES HALL, HANCOCK SHAKER VILLAGE, 1907

½ cup butter
1 cup brown sugar
2 eggs, well beaten
½ cup milk
½ cup hot riced potatoes
1 cup sifted flour

2 teaspoons baking powder
½ teaspoon cinnamon
½ teaspoon cloves
½ teaspoon nutmeg
½ cup grated chocolate
½ cup chopped nut meats

⟨Cream butter and sugar together, add well-beaten eggs, milk, and potatoes. Beat thoroughly. Then add dry ingredients, sifted together, and add chocolate and nut meats. Beat again, turn into a buttered and floured cake pan and bake in moderate 350° F. oven for 55 minutes. Frost with caramel frosting. Makes 1 cake.

CAROLINA CAKE

FRANCES HALL, HANCOCK SHAKER VILLAGE, 1907

1 cup butter	½ teaspoon salt
1½ cups granulated sugar	1 cup sour cream
2 eggs	⅓ cup brown sugar
1 teaspoon vanilla	1 teaspoon cinnamon
2 cups sifted flour	1 cup chopped walnuts
1 teaspoon baking powder	1 teaspoon powdered ginger
1 teaspoon baking soda	

⟨Cream butter and 1 cup of the granulated sugar until light and fluffy. Beat and add eggs and vanilla. Sift together flour, baking powder, baking soda, and salt. Stir alternately with sour cream into egg mixture. Turn half the batter into square baking pan, 13x9½x2 inches, which has been greased and floured.

Combine brown sugar, remaining granulated sugar, cinnamon, nuts, and ginger; sprinkle half over batter in pan. Top with remaining batter; sprinkle with remaining nut mixture. Bake in heated 350° F. oven for 35 minutes. Cool in the pan. Yields 1 cake.

CHOCOLATE POUND CAKE

HANCOCK SHAKER VILLAGE

1 cup butter	½ teaspoon baking powder
½ cup lard	¼ teaspoon salt
3 cups sugar	1¼ cups milk
5 eggs	2 tablespoons grated chocolate
3 cups sifted flour	1 teaspoon vanilla
½ cup cocoa	

⟨This is a round ring-type cake and should be baked in a Sally Lunn-type pan about 9 inches across.

Cream butter, shortening, and sugar together until light and fluffy. Add eggs, one at a time, beating well after each addition. Sift together flour, cocoa, baking powder, and salt; add alternately with milk to egg mixture, stirring after each addition until well blended. Add chocolate. Stir in vanilla.

Turn batter into greased and floured tube-type pan. Bake in preheated 325° F. oven for 1½ hours. Turn onto wire rack to cool. Center can be filled with whipped cream and shaved chocolate or left plain. Makes 1 cake.

CIDER CAKE
NORTH UNION SHAKER VILLAGE, OHIO

1 cup butter
3 cups sugar
4 eggs, beaten
1 teaspoon nutmeg

½ teaspoon salt
1 teaspoon baking soda
6 cups flour, sifted
1 cup cider

⟮Cream butter, gradually add sugar and beat thoroughly; then add beaten eggs. Mix all dry ingredients together. Add flour mixture alternately with cider to butter mixture. Butter two 8 inch long pans; turn batter into pan and bake in moderate 350° F. oven for 1 hour. When cool, place in tightly closed tin or jar. This cake keeps well for weeks. Makes 2 loaves.

CHRISTMAS CAKE
NORTH UNION SHAKER VILLAGE, OHIO

2 cups sugar
1 cup butter
3½ cups flour, sifted before
    measuring
4 teaspoons baking powder
½ teaspoon salt
1 cup milk

1 teaspoon vanilla
    or
1 teaspoon rose water
7 or 8 egg whites, beaten until stiff
    but not dry
½ cup chopped butternut meats
    (walnuts or pecans may be used)

⟮This cake is usually made in layers, the number of layers depending upon size of pans.

Sift sugar and beat the butter until soft. Combine and blend until they are nice and creamy. Sift flour before measuring, add baking powder and salt and resift. Add these ingredients to the sugar and butter, alternately with the milk. Add flavoring. Fold egg whites lightly into the cake batter. Add nuts. Bake in greased tins in a moderate 350° F. oven for about 40 minutes. Remove from oven. Cool and spread with Maple Syrup Icing (see next page).

MAPLE SYRUP ICING

NORTH UNION SHAKER VILLAGE, OHIO

1 cup maple syrup   ¼ teaspoon salt
2 egg whites, unbeaten   ½ cup chopped nut meats

([Cook maple syrup until it forms a firm ball when dropped into cold water. Beat this in a fine stream into the egg whites. Add salt. Beat until mixture stiffens, although this icing remains soft. Spread over cake, scatter nuts on top. Makes enough frosting for 8 inch cake.

CLOVE CAKE

FRANCES HALL, HANCOCK SHAKER VILLAGE

2 eggs   1 teaspoon cloves
1 cup molasses   1 teaspoon cinnamon
½ cup butter   ½ teaspoon soda
1 cup raisins   ¼ teaspoon salt
2 cups flour

([Mix ingredients in the order given. Cake may be flavored with vanilla. Bake 45 minutes at 350°F.

The top should be simply frosted. Make an icing of the whites of 2 eggs and 1½ cups powdered sugar. Spread this on the layers and then cover thickly and entirely with bananas—sliced thin or chopped fine.

COFFEE SPICE CAKE

FRANCES HALL, HANCOCK SHAKER VILLAGE

1 cup butter   2 teaspoons cloves
1 cup sugar   2 teaspoons cinnamon
2 eggs, well beaten   2 teaspoons nutmeg
1 cup molasses   1 cup cold coffee
4 cups flour   1 cup raisins
5 teaspoons baking powder

([Cream butter and add sugar gradually. Add well-beaten eggs. Add molasses. Mix and sift flour and baking powder and spices together. Add to the first mixture alternately with the coffee. Beat. Add raisins. Bake 45 minutes to 1 hour at 350° F. in buttered deep 8 or 9 inch square cake pans. Makes 2 loaves.

SISTER SUSAN'S CREAM LAYER CAKE
HANCOCK SHAKER VILLAGE

Note: All ingredients must be at room temperature.

¾ cup butter
½ cup sugar
3 eggs
⅔ cup sweetened condensed milk

1½ teaspoons vanilla extract
1½ cups flour
3 teaspoons baking powder

[Cream butter and sugar together; beat in eggs, one at a time. Pour in condensed milk; mix well. Add vanilla. Sift together remaining dry ingredients; stir into creamed mixture, a little at a time, beating after each addition until smooth. Spread batter in 2 greased and floured 9x11½ inch round cake pans. Bake in moderate 350° F. oven for 25 minutes. Place pans on wire rack; cool about 30 minutes before removing cake from pans. Cut each layer into 2 layers. Spread each of the 3 layers with Cream Filling. Frost top of cake with Chocolate Glaze. Yields two 9 inch layers.

CREAM FILLING

1 envelope unflavored gelatin
1 cup cold water
⅔ cup sweetened condensed milk
¼ teaspoon salt

2 eggs, slightly beaten
1½ teaspoons vanilla extract
1 cup heavy cream, whipped

[Soften gelatin in cold water in top of double boiler; stir in condensed milk, salt, and eggs. Cook over simmering water 10 minutes until mixture thickens. Remove from heat; cool over ice water. (Let mixture cool until it mounds slightly.) Fold in vanilla and whipped cream. Spoon between cake layers. Yields 3 cups.

CHOCOLATE GLAZE

2 (1 ounce) squares unsweetened
   chocolate
¼ cup butter
3 tablespoons milk

2 cups sifted confectioners' sugar
⅛ teaspoon salt
½ teaspoon vanilla extract

[Melt chocolate in small saucepan over low heat. Blend in butter and milk; remove from heat. Add sugar, salt, and vanilla. Mix well. Yields about 2½ cups.

SHAKER CREAM NUT CAKES

HANCOCK SHAKER VILLAGE

2 eggs
Cream
1 cup sugar
1½ cups cake flour

1½ teaspoons baking powder
½ teaspoon salt
½ cup chopped butternuts or
    walnuts

❡Break 2 eggs in a 1 cup measuring cup, and add enough cream to fill the cup. Beat with beater. Add 1 cup sugar. Combine all dry ingredients and add to the egg-cream-sugar mixture. Add ½ cup chopped nuts. Put in 8 inch square pan. Bake in moderate 350° F. oven for 45 minutes. Yields 1 cake.

QUICK DATE CAKE

FRANCES HALL, HANCOCK SHAKER VILLAGE

⅓ cup soft butter
1⅓ cups brown sugar
2 eggs
½ cup milk
1¾ cups flour

3 teaspoons baking powder
½ teaspoon cinnamon
½ teaspoon grated nutmeg
½ pound dates, stoned and cut in
    pieces

❡Put ingredients in a bowl and beat all together for 3 minutes using a wooden cake spoon. Bake in a buttered and floured 9 inch square cake pan 35 to 40 minutes in a moderate 350° F. oven. If directions are followed, this makes a most satisfactory cake, but if ingredients are mixed in separately, it will not prove a success. Makes 1 cake.

BOILED FRUIT CAKE

ELDRESS GERTRUDE, SABBATHDAY LAKE SHAKER VILLAGE

1 cup water
1 cup sugar
1 cup seedless raisins
½ cup butter
1 teaspoon cinnamon
½ teaspoon powdered cloves

½ teaspoon nutmeg
Citron (optional)
2 cups flour
1 teaspoon baking soda
1 egg, beaten
½ cup chopped nuts

([Boil water, sugar, raisins, butter, and spices together for 10 minutes. Let cool. Sift flour and soda together and add alternately with beaten egg. Add nuts.

This can be baked in a 9 inch loaf pan or in a 9 inch cake pan, but for Christmas gifts we use a tube cake pan and place halves of nuts and candied cherries on top before baking.

Bake in 350° F. oven for 45 minutes. Yields 1 cake.

APPLE GINGERBREAD
SISTER OLIVE, HANCOCK SHAKER VILLAGE

2 tablespoons brown sugar
½ teaspoon baking soda
1 cup bread flour
1 cup whole wheat flour
½ teaspoon each ginger, cinnamon, mace, and salt
¾ cup molasses

¼ cup shortening, melted
¼ cup raisins
2 apples, pared, cored, and cut into eighths
1 egg, well beaten
½ cup milk

([Mix and sift together all dry ingredients, add the molasses and shortening melted. Then add the well-beaten egg, raisins and the milk. Place apples into greased muffin pans. Pour mixture over apples and bake in moderate 350°F. oven about 25 minutes. This recipe makes 6 cakes. Serve hot with whipped cream, or heavy pouring cream, or one of your favorite sauces.

CANADA GINGERBREAD
SABBATHDAY LAKE SHAKER VILLAGE

1 cup butter
2 cups sugar
1 cup molasses
1 teaspoon nutmeg
1 teaspoon ginger
1 teaspoon cinnamon

1 pound raisins, seeded
3 eggs, well beaten
1 cup rich milk
1½ teaspoons soda
5 cups flour

([Beat butter to a cream. Add sugar, molasses, spices and raisins. Add well-beaten eggs, then milk in which the soda is well dissolved. Add flour, sifted, and mix well. Pour into two 9 inch buttered pans. Bake in moderate 350° F. oven for 30 minutes. Yields 2 cakes.

MAPLE SYRUP GINGERBREAD
HANCOCK SHAKER VILLAGE

1 cup maple syrup
1 cup sour cream
1 egg, well beaten
2⅓ cups flour

1¾ teaspoons soda
1½ teaspoons ginger
½ teaspoon salt
4 tablespoons melted butter

⟮Combine the maple syrup, cream, and egg. Mix well. Sift all the dry ingredients and stir into the liquid, beating well. Add butter and beat thoroughly. Pour into well-buttered 9 inch square baking pan. Bake in a moderate 350° F. oven for 30 minutes.

Serve with thick cream and sprinkle with shaved maple sugar. SERVES 6–8.

SISTER EMMA NEAL'S RULE FOR SOFT GINGERBREAD
MT. LEBANON SHAKER VILLAGE

1 cup dark molasses
½ cup shortening
½ cup dark brown sugar
2 eggs
2 cups all purpose flour
2 teaspoons ginger

½ teaspoon allspice
1 teaspoon cinnamon
1 teaspoon baking soda
1½ cups day old buttermilk, or sour
  milk

⟮Pour molasses in bowl, add shortening and mix well. Add sugar and beat 2 minutes until smooth. Add eggs one at a time and blend well. Sift all remaining dry ingredients together, except soda and add to mixture. Add baking soda to buttermilk. Then alternately add buttermilk mix and dry ingredients to molasses mix and continue beating. Grease and dust lightly an 8 inch baking pan. Bake in oven at 375° F. for 25 to 30 minutes or until top center is spongy to the touch.

Another method: Put shortening and molasses in saucepan and cook until boiling point is reached. Remove from fire, add soda and beat vigorously. Then add milk, well-beaten eggs, and remaining ingredients mixed and sifted. Bake 25 minutes in buttered baking pan in moderately hot oven until top center is spongy to the touch.

SISTER RUTH'S GINGERBREAD
HANCOCK SHAKER VILLAGE

1 cup sugar
⅔ cup butter
3 eggs
1 cup molasses

1 cup sour cream
3½ cups sifted flour
1½ teaspoons baking soda
1⅓ cups mincemeat

⟨Cream sugar and butter until fluffy. Add eggs. Stir in molasses and sour cream. Sift together flour and baking soda, combine with molasses mixture. Stir in mincemeat. Turn into a greased 9x13x2 inch loaf pan. Bake in a moderate 350° F. oven about 55 to 60 minutes. Makes 12 three-inch squares.

CHEESE LEMON TOPPING

1 eight ounce package cream cheese
1½ cups confectioners' sugar
1 teaspoon vanilla

1 teaspoon lemon juice
Crystallized ginger

⟨Soften cream cheese to room temperature. Whip. Beat in sugar, vanilla, and lemon juice. Chill about 1 hour. Use to top each serving of gingerbread, garnish with crystallized ginger. Yields 2½ cups.

GINGER POUND CAKE #1
HANCOCK SHAKER VILLAGE

1 cup butter
1 cup sugar
1½ cups flour
2 teaspoons baking powder

4 eggs, beaten
1 cup Canton ginger, cut in small
   pieces

⟨Cream butter and sugar together and beat well. Add flour, which has been sifted with baking powder, alternately with beaten eggs. Add ginger and mix well by beating. Bake in buttered and floured muffin tins in a moderately slow 325° F. oven for 35 to 40 minutes. Insert a straw or cake tester in middle of cake. If it comes out clean the cake is done. Cover with White Mountain Cream (see next page). SERVES 6–8.

WHITE MOUNTAIN CREAM
HANCOCK SHAKER VILLAGE

1 cup sugar
⅓ cup boiling water
1 egg white

1 teaspoon vanilla
    or
½ tablespoon lemon juice

⟮Put sugar and water in saucepan, stir until sugar is dissolved and bring to boiling point. Beat egg white until stiff and add 1 tablespoon boiling syrup. Add 4 more tablespoons of syrup one at a time and continue the beating. Repeat. Continue to let syrup boil and add to egg whites, beating. Add flavoring and spread. Yields 1 cup.

GINGER POUND CAKE #2
THE MANIFESTO AND
MARY WHITCHER'S SHAKER HOUSEKEEPER

2 cups butter
2 cups sugar
3 eggs
2 cups molasses

2 teaspoons soda
2 tablespoons ginger
2 teaspoons nutmeg
3 cups flour

⟮Cream butter thoroughly. Add sugar and cream together. Add eggs and beat again after each egg. Add molasses and soda, spices and flour, beating all the time. The eggs and the beating make the cake light. Turn into a buttered, floured 9 inch square cake pan. Bake at 350° F. for 1 hour. Makes 1 cake.

HICKORY NUT CAKE
CANTERBURY SHAKER VILLAGE

2 cups sugar
⅔ cup butter
3 cups flour
1 teaspoon baking soda
1 teaspoon cream of tartar

1 cup milk
2 cups hickory nut (or walnut) meats
3 egg yolks, beaten
4 egg whites, beaten until stiff

⟮Cream sugar and butter together. Sift dry ingredients together and pour in milk, beating well. Combine flour mixture with creamed butter and sugar. Add nuts. Beat all together well. Add beaten egg yolks to this mixture and fold into it the beaten whites. Turn into 2 buttered and floured 8 inch loaf pans and bake in moderate 350° F. oven for 35 minutes. Makes 2 cakes.

HONEY CAKE

NORTH UNION SHAKER VILLAGE, OHIO

1 cup honey
½ cup butter
1 egg, well beaten
½ cup sugar
2 cups flour

½ teaspoon ginger
½ teaspoon grated nutmeg
½ teaspoon baking soda
2 tablespoons warm water

[Measure honey into bowl. Melt butter and add to honey, working it together. Add egg and beat. Sift all dry ingredients together, except baking soda. Add dry ingredients to batter, beating again. Mix soda with water and beat into batter. Pour into buttered and floured 8 inch square pan. Bake in preheated 300° F. oven for 1 hour or more. Makes 1 cake.

A great many recipes calling for honey have come from North Union (Cleveland). The Shakers had a fine beehouse there and raised honey as a successful industry. Honey Cake is especially good when freshly strained honey is used.

HONEY CAKE WITH ALMONDS

NORTH UNION SHAKER VILLAGE, OHIO

2¾ cups flour
½ teaspoon powdered cloves
1 teaspoon cinnamon
¾ teaspoon each grated nutmeg,
   cream tartar, baking soda
¼ teaspoon salt
⅔ cup butter, melted

1½ tablespoons lard, melted
3 tablespoons dark brown sugar
1 tablespoon white sugar
3 eggs, beaten
1½ cups honey
¾ cup sour cream
Blanched halved almonds

[Sift together first five dry ingredients. Melt shortenings and add to them both sugars. Beat eggs until fluffy, add honey and sour cream and add the butter-sugar mixture to them, stirring vigorously. Gradually stir in dry ingredients. Turn batter into a buttered and floured 9 inch cake tin 2 inches deep and cover top at regular intervals with blanched halved almonds. Bake cake in moderate 350° F. oven for about 35 minutes, or until golden brown. Test center with straw or cake tester. If it comes out clean, cake is done. Remove from pan to cake rack to cool. Put in tightly closed container to ripen for at least 2 days. It will keep for weeks. Makes 1 cake.

HONEY BEE CAKE WITH BUTTERNUTS
HARVARD SHAKER VILLAGE

The Harvard Shaker Village had a fine beehouse as did the Shakers at Cleveland. Other communities raised bees as there was need for great quantities of honey. This delicious pastry is topped with honey and nuts.

1 cup flour	½ cup butter
¼ cup sugar	½ cup sugar
1 teaspoon baking powder	¼ cup chopped butternuts
½ cup butter	½ cup honey
3 tablespoons milk	

([Sift together flour, sugar, and baking powder. Work to a dough with the butter and the milk. Pat into a round and cover with a cloth. Melt butter. Stir in sugar and finely chopped butternuts. Stir over low flame until the mixture is smooth and creamy. Remove from fire, stir until cool. Roll the dough to a quarter inch in thickness. Line a buttered and floured baking sheet with the pastry. Spread honey on top and then the nut mixture. Bake at 350° F. for about 35 minutes. Makes 1 cake.

HONEY POUND CAKE WITH RAISINS
HANCOCK SHAKER VILLAGE

1 cup seedless raisins	3 teaspoons baking powder
1 cup butter	½ teaspoon salt
1 cup honey	1 teaspoon vanilla
4 eggs, lightly beaten	1 teaspoon lemon extract
3 cups presifted flour	¾ cup butternuts

([Rinse raisins, dry, chop fine. Cream butter, gradually add honey and continue to cream. Add eggs, blend. Sift together flour, baking powder, and salt; add to creamed mixture; beat. Add vanilla, lemon extract, raisins, and nuts. Stir well. Pour into 9 inch loaf pan lined with waxed paper. Bake in preheated 300° F. oven for about 2 hours. Makes 1 cake.

OLD-FASHIONED HUCKLEBERRY CAKE
HANCOCK SHAKER VILLAGE

¼ cup butter	½ teaspoon salt
½ cup sugar	2 teaspoons baking powder
2 egg yolks, beaten	2 egg whites, stiffly beaten
1 cup rich milk	1¼ cups huckleberries (or
2 cups flour	blueberries), rolled in flour

¶[Cream butter and sugar together, beat in egg yolks and milk. Sift all dry ingredients together and add to first mixture. Beat well. Fold in egg whites and add huckleberries. Bake in buttered and floured 8 inch cake tin at 400° F. for 40 minutes. Makes 1 cake.

JAM CAKE WITH ROSE WATER CREAM FROSTING[1]
HANCOCK SHAKER VILLAGE

2 cups flour	½ cup butter
1 teaspoon allspice	1 cup sugar
1 teaspoon cinnamon	3 eggs, beaten until light
1 teaspoon grated nutmeg	1 cup blackberry or raspberry jam
1 teaspoon baking soda	¼ cup sour milk or cream
½ teaspoon salt	

¶[Sift together flour, spices, baking soda, and salt. Cream butter until light and add sugar and eggs. Mix together the jam and milk or sour cream. Combine flour mixture and butter, sugar, and eggs. Stir in the jam and cream mixture. Butter and flour one 9 inch layer tin. Spoon into the tin. Bake at 375° F. about 25 minutes.

Use the following frosting for top and sides—or use same jam as was used in batter to frost sides and top. Peach jam can also be used as frosting and is very good when flavored with rose water.

ROSE WATER[2] CREAM FROSTING

4 tablespoons butter	Rose water
¼ cup heavy cream	*or*
Confectioners' sugar	Vanilla or lemon extract
	1 egg yolk (optional)

¶[Melt butter in heavy pan. Remove from heat and add heavy cream. Beat in confectioners' sugar until consistency is thick enough to spread. Flavor with rose water. If rose water is unavailable, flavor with vanilla or lemon extract. Beat until smooth. Add egg yolk to make smoother.

---

[1] These recipes are for 1 layer only—double for 2 layer cake.
[2] Rose water can be purchased already made at specialty shops or some drugstores. It was made by Shakers by distilling petals of roses with water or steam.

JELLY ROLL CAKE
MARIAN SCOTT, THE MANIFESTO

3 eggs, well beaten
1 cup sugar
1 cup flour

1 teaspoon baking powder
½ teaspoon salt
Jelly or maple butter

❨Beat eggs, add sugar and flour sifted with baking powder and salt. Beat all well. Bake in an 18 inch tin 12 minutes at 350° F. Turn onto a towel, spread with jelly or maple butter, while warm. Roll up and wrap in towel until cool. Sprinkle with white or maple sugar. Very good. SERVES 6–8.

HERB JELLY ROLL
CANTERBURY SHAKER VILLAGE

3 eggs
1 cup sugar
½ tablespoon milk
1 cup flour
1 teaspoon baking powder

¼ teaspoon salt
1 tablespoon melted butter
Filling: mint, rosemary, or
    basil jelly

❨Beat eggs until light, add sugar gradually. Add milk and flour which have been mixed and sifted with baking powder and salt. Add butter. Mix well. Line the bottom of a dripping pan with paper; butter paper and sides of pan. Cover bottom of pan with mixture, and spread evenly. Bake 12 minutes in a moderate 350° F. oven. Take from oven and turn out on a paper sprinkled with fine (powdered) sugar. Quickly remove paper and cut off a thin strip from sides and ends of cake. Spread with desired filling—mint, rosemary, or basil jelly—which has been beaten to spread easily. Then roll. Work quickly while cake is warm. After cake has been rolled, roll paper around cake that it may better keep in shape. The work must be done quickly or cake will crack in rolling. SERVES 4.

LEMON CAKE
MT. LEBANON SHAKER VILLAGE

1½ cups butter
1½ cups sugar
2 eggs

1 cup flour
1 teaspoon baking powder
1 lemon

⟨Warm the butter, beat in the sugar, add the eggs. Add the flour sifted with baking powder. Grate the lemon rind, add juice of lemon, and mix well. Beat well. Bake in 8 inch greased loaf pan for about 1 hour in 325° F. oven. Makes 1 cake.

MAPLE SUGAR CAKE
NORTH UNION SHAKER VILLAGE, OHIO

1½ cups maple sugar
½ cup butter
2 eggs, beaten
½ teaspoon salt
1 teaspoon baking soda
1 teaspoon cinnamon

½ teaspoon nutmeg
2½ cups flour, sifted
1½ cups unsweetened applesauce
1 cup chopped raisins
1 cup chopped hickory nut meats

⟨Roll maple sugar until all lumps are crushed. Cream butter, gradually add sugar and beat until creamy. Add beaten eggs and blend thoroughly. Add salt, soda, and spices to flour and sift several times. Now alternately add applesauce and dry ingredients to butter mixture and beat well. Lightly flour chopped raisins; combine with nuts and fold into batter. Turn into buttered 9 inch loaf tin and bake in moderate 350° F. oven for 1 hour. Makes 1 cake.

MAPLE SUGAR SOUR CREAM CAKE
MT. LEBANON SHAKER VILLAGE

1 egg
1 cup maple sugar
1 cup heavy sour cream
2 tablespoons sour milk

1 teaspoon baking soda
½ teaspoon salt
1 cup raisins
2 cups sifted flour

⟨Beat egg, add maple sugar. Combine sour cream, sour milk, soda, salt, and raisins. Add to egg and sugar. Stir well and beat in flour. Beat all well. Put in 8 inch greased loaf pan. Bake in 375° F. oven for 40 minutes. Makes 1 loaf.

NUT LOAF (Cake)
FRANCES HALL, HANCOCK SHAKER VILLAGE

1 cup butter
4 cups sugar
7 cups sifted flour
8 teaspoons baking powder
1⅓ cups fresh milk

8 cups broken up nut meats—use only butternut, hickory, or walnut meats
12 egg whites, beaten stiff

◖Cream butter and sugar. Mix dry ingredients and sift several times. Add alternately with milk to butter mixture. Stir in nut meats. Fold in stiffly beaten egg whites. Turn into 2 buttered 9 inch loaf pans and bake in moderate 350° F. oven for 45 minutes. Makes 2 loaves.

MOTHER ANN'S BIRTHDAY CAKE
FROM SEVERAL SHAKER COMMUNITIES

1 cup best butter (sweet butter, fresh if possible)	3 teaspoons baking powder
2 cups sugar	1 cup milk
3 cups flour, sifted	2 teaspoons vanilla
½ cup cornstarch	12 egg whites, beaten
	1 teaspoon salt

◖Beat butter and sugar into a smooth cream. Sift flour with cornstarch and baking powder. Add flour mixture in small amounts alternately with milk to butter mixture. Beat after each addition, about 200 strokes in all. Add vanilla and lightly fold in the beaten whites of eggs to which the salt has been added. Bake in three 8 inch greased tins in a moderate 350° F. oven for 25 minutes. When cool fill between layers with peach jelly and cover the cake with any delicate icing. Makes one 3 layer cake.

∵

Mother Ann's birthday fell on February 29, but was celebrated on March 1. The above cake was served at supper, following the afternoon meeting commemorating the life of the Shakers' beloved founder, Ann Lee (1736–1784). The original recipe reads: "Cut a handful of peach twigs, which are filled with sap at this season of the year. Clip the ends and bruise them and beat cake batter with them. This will impart a delicate peach flavor to the cake."

OLD RECIPE FROM AN OLD SISTER
FOR AN EXCELLENT AND RATHER
EXTRAVAGANT CAKE
MT. LEBANON SHAKER VILLAGE

2 cups butter	2 cups mixed fruit (raisins, candied fruit, currants, etc.)
2 cups sugar	9 eggs
3 cups flour	Ground cinnamon and ginger

❡Cream the butter and sugar together, then mix in flour and fruits gradually. Beat up the eggs lightly and add to the other ingredients. Season to taste with ground cinnamon and ginger. Beat well. Bake in 9 inch square greased pan in moderately slow 325° F. oven for 1 hour. Makes 1 cake.

They make this at the Springs House, Lebanon, New York.

ANOTHER GOOD CAKE, SAME SISTER
MT. LEBANON SHAKER VILLAGE

1 cup sugar
2 teaspoons spices (allspice, ginger, cinnamon and/or nutmeg)
2 eggs and a little rich milk
1 cup butter

¾ cup flour
1 cup currants
1 cup raisins
Milk

❡Beat sugar, spices, and eggs together, cream the butter and mix with the flour, adding fruit last. Add enough milk to make the mixture a softish dough. Bake in a greased 8 inch tin 2 hours at 325° F. Makes 1 cake.

∴

A little rum poured over a cake after it is cooked makes it moist and gives it flavor. Prick the cake with a knitting needle so that it runs in.

POOR MAN'S CAKE
MARY WHITCHER'S SHAKER HOUSEKEEPER

1 cup sugar
½ cup butter
1 egg, beaten
1 cup milk
2 cups flour

2 teaspoons baking powder
1 tablespoon rose water
        or
1 teaspoon lemon or vanilla extract
1 teaspoon cinnamon

❡Cream together sugar and butter, add egg and milk. Sift together flour and baking powder. Add to first mixture and flavor with rose water. Beat up well. Bake 30 minutes in greased 8 inch square cake tin at 375° F. This is a nice cake and easily made. Makes 1 cake.

POUND CAKE

SISTER ABIGAIL, NORTH UNION SHAKER VILLAGE

1 cup butter
1 cup sugar
5 eggs

1 teaspoon rum to flavor
¼ teaspoon mace
2 cups flour, sifted

([Cream butter thoroughly, and then cream it some more. Gradually work in sugar and beat well. After adding each egg, beat again. Add flavoring and mace and gradually work in the flour. The eggs and the beating furnish the leavening for this cake. Bake in 8 inch greased loaf pan for 45 minutes in moderate 350° F. oven. Makes 1 loaf cake.

PRUNE CAKE

KENTUCKY SHAKERS

3 eggs, beaten
1 cup vegetable oil
1½ cups sugar
1½ teaspoons baking soda dissolved
   in 1 cup buttermilk
1 teaspoon cinnamon

1 teaspoon nutmeg
1 teaspoon allspice
1 teaspoon vanilla
2 cups flour
1 cup cut up cooked prunes
1 cup chopped nuts

([Mix ingredients and pour into two 9 inch greased pans. Bake 45 minutes at 300° F. Makes 2 layer cakes. Serve with sauce below.

SAUCE

1 cup sugar
½ teaspoon baking soda dissolved
   in ½ cup buttermilk

1 tablespoon corn syrup
6 tablespoons butter
1 teaspoon vanilla

([Combine ingredients. Boil about 1 minute. Pour over cake while cake is still warm. Yields about 2 cups.

RAISIN LOAF CAKE

THE MANIFESTO
SABBATHDAY LAKE SHAKER VILLAGE

4 cups brown sugar
2 cups butter
5 eggs, beaten
2 teaspoons lemon extract
1 cup milk

5 cups flour
1 cup raisins
1 teaspoon each cinnamon, cloves,
   nutmeg
2 teaspoons baking powder

⟮Cream sugar and butter together, add eggs, flavoring, and milk. Beat well. Combine flour and raisins, add spices and baking powder, and mix well. Combine two mixtures and beat up well. Turn into 2 buttered and floured 8 inch tins. Bake in 350° F. oven for 40 to 50 minutes. Makes 2 loaves.

MRS. RETALLICK'S CAKE

FRANCES HALL, HANCOCK SHAKER VILLAGE, 1907

½ cup butter
1 cup sugar
2 egg yolks, beaten
⅔ cup sweet cream

2 teaspoons baking powder
2 cups flour
½ teaspoon salt
2 egg whites, stiffly beaten

⟮Cream butter and sugar together, add well-beaten egg yolks. Beat together and add cream. Sift together baking powder, flour, and salt. Add to first mixture and beat well. Fold in stiffly-beaten egg whites. Bake in shallow greased 9 inch pan 20 minutes at 400° F. Can also be baked as cupcakes. Makes 1 cake or 6–8 cupcakes, depending on size.

SIMPLE SPICE CAKE

MT. LEBANON SHAKER VILLAGE

1 cup coffee
1 cup raisins
1 cup brown sugar
2 eggs
2 tablespoons lard

2 cups flour
1 teaspoon baking soda
½ teaspoon salt
1 teaspoon each nutmeg, mace, cloves

⟮Boil coffee, raisins, sugar, and lard a few minutes. Add remaining ingredients and mix well. Bake in a buttered 9 inch loaf tin in a moderate 350° F. oven for 30 to 40 minutes or until a straw or cake tester inserted in the middle of the cake comes out clean. Makes 1 loaf cake.

This may be iced with either a simple Boiled Icing or an Apple Frosting.

BOILED ICING

1 tablespoon cornstarch
1 cup sugar
2 tablespoons water
1 egg white

1½ teaspoons vanilla
or
1½ teaspoons rose water

([Combine cornstarch with sugar, add water and egg white in top of double boiler. Beat hard for 7 minutes over boiling water. Stir in flavoring. Yields about 1 cup.

APPLE FROSTING

A nice apple frosting can be made without cooking, but it takes a lot of beating.

1 cup white sugar	1 apple, grated fine
1 egg white	1 teaspoon cinnamon

([Put all ingredients in a quart bowl and beat 20 minutes. Yields about 1 cup.

WALKER CAKE (Sponge Cake Type)

MT. LEBANON SHAKER VILLAGE
MANUSCRIPT FROM SHAKER MUSEUM
OLD CHATHAM, NEW YORK

"One pound nice sugar, 1 dozen new eggs, 14 ounces flour well sifted, and a very little saleratus. Separate the yolks from the whites very carefully. Beat the whites to a thick froth. Beat the yolks and sugar together well. After this process is over, mix the whole together in haste and put immediately into the oven."

Today the cook would proceed as follows:

12 eggs	½ teaspoon salt
2 cups sugar	1 teaspoon baking soda
1¾ cups flour, sifted twice	1 teaspoon rose water

([The directions are simple and quaint but the procedure is standard: Separate the eggs, beat yolks until frothy, add sugar and beat together well. Beat whites until they are stiff. Sift flour, salt, and baking powder together and gradually mix into egg yolks and sugar, beating the while. Then fold in the whites. Flavor with rose water. Bake for 1 hour in a moderately slow 325° F. oven in a buttered angel cake pan. Bake at 350° F. if using layer tin or muffin tin.

A genuine sponge cake contains no rising properties, but is made light by the quantity of air beaten into both yolks and whites of eggs and the expansion of that air in baking. It requires a slow to moderate oven. All so-called sponge cakes which have the addition of soda and cream of tartar or baking powder require same oven temperature as butter cakes. Failures are usually traced to baking in too slow an oven and removing from oven before thoroughly cooked.

This cake has a small amount of baking powder, but is considered a sponge cake. Amounts may be reduced, if 12 eggs are not at hand, to 1 cup sugar, 6 eggs, 1 cup flour, etc. Makes 1 cake.

SOUR CREAM FILLING FOR CAKE[1]

FRANCES HALL, HANCOCK SHAKER VILLAGE, 1907

1 teaspoon cornstarch	1 cup sour cream
1 cup sugar	1 cup chopped nut meats

❮[Mix cornstarch and sugar, add to sour cream, add nuts. Boil about 20 minutes or until it will set. Yields 1½ cups.

Variation: Substitute 1½ cups maple sugar for the white sugar.

BROWN SUGAR CHEWS (Cookies)

HANCOCK SHAKER VILLAGE

2 cups sifted light brown sugar	2 eggs, well beaten
⅛ teaspoon salt	1 cup chopped nut meats (hickory,
⅛ teaspoon baking soda	butter, or walnuts)

❮[Mix together the sifted brown sugar, salt, and baking soda. Add the well-beaten eggs and mix. Add the chopped nut meats and stir. Pour into a buttered 9x9 inch pan, so cooky mixture will be ½ inch thick. Bake in a very slow 250° F. oven for 55 minutes. Cut into squares when cool. Makes 12–16, depending on size.

Note: Don't get excited because this recipe does not call for flour or baking powder. Their lack is the secret of these delicious, chewy cookies.

---

[1]Sour Cream Filling can be used on any cake as a filling or spread on top as an icing.

BROWN SUGAR CHERRY COOKIES

HANCOCK SHAKER VILLAGE

2 cups packed brown sugar
½ pound butter
2 eggs, beaten
1½ teaspoons baking soda dissolved
    in ½ cup warm water

4 cups flour
½ teaspoon salt
1 teaspoon vanilla
2 cups cherry pie filling

([Heat oven to 400° F. Beat sugar and butter and add beaten eggs and beat together. Add soda and water alternately with flour, salt, and vanilla. Drop dough by teaspoonfuls on cooky sheet, press center with thumb. Fill center with cherry pie filling (about ½ teaspoon). Top each cooky with ½ teaspoon cooky dough. This will spread on top and cherry will show through. Very pretty cooky. Bake on greased cooky sheet 10 to 12 minutes. Makes 6 dozen cookies.

BUTTERNUT SURPRISES

MANUSCRIPT, MT. LEBANON SHAKER VILLAGE

1 egg white
½ teaspoon salt
1 cup brown sugar, sifted

1½ cups chopped butternuts
    (walnuts may be used)

([Beat egg white and salt until very stiff. Gradually add sugar. Beat until stiff and glossy. Stir in nuts. Drop 3 inches apart with a teaspoon onto well-greased baking sheets. Bake in preheated 300° F. oven for 25 to 30 minutes. Remove at once to cool. Makes about 4 dozen cookies.

CHOCOLATE COOKIES

MT. LEBANON SHAKER VILLAGE

1 cup butter
¼ cup sugar
2 eggs
3 squares semi-sweet chocolate

½ cup chopped nuts
2¼ cups flour
1 teaspoon baking soda
1 teaspoon vanilla

⟨[Cream butter and sugar. Add eggs and melted chocolate, mix well. Add all dry ingredients (sifted) and mix. Add vanilla and mix. Drop onto greased cooky sheet. Bake in 375° F. oven 12 minutes. Makes about 4 dozen cookies.

CINNAMON CAKES

SISTER OLIVE, NEW LEBANON SHAKER VILLAGE
MANUSCRIPT FROM SHAKER MUSEUM
OLD CHATHAM, NEW YORK

½ cup butter
1 cup white or brown sugar
2 eggs, beaten
½ cup milk

2¼ cups flour
1¼ teaspoons baking powder
1 tablespoon cinnamon
½ teaspoon salt

⟨[Cream butter and sugar together, add beaten eggs and milk. Sift flour with baking powder, cinnamon, and salt and beat into first mixture. Roll out and cut with nice cooky cutter. These are good for children and should look pretty. Bake at 350° F. on greased baking sheet for 20 minutes. Makes 3 dozen cookies, depending on size.

COCOA AND NUT COOKIES

FRANCES HALL, HANCOCK SHAKER VILLAGE

Same weight of sugar as nuts and white of an egg to a pound. Flavor with cocoa:

2 cups confectioners' sugar, sifted
2 cups ground nuts (hazelnuts or walnuts—no other kind because of oiliness)

8 egg whites, stiffly beaten
2 teaspoons cocoa
½ teaspoon salt

⟨[Gradually fold sugar and hazelnuts into egg whites. Fold in cocoa and salt. Drop by spoonfuls onto greased, floured baking sheets. Bake in preheated 325° F. oven for 10 minutes. Remove from baking sheets at once to cool. Makes 8 dozen cookies.

COCONUT LAYER COOKIES
FRANCES HALL, HANCOCK SHAKER VILLAGE

1½ cups brown sugar
½ cup butter
1⅓ cups flour
2 eggs, well beaten

½ cup heavy cream
1½ cups coconut (short shred)
1 teaspoon baking powder
1 teaspoon vanilla

⟨[Cream sugar and butter, add 1 cup of flour and mix. Put into 8 inch square pan. Bake in moderate 350° F. oven for 20 to 25 minutes. Hold oven temperature to 350° F. Mix other ingredients together. Spread over top. Return to oven and bake 35 to 40 minutes. Leave in pan about 10 minutes and then cut into small squares. Makes about 5 dozen cookies.

COFFEE FRUIT DROPS
HANCOCK SHAKER VILLAGE

2 cups peeled and finely chopped apple
1 tablespoon powdered instant coffee, dissolved in 1 cup water
1 cup sugar
½ cup shortening
1 cup raisins
1 teaspoon cinnamon

¾ teaspoon cloves
¾ teaspoon nutmeg
1 teaspoon vanilla
3 cups flour
1 teaspoon baking soda
¼ teaspoon salt
½ cup chopped walnuts

⟨[Cook apple, coffee, sugar, shortening, raisins, and spices in saucepan gently until apple is tender. Remove from heat and cool. Heat oven to 375° F. Add vanilla to cooked mixture. Blend flour, soda, and salt; stir in. Mix in nuts. Drop by heaping teaspoonfuls on ungreased baking sheet. Bake about 12 minutes. Makes about 6 dozen cookies.

A seeded raisin or nut placed on top of each cooky before baking makes a pretty cooky.

CREAM COOKIES
FRANCES HALL, HANCOCK SHAKER VILLAGE

1 cup butter
2 cups sugar
2 eggs, lightly beaten
2 cups sweet cream
3 cups flour (about)

2 teaspoons baking powder
½ teaspoon salt
Vanilla (optional)
Caraway seeds (optional)

⟨[Cream butter and sugar together well. Add eggs and cream. Beat well. Add flour sifted with baking powder and salt. Flavor with vanilla and add caraway seeds, if you choose. Dough should be stiff enough to roll out on lightly floured board. Cut in nice shapes. Bake in moderate 350° to 375° F. oven about 10 minutes. Sprinkle with extra sugar and cinnamon if you like it. Makes 5–6 dozen cookies.

DATE AND NUT PINWHEEL COOKIES
HANCOCK SHAKER VILLAGE

Filling:

½ pound finely chopped dates	2 tablespoons lemon juice
¼ cup sugar	¼ cup chopped nuts
⅓ cup water	

⟨Combine all ingredients except nuts. Cook for 5 minutes stirring constantly. Remove from heat and add nuts. Let cool.

Batter:

½ cup butter or margarine	½ teaspoon vanilla
½ cup brown sugar	2 cups flour
½ cup white sugar	½ teaspoon salt
1 egg, beaten	½ teaspoon baking soda

⟨Cream the butter with the sugars, add egg and vanilla. Sift flour, salt, and soda together and add to creamed mixture, blend well. Divide dough in half. Roll each piece of dough on waxed paper into rectangle about 11x7 inches. Spread rectangles with date filling. Roll up tightly, beginning at wide side. Wrap each roll in wax paper and chill several hours.

Heat oven to 400° F. Slice cookies ¼ inch thick. Place on lightly greased baking sheet. Bake about 10 minutes or until lightly browned. Makes about 4 dozen cookies.

SISTER OLIVE WHEELER'S GINGER COOKIES
MANUSCRIPT FROM SHAKER MUSEUM
OLD CHATHAM, NEW YORK

2 cups molasses	½ teaspoon salt
1 tablespoon ginger	1 cup sugar
1 tablespoon vinegar	2 eggs, beaten
1 tablespoon baking soda	6 cups flour (about)

⟨Use a good-sized saucepan. Let molasses just come to a boil, remove from fire and add ginger, vinegar, soda (carefully for it will fizz up), salt, sugar, and beaten eggs. Stir in enough flour to roll out easily and cut in shapes at once. Bake at 350° F. for 10 to 12 minutes. Makes 8 dozen cookies.

SISTER OLIVE'S GINGER NUTS

MANUSCRIPT FROM SHAKER MUSEUM
OLD CHATHAM, NEW YORK

½ cup butter or lard
½ cup sugar
½ cup molasses
1 teaspoon baking soda
½ teaspoon salt
1 teaspoon ginger

½ cup boiling water, must be
  boiling
1 egg, well beaten
2½ cups flour, sifted
1 cup broken nut meats

([Cream shortening and sugar, add molasses, soda, salt, and ginger. Now add boiling water. Mix thoroughly, add egg. Beat. Reserve some flour to sprinkle on cake board. Add remaining flour to dough. Roll out ⅛ inch thick. Cut cookies in shapes. Put nut meat on each one or add nuts to dough. Place cookies on greased baking sheet. Bake at 400° F. for about 10 minutes. Makes 7–8 dozen cookies.

GINGER CAKES

SISTER OLIVE, HANCOCK SHAKER VILLAGE

½ cup butter
½ cup brown sugar
1 egg, beaten
½ cup thick sour milk or cream
1 cup molasses
3½ cups flour, sifted before
  measuring

1 teaspoon baking soda
3 teaspoons ginger
1 teaspoon cinnamon
½ teaspoon salt
Raisins

([Cream butter and sugar together. Add egg and beat well. Add sour milk or cream. Add molasses. Sift dry ingredients together and beat in well. Drop by tablespoonfuls on greased cooky sheet, spacing far apart. Put 3 seeded raisins on each. Bake 12 minutes at 350° F. Makes 4½ dozen cakes.

HERB COOKIES

HANCOCK SHAKER VILLAGE

½ cup shortening, butter, or
  chicken fat
½ cup sugar
½ cup molasses
1 egg
2½ cups flour, sifted
2 tablespoons ginger
1 teaspoon cinnamon

¼ teaspoon salt
½ teaspoon baking soda
1 teaspoon cloves
6 tablespoons hot water
2 tablespoons anise
1 tablespoon coriander seeds,
  softened in 2 teaspoons hot
  water and crushed

([Cream shortening, sugar, molasses. Stir in unbeaten egg, and beat well. Sift flour, ginger, cinnamon, salt, soda, and cloves. Add alternately with hot water and cool. Stir in anise and coriander seeds. Drop on baking sheet 2 inches apart. Cook 10 to 12 minutes at 350° F.

Frost with Confectionary Frosting.*

Makes about 4 dozen cookies.

JELLY DOT COOKIES
HANCOCK SHAKER VILLAGE

½ cup butter
½ cup firmly packed light brown
  sugar
¼ teaspoon salt
1 egg yolk

½ teaspoon vanilla
1 cup sifted flour
⅓ cup finely chopped walnuts
Jelly

([In a mixing bowl cream together butter, sugar, salt, egg yolk, and vanilla. Gradually stir in flour, blending well. Cover and chill until firm enough to handle. Work with half of dough at a time, keeping remaining portion refrigerated. Shape 1 well-rounded teaspoon of dough into balls about the size of marbles, roll in nuts. Place 1 inch apart on ungreased cooky sheets, gently press thumb into center of each cooky to make a shallow indentation; fill with jelly. Bake in 350° F. oven for 10 to 12 minutes. Cool on wire rack. Makes 36 cookies.

JELLY JUMBLES
FRANCES HALL, HANCOCK SHAKER VILLAGE

½ cup butter
1 cup sugar
1 egg, well beaten
½ teaspoon baking soda

½ cup sour milk
¼ teaspoon salt
Flour
Currant jelly

([Cream the butter, add sugar gradually, egg, soda mixed with milk, salt and flour mixed, to make a soft dough. Chill and pat out on board. Don't use a roller. Cut with a round shape. On the centers of one-half the pieces put currant jelly. Make three small openings in remaining halves, using a thimble. Put pieces together. Press edges slightly, place on a greased cooky sheet, and bake in a moderately hot 375° F. oven for 15 to 20 minutes. Makes 12–16.

MAPLE SUGAR COOKIES
MRS. TABOR
A NEW HAMPSHIRE SHAKER RECEIPT

2¼ cups sifted flour
¼ teaspoon salt
2 teaspoons baking powder
½ cup shortening

1 cup maple sugar
2 eggs, beaten
2 teaspoons vanilla
1 tablespoon milk

⟮Sift flour, salt, and baking powder together. Cream shortening and sugar together, add eggs and vanilla, then sifted ingredients and milk. Mix together well. Roll out and cut into shapes with a cooky cutter. Sprinkle with additional maple sugar. Bake on greased cooky sheet in moderate 350° F. oven for 12 minutes. Makes 2½ dozen cookies.

MAPLE BUTTERNUT SUGAR COOKIES
MT. LEBANON SHAKER VILLAGE

¼ cup butter, melted
½ cup maple syrup
½ cup flour
¼ teaspoon salt

⅛ teaspoon baking soda
⅛ teaspoon baking powder
½ cup chopped butternuts (walnuts may be substituted)

⟮Combine butter and maple syrup. Sift flour with salt, soda, and baking powder. Blend with first mixture, then add the nuts. Drop by teaspoonfuls onto greased cooky sheet 3 inches apart. Bake at 350° F. for 10 minutes or until lightly browned. Remove from oven, cool on sheet. Then remove to wire rack until cookies are cold and crisp. Keep in tightly covered container. Makes 12–16 cookies.

MARGUERITES #1
MT. LEBANON SHAKER VILLAGE

2 eggs, slightly beaten
1 cup brown sugar
½ cup flour

⅓ teaspoon salt
1 cup chopped nut meats
¼ teaspoon baking powder

⟮To slightly beaten eggs, add remaining ingredients in order given. Pour into buttered 8 inch square pan. Bake 30 to 35 minutes in 350° F. oven. Cut into small squares while warm. Makes a dozen or more squares, depending on size.

MARGUERITES #2—Plain and with Jam
FROM SEVERAL SHAKER COMMUNITIES

2 egg whites
½ cup sugar
2 drops vanilla or lemon extract
        or

1 teaspoon rose water
Sweet crackers (soda or saltine-type
    crackers may be substituted)
½ cup nuts, finely chopped

¶Beat egg whites stiff and gradually add sugar and flavoring. Place a
spoonful of the mixture on a cracker and sprinkle with chopped nuts.
Bake in a moderate 350° F. oven until delicately brown. Makes about 30.

To make Marguerites with jam—add 2 tablespoons of raspberry or
other jam to the beaten egg white and proceed with above recipe.

SWEET CRACKERS
NEW LEBANON SHAKER VILLAGE

2 cups flour
½ cup sour cream

½ cup sugar
½ teaspoon baking soda

¶Mix ingredients well in order given. Mixture will be fairly stiff. Roll
out ¼ inch thick on floured board. Cut in desired shape, freehand with
knife or with cooky cutter. Bake on greased sheet in 350° F. oven for 10
to 12 minutes. Makes 20–24 crackers.

The Shakers made their own crackers.

MARMALADE COOKIES
SISTER OLIVE, HANCOCK SHAKER VILLAGE

2 eggs
1 cup sugar
1 teaspoon vanilla
        or
1 teaspoon rose water
½ teaspoon salt
¼ cup shortening, melted

3 tablespoons orange marmalade
Juice and grated rind ½ lemon
½ cup raisins
1 cup coconut
¼ cup butternuts or walnuts
3 cups flour
2 teaspoons baking powder

¶Beat eggs lightly. Add sugar gradually, then other ingredients except
flour and baking powder. Sift flour with baking powder and add to mixture, stirring thoroughly a few minutes. Drop by spoonfuls on a greased
cooky sheet. Pat down a little with a spoon moistened with milk to form
a glaze. Bake at 400° F. for 10 to 12 minutes. Will yield 40 cookies—
delicious ones.

SOFT MOLASSES COOKIES
SABBATHDAY LAKE SHAKER VILLAGE

2¼ cups flour
¼ teaspoon salt
2 teaspoons baking soda
1 teaspoon ginger
1 teaspoon cinnamon
½ cup lard

½ cup sugar
1 egg, unbeaten
½ cup molasses
½ cup hot water from tap
Raisins

⟨[Sift together flour, salt, soda, and spices. Cream lard and sugar until light, add egg, molasses, and mix well. Add sifted dried ingredients alternately with ½ cup of hot water.

Drop by spoonfuls on ungreased baking sheet. Sprinkle sugar and 3 raisins on each cooky before baking. Bake in 375° F. oven about 10 minutes. This makes 25 large cookies.

INDIAN DOUGHNUTS
THE MANIFESTO, JANUARY 1880

1½ cups boiling milk
2 cups corn meal
2 cups flour
3 teaspoons baking powder
1 teaspoon salt

1½ cups sugar
1 cup butter, melted
3 eggs, beaten
1 tablespoon nutmeg or cinnamon
Deep fat for frying

⟨[Pour boiling milk over corn meal and let cool. Sift together flour, baking powder, salt, sugar, and spice. Add to cooled corn meal, stirring well. Add butter and eggs. Mix well and if necessary add more flour to make dough firm enough to handle, but keep it as soft as possible. Knead slightly. Roll out on floured board. Shape with floured doughnut cutter. Let doughnuts stand before frying in hot deep fat. Makes about 48.

MOLASSES DOUGHNUTS
MT. LEBANON SHAKER VILLAGE

2 eggs
½ cup sugar
½ cup molasses
1 teaspoon baking soda
1 cup sour milk or buttermilk
1 teaspoon baking powder

1 tablespoon butter
½ teaspoon ginger
½ teaspoon cinnamon
2–2½ cups flour (about)
Deep fat for frying

⟨[Beat the eggs well. Add sugar and molasses. Add soda to sour milk and combine with first mixture. Add baking powder, butter, ginger, cinnamon, and enough flour to mix as thick as can be handled. Stir well. Roll out on floured board. Cut with doughnut cutter. Fry in deep hot fat. Makes about 3 dozen.

NUT BALLS
MT. LEBANON SHAKER VILLAGE

⅔ cup shortening
1 cup ground nuts
1 cup flour
⅛ teaspoon salt

3 tablespoons sugar
1 teaspoon vanilla
Confectioners' sugar

⟨Cream shortening and blend well with other ingredients. Form into balls the size of a walnut and bake on buttered cooky sheet in moderate 350° F. oven for 12 minutes. While hot, roll in confectioners' sugar. Very easy and quick to make, delicious and will keep if well tinned. Makes 2½–3 dozen.

POPCORN COOKIES
MT. LEBANON SHAKER VILLAGE

2 eggs, well beaten
1 cup granulated sugar
1 teaspoon vanilla

1½ teaspoons baking powder
½–1 cup flour, sifted

⟨Combine eggs, sugar, vanilla, and enough flour to make dough stiff enough to roll out thin. Roll out on floured board and cut with cooky cutter. Put on greased cooky sheet. Bake at 350° F. for 5 to 8 minutes. Called "Popcorn" cookies because they taste like popcorn. Makes 12–16 cookies.

POTATO CHIP COOKIES
SISTER BERTHA LINDSAY
CANTERBURY SHAKER VILLAGE

1 cup white sugar
1 cup brown sugar
1 cup butter
2 eggs, well beaten
2 cups flour
2 cups oatmeal

2 cups crushed potato chips
1 cup chopped nuts
1 cup dates or raisins
½ teaspoon salt
1 teaspoon baking soda

⟨Cream sugar and butter, add beaten eggs. Mix together all other ingredients and drop by teaspoonfuls on greased baking sheet. Bake at 375° F. for 10 to 15 minutes. Makes about 100.

ROSE WATER COOKIES
HANCOCK SHAKER VILLAGE

1 cup butter
1 cup sugar
2 eggs, beaten light and fluffy
2¾ cups flour
1 teaspoon baking soda
½ teaspoon cream of tartar

2 tablespoons rose water
½ cup chopped orange or lemon peel
Pinch salt
½ cup raisins, plus additional raisins for decoration

([Cream butter and sugar together. Add beaten eggs. Sift together flour, baking soda, and cream of tartar and add. Mix well. Add rose water, fruit peel, salt, and raisins. Blend. Drop on greased cooky sheet. Dot each one with 1 raisin. Bake in 375° F. oven for 20 minutes. Makes 6–7 dozen cookies.

ROSE WATER FLOWER COOKIES
HANCOCK SHAKER VILLAGE

½ cup shortening
1 cup sugar
2 eggs, beaten
2 teaspoons rose water
1 teaspoon milk

2½ cups flour
½ teaspoon salt
3 teaspoons baking powder
Jam or marmalade

([Heat oven to 375° F. Grease small cupcake pans, 2½ inches in diameter—¾ inch deep.

Blend shortening and sugar, add eggs and rose water, and beat thoroughly. Gradually blend in milk and dry ingredients. Chill dough. Roll part of the dough out on a lightly floured board about ½ inch thick. Cut dough in rounds, using a 2½ inch scalloped cooky cutter. Fit the round in cupcake pan. Make imprint in center with finger and put in ¼ teaspoon jam or marmalade. Bake 9 to 12 minutes. Makes about 4 dozen cookies.

EXTRA RICH SOUR CREAM COOKIES
MRS. TABOR
NEW HAMPSHIRE SHAKER RECEIPT

2 cups white or maple sugar
1 cup butter or lard
2 eggs
1 teaspoon baking soda
½ teaspoon salt

1 cup thick sour cream
Rose water, vanilla, or cinnamon (optional)
3 cups flour (at least)

❲[Cream sugar and shortening together well. Add eggs. Beat. Combine soda, salt, and sour cream. Add to egg mixture. Can be flavored with rose water, vanilla, or cinnamon if desired. Add flour, enough to make batter workable to roll. Beat well and roll out. Cut into shapes with cooky cutter. Put on greased cooky sheet and bake in a moderately hot 375° F. oven about 10 minutes. Makes about 5 dozen cookies.

SISTER OLIVE'S JUMBLES (Sugar Cookies)
MANUSCRIPT, MT. LEBANON SHAKER VILLAGE

"One pound and a half of flour—1 pound of sugar—¾ of a pound of butter, 4 yolks, and the whites of 2 eggs. A small teaspoon of perlash. Beat the white of the egg to a froth and put it in the last thing."

1½ cups butter	1 teaspoon baking soda
2 cups sugar	½ teaspoon salt
4 egg yolks, well beaten	2 egg whites, beaten to a froth
3 cups flour, sifted	

❲[Cream butter, add sugar gradually and well-beaten egg yolks. Reserve some flour for cake board. Sift 2½ cups flour with soda and salt. Beat gently into butter-egg mixture. At last fold in whites and mix well. Roll out and shape with cooky cutter. Bake at 350° F. for 10 minutes. Makes about 4 dozen cookies.

"BEST TEAS"
MT. LEBANON SHAKER VILLAGE

2 cups flour	1 egg yolk
½ cup brown sugar	¾ teaspoon water
¾ cup sweet or washed[1] butter	Granulated sugar

❲[Mix and sift flour and sugar together. Work in butter using tips of fingers. Roll to ⅓ inch in thickness, cut into shapes with a pretty fluted cooky cutter. Brush over with egg yolk diluted with water. Put on a greased cooky sheet. Bake in a slow oven (300° to 325° F.) for 10 to 12 minutes and watch to keep from burning. Sprinkle lightly with granulated sugar. These keep well. Makes about 4 dozen cookies.

---

[1]If sweet butter is not available, cut chilled butter into pieces and rinse with cold water several times to remove saltiness.

Pies, Pastries, and Fritters

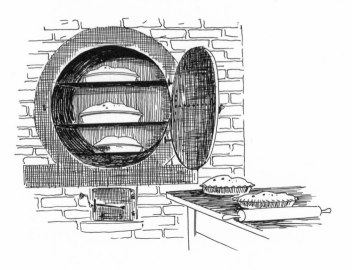

P IES AND OTHER PASTRIES were always on hand in Shaker kitchens
and pantries. Pie was served at breakfast, dinner, and supper, and
certain kinds were made for picnics and other trips, as they
"traveled well." Kitchen deaconesses noted that rye pastry should be
used for "wrapping venison and mutton," white flour crust for pies of
turkey, veal, and lamb, and the shortest wheaten crust for chicken, fish,
quince, and mincemeat. Only the best puff paste would be "ordered for
tarts, delicate pies, and puddings with paste shells." Shaker butter was
used with a lavish hand. They learned to render it by boiling it in water
and removed the pure fat which rose to the top when cold. They did the
same with beef suet and used both of these fats in making pies and
pastries. Chicken fat was treated in the same way for pastry and cakes.
It also made a delicate soap.

We have recounted elsewhere some of the experiences of the South
Union Shakers during the Civil War, and how valiantly the sisters
supplied food for both armies as they came and went through the
Society's property. Another very dramatic account from the same village
was reprinted in an 1894 *Manifesto*. It was dated February 13, 1861, and
told of the confrontation between the Shakers, who were pacifists, and
the soldiers of the federal and Confederate armies, and how food played
an important part in dealing with seven armed robbers.

Early one morning after 36 of the Confederate Cavalry called on
the East family and asked for milk and were supplied with it . . .
seven heavily armed robbers dashed into our Village and demanded
horses. . . . Robbers: "We wish to get some of your fine riding horses."
Brother Urban: "We have none, you took most of our best horses
some time since." Robbers: "They were wagon horses—we want
Cavalry horses. Where is your fine sorrel horse—we have the bay and
now want the sorrel." Brother Urban: "We have a written order

from General Hardee that you are to take no more of our stock."
Robbers: "We do not belong to his brigade. We are Lincolnites."

A company of sisters were called to assist the Brethren and stood
upon the steps of the trustee's office. The Robbers dickered for
horses, cloth, money, silk kerchiefs and the brothers returned their
banter and demands with firmness and great courage. Finally this
rough, ungentlemanly company was invited to accept dinner. They
rudely replied: "We have had our dinner." [After more conversa-
tion] the Brethren now brought several loaves of warm bread, a
bucketful of milk, several pies and some new peach sauce from the
family dwelling. . . . After this simple repast they became more
gentlemanly.

This did not keep them from making off with two horses and threat-
ening to return for cloth and money—but it did deter them from burning the village as they had also promised to do.

PLAIN PASTRY #1
NORTH UNION SHAKER VILLAGE, OHIO

2 cups flour	⅔ cups shortening, chilled
½ teaspoon salt	⅓ cup cold water

⟨[Sift flour with salt into mixing bowl. Cut in shortening with pastry
blender or 2 knives until crumb-like. Add water very gradually by
sprinkling it in. Do not get crumbs too fine or dough too wet. Handle
dough as little as possible. Form lightly into 2 balls and chill. Roll on
a lightly floured board ⅛ inch thick. Yields enough for two 9 inch crusts
or one 9-inch crust and some tart shells.

PLAIN PASTRY #2

2½ cups flour	1 cup shortening
½ tablespoon sugar	2 egg yolks

⟨[Sift flour and sugar together. With a pastry blender or two knives cut
in shortening. Work up to consistency of coarse meal. Drop egg yolks in

a 1 cup measure and fill up with cold water. Add to flour mixture. Mix slowly and gently. Pat dough lightly into a ball. Do not knead. Chill. Roll out on floured board. Divide pastry into two parts, one slightly larger than the other. Place larger one on pie tin for the bottom shell. Use smaller one for top crust. Yields enough for a 9 inch 2 crust pie and some tart shells.

Note: For meat and seafood pies, it is suggested that you make a pastry that contains butter, but not sugar or eggs.

FLAKIER PLAIN PASTRY

MT. LEBANON SHAKER VILLAGE

½ teaspoon salt   Cold water
1½ cups flour sifted   ¼ cup butter
¼ cup lard

⟨[Add salt to flour and sift into bowl. Work in lard with knife. Moisten dough with water so it can be handled easily. Toss out on floured board. Roll out. Dot with butter, fold into three, and roll out again. Divide into 2 pieces for your pies or roll up and fold in cheesecloth. Put in covered tin in cold place until needed.

This is a superior paste. Yields enough for two 8 inch crusts.

SISTER LETTIE'S BUTTER PASTRY

NORTH UNION SHAKER VILLAGE, OHIO

2¼ cups flour, sifted   ⅔ cup unsalted butter, chilled
½ teaspoon salt   ⅓ cup cold water
½ teaspoon baking powder

⟨[The most important point in making a flaky crust is to have the shortening well chilled. This keeps the crumbs from getting too fine.

Sift flour, salt, and baking powder together in a bowl. Use a pastry blender or 2 knives to cut in butter. Add water very slowly drop by drop. Form into 2 balls, chill slightly, and roll out ⅛ inch thick. This crust is especially suited to berry pies. Yields enough for a 9 inch 2 crust pie or a 1 crust pie and some tart shells.

RICH PASTRY FROM SHIRLEY

SHIRLEY SHAKER VILLAGE

2 cups fine flour
½ teaspoon baking powder
½ teaspoon salt
½ cup lard

½ cup butter
Ice water
2 tablespoons butter

([Sift flour, baking powder, and salt into mixing bowl. Cut in lard and butter. Add water slowly. Make a ball and chill. Roll out on a floured board. Dot with extra butter. Roll up like a jelly roll. Chill. Roll out again and cut for 2 crusts. Yields two 8 inch crusts.

PUFF PASTRY

HANCOCK SHAKER VILLAGE

1½ cups flour, sifted once
1 cup sweet butter or washed
  butter (to remove salt), chilled

Cold water

([Resift flour into bowl. Cut in ⅓ of the butter and moisten to a dough with cold water. Roll out on a floured cloth or board. Measure out ⅓ of the remaining butter and dot pastry with it. Roll up dough like a jelly roll. Roll out flat and dot with last ⅓ of butter. Roll up like a jelly roll. Chill. When ready to use roll out on a board. Yields two 8 inch crusts.

ANOTHER RICH PUFF PASTRY

HANCOCK SHAKER VILLAGE

2 cups fine flour
2 tablespoons lemon juice
1 egg yolk
½ teaspoon salt

Cold water
2 cups washed butter (to remove
  salt), chilled

([Put flour sifted once in bowl. Make a depression in center, pour in lemon juice. Add yolk of egg and salt. Add cold water to make a dough. Toss on a floured cloth. Knead, cover, and let stand 5 minutes. Divide butter into 3 parts. Pat, roll out, and dot with butter. Roll up like a jelly roll, chill. Repeat until butter is used up. Roll out and use. Yields two 8 inch crusts.

FLAKE PIECRUST
CANTERBURY SHAKER VILLAGE

⟨Take ½ cup lard to 2 cups of flour—rub well together; take cold water sufficient to make a dough (not too stiff). Roll out and spread with butter. (Total amount of butter needed is about 1½ cups.) Fold over evenly and butter. Make a second fold. Roll out again being careful not to squeeze the butter out. The layers of dough and butter repeated provide the flakiness of the crust.

Use a pinch of ginger in piecrust to eliminate the taste of lard in case it is not fresh. Makes two 8 inch crusts.

·.·

A unique piece of equipment is the large pie oven in the Canterbury Shaker kitchen. Its rotating racks could accommodate 60 pies or dozens of pots of baked beans. It was a clever and ingenious arrangement as the heat was evenly distributed and the baked pies were removed from the oven with no difficulty as each one came to the front. A visitor noted "The immense stove had an oven in which could be stowed away a ten-year-old boy."

SHAKER APPLE PIE
CANTERBURY SHAKER VILLAGE

3 cups peeled sliced sour apples
⅔ cup maple or white sugar
1 tablespoon heavy cream

1 tablespoon rose water*
Pastry* for two 9 inch crusts

⟨Slice apples into mixing bowl and add sugar, cream, and rose water, and mix thoroughly, so that rose water will be distributed evenly. Line the pie dish with favorite pastry. Fill with apple mixture and cover with top crust in which a few small vents have been slashed for steam to escape. Flute the edges well to keep juice from escaping. Bake in a moderate 350° F. oven for 50 minutes. SERVES 6.

·.·

"A good pie is excellent when hot; but the test of a good pie is: How does it eat cold?"

APPLE PIE

HANCOCK SHAKER VILLAGE

Make your own favorite crust recipe.

1 dozen medium green apples	1 tablespoon grated lemon rind
⅔ cup brown sugar	1 tablespoon cornstarch
¼ cup granulated or maple sugar	2 tablespoons melted butter
½ teaspoon nutmeg	1 egg white for glaze (optional)

❨Wash, core, and peel 1 dozen medium apples. Mix all dry ingredients together. Sprinkle over apples. Pour butter over this. (Use egg white glaze if desired.) Bake for ½ hour at 375° F. Drop the temperature to 325° F. for another ½ hour. SERVES 6.

APPLE PIE WITH CHEESE

WATERVLIET SHAKER VILLAGE, NEW YORK

❨Grate ⅔ cup Cheddar cheese generously over pie and heat in 350° F. oven just long enough to make pie hot and melt the cheese. This is good when using day-old pie.

APPLE CUSTARD FOR PIES

HANCOCK SHAKER VILLAGE

Have ready a 9 inch pie tin lined with pastry.*

6 egg yolks	1 teaspoon cinnamon
4 egg whites	*or*
2 cups sugar	1 teaspoon rose water
1 cup melted butter	2 cups sliced, pared, cored apples
Juice 1 lemon	2 egg whites, beaten until they make peaks

❨Beat 6 yolks and 4 whites together. Add sugar and melted butter, lemon juice and flavorings. Add apples and pour into pie shell. Cook in 400° F. oven 10 minutes—reduce to 325° F. and cook another 40 minutes. Cover with beaten egg whites and cook to brown meringue. SERVES 6–8.

APPLE-PORK PIE

MT. LEBANON SHAKER VILLAGE

This is an old deep dish pie and is served either for dessert or in main part of dinner.

1 recipe for 2 crust 9 inch pastry*
2 tablespoons flour
½ cup maple sugar
½ cup white sugar
¼ teaspoon salt
½ teaspoon cinnamon

¼ teaspoon nutmeg
6 tart apples, pared and sliced
½ pound salt pork, cut into thin
    small pieces 1 inch long
¼ teaspoon black pepper
2 tablespoons butter

⟨[Line a cake dish 9x6x2 inches with pastry. Mix flour, sugar, salt, and spices. Combine with apples and place half the mixture in pastry. Cover with half the salt pork. Sprinkle with half the pepper. Repeat layers, using the rest of the apple mixture, salt pork, and pepper. Dot with butter. Fit on upper crust. Slash crust. Bake at 450° F. for 10 minutes, then at 375° F. for 50 minutes. Serve warm. SERVES 6–8.

BLACKBERRY PIE #1

MT. LEBANON SHAKER VILLAGE

⟨[Few things are more acceptable than the old-fashioned blackberry pie. It takes 2 quarts of berries to make a good-sized pie. This is for a 12 inch pie pan.

Pick the berries over carefully, put them in a collander, pour cold water over them, and remove all stems and dust. Then let them drain for at least half an hour. Place berries in a large bowl and squeeze over them the juice of 1 lemon and sugar to taste. Then put in 4 heaping tablespoons of flour and mix it through the berries with the sugar and lemon. The flour thickens the juice of the berries and keeps it from running out of the pie as it bakes. Make a rich pastry,* big enough for a 12 inch pan. Line the pan with the pastry. Then fill with the berries, cover with rest of pastry and put in a hot 425° F. oven for 30 minutes. SERVES 8–10.

Blackberries for winter pies may be prepared by boiling together 14 pounds of berries, 7 pounds of sugar, and 1 pint of vinegar until the berries are just scalded. Place in pint jars and seal. This makes 18 pint jars.

BLACKBERRY PIE #2
HANCOCK SHAKER VILLAGE

1½ cups blackberries
½ cup white sugar
    or
1 cup brown sugar

⅛ teaspoon salt
Water
1 teaspoon butter
Pastry* for two 8 inch crusts

¶[Pick over and wash the berries; be careful to include only those which are ripe. Add sugar and salt. Stew up with enough water to prevent burning. Cook must be the judge of this. When berries are almost done, cooked but not mushy (about 10 minutes), add butter. Line an 8 inch pie pan with pastry, fill with berries, which have been cooled. Arrange strips of pastry in criss-cross pattern over top instead of solid crust. Add a rim about 1½ inches wide around edge. Trim crust at rim of pie pan. Bake 30 minutes in a moderate 350°F. oven. SERVES 6.

BLUEBERRY PIE
HANCOCK SHAKER VILLAGE

2½ cups ripe blueberries, well
    picked over
Flour
½ cup sugar

⅛ teaspoon salt
Pastry* for two 8 inch crusts (See
    Sister Lettie's Butter Pastry*)

¶[Line a deep pie tin with plain pastry, fill with berries slightly dredged with flour. Sprinkle with sugar and salt. Cover with upper crust, which has been pricked. Bake 45 to 50 minutes in a moderate 350° F. oven. For sweetening some prefer to use ⅓ cup molasses and ⅔ cup sugar. Six green grapes, without seeds, cut in small pieces, greatly improve the flavor, particularly when huckleberries are used in place of blueberries. SERVES 6–8.

BUTTERNUT PIE
ENFIELD SHAKER VILLAGE, CONNECTICUT

3 eggs
6 tablespoons sugar
¼ teaspoon salt
¾ cup chopped butternut meats
    (walnuts can be used)

1 teaspoon flour
3 cups sweet milk
Pastry* for one 8 inch crust

¶[Beat together eggs, sugar, and salt. Roll nuts in flour. Add milk. Put in unbaked pie shell. Bake at 400° F. for 10 minutes—then at 325° F. until filling is set, about 30 minutes. SERVES 4–6.

CHERRY PIE
ENFIELD SHAKER VILLAGE, CONNECTICUT

1 cup flour
1 tablespoon brown sugar
1 tablespoon cinnamon
¾ cup ground almonds
½ cup butter
2 tablespoons fine bread crumbs
(crusts removed)

6 eggs
2 cups drained stoned cooked and
    sweetened sour red cherries
1½ cups cherry syrup
1 tablespoon sweet red wine

⟨Combine flour, sugar, cinnamon, and ground almonds. Cream butter and beat into flour mixture with the breadcrumbs. Separate eggs. Add egg yolks to mixture. Whip egg whites until stiff and fold them in. Grease a 9 inch ovenproof dish. Cover bottom with drained cherries. Reserve juice. Cover cherries with the batter. Bake in 325° F. oven 30 minutes until lightly brown on top. Pass whipped cream and heated cherry syrup flavored with wine. SERVES 6.

BLACK CHERRY TURNOVERS
ENFIELD SHAKER VILLAGE, CONNECTICUT

⟨Prepare a double recipe of Plain Pastry #1* and cut out 3 inch rounds. Fill one half with drained, pitted, black, sweet cherries. Sprinkle well with sugar. Fold pastry over to make half moon shape after wetting edges with water. Join edges well by crimping with a common fork to keep in the juice. Prick. Bake in a moderately hot 375° F. oven for 15 minutes. Sprinkle with sugar while still warm and again when serving.

This makes 8 dozen.

CHERRY TARTS
SHAKER FESTIVAL, AUBURN, KENTUCKY

Filling:

1 cup granulated sugar
3 tablespoons cornstarch
¼ teaspoon salt
¾ cup cherry juice
1½ teaspoons fresh lemon juice

⅓ teaspoon almond extract
½ teaspoon red food coloring
3 tablespoons butter
3 cups drained tart canned red
    cherries

❲Mix ¼ cup sugar, cornstarch, and salt; add cherry juice and cook until thick; add remaining sugar and cook until glossy. Remove from heat. Add lemon juice, almond extract, food coloring, and butter. Then add cherries and mix gently.

Pastry:

2½ cups flour, sifted
½ teaspoon salt

⅔ cup shortening, chilled
⅓ cup cold water

❲Sift flour with salt into mixing bowl. Cut in shortening with pastry blender until the particles are pea-size. Add water gradually by sprinkling it in. Do not get the crumbs too fine, and don't get the dough too wet. Handle the dough as little as possible. Form gently into 2 balls and chill. Roll out and fit pastry into tart tins (individual size). Bake in 350° F. oven for 20 minutes.

Pour cherry filling into baked tart shells and garnish with whipped cream. Makes 10–12 tarts.

SHAKER CIDER PIE

SOUTH UNION SHAKER VILLAGE, KENTUCKY

½ cup Boiled Cider
1 tablespoon butter
1 cup maple sugar
¼ cup water
¼ teaspoon salt

2 egg yolks, beaten
2 egg whites, stiffly beaten
1 unbaked 9 inch pie shell*
1 teaspoon nutmeg

❲Put boiled-down cider in saucepan; add butter, sugar, water, and salt. Simmer several minutes. Cool slightly and add beaten egg yolks. Fold in stiffly beaten egg whites. Pour into unbaked pie shell. Dust with nutmeg and bake in moderate 350° F. oven, approximately 20 to 30 minutes, until shell is brown and custard well set. SERVES 6–8.

BOILED CIDER

❲Boiled cider was a staple on grocery store shelves. It was bottled commercially to be used as a sweetener, but it was made by most cooks for their own use. Some condensed it more than others depending on how sweet they wanted it.

Mary Whitcher's directions for making it are short and to the point: "Take 4 gallons of cider and boil it to one gallon." Thus condensed it was used principally to sweeten Shaker applesauce, the manufacture of which was a profitable industry—and was a great saving when used instead of sugar. It was also used in dessert puddings, jellies, and in beverages.

BOILED CIDER PIE WITH BUTTERNUTS

HANCOCK SHAKER VILLAGE

½ cup flour
1 cup maple sugar
½ cup homemade Boiled Cider
1 tablespoon butter

1 cup boiling water
½ cup chopped butternuts
1 unbaked pie shell* for 9 inch pan
Extra pastry*

❨Combine flour and sugar. Sift together. Add cider, butter, water, and nuts and mix well. Beat 20 strokes and put in pie shell. Make lattice top with extra pastry. Bake at 450° F. 10 minutes and 350° F. about 30 minutes. SERVES 6–8.

CLOVE PIE, SOMETIMES CALLED SPICE PIE

HANCOCK SHAKER VILLAGE

4 eggs, slightly beaten
½ cup sugar
¼ teaspoon salt
1¼ teaspoons vanilla
   or
1¼ teaspoons rose water

2½ cups scalding hot milk
Pastry* for 1 crust pie for 9 inch pan
Powdered clove, nutmeg, and
   cinnamon, one or all (amount
   depends on personal taste)

❨Mix beaten eggs, sugar, salt, and vanilla or rose water. Gradually stir in milk; pour at once into pastry-lined pie tin. Sprinkle with powdered spices. Bake in very hot 475° F. oven for 5 minutes. Turn oven down to 425° F. and bake for 30 minutes longer or until knife inserted toward center comes out clean. SERVES 6–8.

∵

There was a cranberry bog on North Mountain, Hancock, near the Saw Mill Shakers. This provided a fine crop of berries in the fall and the Shakers kept them all winter long in a large vessel in the cellar by covering the raw cranberries with water.

SHAKER CRANBERRY PIE
HANCOCK SHAKER VILLAGE

¾ cup sugar
1 tablespoon flour
1 teaspoon vanilla

1 cup raisins
1 cup cranberries
Pastry* for two 9 inch crusts

⟨[Mix sugar with flour and vanilla; sprinkle over fruit and mix well. Bake between 2 piecrusts 45 to 50 minutes in a moderate 350° F. oven. This is a very tasty confection. SERVES 6–8.

CRANBERRY-APPLE PIE
HANCOCK SHAKER VILLAGE

2 nine inch piecrusts*
4 large tart apples, peeled and cored (Gravensteins or Tolmans or your best)
1½ cups cranberries

1 cup maple sugar (if white sugar has to be used add 2 tablespoons maple syrup)
3 tablespoons butter

⟨[Place bottom crust in 9 inch pie tin. Cut apples in quarters and fill plate. Mix cranberries and sugar and let them stand to draw a little juice. Mash just a bit. Cover apples and dot with butter. Put on top crust. Moisten lower rim so edges will cement. Flute to seal. Cut "A" or "C" in top crust to let out steam. Bake at 450° F. for 10 minutes and then reduce heat to 375° F. for 30 minutes. SERVES 6–8.

CRANBERRY TARTS
HANCOCK SHAKER VILLAGE

⟨[Cover cranberries with water. Simmer until tender, about 20 minutes. Drain. Prepare pastry shells not over 2 or 2½ inches in diameter from puff paste.* Prick them on the bottom thoroughly to prevent them from rising and becoming uneven. They can be filled with rice to keep bottoms level. The edges must be left to rise as they please. Place tart pan filled with pastry on baking sheets and bake at 425° F. for 2 to 4 minutes. When cooked fill each cold tart shell with a good tablespoon of sweetened hot, stewed cranberries. Set them away to cool. When serving put a spoon of thick cream, either whipped or naturally thick, in center of cranberries. Serve with Shaker Cream.

SHAKER CREAM

([In summer use milk which is 12 hours old, in winter that which is 24 hours old. Set over slow heat to *bring very slowly almost to boiling point,* keep there 10 to 15 minutes. *Do not allow to boil.* The slower it heats the better. The cream will wrinkle. Do not disturb, but let cool and stand 12 to 24 hours (refrigerated). Then remove cream carefully by rolling. This is a delicious thick mass. It may be whipped, but is best eaten as it is on a dessert, on pastry, or on bread and butter with sugar and cinnamon. Four quarts rich milk makes 2 cups cream.

Note: Pasteurized milk or milk chilled on ice cannot be used.

CUSTARD SPICE PIE
HANCOCK SHAKER VILLAGE

Pastry* for 1 crust pie for 9 inch pan
4 eggs, lightly beaten
½ cup sugar
¼ teaspoon salt

1¼ teaspoons rose water
2½ cups scalding hot rich milk, but not cream
Nutmeg, cloves, cinnamon

([Preheat oven to 450° F. Line a 9 inch pie pan with pastry. Thoroughly mix eggs, sugar, salt, and rose water. Gradually stir in hot milk. Pour at once into pastry-lined pie tin. Sprinkle with mixed spices. Bake in preheated oven for 5 minutes, turn temperature down to 400°F. and bake for about 30 minutes longer or until knife inserted in center comes out clean. SERVES 6–8.

DOLLAR TARTS
HANCOCK SHAKER VILLAGE

([Make your best pastry and cut out rounds just a little larger than silver dollars. Fill center of 1 round with fruit filling, about 1 teaspoon, and season with sugar and spices. Cover with top of pastry. Using fork, seal edges. Bake in 350° F. oven for 10 minutes.

CONCORD GRAPE PIE
HARVARD SHAKER VILLAGE

Concord grapes
4 tablespoons flour
1¼ cups sugar

Pastry* for one 9 inch piecrust/plus
   extra for topping
2 tablespoons butter

⟨Wash enough grapes free of stems to fill 9 inch pie tin and make a rounded mound. Squeeze pulp from grapes into a saucepan, reserve skins. Bring pulp to a boil. Strain out seeds, mix pulp and skins. Stir in 2 tablespoons flour and 1 cup sugar. Line pie tin with pastry, combine ¼ cup sugar and 2 tablespoons flour. Sprinkle on bottom of crust. Add grape filling. Add butter in center of grape mixture. Cover with a lattice topping.

Bake in 450° F. oven for 10 minutes. Reduce heat to 400° F. for 10 minutes and cook for 30 minutes at 350° F. SERVES 6–8.

KENTUCKY PIE
SOUTH UNION SHAKER VILLAGE, KENTUCKY

½ cup butter
3 eggs
3 cups brown sugar
½ cup heavy cream

1 teaspoon vanilla
   or
1 teaspoon rose water
½ teaspoon salt
1 unbaked chilled 9 inch pie shell*
Chopped black walnuts

⟨Cream the butter, eggs and sugar together and add remaining ingredients.

Fill unbaked pie shell, sprinkle top with black walnuts, and bake in a moderate 350° F. oven 30 minutes. SERVES 6–8.

LADIES' FINGERS
SHIRLEY SHAKER VILLAGE

2 egg whites
¾ cup confectioners' sugar
¼ cup finely chopped nuts

Recipe for two 8 inch crusts best
   pastry*

⟨Beat whites of egg until stiff, add sugar gradually, then nuts. Roll out pastry and cut in strips 3½ inches long by 1½ inches wide. Spread with mixture; avoid having it come close to edge. Dust with additional confectioners' sugar and bake 15 minutes in moderate 350° F. oven. SERVES 10–12.

OHIO LEMON PIE
NORTH UNION SHAKER VILLAGE, OHIO

2 lemons, sliced	Pastry* for two 8 inch crusts
2 cups sugar	4 eggs

([This is yet another very old lemon pie recipe which the early Ohio Shakers fashioned frequently.

"Slice 2 lemons as thin as paper, rind and all. Place them in a yellow bowl and pour over them 2 cups sugar. Mix well and let stand for 2 hours or better.

"Then go about making your best pastry for 2 crusts. Line a pie tin with some [pastry for 1 crust]. Beat 4 eggs together. [Arrange slices of lemons in layers in unbaked pie shell, with sugar between each layer. Pour beaten eggs over the lemons and their juice after they are arranged. Add top crust with small vents to let out steam.]

"Place in a hot oven [450° F.] for 15 minutes and then cut down heat [to 400° F.] and bake until tip of a silver knife inserted into custard cames out clean."

Author's Note: The secret in making this pie is to have the lemon slices paper thin just as it says—but fruit and sugar should really stand, mixed, longer than 2 hours for best results—overnight. Additional sugar should be sprinkled over lemon slices when arranging them with the sweetened juice in the pie shell. Do not skip this step. This makes the pie juicy. SERVES 6.

NEW HAMPSHIRE MAPLE PIE
ENFIELD SHAKER VILLAGE, NEW HAMPSHIRE

1¼ cups maple sugar	1 cup sweet cream
½ cup butter	1 unbaked 8 inch pie shell*
1 egg, lightly beaten	

([Combine sugar and butter, add egg, and last the cream. Fill pie shell and bake like a custard pie, at 400° F. for 10 minutes and then at 375° F. for 20 minutes. SERVES 6–8.

SISTER LETTIE'S MAPLE PIE

NORTH UNION SHAKER VILLAGE, OHIO

2 tablespoons butter
1 cup maple sugar
1¼ cups hot milk
3 eggs
2 tablespoons cornstarch

⅛ cup cold milk
½ teaspoon salt
1 unbaked 8 inch pastry* shell
⅛ teaspoon nutmeg

❬Melt butter and blend in maple sugar; gradually add hot milk and stir until sugar is well dissolved. Beat eggs, wet cornstarch with cold milk, and blend with hot mixture. Add salt. Turn into unbaked pie shell and sprinkle with nutmeg. Bake in a 350° F. moderate oven until custard is set, or until a silver knife inserted into it comes out clean. SERVES 6.

MARMALADE OR JAM PIE

HANCOCK SHAKER VILLAGE

¼ cup butter, warmed but not
    melted
⅓ cup sugar

2 eggs, beaten
3 tablespoons marmalade or jam
1 8 inch pastry* shell

❬Cream together well butter and sugar. It must be fluffy. Add beaten eggs and marmalade or jam. Mix all ingredients together. Pile into pastry shell and bake 30 minutes at 350° F. Serve with thick cream. SERVES 6.

. .

Mince pies were baked by the dozen by the Shakers and stored in barrels in some cold place where they froze and kept perfectly until used, when they were thawed out, heated, and eaten good and hot with lemon sauce.

MINCEMEAT FOR PIE

ENFIELD SHAKER VILLAGE, NEW HAMPSHIRE

3 pound beef tongue, boiled and
    chopped fine (cooked round of
    beef may be used instead)
½ pound suet, chopped fine
2 pounds seeded raisins
2 pounds currants
2 pounds white sugar
2 pounds dark brown sugar
½ pound citron, cut fine
¼ pound candied orange peel,
    cut fine

3 pints sour apples, peeled and
    chopped
1 tablespoon cinnamon
1 nutmeg, grated
1 teaspoon allspice
½ teaspoon salt
Rind and juice 2 lemons
1 cup Boiled Cider*
½ cup brandy

❰Blend all ingredients well and put into large crocks to ripen. The boiled-down cider and touch of brandy will keep it from spoiling while ripening. Keep sealed for at least 4 weeks in a cool place before using in pies. Bake between 2 crusts in a 350°F. oven for 45 minutes and serve hot. Use 2–3 cups mincemeat per pie. Recipe makes enough mincemeat for 18 pies. One pie SERVES 6–8.

LEMON SAUCE #1

1 cup Boiled Cider*   3 tablespoons lemon juice
2 tablespoons butter   1 teaspoon salt

❰Boil together above ingredients for 5 minutes. Yields about 1 cup.

LEMON SAUCE #2

½ cup butter   ½ cup boiling water
1 cup sugar   3 tablespoons lemon juice
3 egg yolks, slightly beaten 2 tablespoons grated lemon rind

❰Cream butter, add sugar gradually and slightly beaten egg yolks. Add water and cook over boiling water until mixture thickens. Remove from range, add lemon juice and rind. Serve hot. Yields about 2 cups.

MINCEMEAT PIE WITH PEAR

HANCOCK SHAKER VILLAGE

Mincemeat:
1 cup small seedless raisins   ½ cup lemon juice
½ cup blanched, shredded, toasted   2 cups brown or white sugar
    nuts (almonds or walnuts)   2 teaspoons cinnamon
2 cups peeled, cored, chopped apples 1 teaspoon ground cloves
½ cup candied orange peel   1 teaspoon nutmeg
         or   ½ teaspoon salt
½ cup orange marmalade

Pastry* for 2 crust 9 inch pie   3 tablespoons melted butter
8 pear halves

❰Mix all mincemeat ingredients together well. Put in jars in refrigerator until ready to use. Proceed as for any 2 crust pie.
    Prepare your best pie pastry and line pie pan. Cover the bottom with a layer of sliced poached (or canned) Bartlett or Kieffer pears. (The

Shakers raised both in great quantity.) Over this layer spoon out the mincemeat (given here). Top this with another layer of sliced pears. Cover with top layer of pastry. Cut "PM" or other gashes in top to let steam escape. In each of these cuts pour melted butter—about 3 tablespoons in all. Bake pie in hot 400° F. oven for 35 to 40 minutes and serve while warm. SERVES 8.

PEAR MARMALADE TARTS
HANCOCK SHAKER VILLAGE

([Boil 6 good-sized peeled pears to a pulp (reserve pulp). Weigh, take half this weight in sugar, put it into a saucepan with a very little water, boil it and skim while boiling. When boiled to point where it will spin a thread, add pulp of pears and boil for 5 minutes. Add about 4 drops of essence of cloves. When it is cool, fill 4 cooked tart shells. Cover with 1 cup heavy cream. SERVES 4.

PLUM JELLY TURNOVERS
HARVARD SHAKER VILLAGE

4 egg yolks
2 cups sugar
1 cup heavy cream

½ cup butter, melted
¼ cup plum jelly or jam
Pastry* for 2 crust 8 inch pie

([In top of double boiler blend egg yolks and sugar. Add cream, melted butter, and cut up jelly. Cook 10 minutes. Roll out enough pastry for 2 crusts. Cut rounds 5 inches across. Put a good tablespoon of mixture in center of round, cover with another round. Moisten edges and press together well with tine of fork first dipped in flour. Bake 20 minutes on greased tin sheet in moderate 350° F. oven. Makes 6–8 tarts. SERVES 6–8.

∴

Rhubarb planted by the Shakers at Hancock still grows luxuriously. It is very pink and sweeter than most varieties. The Shakers preserved it by fitting the raw pieces in glass jars, covering with water, and sealing tightly.

RHUBARB PIE
HANCOCK SHAKER VILLAGE

2 cups inch lengths rhubarb, use
   tender pink pieces
1½ cups brown sugar

1 tablespoon flour
3 tablespoons butter
Pastry* for two 8 inch crusts

[Combine rhubarb with sugar and flour, and turn into unbaked shell. Dot with butter, for the butter reduces the acid and takes the place of extra sugar. Cover with top crust, allowing steam vents, and bake in 450° F. hot oven for 15 minutes; reduce heat to 350° F. and bake a few more minutes until well browned. SERVES 6.

Variation: Use 1 cup rhubarb and 1 cup ripe, hulled sliced strawberries.

RHUBARB CUSTARD PIE
HANCOCK SHAKER VILLAGE

1½ cups sugar
3 tablespoons flour
½ teaspoon nutmeg
1 tablespoon softened butter
2 eggs

3 cups 1 inch pieces rhubarb
Pastry* for one 9 inch piecrust
   plus additional pastry for topping
Confectioners' sugar

[Combine sugar, flour, nutmeg, butter, and eggs. Beat until smooth. Put rhubarb into pastry-lined pie tin. Pour sugar-egg mixture on top Cover with lattice topping. Flute edge. Bake at 450° F. for 10 minutes. Reduce heat to 350° F. and bake 30 minutes longer. Sprinkle confectioners' sugar over pie after it comes out of the oven. SERVES 6–8.

RHUBARB AND LEMON PIE
MT. LEBANON SHAKER VILLAGE

3 cups diced rhubarb
Pastry* for two 9 inch piecrusts
   (if lattice topping is used some
   crust will be left over)
1 cup sugar
1 tablespoon flour

1 egg, lightly beaten
1 teaspoon grated lemon rind
½ cup water
1 tablespoon lemon juice
1 tablespoon butter

[Spread rhubarb on pastry-lined 9 inch pie tin. In a saucepan blend sugar and flour. Gradually stir in remaining ingredients. Cook over hot water constantly until thickened and smooth. Remove from heat. Pour over rhubarb. Cover with full crust or lattice crust. Bake at 425° F. for 30 to 40 minutes. SERVES 6–8.

ROSE WATER CREAM PIE
(Also Called Angel Cream Pie)
HANCOCK SHAKER VILLAGE

½ cup sugar
2 tablespoons flour
⅛ teaspoon salt
2 cups light cream, warmed
  slightly

2 teaspoons rose water
2 egg whites, beaten stiff
Unbaked 9 inch piecrust*

⟨[Mix dry ingredients and gradually stir in cream. Add rose water and lastly the stiffly beaten egg whites. Mix lightly but thoroughly. Pour into an unbaked piecrust and bake in a moderately hot 375° F. oven 10 minutes, then reduce heat to 325° F. and bake until well set and lightly brown on top (golden like an angel). Cool before serving. SERVES 6–8.

SOUR CREAM PIE
ENFIELD SHAKER VILLAGE, NEW HAMPSHIRE

1 cup brown sugar
1 tablespoon flour
1½ teaspoons mixed spices
1 cup raisins
1 cup sour cream

2 egg yolks, beaten
1 tablespoon melted butter
1 teaspoon vanilla
Unbaked 8 inch pie shell*
2 egg whites

⟨[Mix dry ingredients and raisins. To sour cream, add egg yolks and butter and flavoring. Stir into dry mixture and mix lightly, but thoroughly. Pour into an unbaked pie shell. Bake 10 minutes at 425° F. then reduce heat to 375° F. Bake about 20 minutes or until custard is firm and knife comes out clean when inserted in middle. Top with meringue made of beaten egg whites. SERVES 6.

SOUR CREAM BUTTERNUT PIE
HANCOCK SHAKER VILLAGE

Pastry* for one 8 inch piecrust
½ cup butter
½ cup brown sugar
¾ cup granulated sugar
4 eggs, lightly beaten

½ cup sour cream
¼ cup light corn syrup
1 teaspoon rose water
⅔ cup chopped butternuts

⟨[Preheat oven to 350° F. Line 8 inch pie tin with pastry. Melt butter in saucepan. Stir in all remaining ingredients except rose water and butternuts. Cook over low heat, stirring constantly for 5 minutes. Remove from heat, stir in rose water and butternuts. Pour into pastry-lined pie tin. Bake in preheated oven for 55 minutes. SERVES 6.

SISTER LIZZIE'S SUGAR PIE
SOUTH UNION SHAKER VILLAGE, KENTUCKY

1 deep unbaked 8 inch pie shell*
½ cup soft butter
1 cup maple or brown sugar
   (white can be used)
¼ cup flour, sifted

2 cups heavy cream
½ teaspoon rose water
   or
½ teaspoon vanilla
⅛ teaspoon nutmeg

([Line a deep pie tin with your best pastry. Cream butter and spread half of it over bottom. Then sprinkle with half the sugar. Repeat this process and sprinkle last layer with flour. Flavor the cream with rose water or vanilla and pour over all. Dust with nutmeg. Bake in hot 450° F. oven for 10 minutes. Reduce heat to 350° F. and bake until a knife blade inserted in the center of the pie comes out clean. This is a delicious pie, especially loved by children, and a good recipe to fall back on when the apple bins are empty in the spring. SERVES 6.

BASIC FRITTER RECIPE
HANCOCK SHAKER VILLAGE

1½ cups flour
2 teaspoons baking powder
¼ teaspoon salt
⅔ cup milk

1 egg, well beaten
Fruit pieces
Deep fat for frying
Sugar

([Mix and sift dry ingredients. Add milk gradually and then the well-beaten egg. Dip peeled fruit pieces into batter, and fry in deep fat. Drain. Sprinkle with sugar. Serve with a sauce or syrup, if desired.

DESSERT FRITTERS

Banana fritters are good served with melted currant jelly, or served with meat as a garnish. Use approximately 1 banana per serving.

Rhubarb fritters are tasty served with a fruit syrup, such as this one: Boil equal amounts of rhubarb and sugar 20 minutes and strain, approximately 1 cup each.

Apple fritters are delicious served with Shaker Applesauce* or Rose Water Cream.*

BLUEBERRY OR APPLE FRITTERS

MT. LEBANON SHAKER VILLAGE

1 cup flour	2 eggs
1 teaspoon baking powder	¾ cup blueberries (chopped,
2 tablespoons sugar	peeled apples may be substituted)
¼ teaspoon salt	Deep fat for frying
½ cup milk	Powdered sugar

⟨[Sift together dry ingredients, add milk and well-beaten egg yolks and beat the batter until smooth. Fold in stiffly beaten egg whites and then fold in blueberries. Drop by spoonfuls into deep hot fat and cook until a delicate brown. Drain on absorbent paper. Dust generously with powdered sugar and serve with Dessert Cream Sauce* or Berry Mountain Blueberry Syrup* and cream.

If apple fritters are made, dust with cinnamon as well as sugar. SERVES 4.

FRIED MOLASSES FRITTERS

SISTER OLIVE, HANCOCK SHAKER VILLAGE

1 cup flour	¼ cup molasses
2 teaspoons baking powder	3 eggs
¼ teaspoon salt	½ cup milk
1 cup corn or rye meal	Powdered sugar

⟨[Mix and sift dry ingredients. Add remaining ingredients except sugar. Beat well. Drop into hot fat and fry to a golden brown. Drain, roll in powdered sugar, and serve. Makes 18–24 fritters. Good with Spiced Sugar for Fritters.

SPICED SUGAR FOR FRITTERS

HANCOCK SHAKER VILLAGE

3 tablespoons powdered sugar or	⅔ teaspoon powdered nutmeg
very fine granulated sugar	⅔ teaspoon powdered cloves
⅔ teaspoon powdered cinnamon	

⟨[Mix well and sift. Sprinkle over fritters while hot.

Puddings and
Cream Desserts

```
┌─────────────────────────────────────────────────┐
│  ┌───────────────────────────────────────────┐  │
│  · :   PUDDINGS AND CREAM DESSERTS   : ·      │  │
│  └───────────────────────────────────────────┘  │
└─────────────────────────────────────────────────┘
```

ANGELS' PINK CREAM

HANCOCK SHAKER VILLAGE

6 egg whites
6 tablespoons powdered sugar
2 tablespoons melted currant jelly

2 cups heavy cream
1 tablespoon rose water

❲Beat the whites of the eggs until stiff, and then sweeten with powdered sugar. Into the egg whites beat the melted currant jelly to give it a pretty pink color. Then whip the cream and flavor it with rose water. Put the whipped cream in a pretty bowl and pour the pink preparation over it. Serve with cake. SERVES 6.

APPLE CREAM

WATERVLIET SHAKER VILLAGE, NEW YORK

1 dozen apples, pared, stewed, and
    strained
6 eggs
1 cup butter

2 cups sugar
1 teaspoon nutmeg
2 teaspoons lemon juice
1 cup heavy cream, whipped

❲Prepare apples, and add the eggs, butter, sugar, nutmeg, and lemon juice. Mix well and bake in a pudding dish for 40 minutes in a moderate 350° F. oven. Chill. Stir in whipped cream before spooning out. SERVES 6–8.

Note: This can be poured into a 9 inch pastry shell and baked as a pie.

BANANA CREAM MOLDED

ENFIELD SHAKER VILLAGE, CONNECTICUT

2½ tablespoons granulated sugar
1 cup light cream
1 envelope plain gelatin
¼ cup milk
2 egg yolks, beaten
½ teaspoon salt

2 large ripe bananas
1 teaspoon rose water
   or
1 teaspoon rum
1½ cups heavy cream

[Mix sugar and light cream together in double boiler and scald in top over boiling water. Soak gelatin in milk. Stir a little of the hot cream mixture into beaten egg yolks. Then add all of this to sugar and cream in double boiler. Add salt. Remove from heat. Add soaked gelatin and stir until completely melted. Cool, stirring to keep smooth. Peel bananas and mash. Stir in cooled custard and add flavoring. Beat heavy cream until stiff and fold into egg-gelatin-banana mixture. Place in a 1 quart mold and refrigerate until well set, about 6 hours. SERVES 6. Serve with fresh cream flavored with rose water or rum.

CHOCOLATE CREAM

NORTH UNION SHAKER VILLAGE, OHIO

½ cup gelatin
Cold water
1 quart milk, scalded
½ cup grated chocolate
½ cup white sugar

10 egg yolks
2 teaspoons vanilla
   or
2 teaspoons brandy

[Soak gelatin in cold water to cover. Add to hot milk and mix in the grated chocolate. Mix sugar and egg yolks together and add to milk mixture. Heat thoroughly to cook all ingredients. Let it thicken. Add vanilla or brandy. Strain. Put in half-cup molds and chill. Serve with sugar and heavy cream. Makes 10 molds.

CHOCOLATE DREAM

HARVARD SHAKER VILLAGE

8 egg yolks
1 cup confectioners' sugar
1¼ cups grated chocolate

½ cup hot coffee
1 teaspoon rum
8 egg whites

❮Place egg yolks and sugar in top of double boiler, over boiling water. Beat constantly. When foamy add chocolate melted in coffee. Continue to beat and heat slowly, until the custard begins to thicken. Add rum and remove from heat.

Beat egg whites until stiff, fold in the chocolate-custard-rum mixture. Serve at once in sherbet glasses or chill and serve with heavy cream flavored with a little rum. SERVES 6–8.

CHOCOLATE WHIP
HANCOCK SHAKER VILLAGE

½ cup water
1 tablespoon gelatin
4 tablespoons sugar
5 tablespoons grated rich chocolate

Rind and juice ½ lemon
1 teaspoon vanilla
2 egg whites

❮Put the water, gelatin, sugar, chocolate, lemon rind and juice into a pan. Heat until sugar and gelatin are dissolved. Allow to cool and add vanilla. Whip whites of eggs very stiffly. When chocolate mixture is cold but not setting, add in spoonfuls to the egg whites. Beat after each spoonful until very stiff. When all the mixture has been added pour into serving dish, chill, and decorate with whipped cream. SERVES 2–4.

GOOSEBERRY CREAM
ENFIELD SHAKER VILLAGE, CONNECTICUT

1 quart gooseberries
2 cups white sugar
1 quart milk
3 eggs

2 tablespoons sugar
2 teaspoons rose water
1 cup heavy cream

❮Stew gooseberries with 2 cups sugar. Strain through a sieve.

Make a custard: bring milk just to a boil, let cool a bit. Beat the eggs well and add sugar to this mixture. Very slowly add the warm milk. Return to medium heat and, stirring constantly, permit it to thicken. Add 2 teaspoons rose water. Cool. Stir custard into cooled gooseberries. Put in glass dish and refrigerate. Garnish with 1 cup whipped cream. SERVES 10–12.

MINCEMEAT CREAM MOLDS
HANCOCK SHAKER VILLAGE

2 tablespoons plain gelatin
½ cup cold rich milk
4 eggs, separated
½ cup sugar
¼ teaspoon salt
2 tablespoons cornstarch
3½ cups scalded milk

1 teaspoon rose water
1½ cups homemade Mincemeat*
2 tablespoons brandy
    or
2 tablespoons rum
4 tablespoons white sugar

([Soften gelatin in cold milk. Set aside. Mix beaten egg yolks, ½ cup sugar, salt, and cornstarch. Add to scalded milk. Cook in a double boiler until mixture coats the spoon. Add softened gelatin and stir until dissolved. Chill until slightly thickened. Add rose water. Fold in mincemeat and brandy or rum. Whip egg whites until soft peaks form. Beat in 4 tablespoons sugar. Fold into mincemeat mixture. Mold and chill. Makes 14 half-cup molds.

Serve with thick cream, runny, specially flavored with brandy.

SOUR CREAM PRUNE WHIP
ENFIELD SHAKER VILLAGE, NEW HAMPSHIRE

2 cups cooked prunes
5 tablespoons sugar
½ cup chopped nuts (optional)
½ teaspoon lemon
    or
½ teaspoon vanilla extract

    or
½ teaspoon rose water
1 cup sour cream

([Remove pits from prunes, chop and beat to a pulp. Add sugar, nuts, and extract and mix thoroughly. Whip cream until stiff with a fork. Add prune mixture in small amounts and mix thoroughly. Chill and serve. SERVES 4.

SPANISH CREAM
MARY WHITCHER'S SHAKER HOUSEKEEPER

⅓ cup gelatin
½ cup cold water
4 cups milk
3 eggs, separated
1 cup sugar

¼ teaspoon salt
2 teaspoons vanilla
    or
2 teaspoons rose water

¶[Put the gelatin in a bowl with half a cupful of cold water, and when it has stood an hour add it to 3 cups of the milk; then place the saucepan in which it is to be cooked (it should hold 2 quarts) into another of boiling water. Beat the yolks of the eggs with the sugar and salt. Beat the whites to a stiff froth. Add the remaining cup of cold milk to the yolks and sugar, and stir all into the saucepan with the milk-gelatin mixture. Cook 5 minutes, stirring all the time; then add the whites and remove from the fire. Add the vanilla or rose water, and pour into molds. Place on ice to harden. Serve with cream. SERVES 4–6.

SPRING CREAM MOLDED
MT. LEBANON SHAKER VILLAGE

⅓ cup brandy
⅓ cup seedless raisins
2 cups heavy cream
½ cup sugar
3 egg yolks

⅛ teaspoon salt
1 tablespoon granulated gelatin
2 tablespoons cold water
¼ cup each: fruit cordial, sherry
    wine, apple brandy

¶[Add brandy to raisins and cook in top of double boiler until raisins are soft. Simmer together over hot water, cream, sugar, egg yolks, and salt until thick; do not boil. Remove from range, add gelatin soaked in cold water. Strain, cool slightly, add flavorings. Stir until mixture thickens. Add raisins. Grease 4 cup mold, fill and chill overnight. Unmold and serve nicely decorated with spring flowers. Pass heavy, runny cream. SERVES 4–6.

SWISS CREAM
MARY WHITCHER'S SHAKER HOUSEKEEPER

½ cup gelatin
¼ cup cold water
1 cup boiling milk

1 cup sugar
2 teaspoons vanilla
4 cups heavy cream, whipped

¶[Soak gelatin 5 minutes in ¼ cup cold water. Add to hot milk. Stir until dissolved (about 2 minutes). Add sugar, stir until dissolved. Set dish in pan of ice water and stir until mixture begins to thicken (about 15 minutes). Add flavoring, fold in whipped cream. Put into molds. Refrigerate 4 hours before serving. SERVES 4–6.

VELVET CREAM

HANCOCK SHAKER VILLAGE

2 tablespoons strawberry jelly
2 tablespoons currant jelly
2 tablespoons powdered sugar

2 egg whites, stiffly beaten
1 cup heavy cream, whipped

⟨Combine the jellies and the sugar. Beat, then fold in egg whites. Fill 4 wineglasses half full of the whipped cream; fill to top with jelly. SERVES 4.

WINE CREAM #1

CANTERBURY SHAKER VILLAGE

4 cups heavy cream
1½ cups powdered sugar
2 glasses white wine (2 cups)

½ cup gelatin
4 cups water

⟨Mix 2 cups cream and sugar together, add the wine. Add rest of cream and beat very hard until it thickens. Boil gelatin and water until it is reduced by half. Strain lukewarm gelatin into cream mixture and set aside to thicken in a serving bowl or in separate sauce dishes.

Decorate in any case with whipped cream. SERVES 6–8.

WINE CREAM #2

MT. LEBANON SHAKER VILLAGE

½ cup gelatin
1 cup white wine
1 lemon, peel and juice

1 cup sugar
3 cups heavy cream

⟨Dissolve gelatin in the wine over the fire. Add peel and juice of the lemon, and when gelatin has dissolved add sugar. Let simmer, then strain. Add cream and beat until cold. Mold and let congeal. Serve with wine sauce. SERVES 4–5.

GINGER CUSTARD

SHIRLEY SHAKER VILLAGE

Canton ginger (preserved ginger)
4 eggs
½ cup sugar
2 cups milk

¼ teaspoon salt
½ teaspoon ginger (powdered)
2 tablespoons rum

⟨[Cut ginger in thin strips and use for garnishing sides of buttered individual molds. Beat eggs slightly, add sugar, milk, seasonings, and rum and strain into greased molds. Set in a pan of hot water and bake in slow 325° F. oven until firm; about 40 minutes. Makes 6 cups.

Serve with Boiled Custard Sauce* flavored with Ginger Syrup.

GINGER SYRUP
HANCOCK SHAKER VILLAGE

⟨[Use syrup from preserved ginger or boil together 1 cup water and 1 cup sugar for 10 minutes; add 2 teaspoons butter, 1 teaspoon powdered ginger. Simmer 2 minutes. Chill for jellied or cold desserts or use warm if dessert is warm. Makes 1½ cups.

MARY WHITCHER'S ORANGE SPONGE CUSTARD
MARY WHITCHER'S SHAKER HOUSEKEEPER

¾ cup sugar
1½ tablespoons butter
1 tablespoon grated orange rind
3 egg yolks, beaten

3 tablespoons flour
⅓ cup orange juice
1 cup milk
3 egg whites, beaten to a froth

⟨[Cream together sugar, butter, and grated orange rind. Add egg yolks and beat well. Stir in flour alternately with orange juice and milk. Beat the egg whites until stiff, but not dry. Fold them into the yolk mixture. Place batter in buttered custard cups or in a 7 or 8 inch ovenproof pudding dish. Set in a pan filled with 1 inch of hot water. Bake about 45 minutes at 325° F. for the cups and about 1 hour for the baking dish, or until set. Serve hot or ice cold with thick cream or Raspberry Sauce, Black Cherry Sauce (see next page), or best of all, cold Orange Sauce.* SERVES 4–6.

RASPBERRY SAUCE
HANCOCK SHAKER VILLAGE

2 cups raspberries
1 cup water

1 cup sugar
½ cup currant jelly

⟨[Cook raspberries in water for 20 minutes. Force pulp through a sieve. Add the sugar and jelly to pulp and any juice. Simmer for another 20 minutes until sauce becomes thick. Chill. Makes about 2 cups.

BLACK CHERRY SAUCE
HANCOCK SHAKER VILLAGE

2 cups cherries
1 cup water

1 cup sugar
½ cup brandy

⟨Cut cherries fine and cook in water until tender. Add sugar and cook until sauce is thick. Add brandy. Serve hot or cold. Makes about 2 cups.

HONEY CUSTARD
HANCOCK SHAKER VILLAGE

5 eggs, lightly beaten
½ cup honey
4 cups scalded milk

¼ teaspoon cinnamon
¼ teaspoon salt

⟨Beat eggs, add honey and scalded milk, cinnamon and salt. Pour into greased custard dishes and bake in pan of water in oven at 325° F. for 40 minutes. SERVES 4–6.

MARY WHITCHER'S APPLE PUDDING
MARY WHITCHER'S SHAKER HOUSEKEEPER

6 large apples
2 cups grated bread crumbs
⅔ cup butter

1 cup sugar
2 teaspoons nutmeg
1 cup cold water

⟨Pare and chop fine 6 large apples. Put in a pudding dish a layer of grated bread crumbs 1 inch deep, then a layer of apples. On this put lots of butter, sugar, and a dusting of nutmeg. Continue as before to repeat the layers and finally pour on a cup of cold water. Bake half an hour at 350° F. or until pudding is golden brown and bubbling. SERVES 4–6.

Serve with Wine Jelly Sauce: Blend together 2 cups heavy cream and ½ cup melted wine jelly. Makes 2½ cups.

SPICED APPLE PUDDING
MT. LEBANON SHAKER VILLAGE

¾ cup butter
1½ cups sugar
1 egg
1½ cups sifted flour
1½ teaspoons baking soda

1 teaspoon cinnamon
½ teaspoon allspice
½ teaspoon ground cloves
4 medium apples, peeled, cored, and chopped

❲Cream butter and sugar in mixing bowl until light. Beat in egg. Sift together all the dry ingredients. Stir into creamed mixture. Stir in apples. Turn into greased oblong pudding pan. Bake in 375° F. oven for 30 minutes.

Serve with heavy cream flavored with maple syrup or vanilla. SERVES 4–6.

APPLE BATTER PUDDING

MANUSCRIPT FROM SHAKER MUSEUM
OLD CHATHAM, NEW YORK

5 tart apples, peeled and chopped	⅓ cup sifted flour
1 cup brown sugar	½ cup sugar
½ teaspoon each cinnamon and nutmeg	¼ teaspoon salt
	1 tablespoon melted butter
2 tablespoons butter	2 eggs, beaten until foamy
¼ cup water	

❲Mix apples, sugar, and spices. Place in buttered pudding dish and dot with butter. Add the water. Sift dry ingredients and beat in melted butter and beaten eggs until mixture is light and fluffy. Spread over apples and bake at 450° F. for 10 minutes. Reduce heat to 350° F. and bake about 40 minutes. Serve warm with Lemon* or Custard Sauce.* SERVES 6.

Variation: Blueberries may be substituted for apples and if so, dust them with flour.

APPLESAUCE PUDDING

SHIRLEY SHAKER VILLAGE

3 cups applesauce	7 eggs, separated
2 cups sugar	1 nine inch piecrust,* baked
1 cup butter, melted	

❲Combine applesauce, sugar, and butter. Beat the yolks of 7 eggs and the whites of 3 together and fold into applesauce mixture. Cook over medium heat until it thickens. Pour into pie shell. Beat whites of 4 eggs until stiff. Spread over filling. Bake at 375° F. for 12 minutes until meringue is set and golden. SERVES 6–8.

BANANA PUDDING

NEW LEBANON SHAKER VILLAGE, 1858

8 bananas, very nice and ripe, skin
  removed
Sugar
Butter
Cinnamon

Lemon juice
1 tablespoon water
  or
1 tablespoon cider

(Cut bananas in half lengthwise. Place in buttered pie dish, sprinkle with sugar, a little cinnamon, dot with a few small pieces of butter, add dash of lemon juice. Add tablespoon of water or cider and bake in moderate 350° F. oven about 45 minutes. Serve hot with thick running cream, or cream whipped up with currant jelly. SERVES 6.

Recipe concludes: "It is not hard to get bananas in Albany. We buy a very large bunch and ripen in the Good Room." (Red skinned bananas seldom seen today were particular favorites.)

BIRD NEST PUDDING

FRANCES HALL, HANCOCK SHAKER VILLAGE

Batter:

1 cup sugar
2 cups sweet milk
2 cups flour
3 teaspoons baking powder[1]

¼ cup butter
2 eggs, beaten lightly
3 sour apples

(Mix batter ingredients together until quite soft and smooth. Cook pared and sliced sour apples, and when nearly done pour over them the batter and steam 1½ hours.

Sauce:

2 egg yolks
1 cup sugar
1 teaspoon cornstarch

1 lemon
½ cup butter
½ cup boiling water

(Beat egg yolks lightly and add the sugar mixed with cornstarch. Add the juice and rind of 1 lemon. Melt butter into boiling water. Stir egg-sugar mixture into boiling water with butter. Allow to thicken. Excellent. Yields 1½ cups sauce.

---

[1] I use 1 teaspoon of cream of tartar and 2 teaspoons of baking soda and like it much better.

BOILED BATTER PUDDING

MANUSCRIPT FROM SHAKER MUSEUM
OLD CHATHAM, NEW YORK

"To a quart of milk put 6 eggs, 8 large spoonfuls flour, teaspoon salt.
Boil an hour and ½. This is nice baked in a dish or in cups. Serve with
a nice sauce."
Directions for today's cook:

1 cup flour	4 cups milk
1 teaspoon salt	6 eggs, well beaten
½ cup sugar	

❨Sift flour and salt together, add sugar. Stir in milk and beaten eggs.
Bring to a boil and cook until thickened. Bake at 400° F. for 30 minutes.
Serve with a nice sauce. SERVES 4–6.

BLACK PUDDING

MT. LEBANON SHAKER VILLAGE

1 cup blackberry jam	2 teaspoons baking powder
½ cup butter	3 eggs, well beaten
1 cup sugar	4 tablespoons water
2½ cups flour	

❨To blackberry jam add butter and sugar creamed together. Add flour
sifted with baking powder. Add eggs beaten with water to a froth and
fold in. Bake 40 minutes in moderate 350° F. oven. SERVES 4–6.

BLACKBERRY PUDDING

MANUSCRIPT FROM SHAKER MUSEUM
OLD CHATHAM, NEW YORK

"Line a buttered pudding dish with nice fresh bread, cut thick without
crust. Have enough sweetened stewed blackberries with plenty of juice
to fill a baking dish. Pour it in and cover with more bread. Pare neatly
round and press down with a plate. Chill. It will turn out in a neat mold
when it is cold. Serve cold with a creamy sauce."

MARY WHITCHER'S BLACKBERRY PUDDING

MARY WHITCHER'S SHAKER HOUSEKEEPER

1½ cups flour
½ teaspoon salt
¼ teaspoon baking soda and ½
   teaspoon cream of tartar
      or
1 teaspoon baking powder

2 eggs, beaten
2 cups rich milk
2 cups blackberries (or blueberries
   or raspberries)
Flour to dredge berries

([Sift all dry ingredients together, add eggs and mix in milk. Beat well
and fold in berries dredged in flour.

Bake in moderate 350° F. oven in greased pudding dish for 1 hour and
10 minutes. A fine sauce should be served with this. SERVES 4–6.

BLUEBERRY PUDDING

HANCOCK SHAKER VILLAGE

2 cups bread crumbs
4 cups milk
4 eggs, separated
1 cup brown sugar
Grated lemon peel

2 tablespoons butter
1½ cups blueberries, ripe
⅓ cup white sugar
4 egg whites
½ cup sugar

([Mix the bread crumbs with the milk and let them set until soft. Beat
the yolks of the eggs and add the brown sugar and the grated lemon
peel. Soften the butter and beat it into the egg mixture, then combine
with the softened crumbs. Fold in 1 cup sweetened berries. Turn the
mixture into a buttered pudding dish with a wide top and bake until
firm about 1 hour in a moderately slow 325° F. oven. Be careful; over-
cooking will make it watery.

Remove from oven and top with remaining ½ cup of blueberries
(they must be ripe) while the pudding is steaming hot. Let it set until
cool. Top with a meringue made by beating the whites of the eggs until
stiff and adding white sugar. Put the pudding in a slow 300° F. oven
until the meringue is golden in color, but not brown. The combination
of cooked and uncooked berries is delicious. SERVES 6.

SHAKER MOUNTAIN BLUEBERRY PUDDING

HANCOCK SHAKER VILLAGE

([Butter 6 small thin slices of nice bread, spread with wild blueberry jam
(or any other jam or jelly), and lay them loosely in a buttered pudding

dish, filling it about half full. Pour over them 1 quart of hot Boiled Custard Sauce* and cool. Cover with a meringue made with 6 egg whites. Brown and serve cold. SERVES 4–6.

BASIC BREAD PUDDING
HANCOCK SHAKER VILLAGE

1 cup bread crumbs	½ teaspoon cinnamon
2 cups milk	½ teaspoon nutmeg
2 eggs, lightly beaten	Sauce of your choice
¼ cup sugar	

⟮Soak crumbs in milk for 20 minutes. Add eggs, sugar, and spices. Mix well, pour into greased 1 quart ovenproof dish, set dish in shallow pan containing hot water. Bake in 350° F. oven for 1 hour. Good with Brandy Sauce* or Hard Sauce*.

Variations: For Chocolate Bread Pudding, add 2 squares of unsweetened chocolate melted and 1 teaspoon vanilla—omit spices and increase sugar to ½ cup. Serve with chocolate sauce.

For Caramel Bread Pudding, melt ½ cup sugar and cook slowly until it browns. Add to milk and crumbs in basic recipe. Proceed from there on.

SISTER CATHERINE'S BREAD PUDDING
PLEASANT HILL SHAKER VILLAGE

3–5 cups diced fresh bread	¼ teaspoon salt
or	3 egg yolks
3½ cups stale bread or stale cake	⅓–½ cup sugar
3 cups warm milk	1 teaspoon vanilla
or	½ teaspoon nutmeg
2 cups milk and 1 cup fruit juice	

⟮Cut bread into slices and trim away crusts. Measure lightly, do not pack. Soak for 15 minutes in milk, add salt. Combine eggs, sugar, and vanilla and beat well, add nutmeg. Pour over the soaked bread. Stir lightly with a fork until well blended. Bake in pudding pan or baking dish, set in a pan of hot water, for about 45 minutes at 350° F. Cover with meringue and bake in 300° F. oven for 15 minutes. Serve with caramel sauce. SERVES 4–6.

MERINGUE

3 egg whites
½ cup sugar

1 teaspoon vanilla
1 teaspoon nutmeg

⟮For meringue beat 3 egg whites until stiff. Add ½ cup sugar gradually and lastly add vanilla. Dust with nutmeg. Drop by spoonfuls on top of pudding.

SISTER MARY'S FAVORITE BREAD PUDDING

HANCOCK SHAKER VILLAGE

2 cups pieces of bread
2½ cups milk
½ cup raisins
¼ cup finely sliced candied fruits

¼ cup chopped almonds (or walnuts)
1 teaspoon cinnamon
4 eggs, well beaten
1 cup sugar

⟮Break odd pieces of bread (no crusts) into boiling milk. Remove from heat. Cover tightly with cloth and allow to soak. The mixture should be solid. Beat all to a soft mush. Add some raisins, finely sliced candied fruits, chopped almonds or walnuts—almonds are best—and cinnamon. Add well-beaten eggs and sugar. Put into a greased baking dish, set in a pan of water. Cover with waxed paper, cook at 325° F. until set, about 1 hour. Serve with heavy cream. SERVES 4–6.

APPLE BREAD PUDDING

MT. LEBANON SHAKER VILLAGE

8 slices toast without crusts, cubed
  (5 cups)
1½ cups hot milk
4 tablespoons melted butter
5 eggs
¼ teaspoon salt
½ cup brown sugar

½ teaspoon cinnamon
¼ teaspoon nutmeg
½ cup raisins
1 teaspoon rose water
4 apples pared, cored, and diced
  (4 cups)
¼ cup brown sugar

⟮Combine 5 cups cubed toast with hot milk and 4 tablespoons butter. Let stand 30 minutes. Beat eggs until light. Add salt, sugar, cinnamon, nutmeg, raisins, rose water, and apples. Add to bread mixture. Turn into buttered 1½ quart baking dish. Sprinkle brown sugar over top. Bake uncovered at 300° F. for 45 minutes. Serve with Apple-Cream Sauce. SERVES 6–8.

APPLE-CREAM SAUCE

1 cup very heavy running cream
1 cup strained applesauce (if applesauce is unsweetened, add ½ cup white sugar)

1 teaspoon rose water
Cinnamon

❨If cream is heavy but runny do not beat. Fold in sweetened applesauce. Add rose water. Sprinkle with cinnamon. Pass in separate little dish.

Variation: Ripe peaches or apricots chopped fine can be substituted for apples. In that case puréed cooked peaches or apricots should be used instead of applesauce in the sauce. Check on sweetness as these two fruits need more sugar than apples. Combine sugar with fruit purée while still warm before folding into the cream. Add 1 teaspoon rose water to the sauce.

∴

The cherry season lasted 6 to 8 weeks in most Shaker communities because of the many varieties in their orchards. One family was very proud of its white cherry trees, and all of the villages canned the fruit in very large quantities. Shaker recipes call for canned cherries, meaning their own home-canned produce, with cans of various sizes. In testing we have specified commercial sizes rather than the contents of a Shaker jar or can.

CHERRY BREAD PUDDING
ENFIELD SHAKER VILLAGE, CONNECTICUT

2 cups new milk (fresh, whole milk)
3 eggs, slightly beaten
2 cups 1 inch cubes crustless day-old bread
½ cup white sugar

¼ teaspoon cinnamon
1 teaspoon rose water
¼ teaspoon salt
1 can (1 pound 4 ounces) tart red cherries and liquid

❨Combine milk and eggs; pour over bread cubes in a mixing bowl. Add ½ cup white sugar, the cinnamon, rose water, and salt. Drain cherries, reserving juice.

Add 1 cup of drained cherries to the bread mixture; toss ingredients lightly to blend. Spread mixture in greased 10x6 inch baking dish. Place dish in shallow baking pan in oven. Pour hot water around the dish 1 inch deep. Bake in moderate oven 350° F. for 40 to 50 minutes or until knife inserted in center and outer edges comes out clean. Serve with Cherry Sauce. SERVES 6–8.

CHERRY SAUCE #1

1 cup cherry juice and water
½ cup brown sugar

1 tablespoon cornstarch
½ cup cherries

❡Add water to cherry juice sufficient to make 1 cup. Mix ½ cup brown sugar and 1 tablespoon cornstarch in a saucepan. Stir in cherry juice. Cook and stir, bringing to a boil. Stir in remaining cherries and simmer, stirring to avoid lumps. Makes 1¾ cups sauce.

CHOCOLATE BREAD PUDDING
WATERVLIET SHAKER VILLAGE, NEW YORK

2 cups milk
1½ squares (1½ ounces) unsweetened chocolate
3 cups 1 inch cubes crustless day-old bread
¼ cup brown sugar
¼ teaspoon salt

1 teaspoon vanilla
1 tablespoon strong coffee (liquid form)
1 cup finely chopped nuts—walnuts or butternuts
2 eggs, slightly beaten

❡Combine milk and chocolate and cook over low heat, stirring until chocolate melts. Place bread cubes in mixing bowl, pour chocolate mixture over. Add brown sugar, salt, vanilla, coffee, nuts and beaten eggs. Mix well to blend. Butter a 10x8 inch baking pan. Spread mixture in pan. Place in larger baking pan. Pour hot water around it to 1 inch deep. Bake in moderate 350° F oven 30 to 35 minutes or until inserted knife comes out clean. Serve with the sauce below. SERVES 6.

SAUCE

1 cup runny heavy cream
¼ cup white sugar

1 tablespoon dry sherry or other wine

❡To the runny heavy cream add sugar and sherry or brandy. Yields about 1 cup.

COLD CHOCOLATE BREAD PUDDING

WATERVLIET SHAKER VILLAGE, NEW YORK

1 cup soft, stale bread crumbs	2 egg yolks, lightly beaten
1½ squares unsweetened chocolate	2 tablespoons butter
1 cup sugar	¼ teaspoon salt
2 cups rich milk	½ teaspoon vanilla

⟨[Add bread, chocolate, and sugar to 1½ cups cold milk, reserving ½ cup. Put in top of double boiler and let cook over boiling water until a smooth paste is formed. Add egg yolks, reserved milk, butter, salt, and stir into hot mixture. Cook until mixture thickens, then add vanilla. Turn into a buttered pudding dish and bake in a moderate 350° F. oven for 20 minutes. Cool slightly, cover with meringue, bake at 350° F. for 8 minutes. Serve very cold. SERVES 4–6.

MERINGUE

3 egg whites	½ teaspoon vanilla
½ cup powdered sugar	

⟨[For meringue beat the whites of 3 eggs until stiff and add gradually ¼ cup powdered sugar. Continue the beating, then fold in another ¼ cup powdered sugar and ½ teaspoon vanilla.

MAPLE BREAD PUDDING

FRANCES HALL, HANCOCK SHAKER VILLAGE

Maple syrup can be substituted for sugar in basic bread pudding or the following dish can be made on top of range when oven is not heated for baking.

¾ cup maple syrup	2 eggs
3 slices bread without crusts	2 cups milk
1 tablespoon butter	¼ teaspoon salt
½ cup nut meats (optional)	¼ teaspoon vanilla
1 teaspoon lemon juice	

⟨[Pour maple syrup into top of double boiler. Butter each slice of bread, cube, and add to syrup. Add nuts and lemon juice. Beat together eggs, milk, salt, and vanilla and pour over bread mixture. Do not stir. Set over gently boiling water and cook 1 hour. This pudding makes its own sauce. Spoon over each serving. SERVES 4–6.

Variation: Substitute ½ cup raisins for nut meats.

BROWN SUGAR PUDDING

SHIRLEY SHAKER VILLAGE

2 cups boiling water	1 cup sifted flour
1½ cups brown sugar	2 teaspoons baking powder
½ cup milk	½ cup seeded raisins
1 tablespoon soft butter	1 teaspoon vanilla

⟨Prepare syrup (or use 2½ cups maple syrup) by combining boiling water and 1 cup of sugar. Bring to boil and simmer. In mixing bowl combine milk, butter, ½ cup brown sugar, flour, and baking powder, beat until smooth. Stir in raisins and vanilla. Pour sugar syrup (or maple syrup) into greased pudding dish, pour batter in center of syrup. Bake at 350° F. for 25 to 30 minutes. SERVES 4–6.

CHERRY PUDDING

WATERVLIET SHAKER VILLAGE, NEW YORK

⟨Beat 2 eggs together without separating and add to 2 cups rich milk. Sift 3 cups of flour with 2 teaspoons of baking powder, add milk and eggs and ½ teaspoon of salt. Beat the batter vigorously; add a cup of sweet cream, or if you wish the pudding fluffy and light, a cup of thick sour cream and ¼ teaspoon of baking soda. Beat this batter well and stir in a quart of luscious rather tart cherries, pitted.

Bake pudding in a deep oven dish at 350° F. SERVES 6–8.

Serve with Cherry Sauce.

CHERRY SAUCE #2

½ cup butter	3 tablespoons boiling water
1 cup powdered sugar	2 teaspoons maraschino syrup
2 egg whites, unbeaten	2 tablespoons chopped cherries

⟨Beat butter and sugar to a cream. Add egg whites and boiling water. Put the bowl containing the sauce into a basin of hot water and stir sauce till it is smooth and frothy. Add finally with care maraschino syrup and chopped cherries. Continue beating a moment. Yields about 2 cups.

CHOCOLATE PUDDING #1
WATERVLIET SHAKER VILLAGE, NEW YORK

¼ cup butter
1 cup sugar
2 egg yolks, beaten until thick
½ cup milk
1¾ cups flour
3 teaspoons baking powder

⅛ teaspoon salt
2 egg whites, beaten stiff
1⅓ squares unsweetened chocolate, melted
½ teaspoon vanilla

⁅Cream butter and ½ of the sugar together. Beat eggs and remaining sugar and combine both mixtures. Add milk alternately with dry ingredients sifted together, then add whites, melted chocolate, and vanilla. Bake in a ring pan (angel cake pan) at 350° F. for 45 minutes. Remove from pan, cool. Fill center with whipped cream and pass chocolate sauce or pour sauce around outside of pudding. SERVES 4–6.

CHOCOLATE PUDDING #2
MARY WHITCHER'S SHAKER HOUSEKEEPER

4 cups milk
1 square semi-sweet chocolate
6 tablespoons sugar
1 tablespoon hot water
4 tablespoons cornstarch

4 eggs, separated
¼ teaspoon salt
2 teaspoons vanilla
or
2 teaspoons rose water

⁅Put the milk on to boil, reserving 1 cupful to mix with the cornstarch. Scrape the chocolate and add 2 tablespoons of sugar and one of hot water to it. Place over a hot fire and stir until dissolved, which will be in about 1 minute. Put this in the boiling milk. Mix the cornstarch with the cold milk. Beat the egg whites to a stiff froth. Beat the yolks of the eggs into this mixture and when the milk is *boiling* stir this mixture, the remaining sugar, and about ¼ of a teaspoonful of salt into it. Cook 6 minutes, stirring all the time; then add the beaten whites. Remove from the fire and add the vanilla or rose water. This pudding can be eaten cold or hot, with or without sugar and cream. SERVES 4–6.

BEST CHOCOLATE PUDDING
MT. LEBANON SHAKER VILLAGE

1 cup grated chocolate
3 egg yolks
2 cups heavy cream

1 tablespoon cornstarch
3 egg whites
1 cup sugar

([Melt chocolate over hot water, add yolks, cook until they thicken. Add cream, thickened with cornstarch. Boil up until it becomes like a custard. Pour in a glass dish and when cold beat the egg whites with sugar until stiff and put on top. Serve very cold. SERVES 4–6.

STEAMED CHOCOLATE PUDDING
HANCOCK SHAKER VILLAGE

3 tablespoons butter
⅔ cup sugar
1 egg, well beaten
2¼ cups flour
4½ teaspoons baking powder

¼ teaspoon salt
1 cup milk
2½ squares unsweetened chocolate, melted

([Cream butter and sugar well, add egg. Mix and sift flour with baking powder and salt and add alternately with milk to first mixture. Add chocolate. Turn into a buttered 4 cup mold. Set mold in large pan with 1 inch of water. Cover and steam 2 hours on top of stove or in oven. Serve with Cream Sauce. SERVES 4–6.

CREAM SAUCE

¼ cup butter
1 cup powdered sugar

½ teaspoon vanilla
¼ cup heavy cream

([Cream butter, add sugar gradually; add vanilla and cream, beaten until stiff. Yields 1-1½ cups.

CIDER PUDDING
MT. LEBANON SHAKER VILLAGE

1 tablespoon granulated gelatin
¼ cup cold water
1 cup boiling water

1 cup sugar (or ½ cup, if boiled cider is used)
¼ cup cider, plain or boiled*
3 egg whites

([Soak gelatin in cold water, dissolve in boiling water, add sugar and cider. Strain and set aside in cool place; occasionally stir mixture and when quite thick, beat with wire spoon or whisk until frothy; add whites of eggs beaten stiff and continue beating until stiff enough to hold shape. Mold or pile by spoonfuls on glass dish. Serve cold with Boiled Custard Sauce.* When cider is not available this makes a nice summer dish if lemon juice is substituted. SERVES 4.

BERKSHIRE CORNSTARCH PUDDING
HANCOCK SHAKER VILLAGE

2 squares unsweetened chocolate	3 tablespoons cornstarch
2¼ cups milk	¼ teaspoon salt
¼ cup sugar	½ teaspoon vanilla

❡Put chocolate and 2 cups milk in double boiler over boiling water. Mix sugar, cornstarch, and salt, and when well blended gradually pour on remaining ¼ cup milk. Add to milk which has been scalded with chocolate and cook 15 minutes, stirring constantly until mixture thickens and afterward occasionally. Flavor and put in a nice glass dish. Chill and serve with sweetened thick cream. SERVES 4.

MARY WHITCHER'S COTTAGE PUDDING
MARY WHITCHER'S SHAKER HOUSEKEEPER

1 tablespoon butter	1 teaspoon baking soda and 2
1 cup sugar	teaspoons cream of tartar
2 eggs, beaten	*or*
1 cup milk	3 teaspoons baking powder
2 cups flour	½ teaspoon salt
	1 tablespoon lemon juice

❡Cream butter and sugar and beat to a froth with the eggs. Then add the milk and lastly the flour sifted with other dry ingredients. Flavor with lemon juice and put in 2 shallow pudding dishes. Bake 30 minutes in a moderate 350° F. oven. Serve with Lemon Sauce.* The pudding is improved by sifting extra sugar over it before baking. SERVES 6.

CRANBERRY PULP PUDDING
HANCOCK SHAKER VILLAGE

❡Combine 1 cup cranberry sauce, 2 cups flour, 2 teaspoons baking powder, 1 teaspoon salt, 2 eggs, and enough sweet milk to make a batter a little thicker than for cakes. Steam 1 hour in well-greased custard cups set in a pan of hot water. Serve with about ½ cup Cranberry Sauce. SERVES 4–6.

CRANBERRY SAUCE

1 cup powdered sugar
2 tablespoons butter
1 egg, beaten

⅓ cup milk
1 tablespoon cranberry juice

❨Cream sugar and butter until very light. Add egg and beat in milk. Beat until sauce is foamy. Add juice. Yields about 1 cup.

FIRMITY

MT. LEBANON SHAKER VILLAGE

3 tablespoons whole wheat granules
2 cups boiling water
2 cups rich milk
½ cup raisins

4 egg yolks
1 cup sugar
1 tablespoon rose water
Heavy cream

❨Add wheat granules to boiling water in a double boiler. Stir and cook until it thickens; then add by degrees 2 cups milk, the raisins, and cook for ½ hour.

Beat egg yolks until light, add them and sugar to other ingredients and cook 2 minutes. Flavor to taste with rose water. Turn out to cool in delicate glass serving dish. Serve icy cold with heavy cream. SERVES 4–6.

SHAKER FLOATING ISLAND

HANCOCK SHAKER VILLAGE

1 tablespoon cornstarch
4 cups whole milk
5 eggs, separated
½ cup sugar

1 teaspoon rose water
or
1 teaspoon vanilla
¼ teaspoon salt
3 tablespoons sugar

❨Combine cornstarch with 2 tablespoons milk. Scald remaining milk in large saucepan. Beat egg yolks in small bowl. Add cornstarch mixture and ½ cup sugar to egg yolks. Stir in half the heated milk. Stir into milk in saucepan. Cook over low heat stirring constantly for 3 minutes. Add ½ teaspoon rose water. Pour into serving dish and cool. Beat egg whites very stiff. Add salt, sugar, and remaining rose water. Drop egg white mixture by spoonfuls into boiling water for 2 minutes. Remove with slotted spoon and float on custard. Chill. SERVES 6.

FUDGE BATTER PUDDING

HANCOCK SHAKER VILLAGE

2 tablespoons melted butter
1 cup sugar
1 teaspoon vanilla
1 cup sifted flour
3 tablespoons cocoa
1 teaspoon baking powder
¾ teaspoon salt

½ cup milk
½ cup chopped nuts
5 tablespoons cocoa
or
5 tablespoons grated chocolate
1⅔ cups boiling water

⟨Mix butter, ½ cup sugar, and vanilla together. Sift flour, 3 tablespoons cocoa, baking powder, and ½ teaspoon of salt together and add alternately with milk to first mixture. Mix well and stir in nuts.

Mix together ½ cup sugar, 5 tablespoons cocoa (or 5 tablespoons grated chocolate), ¼ teaspoon salt, and boiling water. Turn into 10x6x2 inch baking dish or pudding pan and drop batter by tablespoonfuls on top. Bake in moderate 350° F. oven for 40 to 45 minutes. Serve warm in baking dish—pass cream. SERVES 6.

Note: This pudding when baked has a chocolate sauce on bottom and cake on top. The sauce becomes thick if pudding gets too cool. Serve warm with thick cream—whipped or runny.

STEAMED GINGER PUDDING

HANCOCK SHAKER VILLAGE

1 cup butter
2 teaspoons sugar
2 eggs, well beaten
1 cup milk
2½ cups flour

3 teaspoons baking powder
¼ teaspoon salt
½ cup pieces preserved Canton
    ginger
1 teaspoon ginger syrup

⟨Cream butter and add sugar gradually. Add well beaten eggs: then add milk alternately with flour, mixed and sifted with baking powder and salt. Add ginger and ginger syrup and turn into a buttered mold. Steam 2¾ hours on rack in a kettle on top of stove. Add boiling water to come halfway up mold. Cover tightly. Adjust to keep water boiling throughout steaming time. Add water if necessary. Remove from mold and serve with Dessert Cream Sauce,* Boiled Custard Sauce,* or Hard Sauce.* SERVES 4.

GINGER FLUFF

HANCOCK SHAKER VILLAGE

2¼ cups flour, sifted
1½ teaspoons baking soda
½ teaspoon salt
1½ teaspoons ground ginger
½ cup butter

½ cup sugar
2 eggs, beaten
½ cup molasses
½ cup sour cream

⟮Sift flour, soda, salt, and ginger together. Cream butter and sugar together until light. Add beaten eggs and mix thoroughly. Stir in molasses. Add sifted dry ingredients alternately with sour cream beginning and ending with flour mixture. Turn into greased and floured 1 quart tin and bake in moderate 350° F. oven for 45 minutes. Serve very hot with Lemon Sauce.*

GOLDEN PUDDING

HANCOCK SHAKER VILLAGE

½ cup flour
¼ cup sugar
½ teaspoon salt
¼ cup suet

1 tablespoon baking powder
3 tablespoons milk
3 tablespoons jam, marmalade or
   maple syrup

⟮Mix dry ingredients and suet together with milk, put jam in bottom of greased pudding dish, put in the mixture (which must be stiff), and steam 1½ hours in a mold set on a rack in a kettle on top of stove. Add boiling water to come halfway up mold. Cover tightly. Adjust to keep water boiling throughout steaming time. Add water if necessary. SERVES 4.

GOOSEBERRIES IN BATTER PUDDING

ENFIELD SHAKER VILLAGE, CONNECTICUT

⟮Make a batter by combining ½ cup flour and ½ teaspoon salt; make a well in the flour and stir in 1 beaten egg. Add 1 cup milk and stir slowly. Beat the batter and let it stand for half an hour. Beat again and pour over 2 cups berries. Bake 30 to 40 minutes at 350° F. until golden brown. Dredge with sugar and cut in neat pieces. SERVES 6–8.

BAKED INDIAN PUDDING
FRANCES HALL, HANCOCK SHAKER VILLAGE

Each New England Shaker village had its favorite recipe for Indian pudding. We chose the following one with variations.

5 cups milk	A little allspice
4 tablespoons Indian meal (corn)	1 tablespoon butter
¼ teaspoon nutmeg	½ cup molasses
½ teaspoon cinnamon	¾–1 cup sugar
¼ teaspoon ginger	2 eggs, well beaten
1 teaspoon salt	

⟨Heat 4 cups of the milk and sprinkle the corn meal in slowly. Cook for a few minutes. Remove from fire and add other ingredients. Then add 1 cup cold milk; pour into a buttered 2 quart ovenproof dish and bake slowly at 300° F. for about 3 hours. Serve with cream or Hard Sauce.*

Variation #1:

5 cups milk	1 teaspoon allspice
4 tablespoons Indian meal (corn meal)	½ teaspoon cinnamon
	½ teaspoon ginger
½ cup molasses	2 eggs, well beaten
½ teaspoon salt	¾–1 cup sugar

⟨Scald 2 cups milk and add corn meal. Cook ½ hour in double boiler. Cool and add 2 cups cold milk, molasses, salt, all the spices, eggs, and sugar. Stir up well. Bake ½ hour in greased 2 quart baking dish at 300° F. Add 1 cup cold milk and bake slowly at 300° F. for 2 hours.

Variation #2:

⟨Proceed as for above. Grease baking dish, arrange 3 sweet apples, peeled, cored, sliced on bottom. Pour pudding over. Maple sugar can be used instead of white sugar. Serve with Apple Ice Cream.*

JAM SPONGE PUDDING
HANCOCK SHAKER VILLAGE, 1887

1 cup any kind jam	¼ cup granulated sugar
½ cup flour	¼ cup ground nuts (almonds best,
Pinch salt	but hazelnuts will do)
1 teaspoon baking powder	1 egg
¼ cup butter	2 tablespoons milk

⟮Spread the jam in the bottom of a buttered 8 inch pie pan. Mix flour, salt, and baking powder and sift them together. Then mix in the butter. Stir in the sugar, almonds, then add the well-beaten egg and the milk. Put this mixture on the jam and bake in a moderate 350° F. oven for half an hour. SERVES 4.

LEMON CURD
(Sometimes Called Lemon Cheese)
HANCOCK SHAKER VILLAGE

2 cups butter   6 lemons
4 cups white sugar   6 eggs

⟮Use a double boiler and put butter in the inner pan, add white sugar. While these are melting, grate the rind of 4 lemons into a cup, and into another cup put the juice of the 6. (The rinds of 2 lemons are not used.) Thoroughly beat the eggs. When the sugar and butter are properly melted, stir the grated lemon rind into the mixture, then the juice, and lastly the eggs. Cook while it thickens. Should be moderately firm when cold. Makes 8–10 cups. Can be eaten with cream or used as a tart filling.

KENTUCKY PUDDING
MANUSCRIPT FROM SHAKER MUSEUM
OLD CHATHAM, NEW YORK

"1 teacup of butter, 1 of cream, 2½ cupfuls sugar, yolks of 4 eggs well beaten, 1 tablespoon flour. Flavor to taste with bourbon. Bake in a rich paste."

Directions for today's cook:

1 cup butter   1 tablespoon flour
2½ cups sugar   1 tablespoon old bourbon
1 cup heavy cream   1 unbaked 8 inch pie shell*
4 egg yolks, well beaten

⟮In small saucepan melt butter, add sugar and cream. Bring just to the boil. In mixing bowl beat eggs, stir in flour and first mixture. Add old bourbon and pour into pastry-lined pie tin. Bake at 375° F. for 35 minutes or until set. SERVES 4–6.

KENTUCKY LEMON PUDDING

MANUSCRIPT FROM SHAKER MUSEUM
OLD CHATHAM, NEW YORK

¾ cup butter
2½ cups sugar
1 tablespoon lemon juice
3 eggs, beaten

1 teaspoon vanilla
¼ teaspoon salt
1 unbaked 8 inch pastry* shell

⟨[Melt butter, stir in sugar and lemon juice. Bring to boil. Remove from heat. Add eggs, vanilla, and salt. Turn into pastry-lined 8 inch pie tin. Bake at 375° F. for 35 minutes. SERVES 4–6.

LEMON MERINGUE PUDDING

HANCOCK SHAKER VILLAGE

2 cups milk
1 cup fine fresh breadcrumbs
1 tablespoon butter
½ cup sugar

2 eggs, separated
Grated rind and juice 1 lemon
1 tablespoon confectioners' sugar

⟨[Warm milk and pour on bread crumbs. Beat butter and sugar to a cream, add egg yolks and grated rind of lemon and mix with milk and breadcrumbs. Bake at 350° F. until slightly brown, about 20 minutes. Beat egg whites to a stiff froth with a tablespoon of confectioners' sugar and juice of the lemon. Put on top of mixture, brown slightly. Excellent hot or cold, with or without cream. SERVES 4.

MAPLE NUT PUDDING

FRANCES HALL, HANCOCK SHAKER VILLAGE

1½ cups brown sugar
2 cups boiling water
⅓ cup cornstarch
¼ cup cold water
3 egg whites

½ cup broken up English walnut
    meats
3 tablespoons maple syrup
¼ teaspoon salt

⟨[To the brown sugar add boiling water and cornstarch diluted with cold water. Cook over flame until mixture thickens, stirring constantly. Then cook in double boiler, 15 minutes, stirring occasionally. Remove from range and add whites of eggs, beaten until stiff, nut meats, maple syrup, and salt. Mold and chill. Serve with Custard Sauce* made of yolks of eggs. SERVES 4–6.

MOLASSES PUDDING

MANUSCRIPT FROM SHAKER MUSEUM
OLD CHATHAM, NEW YORK

2½ cups sugar
1 cup molasses
3 eggs, separated

1 teaspoon butter
2 teaspoons heavy cream
1 unbaked 8 inch pastry* shell

⟨Combine sugar and molasses. Beat in beaten yolks. Add butter and cream. Heat for 10 minutes. Fold in stiffly beaten whites. Pour into pastry-lined pie tin. Start baking in a 400° F. oven for 10 minutes, then reduce to 350° F. until knife inserted in center comes out clean—about 20 minutes more. SERVES 4–6.

MOUNTAIN DEW PUDDING

FRANCES HALL, HANCOCK SHAKER VILLAGE

3 tablespoons sugar
2 egg yolks
½ cup finely rolled cracker crumbs
4 teaspoons coconut

1 tablespoon lemon juice
2 cups milk
2 egg whites
1 cup sugar

⟨Cream sugar and yolks together, adding cracker crumbs and mixing well. Add coconut, lemon juice, and milk and beat well 2 minutes. Pour into greased pudding dish. Frost with meringue of the 2 egg whites beaten stiff with 1 cup sugar. Bake 30 minutes at 350° F. SERVES 4.

∴

Gail Borden worked at the New Lebanon Shaker Village perfecting his process to condense milk. The Shakers' fruit condenser was the model for Borden's invention. The Shakers used condensed milk as soon as it was marketed and this dessert was a favorite.

MT. LEBANON PUDDING

MT. LEBANON SHAKER VILLAGE

⟨Boil unopened can of condensed milk in boiling water for 4 hours. When well chilled, open and slide onto glass plate. Delicious. SERVES 4.

NUT PUDDING
MT. LEBANON SHAKER VILLAGE

½ cup crustless day-old bread cubes
1½ cups milk
3 eggs
⅔ cup white sugar

½ cup finely chopped butternuts or walnuts
⅔ cup butter
Fine breadcrumbs and butter for topping

[Soak bread in the milk. Separate eggs, beat yolks with the sugar until they are light and creamy. Add the bread, nuts, and softened butter. Beat well together. Beat the egg whites until stiff. Fold them into mixture. Butter a baking dish. Fill with the mixture. Top with fine breadcrumbs and dot with butter. Bake in 325° F. oven for 30 minutes. Serve with heavy sweetened cream. SERVES 4.

ORANGE MARMALADE PUDDING
HANCOCK SHAKER VILLAGE

½ cup butter
⅔ cup flour
1 teaspoon baking soda
¼ cup milk

4 tablespoons orange marmalade
3 egg yolks
½ cup sugar
3 egg whites

[Melt butter, add flour and soda, and stir well to blend. Pour on milk, stirring constantly, and bring to boiling point. Add marmalade to egg yolks, beat until thick. Add sugar, beat again. Combine mixtures and fold in stiffly beaten whites. Turn into buttered mold and steam on a rack in a kettle on top of stove. Add boiling water to come halfway up mold. Cover tightly. Adjust to keep water boiling throughout steaming time. Add water if necessary. Steam 1 hour. Serve with Orange Sauce.* SERVES 4.

Variation: Another preserve such as cherry, strawberry, or raspberry could be substituted for marmalade, but add a little juice to make consistency less condensed. In that case another suitable sauce should be served, or serve with Honey Pudding Sauce.*

ORANGE PUDDING
HARVARD SHAKER VILLAGE

4 large oranges
1 cup white sugar
1 quart milk
2 tablespoons cornstarch

3 egg yolks, beaten lightly
1 unbaked 8 inch pastry* shell
4 eggs whites, beaten stiff
Powdered sugar to taste

([Peel, seed, and cut in small pieces 4 good-sized oranges. Add a cupful of white sugar and let it stand awhile. Into a quart of nearly boiling milk stir 2 tablespoons cornstarch mixed with a little water and the yolks of 3 lightly beaten eggs. When cooked to the consistency of thick custard, put away to cool. When cool, mix with the orange and sugar. Cook the above pudding in a pastry shell for 35 minutes at 350° F. When done, make a meringue with whites of 4 eggs beaten stiff with powdered sugar to taste. Spread on pudding and return to oven to brown lightly. This pudding is very similar to a lemon meringue pie. SERVES 4–6.

POOR MAN'S PUDDING
MARY WHITCHER'S SHAKER HOUSEKEEPER

⅔ cup flour
¼ teaspoon salt
½ teaspoon baking soda
1 cup raisins

1 cup sour milk
1 cup molasses
2 eggs, beaten until light

([Sift dry ingredients together and add raisins. Stir in sour milk and molasses and beat well. Since the eggs make this pudding light be sure they are beaten well. Beat into mixture and pour into greased pudding dish. Bake at 325° F. for 40 minutes or put mold into pan of water in 400° F. oven and steam 1½ hours. Pudding can also be steamed on top of stove. See Orange Marmalade Pudding* for directions. Serve with Honey Pudding Sauce.* SERVES 4–6.

RASPBERRY PUDDING WITH BOILED CUSTARD SAUCE*
HANCOCK SHAKER VILLAGE

2 cups raspberries
2 cups water
1 cup sugar

4 tablespoons cornstarch
½ teaspoon salt
Boiled Custard Sauce*

([Boil berries in water, add sugar. Cook until sugar melts. Rub cornstarch in a little water until smooth. Stir into boiling fruit. Add ½ teaspoon of salt.

Pour into individual buttered custard cups. Cool in refrigerator. Unmold onto separate plates or on a platter. Surround with Boiled Custard Sauce. Do not pour sauce over the fruit mold as it is not so pretty. Raspberry mold must look as if it were floating in sauce. Flavor custard sauce with cinnamon *or* vanilla but not both, or rose water. SERVES 4.

RHUBARB SCALLOP WITH MERINGUE
FRANCES HALL, HANCOCK SHAKER VILLAGE

1 cup granulated sugar
Grated rind 1 orange
1 teaspoon salt
1 cup cooked rhubarb, unsweetened

1 six inch white cake or pound cake
2 egg whites
2 tablespoons powdered sugar

⟨Add sugar, orange rind, and salt to rhubarb and mix well.

Cut cake in thin slices. Line bottom of greased 9 inch baking dish with 3 or 4 slices. Cover with ¼ of rhubarb mixture. Continue to make alternate layers of cake and fruit until all material is used. Cover, bake in moderate 350° F. oven for 30 minutes.

Beat egg whites until stiff, add powdered sugar slowly, beat until blended. Pile on baked pudding and bake 15 minutes longer or until meringue is lightly browned. Serve plain or with Custard Sauce* or heavy cream.

Sponge cake, pound cake, or any plain leftover cake may be used. SERVES 6–8.

∴

In cooking rhubarb to eat as a dessert sauce, cover cut up fruit with boiling water and let stand for 15 minutes. Drain. Then add sugar and cook. This reduces amount of sugar needed.

RHUBARB YORKSHIRE
HANCOCK SHAKER VILLAGE

⟨Heat ¼ cup butter in a 1 quart dish in a hot 425° F. oven until butter bubbles. Meanwhile beat 2 eggs with ¾ cup milk. Gradually beat in ¾ cup flour sifted with ½ teaspoon salt. Pour batter into bubbling butter. Drop into center of batter 1 cup ¾ inch lengths rhubarb.

Bake in 425° F. oven for 25 minutes or until crust is browned. Serve in dessert dishes and spoon on this hot topping:

Melt ⅓ cup butter. Stir in about a cup of brown sugar. Cook until it becomes a thick syrup. Spread over the pudding and pass heavy cream. SERVES 4–6.

Variation: Apples can be substituted for rhubarb.

RICE PUDDING
WATERVLIET SHAKER VILLAGE, NEW YORK

½ cup sugar
1 quart milk
¼ cup uncooked rice

Pinch salt
1 teaspoon cinnamon

❨Mix all together and bake slowly for 4 hours. Stir occasionally during first 2 hours—then *do not touch.* Pudding will be pink—oven should be 250° F. Serve with heavy cream. SERVES 2–3.

ROSE CREAM PUDDING
MT. LEBANON SHAKER VILLAGE

❨To 1 cup of boiled white rice add, by folding in, the whites of 6 eggs, beaten stiff and sweetened to taste. Add 3 tablespoons sweet rich heavy cream last. Flavor with rose water. Mix carefully and lightly. Serve chilled. SERVES 4–6.

MARY WHITCHER'S ROCK CREAM PUDDING
MARY WHITCHER'S SHAKER HOUSEKEEPER

❨This will be found to be a very ornamental as well as a delicious dish for a supper table. Boil a cup of the best rice until quite soft, in whole milk. Sweeten with powdered sugar and pile it upon a dish. Lay on it in different places square lumps of either currant jelly or preserved fruit of any kind; beat up the whites of 5 eggs to a stiff froth with a little powdered sugar and flavor with either orange-flower water or rose-flower water. Add to this when beaten very stiff about a tablespoon of rich heavy cream, and drop it over the rice, giving it the form of a rock of snow. SERVES 6–8.

SPONGE PUDDING

SHIRLEY SHAKER VILLAGE

⟪Mix ¼ cup of sugar, ½ teaspoon of salt, and ½ cup of flour. Blend with ½ cup of cold milk. Stir slowly into 2 cups of hot milk. Cook until thick and smooth. Then add ¼ cup of butter and 1 teaspoon of vanilla. When well blended, stir this mixture into the beaten yolks of 4 eggs. Then fold in the stiffly beaten whites of 4 eggs.

Pour the pudding into a shallow greased baking dish. Place in a pan of hot water and bake for 1 hour in a moderately hot 400° F. oven. Serve with Currant Sauce* or Hot Maple Sauce.* SERVES 4.

STEAMED PUDDING

SABBATHDAY LAKE SHAKER VILLAGE

1 cup molasses	1 teaspoon mixed spices, such as
1 cup sweet milk	cinnamon, nutmeg, mace
1 cup raisins	1 teaspoon baking soda
½ cup butter	½ teaspoon salt
	4 cups flour

⟪Mix all together thoroughly and steam 3 hours in greased mold in pan of water in 350° F. oven. Use other fruit beside raisins if you wish. SERVES 4–6.

SUET PUDDING

HANCOCK SHAKER VILLAGE

3 cups flour	1 teaspoon cinnamon
1 teaspoon baking soda	1 cup molasses
1½ teaspoons salt	1 cup milk
½ teaspoon each ginger, cloves, nutmeg	1 cup finely chopped suet

⟪Mix and sift dry ingredients. Add molasses and milk to suet; combine mixtures. Turn into buttered mold, cover and steam 3 hours in pan of water set in 350° F. oven. Serve with a nice sauce such as Apples and Rum,* chilled Boiled Custard,* Hard,* or Foamy.* SERVES 4–6. Raisins and currants may be added or a special sauce for suet puddings given below.

SAUCE

½ cup butter
1 cup brown sugar
4 tablespoons heavy cream

1 teaspoon vanilla
or
2 tablespoons dry wine or brandy

⟬Cream butter and sugar together, gradually adding cream, and flavoring drop by drop, to prevent separation. Yields 1½ cups sauce.

SUMMER PUDDING
(A Molded Pudding)
MT. LEBANON SHAKER VILLAGE

⟬Made with raspberries, currants, blackberries, or blueberries.

In a greased 4 to 6 cup mold lined with unbuttered bread without crusts, add layers of one of the fruits, sugar, more bread, and repeat. Stand overnight to draw out juice. Next day—unmold—slice. Serve with heavy cream. SERVES 4–6.

SWEETMEAT PUDDING
MT. LEBANON SHAKER VILLAGE

⟬Pastry* for two 9 inch bottom crusts. Spread over each crust a nice cherry preserve or another acid preserve—but cherry is best. Beat 4 eggs, 2 cups sugar, 1 teaspoon melted butter, and 1 teaspoon of flour together. Pour this mixture over the preserves in each pie shell and bake. Spread a meringue made of 2 beaten egg whites sweetened with ½ cup sugar over the puddings and brown lightly.

Bake at 400° F. for 10 minutes—then reduce to 350° F. for 20 minutes—but watch so meringue is not too brown. Makes 2 pies, each serving 6–8.

MARY WHITCHER'S ORANGE SOUFFLÉ
MARY WHITCHER'S SHAKER HOUSEKEEPER

5 eggs, separated
¼ cup granulated sugar
2 cups milk

½ teaspoon salt
5 oranges
3 tablespoons powdered sugar

❡[Beat the yolks of 5 eggs and the whites of 2, with the granulated sugar. Bring the milk to a boil and stir in the egg-sugar mixture. Stir for about 2 minutes, until it begins to thicken. Add the salt and set aside to cool. Pare the oranges, remove the seeds, cut up the pulp fine, and put in a glass dish. Pour on the cold custard. Just before serving, beat the 3 remaining whites with the powdered sugar, and heap upon the custard. Serve very cold. SERVES 4–6.

MARY WHITCHER'S RICE AND ROSE WATER SOUFFLÉ

MARY WHITCHER'S SHAKER HOUSEKEEPER

½ cup rice
1 cup cold water
1 quart rich milk
4 tablespoons sugar

1 teaspoon salt
6 egg yolks, beaten
1 tablespoon rose water
6 egg whites, beaten to a stiff froth

❡[Wash rice and put it on to boil with water. As soon as the water is all absorbed, add milk and cook 1 hour in a double boiler; then add sugar, salt, and the beaten egg yolks. Let the mixture cool. Then add 1 tablespoon of rose water and the egg whites beaten to a stiff froth. Turn into a buttered pudding dish and bake in a moderate 350° F. oven for 25 minutes. SERVES 6.

Candies and Maple Desserts

Sister Lydia loves her work,
The nicest things she makes
She knits fur caps and nice fur gloves,
and moulds out sugar cakes.
—Sister Genevieve DeGraw
Mt. Lebanon Shaker Village, 1898

MAPLE TREES were planted in large groves in Shaker communities. A most useful tree, it furnished wood for the cabinet makers and rich ingredients for the Kitchen Sisters. In the early days white and even brown sugar was scarce, but maple sugar, maple syrup, molasses, and honey were readily available for sweet concoctions. The sale of maple products was most profitable, with thousands of gallons being harvested by each community annually. Letters in *The Manifesto* record: "we have collected 3,536 gallons so far and the end is not in sight," and again: "this has been one of the best maple harvests in years—quality excellent Grade A and extra fancy." Sap buckets had to be scrubbed spotlessly clean, hung on the trees, watched carefully, and emptied without loss. But there was some fun, too. Sugaring-off parties were a relief from the hard labor involved, and the account of this young sister is a record of some fun in the daily routine.

"The Sugar Making season was another time of fun and frolic and labor all melted into one. At North Union we made gallons of luscious syrup which we had every Sabbath breakfast on golden hot cakes. While the brethren tapped the trees, carried the buckets and filled the large sap kettles, the sisters stirred and strained and sealed into jugs the rich harvest. Again they boiled down the syrup and measured it off into large cakes of dark sugar. We children did our mite toward the harvesting and were allowed a certain fee in boiling syrup which we dropped bit by bit on the remnants of snow along the hedgerows. These golden pellets of sweet wax were ample pay for long hard days of labor in the woods each spring.

"Our camp of a thousand sugar maples was on the side of a hill about two miles from the settlement. Here the great sheet-iron kettles were in later years arranged one above another and connected with pipes and faucets. In the early spring a detachment of sisters went out and washed all the wooden buckets before they were hung on the camp and then brought by ox sled to the sugar shop where a certain amount was made into sugar. . . . Shaker syrup is remarkably fine because it is clarified by the addition of milk—one quart to twelve gallons of syrup but it must be put in at just the right moment in order to produce the right results. The syrup was stored in two gallon jugs, sealed with resin and one of these jugs was opened every Sabbath morning for the family breakfast. . . . When all the sap was in, there came another day of bucket washing and the older ones and the lunch coming along on an ox sled. When we reached the camp we found roaring fires under the sap kettles to supply us with hot water for it was no small task to wash a thousand sticky wooden pails. We fell to and scrubbed and rinsed for when they were all stacked away each in its proper place, we had our playtime. The more sedate sisters walked among the trees and communed with nature but we younger ones swung on the branches and played bean-bags and romped like real girls. The presence of the brethren added real zest to our pleasuring. The older boys broke steers at camp and they were certain to be exercising their teams on that particular day! Those who were skilled in whittling and wood working had fine new yokes and sledges for the occasion. Of course we were forbidden to speak to them unless it was absolutely necessary! At dusk we rode home over the rough log roads in the ox sleds and suddenly realized how tired we were; on falling asleep that night we would dream of lurching and plunging steers, maple candy, swings and the fascinating young brethren! !"

In most of the Shaker communities the sisters made excellent candies which were much sought after by the World. A Hancock note says:

"Visitors have cleaned us out of candy and we have Christmas orders to keep us busy for weeks on end—how will we ever fill them all—we did last year, but now there is even more demand.

"Crystallized fruits, fruit peels, sugared nuts, and rock candy put up in pretty boxes are much asked for, also peppermints plain and with chocolate. The horehound candy is excellent for coughs. It is a great favorite."

HOREHOUND CANDY #1
HANCOCK SHAKER VILLAGE

3 tablespoons dried horehound herb, leaf, stem, and flowers
2½ quarts boiling spring water or rain water
½ cup fresh lemon thyme leaves
3 cups granulated sugar

1 teaspoon cream of tartar to 2 cups of the horehound brew
1 teaspoon butter
1 teaspoon lemon juice
Confectioners' sugar

⟨Steep horehound in boiling water, let it stand 5 minutes; add lemon thyme and let stand another 5 minutes. Strain and squeeze through cheesecloth. Allow tea to settle. Then decant, pour clear tea into another vessel without disturbing sediment which has fallen to the bottom of the brew. Add 3 cups of granulated sugar, and to every cup of horehound tea add 1 teaspoon of cream of tartar. Boil to 240° F. and add teaspoon of butter and continue boiling without stirring until the temperature reaches 312° F. Remove from the fire and add 1 teaspoonful lemon juice. Pour into a buttered pan. When cool, mark into squares. Roll squares in confectioners' sugar and pack in airtight jars. Excellent for sore throats. Makes about 1 pound.

HOREHOUND CANDY #2
HANCOCK SHAKER VILLAGE

2 cups boiling water
1 square inch prepared, pressed horehound (a large piece of fresh root, cleaned and pressed)

3 cups sugar
½ teaspoon cream of tartar
Sugar

⟨Pour boiling water over horehound which has been separated into pieces; let stand 1 minute, then strain through double cheesecloth. Put in a granite kettle with 3 cups sugar and cream of tartar, boil until mixture becomes brittle when tried in cold water. Turn into a buttered pan, cool slightly, then mark in small squares. For horehound drops, take up squares when still somewhat soft, shape into balls and roll in sugar. Will keep if tinned. Makes about 1 pound.

APPLE LEATHER
MT. LEBANON SHAKER VILLAGE

2 tablespoons unflavored gelatin
½ cup cold Shaker Applesauce,*
  strained
¾ cup hot applesauce, strained

2 cups sugar
1 cup chopped walnuts or butternuts
1 tablespoon vanilla
Confectioners' sugar

❨Soak gelatin in ½ cup cold applesauce for 10 minutes. Combine the hot applesauce with the sugar and boil 10 minutes. Add gelatin mixture and simmer 15 minutes, stirring constantly. Remove from heat, then add nuts and vanilla. Pour into lightly buttered 9x9 inch pan and let set overnight. Cut in squares and roll in confectioners' sugar. This makes a very chewy candy and therefore is called "leather." Makes 16–18 pieces.

BUTTER SCOTCH
FRANCES HALL, HANCOCK SHAKER VILLAGE

2 cups brown sugar
2 tablespoons vinegar
1 cup butter

1 cup water
½ tablespoon vanilla

❨Boil ingredients together without stirring until mixture becomes brittle when tried in cold water. Pour into a buttered pan to ⅓ inch in thickness—cool slightly and mark in squares. When cool wrap each little piece in wax paper. The neatness of the candy makes an appealing sale. Makes 12–16 pieces.

Variation: Use 1 cup white sugar in place of brown sugar, ¼ cup of molasses, 1 tablespoon vinegar, 2 tablespoons boiling water, and ½ cup butter. Cook a vanilla bean with other ingredients and proceed as for other Butter Scotch. This gives a variety if too much molasses is on the shelf.

CHOCOLATE CREAM CANDY
HANCOCK SHAKER VILLAGE

1 tablespoon butter
2 cups white sugar
⅔ cup milk

2 squares unsweetened chocolate
1 teaspoon vanilla

❨Put butter into granite saucepan; when melted add sugar and milk. Heat to boiling point. Add chocolate and stir constantly until chocolate is melted. Boil 13 minutes, remove from fire, add vanilla and beat until creamy and mixture begins to sugar slightly around edge of saucepan. Pour at once into a buttered pan, cool slightly, and mark in squares. Omit vanilla if desired and add, while cooking, ½ teaspoon cinnamon. Makes 12 pieces.

CHOCOLATE CREAM DROPS
MARY WHITCHER'S SHAKER HOUSEKEEPER

2 cups sugar
½ cup flour
1 tablespoon oil of peppermint

2 squares chocolate, grated and melted

❨These are simple but delicious. Boil together for 4 minutes sugar and flour and beat to a cream. When nearly cold, flavor to taste. Mold in little balls and roll in grated and melted chocolate. Makes a dozen or so, depending on size.

CORN BALLS
FRANCES HALL, SOLD IN HANCOCK SHAKER VILLAGE STORE

2 cups sugar
1½ cups water
½ cup white corn syrup

⅓ teaspoon each salt and vinegar
1 tablespoon vanilla
5 quarts popped corn

❨Bring to boil sugar, water, and corn syrup without stirring and boil for 10 minutes. Add remaining ingredients except corn and boil another 10 minutes. (Mixture should be brittle when tested in cold water.) Have corn in a large pan; pour syrup on gradually, using a spoon all of the time to turn corn so that it may be evenly coated. Make into balls and let stand in a cold place until brittle. Wrap in waxed paper and tie at throat with colored thread. Makes 24–30 balls, depending on size.

CANDIED SWEETFLAG

ETHEL PEACOCK, SABBATHDAY LAKE SHAKER VILLAGE

([Scrape the flag root with great care. Cut in thin slices across root. Boil gently in equal parts of milk and water for 2 hours. Drain well and add to heavy syrup—made by boiling equal parts sugar and water 5 to 10 minutes. Add flag and boil until syrup is absorbed. Place on waxed paper and while hot, powder generously with granulated sugar.

Sweetflag is the root of citron grass and is related to the spice calamus mentioned in the Scriptures.

Angelica is another plant which is candied and used as a sweetmeat. The root is candied and used for flavoring puddings and sauces, and it is delicious.

MAPLE FUDGE

HANCOCK SHAKER VILLAGE

2 cups white sugar
2 cups maple syrup
2 egg whites

1 cup chopped nuts
1 cup raisins (optional)

([Boil sugar and syrup until it hairs (threads). Then pour over the stiffly beaten egg whites. Beat in earnest. Must hold shape. Add nuts (and raisins). Turn into buttered pan to cool and cut in squares—or drop from teaspoon on wax paper. Makes 12–18 pieces.

SOUR CREAM FUDGE

FRANCES HALL, HANCOCK SHAKER VILLAGE

2 cups sugar
2 tablespoons white corn syrup
1½ heaping tablespoons cocoa
½ cup sour cream

1 teaspoon vanilla
½ cup butter
½ cup chopped nuts

([Combine ingredients and put mixture in heavy saucepan. After it begins to bubble allow to cook 2 minutes; then set in cold water 2 minutes, take out, and beat until thick. Add nuts. This is very creamy and keeps moist a long time. Makes 12–16 pieces.

CANDIED LOVAGE ROOT

HANCOCK SHAKER VILLAGE

2 cups finely cut scraped fully ripe lovage root
2 cups sugar

2 cups water
2 tablespoons sugar

〖The root should be dug in the fall, scraped and cut fine, crosswise. Boil for several hours at low heat—changing water 3 times. Strain. Boil until clear in heavy syrup made by cooking equal amounts of sugar and water together until thick. Spread on buttered cooky sheets and dust well with sugar. When dry, cut in strips and roll in sugar. Pack in tin boxes.

CANDIED MINT LEAVES

HANCOCK SHAKER VILLAGE

3 drops oil of peppermint
½ cup very fine granulated sugar

1 egg white, beaten until stiff
2 cups fresh mint leaves

〖Mix oil of peppermint with sugar (do not use confectioners' sugar.) Dip leaves in stiffly beaten egg white and then in sugar. Dry on waxed paper and store in small boxes between layers of waxed paper. These keep well several months.

Other instructions read: "Wipe fresh mint leaves, remove from stems and brush each leaf with white of egg beaten until stiff. Dip in ⅓ cup granulated sugar flavored with 5 drops oil of spearmint. Place closely together on a cake rack covered with paraffine paper and let stand in a slow oven until dry. If leaves are not thoroughly coated, the process may be repeated."

MOLASSES CANDY

**Receipt Written by Sally Ceeley
After 80 Years of Age**

MT. LEBANON
MANUSCRIPT FROM SHAKER MUSEUM
OLD CHATHAM, NEW YORK

¾ cup molasses
½ cup sugar

1 teaspoon vinegar
1 tablespoon butter

〖Boil the above on a hot fire just 10 minutes, stirring it all the time. Then set aside to cool. Pull it as soon as hard enough, or if you prefer, stir in nut meats before cooling and beat hard before pulling.

CANDIED ORANGE OR LEMON PEEL
HANCOCK SHAKER VILLAGE

❨To candy orange or lemon peel, soak the peels in cold water changing water frequently till they lose their bitterness, then put them into syrup (see recipe below) for about 30 minutes until they become soft and transparent. Then take out and drain. Boil with sugar, expose to air till they crystallize, then sprinkle with sugar. Or as follows:

Remove peel from 4 thin-skinned oranges in quarters (or use 6 lemons). Cover with cold water and bring to boiling point. Cook slowly until soft. Drain, remove white portion using a spoon and cut orange or yellow portion in thin strips using scissors. Boil ½ cup water and 1 cup sugar until syrup will thread when dropped from tip of spoon. Cook strips in syrup 5 minutes, drain. Coat with fine granulated sugar. Makes about 1 pound.

CHOCOLATE-DIPPED ORANGE PEEL

❨Follow directions for candied orange peel, leaving on a considerable amount of the white portion. Melt chocolate for dipping in small saucepan. Place in a large saucepan containing hot water for about 10 minutes. Remove from range and beat until cool. Dip each piece of candied orange peel separately in chocolate. Put on paraffin (wax) paper. Let stand until cool. Four oranges make about 1 pound.

SYRUP FOR CANDIED NUTS AND ORANGE PEEL AS DONE BY THE SHAKERS
FRANCES HALL, HANCOCK SHAKER VILLAGE

❨Use 3 or 4 pounds of maple sugar (light brown sugar can be used instead), add a cup of water—let melt and then bring to a boil. Let boil until syrup is heavy enough to coat the nuts. Try just a few. If syrup clings well as you stir, it is ready. Drop syrup-coated nuts into granulated sugar. Stir around well. Then finish off in confectioners' sugar. This amount of syrup will candy about 4 pounds of nut meats.

Orange peel should be boiled until tender, drained, any excess white removed, and then cut in strips with sharp scissors before dipping in the syrup. Sugaring process is the same for nuts, orange, lemon, or grapefruit peel, but white sugar should be used for candied fruit peel.

Better amounts for today's cook:

2 cups maple sugar   1 cup maple syrup

⟨Boil together until it hairs (spins a thread which will float in the air). Place small quantity of nuts (butternuts, pecans, or English walnuts) in a pie tin, dip over them a small amount of the slightly cooled syrup. Coat nuts completely—then drop into granulated sugar and shake until well covered. Then dry off with confectioners' sugar. This amount of syrup will candy 1 pound of nut meats.

JELLIED ORANGES
HANCOCK SHAKER VILLAGE

2 cups orange sections, meat and   4 tablespoons granulated gelatin
  peel   1 cup sugar
3 cups boiling water   2 tablespoons lemon juice

⟨Peel oranges nicely, discarding peel. Separate into sections. Cover with 1 cup boiling water and let sit 20 minutes. Drain. Soften gelatin in 2 cups boiling water. Add sugar and lemon juice. Put oranges in gelatin mixture, turn into bowl. Chill. Makes 2 cups.

Orange sections can be simmered in liquid syrup made by softening 4 tablespoons gelatin and 1 cup sugar to 2 cups boiling water. When sections are dipped and coated with syrup they can be rolled in sugar. A nice candy.

PEACH OR APRICOT CONFECTION
HANCOCK SHAKER VILLAGE

1 pound peeled, stoned peaches or   ½ cup sugar for each pound of fruit
  apricots

⟨Combine fruit and sugar in heavy kettle, simmer until quite dry. Mash fruit to a smooth paste.

Butter a large board and spread cooked fruit on it in a thin sheet. Put board in sun to dry. Cut confection in squares or fancy shapes. Sprinkle with sugar.

To keep—roll up in one piece and wrap in a cloth. Store in a cool, dry place.

This is chewy and tart. Makes 12–18 pieces.

CRYSTALLIZED ROSE PETALS

HANCOCK SHAKER VILLAGE

⟨Use only perfect rose petals—fairly large in size. Brush each petal with well-beaten egg white, stroking it on with a small brush kept just for this purpose. Sprinkle sugar on a plate, put petal moist side down on it. Coat second side and sprinkle with sugar. Sift additional sugar over all. Put in a warm place near the stove to dry. Violets and mint leaves can be treated in the same way. Store between wax paper sheets in a dry tin box.

TAFFY

FRANCES HALL, HANCOCK SHAKER VILLAGE

1 cup sugar	⅛ teaspoon salt
½ cup honey	1 tablespoon butter

⟨Cook all together until a ball is formed when dropped in cold water. Pour on buttered platter until cool enough to pull. Butter hands and pull until hard. All taffy takes two people to pull unless you have a hook set in the wall to secure one end of the taffy. When taffy is cool cut with scissors and wrap in paper twisting both ends. Makes about 2–3 dozen.

SHAKER MOLASSES TAFFY

NORTH UNION SHAKER VILLAGE, OHIO

1 cup molasses	2 tablespoons butter
1 cup sugar	1 teaspoon baking soda
1 cup thin cream	1 cup chopped walnuts

⟨Cook molasses, sugar, and cream until a ball is formed when dropped in cold water. Remove from heat and add butter, soda, and nuts. Pour on a buttered platter until cool enough to pull. Pull to make light. Some like to pull this a bit before adding nuts. In this case, nuts are folded in toward end of pulling; when hard cut into desired lengths with scissors. Makes 4–6 dozen, depending on size.

MAPLE CREAMS
REBECCA HATHAWAY, CANTERBURY SHAKER VILLAGE

3 cups maple sugar
1 cup heavy cream

½ teaspoon maple flavoring
1 cup chopped butternuts

([Cook sugar and cream until a soft ball is formed when tested in cold water. Cool and beat until very creamy, add maple flavoring. Have platter buttered, sprinkle with nut meats, and pour maple cream over nuts. When cold, cut in squares. Makes 12–18 pieces.

DUMPLINGS COOKED IN MAPLE SYRUP
HANCOCK SHAKER VILLAGE

2 cups flour, sifted
6 teaspoons baking powder
1 teaspoon salt
1 teaspoon nutmeg or allspice
1 tablespoon sugar

2 eggs
Milk, about ¾ cup
1 tablespoon water
2 cups maple syrup

([Sift flour with baking powder, salt, spice, and sugar. Break eggs into 1 cup measure and fill with milk; beat well and mix into dry ingredients. Add water to syrup and bring to a boil in a 12 inch skillet. Dip tablespoon into warm water, then fill it with batter and drop into syrup. Do not cook too many at a time; dumplings must not touch. Cover tightly and cook 2 minutes. Turn dumplings and cook 2 minutes longer. Serve very hot with flavored cream. Serve syrup left in pan with dumplings as a sauce. Makes 12–15 dumplings.

MAPLE MOLD WITH CUSTARD SAUCE
A NEW HAMPSHIRE SHAKER RECIPE

1½ cups brown sugar
7 tablespoons cornstarch
¼ cup cold water
2 cups boiling water

¼ teaspoon salt
3 egg whites
½ cup chopped nuts
2 tablespoons maple syrup

([Mix sugar and cornstarch and stir into a smooth paste with cold water. Stir vigorously while adding boiling water. Cook 15 to 20 minutes in a double boiler. Add salt to egg whites and beat until stiff. Combine with cornstarch mixture—add nuts and maple syrup. Pour into a 4 cup ring mold and chill. Unmold and serve with Custard Sauce (see next page) in center.

CUSTARD SAUCE

2 egg yolks
2 tablespoons sugar
1 cup milk, scalded

Few drops vanilla or rose water (or
 maple syrup)

([Beat yolks with sugar. Add carefully to scalded milk. Cook over boiling water until custard coats the spoon. Remove immediately, flavor and cool. Makes 1½ cups sauce.

MAPLE MOUSSE
FRANCES HALL, HANCOCK SHAKER VILLAGE

1 cup maple syrup
4 eggs, separated

2 cups heavy cream, whipped

([In top of double boiler, combine maple syrup and egg yolks. Cook over low heat stirring constantly for 10 minutes or until thickened. Remove from heat and cool. Beat egg whites until stiff but not dry. Fold in whipped cream. Beat custard until light and stir into egg white mixture. Pack into a 6 cup mold and freeze. SERVES 6.

MAPLE RICE SNOW
THE MANIFESTO, 1878

2 cups maple syrup
2 teaspoons cornstarch
4 cups cooked rice

1 cup whipped cream (about)
1 teaspoon nutmeg

([Boil syrup and stir in cornstarch. When it is thickened, cool. Combine with cooked rice and beat well. Put in glass dish and chill. Cover over with cream and sprinkle with nutmeg. SERVES 4–6.

MAPLE SYRUP MOLD
A NEW HAMPSHIRE SHAKER RECIPE

1 tablespoon gelatin
½ cup milk
1 cup maple syrup

5 egg yolks, beaten
1½ cups heavy cream, whipped

⟨Soak gelatin in milk. Heat cup of maple syrup in top of double boiler and add beaten egg yolks. Add gelatin and milk and continue beating until thick. Cool. Add whipped cream. Pour into a melon mold and place in refrigerator until firm. Serve with runny cream. SERVES 4.

MAPLE SYRUP ON SNOW
HANCOCK SHAKER VILLAGE

⟨So many times during a snowy winter people talk of "syrup on snow" and no one can quite remember how they used to do it. This is how the Shakers did it:

"Boil maple syrup until it spins a thread, then it will form a soft gummy covering when dropped upon snow and will become brittle.

"Gather pure, clean, freshly fallen snow in tin cake or pie pans. Place the hot maple liquid in a white pitcher. Pour over the clean snow. Make artistic patterns in the snow.

"Sour pickles and salted, butter crackers, raised doughnuts and coffee are served with this. Good!"

Ices and
Fruit Desserts

SHAKER BOILED APPLES

MARY WHITCHER'S SHAKER HOUSEKEEPER

"About the nicest morsel that ever tickled the palate is a boiled apple. Not boiled like a potato nor steamed like a pudding, but as follows:

"Place a layer of fair-skinned Baldwins, or any nice varieties, in the large stew pan, with about a quarter of an inch of water. Throw on about half a cup of sugar to 6 good-sized apples and boil until the apples are thoroughly cooked and the syrup nearly thick enough for jelly.

"After one trial, no one would for any consideration have fair-skinned apples peeled. The skins contain a very large share of the jelly making substance, and impart a flavor impossible to obtain otherwise. It is also said that 'a wise housekeeper instead of throwing away the skins and cores of sound pie apples would use them for jelly. A tumblerful of the richest sort can thus be obtained from the dozen apples. Boil the skins, etc., a few minutes and strain. Add a little sugar to the liquid and boil until right to turn into the tumbler.' "

Directions for today's cook:

6 Baldwin apples (red cooking   1 cup cold water
  apples)   ½ cup sugar

❲Remove cores, place in saucepan with about ½ inch of water. Pour over apples ½ cup sugar and gently boil about 20 minutes or until apples are tender. Turn apples carefully several times. The syrup should turn as thick as jelly. Pour over apples. Thick cream may be passed. SERVES 6.

BAKED APPLES

ALFRED SHAKER VILLAGE

6 medium-size apples
3 teaspoons sugar
1 teaspoon ground cinnamon
6 small pieces lemon or orange peel
2 eggs, beaten

2 cups sweet milk
2 tablespoons sugar
1 tablespoon flour
1 teaspoon rose water

¶Pare and core the apples. Place apples in a baking dish. Fill up each hole in the apples with ½ teaspoon sugar, ⅛ teaspoon cinnamon, and a small piece of lemon or orange peel. Make a rich custard by cooking eggs and milk together slowly on low heat. Add 2 tablespoons sugar and 1 tablespoon flour. Stir to keep smooth consistency. Add rose water. Beat and pour over apples. Bake at 350° F. for 20 minutes. Serve with thick cream. SERVES 6.

BAKED APPLES WITH HONEY AND CIDER

HANCOCK SHAKER VILLAGE

¶Slice 6 green apples 1 inch thick, no less (if not green should be tart). Put apple slices in a buttered baking dish and sprinkle with ¼ teaspoon of cinnamon and ¼ teaspoon of cloves or nutmeg. Drip honey over apple slices. Do not spare honey. Pour into dish just enough hot Boiled Cider* to fill dish ½ inch.

Bake in moderate 350° F. oven 20 minutes or until tender. Serve with Shaker Cream.* SERVES 4.

SISTER REBECCA'S BAKED MAPLE APPLES

CANTERBURY SHAKER VILLAGE

6 firm tart apples
4 tablespoons shaved maple sugar

3 tablespoons butter
1 cup boiling water

¶Pare, quarter, and core the apples. Place in an earthenware pie plate or other ovenproof dish which can also come to the table.

Mix the maple sugar, butter, and boiling water and boil for 5 minutes. Pour this mixture over the apples. Place in a moderate 350° F. to 375° F. oven and bake until apples are soft, approximately 20 minutes. Baste occasionally with hot syrup.

This makes a delicious dessert served with heavy cream. It may also

be served in the baking dish with pork or fowl or duck or goose.
SERVES 4–6.

SAUTÉED APPLES WITH HONEY AND CREAM SAUCE
HARVARD SHAKER VILLAGE

4 nice apples, pared, cored, and
 chopped
½ cup butter, melted
½ teaspoon salt
½ teaspoon nutmeg

½ cup honey
1 tablespoon cornstarch
½ cup cider
½ cup heavy cream

([Sauté apples in butter, slowly and covered in a saucepan. When apples
are soft (but not mushy) remove cover and let some moisture go. Add
salt, nutmeg, and honey and cornstarch and stir well while it simmers.
Add cider and reduce liquid to consistency of thick applesauce. Remove
from fire and add cream. Makes about 6 cups.

APPLE DUMPLINGS COOKED IN MAPLE SYRUP
REBECCA HATHAWAY, CANTERBURY SHAKER VILLAGE

2 cups flour, unsifted
1 teaspoon cream of tartar and ½
 teaspoon baking soda
     or
1½ teaspoons baking powder
1 teaspoon sugar

1 teaspoon salt
¾ cup milk
½ cup peeled chopped apples
2 cups maple syrup and 1 tablespoon
 water

([Mix and sift dry ingredients together. Add milk and apples and mix
well. Drop by spoonfuls into boiling maple syrup. Cook 10 minutes in
syrup, which must boil all the time. Makes 24.

APPLE FLOAT
PLEASANT HILL SHAKER VILLAGE

4 egg whites
6 tablespoons sugar (about)

1 cup unsweetened applesauce
Grated nutmeg

([Beat egg whites until stiff and add 6 tablespoons sugar; then beat again,
hard. Add the applesauce a little at a time, beating all the while. Add
more sugar or not according to tartness of applesauce. Grate in nutmeg
to taste and mix well. Serve float from a pretty glass bowl. Serve with
thick cream. Or have ready some rounds of best pastry cooked to a
golden color, top with the apple float and pass a pitcher of thick cream.
This is sometimes called "Apple Toast." SERVES 4.

APPLE FOAM
WATERVLIET SHAKER VILLAGE, NEW YORK

⟮Boil 12 apples till soft, take off the peel, and press through a sieve. Add 1 cup of sugar, cool. Beat whites of 2 eggs until stiff and fold into apple-sugar mixture. Heap in a glass dish, chill, and cover with thick cream whipped and flavored with rose water. This should all be well chilled. SERVES 6–8.

BAKED BANANAS IN CIDER
HANCOCK SHAKER VILLAGE

4 firm red-skinned bananas (yellow-skinned bananas may be used)
Lemon juice
3 tablespoons melted currant jelly

3 tablespoons cider, heated
2 tablespoons melted butter
Brown sugar
1 cup heavy cream
½ cup grated coconut

⟮Slice the peeled bananas in half lengthwise and arrange in buttered baking dish. Sprinkle with lemon juice to keep from discoloring. Combine jelly, cider, and melted butter and pour over bananas. Bake 20 to 25 minutes at 350° F. Baste occasionally. Sprinkle with brown sugar and broil top just before serving.

Combine cream and coconut, let stand 15 minutes. Pass with bananas. SERVES 4.

BAKED BANANAS WITH CURRANT JELLY
SHIRLEY SHAKER VILLAGE

6 firm bananas, not overripe
1 cup currant jelly, mixed with ½ cup cider
4 tablespoons butter

1 cup cake crumbs
1 cup rich heavy cream
½ cup chopped butternuts (or walnuts or almonds)

⟮Peel bananas and arrange side by side in a buttered baking dish. Spoon jelly beaten up in cider over bananas. Dot with butter. Bake 20 minutes at 375° F., basting when necessary. Sprinkle with good cake crumbs (this is a nice way to use up last few pieces of cakes). Cook 5 minutes longer. Serve at once and pass cream mixed with chopped nuts. SERVES 4.

BLUEBERRY TOAST
HANCOCK SHAKER VILLAGE

1 quart blueberries (raspberries can
   be substituted)
1 cup sugar
6 slices white bread
1½ cups milk

1 egg yolk, beaten
6 tablespoons butter
Powdered sugar
Ground cinnamon
Thick cream

❲Wash blueberries and put in saucepan with sugar. Let boil over low heat 6 minutes or until tender. Trim crusts from bread and dip bread in mixture of milk and beaten egg as for French toast. Fry bread in butter and remove to warm platter. Top with stewed blueberries. Dust with powdered sugar and cinnamon. Put a tablespoon of whipped cream on top or pass heavy cream in a pitcher. SERVES 4–6.

Plain buttered toast can be used in place of French toast.

CHERRY AND RICE COMPOTE
ENFIELD SHAKER VILLAGE, CONNECTICUT

4 cups stoned, stewed cherries and
   the juice (see below)
2 cups cooked rice
3 cups milk
½ cup sugar

1 tablespoon butter
1 tablespoon gelatin
½ cup warm water
1 teaspoon rose water
1 cup heavy cream, whipped

❲To cooked rice add milk, sugar, and butter. Beat in gelatin melted in warm water and rose water. Fold in whipped cream and stewed cherries. Arrange in a glass serving dish and chill until firm. Pass heavy cream in pitcher. SERVES 8.

STEWED CHERRIES FOR COMPOTE

❲Simmer 2½ cups sugar with 2 cups water 10 minutes. Add to the syrup 4 cups of cherries, measured after they are stalked and pitted. Let stew 20 minutes. Yields 4 cups.

FRIED FRESH PEACHES

HARVARD SHAKER VILLAGE

2 tablespoons butter	12 teaspoons brown sugar
6 peaches	Rose water

([Pare, split, and stone the peaches. Melt butter in an iron skillet and add the peaches.

Fill the hollows with brown sugar and a drop of rose water. Simmer until well cooked.

Serve with meats as a garnish or as a dessert with whipped cream or ice cream. SERVES 4–6 as dessert. Use halves as garnish to serve 6.

HONEYED PEARS

OHIO SHAKERS, THE MANIFESTO

([Remove stems from pears. Rub well with soft, clean cloth. Pears should be ripe, but not past their peak. Arrange fruit in large glass bottle which can be covered airtight. Completely cover fruit with strained honey. Let it stand in dark cupboard for one month, or longer.

Serve in fruit dish and pass thick cream. Allow 1 large pear per person. If pears are small, allow at least 2.

SPICED RHUBARB

HARVARD SHAKER VILLAGE

2 cups small lengths young, tender rhubarb	Sugar or honey to taste
1 teaspoon cloves	Cornstarch to thicken

([Cover washed rhubarb with water. Add spice, sugar, or honey to taste. Stew until very soft, about 15 minutes. Rub through a sieve. Return to the pan. Thicken with cornstarch mixed smooth with cold water. The amount of cornstarch will depend on whether you want the dessert thick or thin. Cook 10 minutes longer.

Serve with sour cream slightly sweetened with brown sugar. SERVES 4.

SNOWBALLS WITH STRAWBERRY SAUCE

MT. LEBANON SHAKER VILLAGE

½ cup fat
¾ cup sugar
⅔ cup milk
2 cups flour

2 teaspoons baking powder
⅛ teaspoon salt
4 egg whites, stiffly beaten

❨Cream fat and sugar, add liquid alternately with the sifted dry ingredients. Fold in stiffly beaten whites last. Turn into buttered custard cups or buttered molds. Steam on a rack in a covered kettle on top of stove (see Steamed Ginger Pudding,* for steaming directions) about 45 minutes. Serve with a Fruit Sauce or a Foamy Sauce or both. SERVES 6.

Fruit Sauce:

Use fruit preserve, such as strawberry preserves. Melt it with a little currant or apple jelly, add rose water, and if necessary a little water to obtain desired consistency.

Foamy Sauce:

Add 2 well-beaten eggs, ½ teaspoon vanilla or rosemary, and some nutmeg to the following: ⅓ cup butter and 1 cup powdered sugar creamed together. Beat well over hot water 2 or 3 minutes. If too runny, add more sugar. Yields 1½ cups.

To serve, arrange Snowballs on platter, surround with Fruit Sauce and pass Foamy Sauce, or cover snowballs with Foamy Sauce.

CIDER JELLY

MT. LEBANON SHAKER VILLAGE

¾ cups granulated sugar
Grated rind and juice 2 lemons
2½ cups cold water
4 cups cider

3 envelopes plain gelatin
1½ cups warm water
2 egg whites, beaten stiff

❨Mix together sugar, lemon rind and juice, cold water, and cider. Heat and when warm stir in gelatin which has been melted in the 1½ cups of warm water. Bring to a boil and stir to make smooth. Remove from heat. Add stiffly beaten whites to mixture. Stir and cool. Pour into 1½ quart mold.[1] Refrigerate when cool. Let set 4 hours. Serve with sweetened whipped cream. SERVES 4.

---

[1]It may need straining before molding.

BOILED CIDER JELLY

HANCOCK SHAKER VILLAGE

2 tablespoons granulated gelatin
½ cup cold water
1 cup boiling water

1 teaspoon lemon juice
2 cups Boiled Cider*
Sugar to taste

⟦Soak gelatin in cold water. Add boiling water to dissolve it. Strain if necessary. Cool. Add lemon juice and Boiled Cider.* This is sweet, extra sugar may not be needed. Turn into 4 cup mold and chill. Serve with heavy cream. SERVES 4.

LEMON JELLY

FRANCES HALL, HANCOCK SHAKER VILLAGE

1 cup plain gelatin
2 cups cold water
1 quart boiling water

1½ cups sugar
Juice 6 lemons

⟦Soak the gelatin in the cold water. Pour over this the boiling water, add the sugar, and stir until dissolved. Add the lemon juice and strain into molds. Makes 8 molds.

According to Frances Hall, the Shaker sisters in Hancock Village were "called upon to furnish a great quantity of this during the haying."

JELLIED PRUNES

SHIRLEY SHAKER VILLAGE

⅓ pound prunes
2 cups cold water
Boiling water
2½ tablespoons granulated gelatin

½ cup cold water
1 cup sugar
¼ cup lemon juice

⟦Pick over, wash, soak prunes for several hours in 2 cups cold water (some prunes on the market today will not need to soak so long) and cook in same water until soft. Remove prunes, reserve prune water.

Stone prunes and cut in quarters. To prune water add enough boiling water to make 2 cups. Soak gelatin in ½ cup cold water, dissolve in hot liquid. Add sugar, lemon juice, then strain. Add prunes, mold and chill. Stir twice while cooling to prevent prunes from settling. Apricots can be substituted for prunes.

Serve with cream sauce flavored with brandy. SERVES 4.

JELLIED WALNUTS
MT. LEBANON SHAKER VILLAGE

1 tablespoon granulated gelatin
¼ cup cold water
⅓ cup boiling water
¾ cup sugar

½ cup dry sherry wine
½ cup orange juice
3 tablespoons lemon juice
Walnuts or butternuts

([Soak gelatin in cold water and dissolve in boiling water. Add sugar, wine, and juices. Cover bottom of shallow dish or individual molds with half the mixture. When nearly firm, place over it the halves of the nuts, placed 1 inch apart. Cover with remaining mixture. Chill. If in large dish, cut in squares. Serve with cream sauce, heavy cream or whipped cream, sweetened and flavored. SERVES 4.

WINE JELLY
MARY WHITCHER, CANTERBURY SHAKER VILLAGE

2½ tablespoons granulated gelatin
½ cup cold water
1⅔ cups boiling water
1 cup sugar
⅓ cup orange juice

3 tablespoons lemon juice
½ cup dry sherry wine
½ cup brandy
Red fruit juice—to color (optional)

([Soak gelatin 5 minutes in cold water, dissolve in boiling water; add sugar, fruit juices, sherry, brandy, then color with red fruit juice. (This is made by squeezing raspberries through a sieve and bottling.) Without the red, jelly will be golden. Make the day before serving so it will set pleasantly. Serve with Cream Sauce.* SERVES 4.

MARY WHITCHER'S LEMON JELLY
MARY WHITCHER'S SHAKER HOUSEKEEPER

([Make the same as Wine Jelly, using the juice of 8 lemons instead of orange juice, and 1 pint more water instead of the wine. Serve with rich cream. SERVES 4–6.

ICE CREAM

MANUSCRIPT FROM SHAKER MUSEUM
OLD CHATHAM, NEW YORK

1 quart thick yellow cream   1½ cups sugar
2 egg yolks

⟨[Bring cream to a boil. Beat yolks and sugar together. When cream boils put them into it. Remove from heat immediately after putting in the yolks and sugar, and strain. Beat up well and freeze. Makes 1 quart.

SHAKER ICE CREAM

THE SISTER AMELIA J. CALVER BOOK
MT. LEBANON SHAKER VILLAGE

4 tablespoons cornstarch   8 egg whites, beaten to stiff froth
4 quarts milk   1 tablespoon vanilla
1 teaspoon salt   or
8 egg yolks, well beaten   1 tablespoon rose water
4 cups sugar   1 quart heavy cream

⟨[Cook cornstarch thoroughly in the milk, add salt, the well-beaten yolks, and sugar. Set aside to cool. When ready to freeze, fold in beaten whites and flavoring. If you wish to whip the cream, do so a little at a time so it will not turn to butter and do not touch the beater to the bottom of the bowl. Freeze. Makes 4½ quarts.

APPLE ICE CREAM

HANCOCK SHAKER VILLAGE

This is used to top servings of Baked Indian Pudding.*
  To 1 quart of rich vanilla ice cream add the following:

1 tablespoon cinnamon   1 teaspoon salt
1 cup shaved maple sugar   1 cup grated raw peeled cored apples
    or
1 cup granulated sugar

⟨[Add cinnamon to sugar and salt. Combine with apples (if they are grated it is best). Work quickly so they won't discolor. Fold this mixture into quart of softened vanilla ice cream. Serve on top of hot Baked Indian Pudding* or hot gingerbread.

APRICOT ICE CREAM
HANCOCK SHAKER VILLAGE

3 cups light cream
⅔ cup sugar
5 egg yolks, well beaten
1 cup sweetened apricot purée

1 teaspoon each lemon juice, orange juice
2 tablespoons rose water

❰[Combine cream and sugar, bring to a boil. Add some of this mixture to beaten egg yolks. Then add this to first mixture. Mix well. Strain and cool thoroughly. Stir in remaining ingredients. Freeze in hand freezer or in the refrigerator. Makes 1 quart.

Variation: Peach purée can be substituted for apricot.

ICED LEMON VELVET
MANUSCRIPT FROM SHAKER MUSEUM
OLD CHATHAM, NEW YORK

Juice and grated rind 6 lemons
½ cup boiling water
4 cups sugar

1 quart milk
1 quart heavy cream, whipped

❰[Put lemon rind and juice in large mixing bowl. Add water and stir in sugar. Stir until dissolved and cool. Stir in milk and fold in cream. Freeze until firm. Turn into mixing bowl and beat until smooth. Return to freezer until hard. SERVES 12.

Variation: Oranges may be used in place of lemons.

PINEAPPLE ICE CREAM
MANUSCRIPT FROM SHAKER MUSEUM
OLD CHATHAM, NEW YORK

❰[Pare a ripe juicy pineapple, chop it up fine, and pound it to extract the juice. Cover it with sugar and let it lie in a china bowl. When the sugar has entirely dissolved, strain the juice into a quart of good thick cream, and add a little less than a pound of loaf sugar. Beat up the cream and freeze it in the same manner as common ice cream. Makes 1½ quarts.

ROSE WATER FROZEN CREAM
HANCOCK SHAKER VILLAGE

1 tablespoon flour
1½ cups granulated sugar
1 teaspoon salt
2 egg yolks, slightly beaten

2 cups scalded milk
4 cups light cream
1 tablespoon rose water

⟨Mix flour, sugar, and salt, add slightly beaten egg yolks, stir until smooth. Add scalded milk slowly. Cook in top of double boiler until thick. When cool, add cream and rose water. Pour into ice cream freezer and freeze. Makes 2 quarts.

VANILLA ICE CREAM
MT. LEBANON SHAKER VILLAGE

6 eggs
3 cups sugar

8 cups cream
3 teaspoons vanilla

⟨Beat the eggs and gradually add the sugar and part of the cream. Beat, add 3 teaspoons of flavoring. Put in rest of cream, beat again, and freeze. Makes about 2 quarts.

WATER ICES
LUCY A. SHEPARD, 1860
MANUSCRIPT FROM SHAKER MUSEUM
OLD CHATHAM, NEW YORK

⟨Water ices are made with the juice of the orange, lemon, raspberry, currant, or any other sort of fruit, sweetened and mixed with a pint of water (2 cups). To make orange-water ice, mix with 1 pint (2 cups) of water, 2 cups strained juice of 3 fine oranges and that of 1 lemon. Rub some fine sugar on the peel of the orange to get oil from peel. Make it very sweet and freeze. Lemon ice is made in the same manner. Freeze like ice cream.

If made from jams, you must rub them through a sieve, adding thick boiled syrup and lemon juice and for pink, some jelly coloring, and the white of an egg whipped up before you add it to the best half of a pint of spring water. If of jam, you must have a good pint of mixture in all to make a quart mold. If from fruits with syrup, you will not require water.

CRANBERRY ICE
FRANCES HALL, HANCOCK SHAKER VILLAGE

4 cups cranberries
2½ cups water
3 cups sugar

1 tablespoon gelatin
1 tablespoon lemon juice

❮[Boil together cranberries and 2 cups of water. Bring to boil and cook until cranberries are soft, about 30 minutes. Put them through a sieve, then return pulp and juice to saucepan, add sugar and heat 2 minutes. Soften gelatin in remaining water; when dissolved add with lemon juice to cranberry mixture. Beat well. Freeze to mushy consistency, beat again, and refreeze. SERVES 6, but double for Thanksgiving.

GRAPE ICE
HANCOCK SHAKER VILLAGE

2 tablespoons gelatin
Juice 4 lemons
1½ cups sugar

4 cups juice from 4 pounds fresh,
    ripe, blue grapes
4 egg whites

❮[Soften gelatin in lemon juice; dissolve sugar in grape juice and combine both mixtures. Bring to a boil and remove from heat. Chill and beat. Beat egg whites stiff and fold into grape juice. Freeze. When mixture is mushy beat once more and freeze. SERVES 8.

Variation: Other fruit juices can be used instead of grape.

LEMON ICE
MANUSCRIPT FROM SHAKER MUSEUM
OLD CHATHAM, NEW YORK

8 juicy lemons
4 cups sugar

2 cups water
2 egg whites

❮[Roll lemons till well bruised and soft. Squeeze out the juice. Add white sugar to make a thick syrup. Add cold water and bring to a boil, then set aside to cool. Put into the freezer and when nearly frozen add the whites of 2 eggs beaten to a stiff froth; stir well and freeze until firm. SERVES 6–8.

Variation: Oranges can be substituted for lemons.

RASPBERRY ICE

MANUSCRIPT FROM SHAKER MUSEUM
OLD CHATHAM, NEW YORK

1 tablespoon gelatin
1 cup hot water
2 cups raspberry juice

2 cups sugar
¼ cup lemon juice
2 egg whites

[Dissolve gelatin in water. To the juice of ripe raspberries add sugar and water with gelatin. Add lemon juice and let this stand. Add stiffly beaten egg white. Strain through a fine sieve and freeze. SERVES 4.

SUMMER SHERBET

MANUSCRIPT FROM SHAKER MUSEUM
OLD CHATHAM, NEW YORK

2 cups sugar
2 cups water
1 cup fresh orange juice
⅓ cup lemon juice

4 tablespoons currant jelly
2 medium bananas, mashed
2 egg whites, stiffly beaten

[Combine sugar and water and bring slowly to boil, then simmer for 15 minutes and cool. Stir fruit juices and jelly into this syrup. Freeze until mushy. Put in mixing bowl, beat well, and fold in bananas and egg whites. Return to freezer and freeze until firm. Make plenty of this, it is a great favorite. Makes about 1 quart.

Jams, Jellies, and Preserves

·: JAMS, JELLIES, AND PRESERVES :·

IT IS IMPOSSIBLE to estimate the production of the Shaker canning industry. Nothing in this field can be compared with it until the mid 1800s when commercial companies became prominent. Not that this Shaker endeavor was ever considered anything but commercial by them. Large crops of vegetables and fruits were planted and well tended to produce as much surplus as possible. Canned goods were advertised and careful records kept in order to promote better and larger sales. "Household industries," as this activity was known, consisted of the preparation for sale of wines, sauces, jellies and preserves, maple syrup, maple sugar, applesauce, dried apples and dried corn, tomato sauce and tomato catsup (or ketchup); "cucumber pickles, a big seller, and other relishes and compounds." These were sold as early as 1811 by the bottle and by the gallon. From office stores sisters sold in great quantities preserved or sugared sweetflag, ginger, sugared butternuts and walnuts, and candied lemon and orange peels.

Currants, crab apples, apples, plums, cranberries, quince, grapes, raspberries, strawberries and many other fruits were preserved in quart containers as were boiled cider and boiled cider applesauce. Kitchens were busy all summer long with this activity for nothing went to waste.

Kitchen sisters were not permitted to blanch the fruit in order to remove the skins but had to peel the skins carefully and nothing short of perfection was accepted. A former Shaker recalled the acute discomfort which came with peeling peaches and inhaling the fuzz during the canning season. She said that one summer when the peach crop was much more abundant than usual the family had some very large orders for canned peaches to fill. As a result she served in the kitchen for a longer period than was normal and developed an irritating allergy from the peach fuzz. In a burst of anger and frustration one day, she threw drown her knife and burst into tears. At once the deaconess in charge took her out of the kitchen and without remonstrating put her to work copying the following couplet until she calmed down:

> Of all bad things by which mankind are curst,
> Their own bad tempers surely are the worst.

She thought it was composed especially to suit the moment by the deaconess, whom she loved and admired. In later years she found it came from a *Manifesto* (August 1895 and attributed to "Cumberland").

If one considers the tremendous amount of work involved with canning, one becomes aware of the lack of idleness in the Shaker communities, an awareness which one Shaker youth with a sense of humor noted in verse:

> I'm overrun with work and chores
> Upon the farm or within doors
> Whichever way I turn my eyes;
> Enough to fill one with surprise,
> How can I bear with such a plan?
> No time to be a gentleman!
> All work-work-work, still rushing on,
> And conscience too, still pushing on,
> When will the working all be done?
> When will this lengthy thread be spun?
> As long as working is the cry
> How can I e'er find time to die?
>
> > Written in 1807 by Isaac N. Youngs,
> > the chief clock maker at New Lebanon,
> > when he was a lad of fourteen.

HANCOCK FRUIT COMPOUND

HANCOCK SHAKER VILLAGE

2 tablespoons salt
1 quart water
7 cups sliced peeled fresh peaches
¼ cup water
3 cups sugar
1½ cups cider vinegar
2 large cloves garlic

1 cup chopped onions
1 teaspoon ground ginger
¼ teaspoon crushed red pepper
¾ cup lemon juice
1 cup raisins
½ cup chopped preserved ginger

¶Add salt to a quart of water. Pour over peaches and let stand 1 day. Drain.

Mix ¼ cup water, sugar, and vinegar and garlic. Bring to a boil. Add peeled sliced peaches and cook until they are clear, about 40 to 45 minutes. Remove peaches. Add onions, spices, lemon juice, and raisins to syrup. Cook until thickened, 12 to 15 minutes. Add peaches and ginger and bring to the boiling point.

Fill hot sterilized ½ pint jars and seal. Makes 6 jars.

Should be darkish in color, not a light peach shade.

APPLE GINGER
SHIRLEY SHAKER VILLAGE

3 pounds apples
3 cups brown sugar
1½ lemons

2 tablespoons powdered ginger
1 teaspoon salt

¶Pare and chop apples—there should be 6 cups. Put in a saucepan and add sugar, juice and rind of lemons, the ginger and salt. Add just enough water to keep from burning, cover and cook very, very slowly for 4 hours, adding water as necessary. Great care must be taken to keep from scorching.

Eat as is, or turn into a crock or jelly tumblers. It may be kept several weeks. Makes 1½–2 pints jelly glasses.

∙ ∙

Sister Marcia of Mt. Lebanon Shaker Village wrote about the famous Shaker apple orchards and how many new species were introduced. Among these was the quince apple, especially adapted to drying and used in Shaker applesauce.

"As soon as the apple harvest opened in late August we often held several apple-paring bees a week where we pared, quartered, and sliced 10 to 20 bushels for dried apples in a single evening. The Bretheren join us in this chore."

SHAKER APPLESAUCE #1
ETHEL PEACOCK, SABBATHDAY LAKE SHAKER VILLAGE

2 pounds dried apples, peeled,
  cored and sliced
⅓ gallon water

⅔ gallon Boiled Cider,* boiled down
  from 2 gallons fresh cider
(2 cups sugar may be used in place
  of cider)

([Soak apples overnight in water. In the morning add the boiled-down cider to the soaked (approximately 2 cups) apples. Cover tightly and simmer for 3½ hours; add sugar if desired. Do not stir, for the apple slices should remain whole and float in the rich dark syrup. Put in sterilized jars. Makes 2 pints.

SHAKER APPLESAUCE #2
MT. LEBANON SHAKER VILLAGE

2 pounds apples, peeled and sliced thick
⅔ gallon Boiled Cider,* boiled down from 2 gallons fresh cider

(1 cup sugar may be used in place of cider)

([Add apple slices to boiled down cider; simmer until apples are tender. Do not stir, for apple slices must remain whole. Add sugar, if desired, but the concentrated cider is very sweet. Put in sterilized jars. Makes 2 pints.

SHAKER APPLESAUCE #3
HANCOCK SHAKER VILLAGE

This may be the simplest and best.

2 pounds sweet apples

1 cup thick Boiled Cider,* boiled down from 1 quart fresh cider

([Peel and quarter apples. Just cover with hot water. Add cider and let simmer until the apples are done but not mushy. Put in sterilized jars. Makes 4 eight-ounce jars—2 pints. In the old days boiled cider was sold by the bottle in grocery stores; however, it is easy to make by boiling down fresh cider until it is thick as molasses.

AMELIA'S CHERRIES
NORTH UNION SHAKER VILLAGE, OHIO

2 pounds white or brown sugar
1 quart white vinegar
2 sticks cinnamon

2 teaspoons whole cloves
2 quarts cherries with stems
Peel ½ lemon

([Bring to a boil sugar dissolved in vinegar, add spices. Put cherries in sterilized quart containers; add lemon peel. Pour over hot sugar, vinegar, and spice mixture. Seal jars. Store in cool place until ready to use. Do not use for 2 months. Makes 2½ quarts.

SPICED CHERRIES
ENFIELD SHAKER VILLAGE, CONNECTICUT

3 sticks cinnamon
6 whole cloves
1 tablespoon whole allspice

6 cups sugar
1½ cups vinegar
6 cups stemmed pitted cherries

❮Tie the spices in a muslin bag and boil them with the sugar and vinegar for 5 minutes. Put in the stemmed pitted cherries for 10 minutes to allow their juice to mix with the syrup. Strain them through a colander. Put the syrup back on the stove and boil it down until it jellies. Test a little in cold water to see if it jells. Return fruit to the syrup. Boil up and put in sterilized jars. Makes 6 pint jars.

CURRANT PRESERVES
HANCOCK SHAKER VILLAGE

❮To each pound of currants allow ¾ of a pound of sugar. Put the currants in a kettle and mash them a little so that there will be juice enough to cook them without using water. Stir them to prevent scorching. Cook 15 minutes and then add sugar to taste. Let them boil hard 1 minute. Put them in hot sterilized 1 pint jars and seal at once. Makes 1 pound of fruit.

DAMSON PLUM CHEESE
MANUSCRIPT FROM SHAKER MUSEUM
OLD CHATHAM, NEW YORK

❮Boil 2 pounds of plums in sufficient water to cover. Strain the pulp through a coarse sieve. (Two pounds of plums yields 2 cups pulp.) To each 2 cups pulp add ½ cup sugar. Boil till it begins to candy on the sides, then pour into the molds. Other kinds of plums and cherries and several kinds of fruit can be used this way. If poured into sterilized jars, this will keep well. Makes 1 pint.

STORE FIGS BOILED IN CIDER
SHIRLEY SHAKER VILLAGE

《Buy nice big dried figs in a wooden box. Cover with fresh cider and let stand 12 hours. Place in iron pan on top of stove and boil slowly until the figs are soft and cider is dark and rich. Eat with heavy cream.

SPICED GRAPES
THE MANIFESTO, SEPTEMBER 1880

2 quarts stemmed seeded grapes
2 ounces (4 tablespoons) ground
  cloves

2 ounces (4 tablespoons) cinnamon
3½ pounds sugar

《Boil all together 2 hours until thick. Pour into hot sterilized jars and seal. Makes about 7–8 six ounce jars.

BRANDIED PEACHES
HANCOCK SHAKER VILLAGE

4 pounds peaches
1 quart water
4 cups sugar

2 cups water
1 cup brandy

《Combine peaches and water and simmer 2 minutes. Remove skins. Return peaches to kettle, add sugar and 2 cups of water. Simmer until sugar has thickened the juice. Add 1 cup of brandy. Bottle and seal in hot sterilized jars while hot. Do not use for 3 months. Makes 2 quarts.

PEAR HONEY
HANCOCK SHAKER VILLAGE

1 cup water
6 cups sugar
12 pears, peeled

4 drops essence of cloves
Few drops yellow food coloring
  (optional)

《Boil water and sugar together until it spins a thread. Stir in pears and stew slowly for 1 hour. It should be on low heat and stirred to keep from scorching. When it is thick and jellied, add flavoring and a few drops of yellow food coloring, if desired. Pour into hot sterilized jars. Seal. Yields 6 six ounce jars.

PINEAPPLE PRESERVE
MANUSCRIPT FROM SHAKER MUSEUM
OLD CHATHAM, NEW YORK

([Pare the pineapples and either grate them or chop them very fine. Add a pound of sugar to a pound of the pineapple. Boil from 15 to 20 minutes. Put up in small sterilized bottles, cork and seal well to keep out the air. One pound of pineapple will yield about 3 six ounce jars.

QUINCE HONEY
MT. LEBANON SHAKER VILLAGE

1 cup water
6 cups sugar
6 quinces, chopped fine

3 apples, peeled, cored, and
    chopped fine

([Combine water and sugar in large pot. Cook over low heat stirring occasionally until sugar is dissolved. Bring to a boil and boil hard for 5 minutes. Stir in quinces and apples; boil for 15 minutes. It should be thick, cook until it is thick and jellied. Pour into hot sterilized jars and seal at once. Yields 3–4 six ounce jars.

TOMATO HONEY #1
HANCOCK SHAKER VILLAGE

1 pound small tomatoes
2 cups honey
¼ cup preserved ginger

1 teaspoon powdered ginger
2 lemons

([Cover tomatoes with boiling water, remove skins, drain. Add honey, cover, and let stand overnight. In the morning pour off syrup and boil it until quite thick. Skim and then add tomatoes, preserved ginger, powdered ginger, and lemons sliced and seeded. Cook until tomatoes have a transparent appearance. Seal in sterilized jars. Yields 3 six ounce jars.

TOMATO HONEY #2

MT. LEBANON SHAKER VILLAGE

⟨Take 12 pounds tomatoes to 8 pounds white sugar. Mash or grate tomatoes thoroughly, then put into a strainer small quantities at a time; rub pulp through, leaving the skins. Add the sugar to the juice and let it stand 1 hour or until sugar is thoroughly dissolved, stirring it occasionally. Boil tomato-sugar mixture in a kettle over a slow fire about ¾ of an hour, or more if needed, stirring it often. If the scum rises, take it off. The mixture should be thick. Bottle while hot in sterilized jars and seal. Makes about 12 six ounce jars.

SPICED TOMATOES

THE MANIFESTO, SEPTEMBER 1880

⟨To 12 cups of chopped fruit allow 8 cups of white sugar, 4 cups cider vinegar, not too strong, 2 tablespoons each of ground cinnamon, cloves, and allspice; cook together in a porcelain kettle 1 hour (or more if mixture remains too thin), then put in sterilized jars and cover tightly. Nice with meat. Twelve cups fruit yields 10 pints.

BEST PICKLES

HANCOCK SHAKER VILLAGE

20 medium-size cucumbers	2 tablespoons pickling spices
Salt	5 teaspoons salt
8 cups sugar	4 cups vinegar

⟨Cover whole cucumbers with salted boiling water. Allow to stand until next morning. Drain, reserving water. Repeat this procedure on next three mornings, using the original water. The brine gets stronger each day. On fifth day, drain and slice in half-inch pieces. Combine sugar, spices, salt, and vinegar. Bring to boil and pour over cucumbers. Let stand 2 days. On third day, bring to boiling and seal in hot sterilized pint jars. Makes 7 pints. Makes very crisp, transparent pickles. Keep same water for 4 days, bringing it to boil each day.

MARY WHITCHER'S SWEET PICKLED FRUIT

MARY WHITCHER'S SHAKER HOUSEKEEPER

7 pounds fruit, either crab apples, Seckel pears, or plums	4 sticks cinnamon
7 cups sugar	¼ cup cassia buds
8 cups vinegar	*or*
	¼ cup cloves

([If crab apples or plums are used, wash but do not pare. If pears are preferred, pare but leave on stems. Combine sugar, vinegar, and spices and boil 5 minutes. Add fruit and cook slowly until fruit is tender, but not soft. Let stand in syrup overnight. Drain off syrup and cook until of honey consistency. Pack fruit in sterilized pint jars, cover with boiling syrup and seal at once. Makes 7 pints.

PICKLED BEETS

HANCOCK SHAKER VILLAGE

([Wash 2 pounds very small beets but do not cut off any of the rootlets. Boil or bake until tender, peel or rub off the outside with a coarse cloth. If beets are large, cut them in slices; if very small beets are used, leave whole. Put them into a sterilized jar with 4 cups cold boiled vinegar, black pepper, and 2 teaspoons ginger. This is one of the most ornamental pickles brought to the table. When serving, add caraway seeds or caraway powder (made by pounding the seed fine) to taste. Yields 4 half pint jars.

PICKLED CELERY

MT. LEBANON SHAKER VILLAGE

([Cut up finely 6 heads of cabbage, 6 heads of celery, put them in a crock; pour boiling salted water over all. Let stand 2 days. Drain. Put in a pan. Combine 2 ounces turmeric, some scraped fresh horse-radish, 6 or 8 blades of mace, broken cinnamon sticks, white ginger root, and 1 tablespoon celery seed; mix all these with the cabbage and celery. Put on the fire 1 quart of vinegar, made very sweet with sugar, and a handful of whole black peppercorns. Let it come to a boil and pour over the cabbage and celery. Bottle in sterilized jars and store. Makes 12 quarts.

AMELIA'S PICKLED GRAPES
NORTH UNION SHAKER VILLAGE, OHIO

16 cups stemmed half-ripe grapes
8 cups brown sugar
2 quarts wine vinegar

½ cup each whole cloves, whole allspice, and pieces stick cinnamon
or
8 drops oil of spices

⟨[Do not use ripe grapes, a half-ripe Catawba is most suitable. Place grapes in jars. Make a syrup of sugar, vinegar, and spices, or better yet use 8 drops of oil of spices. This will give a very clear pickle. Pour hot syrup over grapes in sterilized jars and seal. Excellent with ham or fowl. Makes about 6–8 pints.

PICKLED PEACHES
SHIRLEY SHAKER VILLAGE

⟨[Take large freestone peaches, almost ripe enough to be eaten with cream. Put them in brine[1] for 2 days. Wipe dry. Pry peaches open without cutting them in half. Remove seed and fill cavity with mixture of chopped horse-radish, white and black mustard seeds, celery seeds, chopped garlic or onion, powdered cloves, allspice, nutmeg, powdered ginger, pepper, cinnamon, and sugar. Cover with cold vinegar. Keep peaches well covered with mixture and the jar closely covered.

AMELIA'S PICKLED PEACHES
NORTH UNION SHAKER VILLAGE, OHIO

7 pounds ripe peaches
¼ cup whole cloves
¼ cup pieces stick cinnamon

¼ cup whole allspice
8 cups sugar
1 quart vinegar

⟨[Wipe all the fuzz from peaches and insert 3 cloves in each one. Put the remaining spices in a muslin bag. Place the bag in the sugar and vinegar and boil 10 minutes. Pour while very hot over peaches. Do this three mornings in succession, heating syrup to boil each time. The

---

[1] Brine is 1 cup salt dissolved in 2 quarts boiling water which has settled for 2 days.

fourth morning scald fruit in syrup; pack in sterilized jars, cover with syrup, and seal. Makes 6 pints.

HOT PICKLED PEARS
HANCOCK SHAKER VILLAGE

4 cups sugar
1 tablespoon turmeric
4 tablespoons celery seeds
8 tablespoons flour
4 tablespoons salt
3 tablespoons dry mustard

4 quarts unpeeled coarsely ground preserving pears
1½ quarts coarsely ground onions
8 red peppers, coarsely ground
8 green peppers, coarsely ground
2 quarts apple cider vinegar

❡Mix all dry ingredients together and add to mixture of pears and vegetables. Add vinegar and cook approximately 20 minutes or a little longer after mixture comes to a boil. Seal in sterile jars. Makes about 3 dozen 6 ounce jelly glasses.

HANCOCK PICKLED PUMPKIN
HANCOCK SHAKER VILLAGE

Peel and cut in 1 inch squares 12 cups of yellow pumpkin. Cover with 10 cups of sugar and let stand overnight. In the morning add 2 cups white vinegar, a spice bag of 2 tablespoons of whole cloves and 6 sticks of cinnamon. Bring slowly to a boil. Cook until pumpkin is clear and syrup is thick. Discard spice bag. Pack pumpkin in sterilized pint jars, pour hot liquid over it and seal. Makes 6 pints.

Variation:

2 tablespoons whole cloves
2 tablespoons pieces stick cinnamon
8 cups white sugar

1 quart cider vinegar
10 cups 1 inch cubes pared pumpkin

❡Tie spices in double thickness of cheesecloth. Combine sugar and vinegar in large saucepan. Add spice bag; bring to a rolling boil. Add pumpkin, cook until tender. Remove spice bag. Spoon pumpkin into sterile pint jars; cover with syrup. Seal at once. Makes 5 pints.

PICKLED WALNUTS
MT. LEBANON SHAKER VILLAGE

Gather walnuts about June 10 when they are green and young enough for a big needle to pass through them. Make a brine to cover them entirely with 6 ounces salt to 1 quart of water. Lay them in this brine for two weeks, removing scum as it appears. Take them out, and scrape them, and rub them with a coarse towel. Put them in fresh water for 3 days, changing the water daily. Put garlic, allspice, and black pepper into vinegar and pour it boiling on the walnuts. Cloves added are an improvement.

For 100 walnuts:

½ gallon vinegar
1 teaspoon salt
3 ounces bruised ginger root

¼ ounce cloves
A blade or two of mace

❮Put nuts in stone jar. Add salt, ginger root, cloves, and mace to vinegar. Cover nuts entirely with vinegar mixture. Put lid on jar. It is said the nuts will keep like this for 10 years.

APPLE CATSUP
THE MANIFESTO

Pare and core 12 sour apples. Stew with water until soft. Rub through a sieve. To each quart of apple pulp add this mixture:

1 cup sugar
1 teaspoon pepper
1 teaspoon powdered cloves
1 teaspoon dry mustard

2 teaspoons cinnamon
1 tablespoon salt
2 onions, finely chopped
2 cups cider vinegar

❮Add mixture to apple pulp, bring to a boil, and simmer 1 hour. Bottle in sterilized jars, cork, and seal while hot. Makes 3 pints.

CUCUMBER CATSUP
WATERVLIET SHAKER VILLAGE, NEW YORK

48 cucumbers, unpeeled
14 onions
6 green peppers
6 teaspoons black pepper

2 cups vinegar
8 teaspoons salt
1 cup sugar
Dill seed to taste

([Grate the cucumbers. Chop onions and peppers very fine and drain cucumbers, onions, and peppers through a colander for 2 hours before seasoning. Boil vinegar. Add vegetables and seasonings to it. Bottle in sterilized jars while very hot and seal. Makes 15 pints.

GOOSEBERRY CATSUP
HANCOCK SHAKER VILLAGE

10 cups gooseberries	1½ tablespoons cinnamon
8 cups sugar	1 tablespoon cloves
2 cups cider vinegar	1 tablespoon allspice

([Pick over, wash, and drain gooseberries. Put in kettle, add sugar, vinegar, and spices. Bring to boiling point and let simmer 2 hours. Fill sterilized bottles and seal.

Gooseberries are sometimes hard to find, but this recipe makes the hunt worthwhile. Makes 4–5 pints.

GRAPE CATSUP
HANCOCK SHAKER VILLAGE

([Use recipe for Gooseberry Catsup* substituting 10 cups grape pulp (without seeds and skins) for gooseberries. Simmer only 30 minutes.

AMELIA'S GRAPE CATSUP
NORTH UNION SHAKER VILLAGE, OHIO

5 pounds grapes, stemmed (10 cups)	1 tablespoon allspice
1 tablespoon ground cloves	1 teaspoon salt
1 tablespoon cinnamon	4 cups maple or brown sugar
1 tablespoon pepper	1 cup best wine vinegar

([Cover grapes with water in enamel pot and simmer 10 minutes. Put through a sieve. Add spices, salt, sugar, and vinegar. Boil gently until thick. Pour into hot sterilized containers and seal. Makes 4–5 pints.

TOMATO CATSUP

THE MANIFESTO, SEPTEMBER, 1880

24 ripe tomatoes
3 tablespoons salt
1 teaspoon cayenne pepper
1 teaspoon black pepper
2 tablespoons whole allspice

2 tablespoons whole cloves
2 tablespoons grated nutmeg
1 cup maple syrup
½ cup brandy

⟨[Wash the tomatoes, put them into a kettle, and mash as fine as possible; add the salt and spices and boil 2 hours. Then strain through a sieve, carefully rubbing through the pulp. Put back and boil. Add 1 cup maple syrup. At the end of 4 hours remove. Add ½ cup brandy. When cold, bottle in sterilized jars and seal. Keep in a cool dry place.

When boiling, stir almost constantly to prevent browning. Makes 1½ pints.

CELERY RELISH

THE MANIFESTO

1½ cups chopped celery
4 teaspoons powdered sugar (or less according to taste)

1 teaspoon salt
½ teaspoon dry mustard
¼ cup vinegar

⟨[Mix ingredients in order given. Cover and let stand in a cold place 1½ hours. Drain off the liquid before serving. When preparing celery include some of the small tender leaves. Makes 1½ cups.

CORN RELISH

HANCOCK SHAKER VILLAGE

4 cups skinned and chopped onions
4 cups peeled and chopped ripe tomatoes
4 cups peeled and chopped cucumbers
4 cups corn cut from cob

4 cups chopped cabbage
4 cups sugar
1 tablespoon salt
1 tablespoon celery seeds
1 teaspoon turmeric
4 cups vinegar

⟨[Mix vegetables together in large saucepan. Add remaining ingredients and bring to a boil. Reduce heat and simmer 20 minutes uncovered. Put into sterilized glass containers; seal. Makes about 2 quarts.

CRANBERRY RELISH
SHAKER FESTIVAL, AUBURN, KENTUCKY

2 oranges
2 cups raw cranberries
3 sour apples

1 cup grated pineapple
2 cups sugar

❨[Remove and discard peel from 1 orange. Put cranberries, oranges, and apples through coarse cut of food grinder. Add pineapple and sugar and let stand in cool place 6 hours before using. Do not cook. Makes 4–6 cups.

INDIA RELISH
SOUTH UNION SHAKER VILLAGE, KENTUCKY

8 pounds very small green tomatoes
8 cups brown or maple sugar
2 cups water
3 sticks cinnamon
2 tablespoons ginger

3 lemons, cut very thin
2 cups shredded citron
3 cups seedless raisins
Peel 1 small orange

❨[Wash tomatoes and cut in quarters. Make syrup of sugar and water. Add tomatoes, cinnamon, ginger, lemons, citron, raisins, and orange peel. Boil slowly until fruit is clear and thick. Pour into sterilized containers and seal. This is excellent with cold meat. Makes 12 pints.

RHUBARB CHUTNEY #1
HARVARD SHAKER VILLAGE

8 cups cut up rhubarb
2 cups sugar
4 cups cut up onions
4 tablespoons salt

4 tablespoons black pepper
2 tablespoons cayenne pepper
1 cup cut up raisins
2 cups or less vinegar

❨[Cook rhubarb and sugar together for 1 hour. Mix other ingredients and add to rhubarb and sugar. Cook slowly for 4 hours. Let stand overnight. Simmer next morning. The chutney should be very thick and a dark rich color. Makes about 4 pints. Reduce amount of both peppers if you like a less spicy chutney.

RHUBARB CHUTNEY #2
CANTERBURY SHAKER VILLAGE

2 quarts diced rhubarb
1½ quarts diced onions
2 cups seedless raisins
7 cups white sugar
1 quart cider vinegar

2 tablespoons salt
2 teaspoons ground cinnamon
1 teaspoon ground cloves
⅛ teaspoon ground red pepper
2 teaspoons ground ginger

《Combine ingredients in a large heavy kettle and cook gently about 45 minutes or until fairly thick sauce is formed, stirring often. Let stand 1 hour. Return to heat and barely simmer for 4 hours. That is the secret. Mixture must be thick and dark. Makes 2 pints.

HANCOCK TOMATO CHUTNEY
HANCOCK SHAKER VILLAGE

12–15 medium-sized ripe tomatoes
3 cups peeled cored chopped tart
    apples
3 large onions, finely chopped
1½ tablespoons salt
1¼ cups cider vinegar

1½ cups brown sugar
1 teaspoon cinnamon
1 teaspoon dry allspice
1 teaspoon dry mustard
1 teaspoon cloves
1 or 2 tablespoons pickling spice

《Scald, skin, and chop tomatoes. Add apples, onions and remaining ingredients. Tie pickling spice in a muslin bag and add. Stir well and let stand for an hour. Put over heat and cook slowly until thick. Makes 2½–3 pints.

∵

In putting up jellies turn at once into sterilized glasses and let them remain in the sun under a net for several days. Then cover jelly directly with a paper dipped in brandy and paste paper over the top of the glasses.

Equal parts of red and white currants or currants and raspberries in equal parts make a delicious jelly.

Visitors to Canterbury, New Lebanon, Hancock, and other Shaker villages fifty years ago recall the rows upon rows of jellies, jams, and marmalades all capped with little paper covers neatly tied around with cord.

CHERRY JAM
LUCY A. SHEPARD, MT. LEBANON SHAKER VILLAGE

4 pounds cherries, pits removed
2 pounds fine white sugar

2 tablespoons red currant juice
or
2 tablespoons currant jelly

❡Boil the whole together rather fast until it stiffens and fruit is very soft. Then put into hot sterilized jam glasses for use. Seal. Makes 4 pints.

AMELIA'S SOUR CHERRY JAM
NORTH UNION SHAKER VILLAGE, OHIO

½ cup cracked cherry pits
16 cups (4 quarts) pitted sour
   cherries

3 quarts (12 cups) white sugar

❡Add cracked pits tied in cheesecloth to the pitted cherries and sugar. Cook together for 1½ hours, or until the jam thickens and the cherries take on a dark color. Remove bag of pits and pour jam into scalded sterilized jars and seal. This is a very rich and tasty confection. Makes 6–8 pints.

GINGER PEACH JAM
HANCOCK SHAKER VILLAGE

3 pounds peaches (about)
¼ cup lemon juice
1 package powdered pectin (used

by Hancock Shakers during
World War I)
5 cups sugar

❡Sort and wash fully ripe peaches. Remove stems, skins, and pits. Crush the peaches.

Measure crushed peaches into a kettle. There should be 3¾ cups. Add the lemon juice and pectin and stir well. Place on high heat and, stirring constantly, bring quickly to a full boil with bubbles over the entire surface.

Add the sugar, continue stirring, and heat again to a full bubbling boil. Boil hard for 1 minute, stirring constantly.

Remove from heat; skim and stir alternately for 5 minutes. Ladle jam into hot sterilized containers and seal immediately. Makes about 8 six ounce glasses.

To the recipe above, add 1 to 2 ounces of finely chopped candied ginger, the amount depending on the spiciness desired. Combine ginger with the crushed peaches before adding the pectin.

RHUBARB JAM OR CONSERVE

ELDRESS EMMA B. KING
OF CANTERBURY SHAKER VILLAGE AND
ELDRESS GERTRUDE SOULE
OF SABBATHDAY LAKE SHAKER VILLAGE

1 pound seedless raisins
3 medium-sized onions, peeled and chopped
2⅓ cups sugar
3 cups vinegar
2 tablespoons salt

1 teaspoon black pepper
2 tablespoons allspice
2 tablespoons ginger
8 cups ½ inch pieces rhubarb
2 cups peeled cored apples, finely chopped

❲Put raisins and onions through food chopper. Bring to a boil the sugar, vinegar, and seasonings. Add raisins, onions, and rhubarb and apples. Simmer this mixture very slowly all day and overnight, until it becomes very black and very thick. Pour into sterilized jars. Makes 4 pints.

RHUBARB AND CHERRY JAM

HANCOCK SHAKER VILLAGE

5 cups thinly sliced rhubarb
4 cups sugar

1 teaspoon butter
2 cups pitted stewed cherries

❲Boil all ingredients gently for 3 hours, let stand overnight. In morning, bring to a boil, for 5 minutes. Put in sterilized jar. Seal. Makes four eight ounce jars.

Variation: Stew rhubarb, sugar, and butter together (omit cherries). Boil 5 minutes. Stir in 1 package cherry Jell-o. Boil 2 minutes. Put in sterilized jars. Seal.

ROSE HIP JAM

HANCOCK SHAKER VILLAGE

After first frost, collect rose fruit before frozen, but after turning red.

Ratio is: 2 cups hips to 1 cup water.

❲Place hips and water in heavy pan and simmer until fruit is tender. Rub through a fine sieve. Measure and add fine sugar, 2 cups, and 1 tablespoon rose water to each 2 cups of pulp. Simmer until thick. Put into sterilized jars. Seal. Makes two 8 ounce jars.

SHAKER TOMATO JAM
HANCOCK SHAKER VILLAGE

4 pounds ripe tomatoes   8 lemons
16 cups sugar   3 sticks cinnamon
4 large oranges

❲Scald tomatoes to remove skins and chop fine. Add sugar, the juice and grated rind of oranges and lemons, and cinnamon and cook until it jells on spoon. Skim, pour, and seal. This makes a most appetizing, bright pink confection. Put into sterilized jars. Seal. Makes 4–5 pints.

APPLE JELLY
HANCOCK SHAKER VILLAGE

Basis for many other jellies:

8 pounds firm tart apples   Sugar
4 cups water

❲Wash, core, and slice apples (do not peel) and put them with water in large pot. Bring to boil and cook over low heat 15 minutes or until soft. Remove from heat, pour through a jelly bag or large sieve lined with several layers of cheesecloth. Allow juice *to drip* into container below. (Do not squeeze, this will make jelly cloudy.)

Measure juice. Add ¾ cup sugar for every cup of juice. Boil 20 minutes and skim surface. Add cinnamon to flavor, pour into hot sterilized jars, seal at once. Makes about 4 pints.

Mint Jelly:

Follow above rule, omit cinnamon, and add large bunch of fresh mint, leaves bruised. After juice and sugar have been boiled together, simmer in apple juice until desired flavor is obtained, about 5 minutes. Add 2 tablespoons lemon juice and few drops green food coloring. Turn into sterilized glass jars and seal. Put in a sunny window and let stand 24 hours.

Basil Jelly:

Substitute green basil leaves, bruised and stewed with apple juice. Omit cinnamon and lemon juice and use pink food coloring. Boil up, pour into sterilized glasses, and seal. Substitute thyme leaves to make Thyme Jelly (use green food coloring).

Rose Geranium Jelly:

Follow recipe for Mint Jelly but use rose geranium leaves in place of mint—omit lemon juice, use pink coloring. Heat and pour into sterilized glass jars—fill halfway up and let stand 30 minutes. Put a small geranium leaf on jelly—complete filling glass jar with hot jelly and seal.

MARY WHITCHER'S CINNAMON JELLY
MARY WHITCHER'S SHAKER HOUSEKEEPER

4 pounds firm tart apples	Sugar
2 cups water	Powdered cinnamon

❨Wash, core, and slice apples. Add water and in a large pot bring to a boil. Cook over low heat 15 minutes or until soft. Remove from heat and pour through jelly bag or large sieve lined with several layers of cheese-cloth. Allow juice to drip into container. Measure juice, return to pot. Add ¾ cup sugar and ½ teaspoon cinnamon for every 1 cup of juice. Cook over low heat, stirring until sugar is dissolved. Boil rapidly to jelly stage. Skim surface. Color lightly by adding a few drops of red food coloring just to make jelly a pretty pink. Pour into sterilized jars; seal at once. Make 2 pints or 4 jelly jars.

CRANBERRY JELLY
FRANCES HALL, HANCOCK SHAKER VILLAGE

4 cups raw cranberries	2 cups sugar
2 cups boiling water	

❨Boil cranberries with water, stir to prevent their burning. Strain through a sieve, add sugar, and again boil until thick. Pour into a quart mold and refrigerate until cold, when it can be turned out. Use a fancy mold for Thanksgiving table.

If whole sauce is wanted, do not strain, but use same amounts. Do not let it boil over. Makes 1–1½ quarts.

GREEN GRAPE JELLY
(Wild Grapes Make Best Jelly)
MT. LEBANON SHAKER VILLAGE

⟨Pick the grapes from the stems and put into a preserving kettle that will hold about 2 quarts; add 2 cups of cold water. Boil until the fruit is thoroughly scalded. Press very gently through a flannel jelly bag. To every 2 cups of juice, add 2 cups of white sugar; boil 10 minutes. Boil 1 pint at a time and use a porcelain-lined kettle. The jelly will be light green or yellow. Adding a handful of ripe grapes will make jelly a delicate pink. Seal in sterilized jars.

If ripe Concord grapes are used, the jelly will be purple and also very pretty. Makes 4 pint jelly jars.

RASPBERRY JELLY
SHIRLEY SHAKER VILLAGE

⟨Take equal quantities of raspberries and currants, using 1 pound of sugar to 1 pint of juice. Make according to the recipes already given. Blackberry jelly can be made in the same way. Seal in sterilized jars. Makes two 8 ounce jars.

RHUBARB JELLY
HANCOCK SHAKER VILLAGE

⟨Cut up the rhubarb without peeling. Steam till very soft. Then lay it on a hair sieve to drain overnight, until the juice is out. It may be pressed a little at last.

To a pint of juice allow a scant 2 cups of sugar.

Boil the juice and skim. Heat the sugar in the oven while the juice is boiling. Add the hot sugar to the juice and boil till it forms jelly when tried in cold water.

This looks and tastes like guava jelly and keeps well.

Seal while hot in sterilized glass jars. Makes 1 pint.

CARROT MARMALADE
SABBATHDAY LAKE SHAKER VILLAGE

3 cups pared chopped cooked carrots
2 tablespoons grated lemon rind
⅓ cup lemon juice

3 tablespoons grated orange rind
½ cup orange juice
6 cups sugar

❲Combine all ingredients in large saucepan. Cook slowly 45 minutes or until it jells on spoon. Skim, pour into sterilized containers; seal. Makes about 1 quart.

CURRANT MARMALADE
SHIRLEY SHAKER VILLAGE

❲Strip the currants from the branches and soak them in boiling water until they break. Then place them in a sieve to drain and when they are cold press through the sieve to clear off the seeds. Then mix together equal parts fruit pulp and sugar and bring to a boil. Simmer until marmalade is quite thick. Add brandy to taste and simmer a few minutes more. Pour into sterilized ½ pint marmalade jars, and seal carefully.

HANCOCK TOMATO MARMALADE
HANCOCK SHAKER VILLAGE

3 quarts skinned and sliced green tomatoes
6 cups sugar
1 teaspoon salt
4 lemons

2 cups water
1 ginger root grated
    or
2 tablespoons chopped preserved ginger

❲Combine tomatoes, sugar, and salt in large kettle. Peel the lemons. Shred peel and add to tomatoes. Remove seeds from lemon pulp, chop pulp, and with remaining ingredients add to mixture in kettle. Bring mixture to a boil. Boil rapidly, stirring often until it thickens, 45 minutes or longer. Don't cover kettle.

Pour marmalade into 5 hot sterilized 1 pint jars and seal. Yields 5 pints. Store in a cool, dry, dark place.

Sauces

APPLESAUCE TO SERVE WITH HAM
HANCOCK SHAKER VILLAGE

〖Follow recipe for Shaker Applesauce.* Use 4 cups of the applesauce and to this add 1½ cups onions which have been cooked to a purée in 2 tablespoons butter. Add 1 cup fresh cider and cook down. At very last, add 1 teaspoon horse-radish and 2 to 4 tablespoons heavy cream. Mix gently.

Apples should be kept in nice firm slices and not mashed up. Makes about 6 cups.

SPECIAL APPLESAUCE
FOR PORK, CHICKEN, OR DUCK
SHIRLEY SHAKER VILLAGE

〖Core, but do not pare, 4 apples. Cut into quarters and cover with boiling water. Add a small piece of stick cinnamon and 2 cloves. Cook until apples are tender. Rub through a sieve. Return to fire and add 1½ tablespoons sharp cider and ½ cup brown sugar. Cook 10 minutes. Add 1 tablespoon of butter. Serve hot. Yields 1 cup.

BLACKBERRY SAUCE
MANUSCRIPT FROM SHAKER MUSEUM
OLD CHATHAM, NEW YORK

14 cups blackberries
6 cups sugar
1 cup vinegar

Whole cloves, allspice, or broken cinnamon sticks

〖Put berries, sugar, and vinegar in kettle and cook until soft, about 25 minutes. Mash and pass through a coarse sieve. Combine pulp with juice and add spices, tied in a bag. Cook to desired thickness. Remove spice bag. Serve hot or cold. Makes 4–6 cups.

BLUEBERRY SAUCE

WATERVLIET SHAKER VILLAGE, NEW YORK

1 cup sugar
1 tablespoon cornstarch
1 cup boiling water

2 cups fresh blueberries
1 tablespoon grated lemon rind
1 tablespoon lemon juice

⁅In a saucepan mix together sugar and cornstarch. Add boiling water and cook over low heat 5 minutes, or until thick. Mash blueberries until very soft, add to sugar mixture. Add lemon rind and juice. Cook 5 minutes. Serve hot or cold. Makes 2 cups.

BREAD SAUCE

MT. LEBANON SHAKER VILLAGE

2 cups milk
½ cup fine dry bread crumbs
1 onion
6 cloves
½ teaspoon salt

¼ teaspoon pepper
½ teaspoon thyme (optional)
½ cup coarse dry breadcrumbs
3 tablespoons butter

⁅Cook milk 30 minutes in top of double boiler with fine breadcrumbs and onion stuck with cloves. Remove onion and cloves, add salt and pepper, and thyme if desired. Brown coarse breadcrumbs in butter and sprinkle over the sauce. Makes 1 cup.

DRAWN BUTTER SAUCE

MARY WHITCHER, THE MANIFESTO

½ cup butter
3 teaspoons flour
5 teaspoons cold water
½ teaspoon salt
½ teaspoon pepper
1 hard-boiled egg, chopped
 (optional)
 or
½ cup chopped parsley (optional)

or
1 cup chopped oysters flavored
 with 2 tablespoons heavy cream
 and 2 tablespoons dry sherry
 (optional)
 or
2 tablespoons drained capers and
 1 tablespoon lemon juice
 (optional)

⁅Heat butter and add flour, cold water, and seasoning. Simmer over low heat. If Drawn Butter Sauce is to be used with fish add very finely chopped hard-boiled egg or parsely. If used with boiled fowl add oysters. If used with lamb, add capers and lemon juice.

CAPER SAUCE #1
MT. LEBANON SHAKER VILLAGE

❲Melt 2 tablespoons butter, add 2 tablespoons flour, and simmer. Add 1½ cups of liquid (½ heavy cream and ½ lamb or mutton stock). Stir in 2 egg yolks and remove from heat. Add 2 teaspoons capers, 1 teaspoon lemon juice, and 1 teaspoon chopped parsely or tarragon. Makes 1½ cups.

CAPER SAUCE #2

❲Melt 2 tablespoons butter. Cook slowly and add 2 tablespoons flour. Cook thoroughly 2 minutes. Add ½ cup boiling beef stock (bouillon) and beat to make smooth. Beat together 2 egg yolks, 1½ tablespoons warm heavy cream, and 1 tablespoon capers, and add to sauce. Makes 1 cup.

CAPER SAUCE #3

❲Cook together 2 tablespoons each of melted butter and flour. Gradually add 2 cups clear lamb or mutton stock (if lamb stock is not available, use beef bouillon). Add 2 thin slices of peeled lemon, ½ teaspoon dry mustard, and 2 teaspoons vinegar. Cook for 1 minute. Just before serving, stir in 2 teaspoons butter, 4 tablespoons chopped capers, and 1½ tablespoons hot heavy cream. Makes 2 cups.

"CATCHUP" SAUCE
MT. LEBANON SHAKER VILLAGE

❲Cook 1 teaspoon melted butter and 1 teaspoon flour together. Add 1 cup pan drippings and cook to thicken. Use beef pan drippings, even if sauce is to be used with mutton. Add ½ cup thick tomato catsup and bring to a boil. Add salt and pepper and strain. Makes 1½ cups sauce.

HANCOCK CHILI SAUCE

HANCOCK SHAKER VILLAGE

24 ripe tomatoes
2 large onions, chopped fine
4 cups vinegar
1 cup maple syrup
or
1 cup brown sugar

1 tablespoon salt
4 teaspoons powdered cloves
4 teaspoons cinnamon
4 teaspoon allspice
4 teaspoons nutmeg

❲Peel tomatoes by dipping in boiling water. Cut them up. Put in preserving kettle with all ingredients and boil 5 hours, watching and stirring often as tomatoes will burn easily. If too liquid remove some of juice as sauce should be thick. Bottle in sterilized jars and seal. Makes 6 pints.

SISTER EMMA'S CHOCOLATE SAUCE

MT. LEBANON SHAKER VILLAGE

2 cups milk
1½ tablespoons cornstarch
2 squares (1 ounce each) unsweetened
chocolate
4 tablespoons powdered sugar

2 tablespoons hot water
2 eggs, separated
⅔ cup powdered sugar
1 teaspoon vanilla

❲Scald 1¾ cups milk, add cornstarch diluted with remaining milk and cook 8 minutes in top of double boiler. Melt chocolate, add 4 tablespoons sugar and hot water. Stir until smooth, then add to cooked mixture. Beat white of eggs stiff, add powdered sugar, and continue beating. Then add unbeaten egg yolks and stir into cooked mixture. Cook 2 minutes, add vanilla, and cool before serving. Makes 2 cups sauce.

EXCELLENT CHOCOLATE SAUCE

WATERVLIET SHAKER VILLAGE, NEW YORK

2 ounces sweet chocolate
1 tablespoon granulated sugar
¼ cup milk
1 teaspoon arrowroot (or cornstarch)
¼ cup heavy cream

¼ teaspoon salt
1½ tablespoons butter
¼ cup powdered sugar
½ teaspoon vanilla

⟨In a double boiler (over hot water) cook chocolate, granulated sugar, and milk, 5 minutes. Add arrowroot, cream, and salt mixed together. Cook 10 minutes. Melt butter, add powdered sugar, and cook until caramelized, stirring constantly. Add to chocolate-arrowroot-cream mixture and flavor. Chill. This sauce takes pains, but is well worth it. Makes about 1 cup.

SISTER EMMA'S HOT CHOCOLATE SAUCE
MT. LEBANON SHAKER VILLAGE

1 square (1 ounce) unsweetened
  chocolate
1 tablespoon melted butter

½ cup boiling water
1 cup sugar
½ teaspoon vanilla

⟨Melt chocolate in top of double boiler over boiling water. Add butter and when blended pour on gradually, while stirring constantly, boiling water. Then add sugar. Bring to the boiling point. Let boil 14 minutes. Cool slightly and flavor with vanilla. Makes about 1 cup.

CIDER SAUCE
HANCOCK SHAKER VILLAGE

1 tablespoon butter
¾ tablespoon flour

1½ cups Boiled Cider*, boiled down
  from 3 cups fresh cider
2 tablespoons sugar

⟨Blend butter and flour over low heat. Add cider gradually. Add sugar. Boil 5 minutes, stirring to keep smooth. Serve hot. Makes 1½ cups.

CRANBERRY SAUCE
MARY WHITCHER'S SHAKER HOUSEKEEPER

⟨Discard the poor fruit and wash the rest. Put in the preserving kettle 1 quart of berries with 1 cup of water. Now put the sugar on top of the berries, allowing 2 cups of sugar to a quart of berries. Set on the fire and stew 20 minutes. Stir often to prevent burning. They will not need to be strained and will preserve their color, cooked in this way. Never cook cranberries before putting in the sugar. One quart of berries yields 3–4 cups sauce.

MAPLE-CRANBERRY GLAZE FOR HAM
HANCOCK SHAKER VILLAGE

([Stir over low heat until blended and smooth: ½ cup maple syrup, 1 cup strained cranberry sauce, 1 tablespoon vinegar or cider. If cider, add 1 tablespoon lemon juice. Yields 1 cup.

Pour over ham during last 10 minutes of baking.

Variation: Use 2 cups whole Cranberry Sauce* and double the recipe. After basting ham, remove the sauce and pass in separate dish.

DESSERT CREAM SAUCE #1
HARVARD SHAKER VILLAGE

¾ cup thick cream
⅓ cup powdered sugar (or granulated, sifted fine)

½ teaspoon vanilla (other flavoring such as rose water, maple syrup, brandy, cider, or fruit juices may be substituted for vanilla)

([Have cream at room temperature. Add sugar, vanilla, or other flavoring. Mix gently. Let stand a few minutes and then refrigerate. Makes 1 cup.

DESSERT CREAM SAUCE #2
SHIRLEY SHAKER VILLAGE

1 egg, separated
1 cup confectioners' sugar
½ cup thick cream

½ teaspoon vanilla (or other flavoring)

([Beat white of egg until stiff. Add well-beaten yolk of egg and sugar, gradually. Beat cream until stiff, combine mixtures and flavor. Makes 2 cups.

ENGLISH CREAM
MT. LEBANON SHAKER VILLAGE

([The milk must be new—perfectly fresh and sweet. Set in a large broad milk pan in a cool place (not freezing) for 10 to 12 hours. Then in the same pan, bring to a boil, but do not boil or it will curdle. Keep in same vessel and set in a cool place 6 hours longer. Skim off cream and use with tarts, open pies, and puddings. One quart of milk yields about 2 cups cream.

Note: Cannot be made with homogenized milk.

CUCUMBER SAUCE TO SERVE WITH FISH
HARVARD SHAKER VILLAGE

([Peel and seed 4 cucumbers. Chop or cut meat into small pieces. Put in pan and pour over 2 or 3 cups of boiling water to cover. Let stand for 10 minutes. Drain very well. Chill. Add 1 teaspoon each of chives, basil, 1 teaspoon sugar, 1 teaspoon horse-radish, and 1 cup of sour cream; salt and pepper. Makes 2 cups.

CURRANT SAUCE #1
THE MANIFESTO, 1899

6 cups currants	1 tablespoon each cloves and
3 cups sugar	cinnamon
1 cup vinegar	½ teaspoon salt

([Mix all together and boil ½ hour. Serve with meat or game. Makes 3–4 cups.

CURRANT SAUCE #2
MT. LEBANON SHAKER VILLAGE

([Whip one 8 ounce glass of currant jelly with a fork until soft. Add ½ teaspoon grated lemon rind and brandy to taste. Makes 1 cup.

BOILED CUSTARD SAUCE
HANCOCK SHAKER VILLAGE

3 egg yolks	2 cups scalded milk
¼ cup sugar	½ teaspoon vanilla
⅛ teaspoon salt	

([Beat eggs slightly using a fork, add sugar and salt while gradually adding hot milk. Cook in top of double boiler over boiling water. Continue stirring until mixture thickens to your liking. Chill. Flavor after sauce has been chilled.

If using above as a dessert instead of a sauce, it should be of thicker consistency, which means longer cooking, but be careful for overcooking will curdle the custard.

HOT DILL SAUCE
HARVARD SHAKER VILLAGE

To use with poached white fish, grilled lamb chops, or hot tongue.

⅓ cup chopped onion
1½ tablespoons butter
1½ tablespoons flour
1 cup rich milk
Salt and pepper to taste

2 tablespoons sour cream
1 teaspoon chopped fresh dill
      or
2 teaspoons dried dill

([Cook onion in butter until tender, add flour and cook 2 minutes over low heat. Add milk, stirring constantly until mixture thickens. When very hot, remove from stove and add salt, pepper, and sour cream. Beat well. Stir in dill. Makes 1½ cups.

DILL SOUR CREAM SAUCE
HANCOCK SHAKER VILLAGE

1½ cups sour cream, room
   temperature
½ teaspoon salt
¼ teaspoon pepper

3 teaspoons chopped fresh dill
   leaves
      or
1½ teaspoons powdered dried dill
   leaves

([Mix all ingredients together in order given. Chill. Makes 1½ cups.

EGG SAUCE
HANCOCK SHAKER VILLAGE

2 tablespoons butter
2 tablespoons flour
1 cup light cream
2 hard-boiled eggs, whites chopped,
   yolks riced or coarsely crumbled
½ teaspoon salt
¼ teaspoon white pepper

1 tablespoon chopped minced
   parsley
1 tablespoon chopped minced
   chives
1 teaspoon dry mustard
1 teaspoon brown sugar

❨[Melt butter, add flour, cook 5 minutes, slowly. Gradually add light cream, stirring constantly, and simmer 10 minutes. Blend in eggs, seasonings, herbs, mustard, and sugar. If too thick add more cream. Cook over low heat 3 minutes. Makes 1½ cups.

FISH SAUCE
SISTER OLIVE, HANCOCK SHAKER VILLAGE

❨[Combine 1 cup of cream, 2 well-beaten eggs, juice of ½ lemon, salt, and pepper. Put on the fire and stir constantly at low heat until it thickens. A bit of dry mustard might be added if a sharper taste is desired. Serve over boiled fish. Makes 1½ cups sauce.

GINGER SAUCE FOR PORK OR HAM
HANCOCK SHAKER VILLAGE

2 tablespoons chopped onions	1 teaspoon powdered ginger
2 tablespoons melted butter	1 tablespoon chopped ginger
1 tablespoon sugar	1 tablespoon flour
½ teaspoon salt	1 cup cider or orange juice
¼ teaspoon pepper	½ cup heavy cream

❨[Sauté onion in melted butter until soft. Add sugar, salt, pepper, powdered ginger, chopped ginger and blend well; add flour and cook 2 minutes. Stir briskly and add cider or juice; simmer 5 minutes and let boil up once. It should be smooth. Remove from heat, add cream, and serve hot or warm. If sauce is to be used cold, cool off before beating in cream. Makes about 2 cups.

CREAM GRAVY
HANCOCK SHAKER VILLAGE

3 tablespoons flour	1½ cups milk
3 tablespoons salt pork fat	½ cup heavy cream

❨[Cook flour in fat until bubbles appear; simmer 2 minutes. Add milk and bring up to a boil, stirring all the time to keep it smooth and free of lumps. Remove from the heat and add cream. Stir briskly and serve in a bowl at breakfast when bacon is served. This is also good with fried pork and with little pancakes. Serve separately in a bowl. Makes 2 cups gravy.

CHESTNUT GRAVY TO USE WITH VEGETABLES

ELDER FREDERICK W. EVANS
MT. LEBANON SHAKER VILLAGE

⟮Add ¾ cup of mashed cooked chestnuts to 2 cups White Sauce #2* made with cream. Add salt and pepper. This is excellent to pass with boiled Brussels sprouts, cabbage, onions, and potatoes. It improves winter fare.

SALT PORK "MILK" GRAVY SAUCE

MARY WHITCHER'S SHAKER HOUSEKEEPER

⟮Sauté ¼ pound lean salt pork until golden brown. Drain, reserving fat. Chop up pork and set to one side. Measure off 3 tablespoons of strained pork fat, add 3 tablespoons flour, and cook 5 minutes gently. Add 2 cups top milk. Add 1 tablespoon minced chives and salt and pepper to taste. Cook slowly another 5 minutes. Add reserved chopped pork. Remove from stove and add ¼ cup heavy cream just before serving. Makes 2½–3 cups gravy.

HARD SAUCE

WATERVLIET SHAKER VILLAGE, NEW YORK

¼ cup butter
1 cup powdered sugar
       or
1 cup fine granulated sugar
2 tablespoons brandy

or
2 tablespoons dry sherry wine
2 egg yolks, beaten
½ cup heavy cream
2 egg whites, well beaten

⟮Cream butter and sugar, add brandy gradually. Put over hot water and add yolks very slowly, cooking over low heat until sauce thickens. Add cream and when sufficiently thick pour mixture over stiffly beaten egg whites. Makes 2 cups.

UNCOOKED HARD SAUCE

HANCOCK SHAKER VILLAGE

½ cup butter
1 cup fine sugar

3 tablespoons dry sherry wine
½ teaspoon nutmeg

❲Cream butter and sugar gradually and add wine slowly. Pile onto glass dish, sprinkle with nutmeg. Chill. Makes 1½ cups.

SIMPLE HARD SAUCE
SHIRLEY SHAKER VILLAGE

½ cup butter
1 cup confectioners' sugar

¾ cup granulated sugar
1 teaspoon vanilla

❲Cream butter and add sugars gradually. Beat well to make smooth and fluffy. Add flavoring. Makes 2 cups.

HONEY PUDDING SAUCE
HANCOCK SHAKER VILLAGE

2 egg whites

2 cups honey

❲Combine honey and egg whites and beat vigorously until the mixture forms a light fluffy sauce. Serve cold on puddings. Makes 2 cups.

.·.

"The horse-radish root we grow with success and consider it favorable. It is also a good seller."

HORSE-RADISH SAUCE #1
HANCOCK SHAKER VILLAGE

Horse-radish was grown as a root crop and sold by the Shakers freshly grated and also prepared in vinegar and bottled. The following measurements have been reduced from the vast amount used for commercial purposes, but the procedure is the same.

8 tablespoons grated horse-radish
   root
5 tablespoons vinegar

1½ teaspoons salt
Few grains cayenne

❲Mix all ingredients and bring to a boil. Remove at once from the heat. Let stand 10 minutes. Bottle in sterile jars and store. Makes about 1 cup.

HORSE-RADISH SAUCE #2
SHIRLEY SHAKER VILLAGE

1 teaspoon dry mustard
2 tablespoons heavy cream
1 tablespoon vinegar
½ teaspoon salt

½ teaspoon white sugar
1 tablespoon freshly grated
  horse-radish
1 tablespoon brown sugar

([Mix in order given and put in cool place for several hours before using. Makes ¾ cups.

HORSE-RADISH SAUCE #3
HANCOCK SHAKER VILLAGE

2 tablespoons Made Mustard*
2 tablespoons white sugar
½ teaspoon salt

1 tablespoon vinegar
2 tablespoons grated horse-radish

([Mix mustard, sugar, salt, and vinegar and pour over grated horse-radish. Let stand for 2 hours. Excellent with beef. Makes ¾ cup.

HORSE-RADISH SAUCE #4
HANCOCK SHAKER VILLAGE

([To 1½ cups of sour cream at room temperature add 2 teaspoons fresh horse-radish, 1 tablespoon drained capers, and salt and pepper to taste. Makes 1⅓ cups.

HORSE-RADISH SAUCE #5
HANCOCK SHAKER VILLAGE

1 cup white sauce (use North Union
  Sauce* or White Sauce #1*)
3 tablespoons freshly grated
  horse-radish
1 teaspoon sugar

2 tablespoons vinegar
½ teaspoon dry mustard
⅛ teaspoon powdered thyme
½ cup chopped hard-boiled egg
  (optional)

⟨Mix in order given. Heat but do not boil. Serve hot with fish or meat. Makes 1½ cups.

SOUR CREAM HORSE-RADISH SAUCE
HANCOCK SHAKER VILLAGE

½ cup heavy cream, slightly soured
6 tablespoons prepared horse-radish
½ teaspoon dry mustard

1 teaspoon each sugar, salt, and pepper

⟨Whip cream until stiff. Drain horse-radish. Mix with mustard, sugar, salt, and pepper. Fold into cream. Makes 1¼ cups.

HORSE-RADISH CREAM DRESSING
HANCOCK SHAKER VILLAGE

½ cup heavy sweet cream
3 tablespoons vinegar
¼ teaspoon salt

⅛ teaspoon pepper
2 tablespoons grated horse-radish root

⟨Beat cream until it begins to thicken. Add vinegar gradually while continuing to beat. When mixture is stiff, add seasonings and fold in grated horse-radish. Makes about 1 cup.

LEMON SAUCE FOR PUDDING
SABBATHDAY LAKE SHAKER VILLAGE

½ cup butter
1 egg, beaten
1¼ cups sugar (about)
1 teaspoon grated lemon rind

3 tablespoons lemon juice
1 teaspoon nutmeg
½ cup boiling water

⟨In the top of a double boiler beat the butter to a cream, add the beaten egg and also the sugar gradually. Then beat in the lemon rind and juice and nutmeg. Put over boiling water, add ½ cup of boiling water, stir and cook until it thickens. Makes 2 cups.

HANCOCK LEMON SAUCE

FRANCES HALL, HANCOCK SHAKER VILLAGE

½ cup sugar
1 tablespoon cornstarch
1 cup boiling water
2 tablespoons butter

1½ tablespoons lemon juice
½ teaspoon nutmeg
¼ teaspoon salt

([Mix sugar and cornstarch, add water gradually, stirring constantly; boil 5 minutes, remove from fire, add butter, lemon juice, nutmeg, and salt. Cook until thickened. Makes 1 cup.

Vanilla Sauce:

Substitute 1½ tablespoons vanilla for lemon juice and omit nutmeg.

Rose Water Sauce:

Add 1½ tablespoons rose water and leave out nutmeg and lemon juice.

LEMON EGG SAUCE

MT. LEBANON SHAKER VILLAGE

½ cup butter
1 cup sugar
3 egg yolks

⅓ cup boiling water
3 tablespoons lemon juice
1 tablespoon grated lemon rind

([Cream butter and sugar and beat in yolks. Add boiling water and cook in top of double boiler over boiling water. Remove from fire, beat up and add lemon juice and rind. Makes 1½ cups.

SHIRLEY LEMON SAUCE

SHIRLEY SHAKER VILLAGE

¾ cup sugar
¼ cup water
1 tablespoon fresh lemon balm or
    lemon verbena

2 tablespoons butter
1 tablespoon lemon juice

([Make a syrup by boiling sugar and water 5 minutes. Add balm or verbena and steep 5 minutes. Remove from fire and discard the herb. Add butter and lemon juice. Cook until thickened. Makes about 1 cup.

HOT MAPLE SAUCE
ENFIELD SHAKER VILLAGE, NEW HAMPSHIRE

⟨Add a very little water to a pound of maple sugar and boil until it reaches the "thread" stage. Add a ½ cup butter and ½ cup of English walnut meats broken into small pieces. There should be sufficient nuts to make sauce quite thick. Serve hot with vanilla ice cream or very slightly sweetened blancmange or custard. Makes about 2 cups.

MAPLE OR MOLASSES SAUCE
CANTERBURY SHAKER VILLAGE

1 cup maple syrup or molasses
2 tablespoons butter

2 tablespoons lemon juice
or
1 tablespoon vinegar

⟨Boil maple syrup or molasses 5 minutes, remove from fire and add butter and lemon juice or vinegar. Makes about 1 cup.

SAUCE MAYONNAISE
MARY WHITCHER'S SHAKER HOUSEKEEPER

⟨Mix together yolks of 2 raw eggs (not a particle of the white or your sauce will curdle) and 1½ teaspoons of Made Mustard.* Add very slowly 1 cup the best salad oil, stirring constantly, until you can tip the dish without spilling. Then add 1 tablespoon vinegar, cayenne and black pepper to taste, and ½ teaspoon salt. Stir briskly until quite light colored and serve on cold vegetables, fish, and salads. Makes 1 cup.

MINT SAUCE FOR KEEPING
HARVARD SHAKER VILLAGE

2 cups sugar
2 cups vinegar

½ cup chopped mint leaves

⟨Boil sugar and vinegar. Pour over chopped mint. Seal in sterilized air-tight bottles. Makes 2 cups.

MINT DRESSING FOR RACK
OF MUTTON OR LAMB
HANCOCK SHAKER VILLAGE

1 cup minced onion
1 cup finely chopped celery
1 cup slivered almonds
1 cup butter
1 cup purée of peas
2 tablespoons finely chopped
   fresh mint

½ teaspoon pepper
1 tablespoon salt
12 cups ¼ inch dry bread cubes
1 cup beef or chicken bouillon
   or stock

❛[Sauté onion and celery and almonds in butter, add purée of peas. Do
not brown. Add mint and seasonings to bread cubes. Add vegetable mixture and broth to moisten. Toss lightly to mix. Cool completely. Makes
15–16 cups.

MINT DRESSING FOR LAMB
HANCOCK SHAKER VILLAGE

4 tablespoons melted butter
2 tablespoons chopped onions
½ teaspoon salt
¼ teaspoon pepper
1 tablespoon brown sugar
2 tablespoons tarragon vinegar

2 cups fine bread crumbs
1 cup chopped fresh mint
1 cup liquid added if above is too
   dry (liquid can be all cider or ½
   butter and ½ cider; apple juice;
   or ½ water and ½ sherry)

❛[In melted butter, sauté onions until very soft. Add salt, pepper, sugar,
and vinegar. Blend and add crumbs, and chopped mint. It should be on
the dry side. Put on platter of sliced cooked lamb to surround the meat
as a garnish-dressing. Yields 2 cups.

MINT SAUCE FOR LAMB
HARVARD SHAKER VILLAGE

2 tablespoons dry mustard
2 tablespoons salt
2 cups sugar
2 small white onions, chopped
1 cup seeded raisins, chopped
2 cups tart apples, peeled, cored,
   chopped

1 cup chopped ripe tomatoes
6–8 small red peppers, seeded,
   chopped
1 cup finely chopped mint leaves
8 cups cider vinegar

❛[Mix all ingredients except vinegar together in an earthenware crock or large bowl. Mix well and let stand an hour or so. Bring vinegar to a boil and cool; add to other mixture. Stir well and enjoy. This will keep without refrigeration. Makes 5–6 cups.

MOLASSES SAUCE
SISTER OLIVE, HANCOCK SHAKER VILLAGE

⟨Mix 1 cup molasses, 1 tablespoon vinegar, ½ teaspoon of salt, and 1 tablespoon butter. Boil 10 minutes. Makes 1 cup.

.·.

Mustard grew wild and was also cultivated by the Shakers as a crop. The seeds were gathered when the plant ripened. They were dried and powdered to be used as seasoning. The two species of mustard used were *Brassica alba,* which yielded white seeds, and *Brassica nigra,* black seeds.

MADE MUSTARD
HANCOCK SHAKER VILLAGE

⟨Pour a very little boiling water over 3 tablespoons of dry mustard. Add ½ teaspoon salt, a tablespoon of olive oil, stirred in slowly; and 1 teaspoon sugar. Add 1 well-beaten egg yolk. Cook together until it thickens and pour in vinegar to taste. It is best eaten after blending several days. Egg can be omitted. Makes ½ cup.

.·.

Prepared mustard can of course be bought, the milder varieties often being called French or German mustard. English mustard is somewhat sharper. To mix ordinary mustard for your own use, use the following recipes.

PREPARED MUSTARD #1
HANCOCK SHAKER VILLAGE

3 tablespoons dry mustard   1 egg, slightly beaten
1 teaspoon salt   1 cup vinegar
1 tablespoon sugar   1 tablespoon olive oil

⟨Mix dry ingredients. Slowly add egg, then vinegar, mixing smooth. Set over low fire and cook 4 minutes, stirring constantly. Let cool, beat in oil. This is mild. Makes 1 cup.

PREPARED MUSTARD #2
HANCOCK SHAKER VILLAGE

1 teaspoon mustard
½ teaspoon salt
1 teaspoon sugar
2 tablespoons heavy cream
　　or

2 tablespoons evaporated milk
1 teaspoon vinegar
6 tablespoons salad oil

〖Follow directions for Prepared Mustard #1. This is also mild. Yields ½ cup.

PREPARED MUSTARD #3
HANCOCK SHAKER VILLAGE

2 teaspoons sugar
¼ teaspoon salt
2 tablespoons salad oil

¼ cup vinegar
¼ cup dry mustard

〖Mix sugar and salt. Add oil and mix until smooth. Mix vinegar and mustard together until smooth. Combine mixtures. This makes a rather sharp mustard. It may be thinned with hot water or made milder by more oil. Yields ½ cup.

PREPARED MUSTARD #4
HANCOCK SHAKER VILLAGE

½ cup dry mustard
½ cup flour
½ teaspoon salt
¾ cup boiling water
2 small onions, minced

2 tablespoons vinegar
2 tablespoons tart catsup
　(cook's choice)
½ cup boiling water (about)

〖Mix mustard, flour, and salt. Add ¾ cup boiling water slowly, mixing until smooth paste. Cook onions, vinegar, and catsup together for 10 minutes. Pour over paste and mix well, adding boiling water until mixture is of desired consistency. Bottled, this will keep for months. A small onion crushed in the bottom of each bottle is an addition liked by many. Yields 1 cup.

PREPARED MUSTARD #5
HANCOCK SHAKER VILLAGE

½ cup dry mustard
¼ cup sifted flour
½ cup sugar (or less, depending
on taste)

¼ cup milk
¼ cup vinegar

⟪Combine dry ingredients in a small saucepan. Gradually stir in milk and vinegar, stirring constantly over low heat until thick and smooth. Remove from heat and continue to stir until mixture is cool. Bottle securely and refrigerate for 2 weeks to ripen. Makes 1½ cups.

MUSTARD SAUCE–HOT
HANCOCK SHAKER VILLAGE

⅓ cup sugar
½ cup dry mustard
¼ teaspoon salt

½ cup vinegar
1 egg, lightly beaten
1 cup mayonnaise

⟪Mix sugar, mustard, and salt in top of double boiler. Stir in vinegar, egg and cook over hot water stirring constantly until mixture is smooth and thick. Remove from heat and stir in mayonnaise. Serve at once. Makes 2½ cups.

MUSTARD SAUCE–COLD
HANCOCK SHAKER VILLAGE

¾ cup mayonnaise
2 teaspoons prepared horse-radish

2 tablespoons prepared mustard
1 teaspoon sugar

⟪Blend all ingredients together. Chill. Makes 1 cup.

MUSTARD SAUCE
HARVARD SHAKER VILLAGE

2 teaspoons prepared mustard
½ teaspoon salt
½ teaspoon pepper
2 tablespoons flour
1 teaspoon brown sugar

¾ cup chicken broth
2 tablespoons vinegar
2 egg yolks
1 tablespoon chopped chives
2 tablespoons finely chopped raisins
(optional)

([Mix dry ingredients together in heavy saucepan over low heat. Add broth and vinegar and cook slowly to thicken. Add some of this mixture to egg yolks, then combine all together. Cook, stirring continuously; watch so it will not burn. Add chives. (Two tablespoons finely chopped raisins are especially good if serving with tongue.) Yields 1 cup.

MUSTARD SAUCE WITH CIDER

HANCOCK SHAKER VILLAGE

1 pint heavy cream
½ cup white or brown sugar
4 tablespoons dry mustard
Salt to taste
⅔ cup dry cider (not apple juice)

1 tablespoon lemon juice
    or
1 tablespoon vinegar
2 egg yolks

([Heat half the cream and all the sugar in the top of a double boiler over hot, not boiling, water. Stir well. Mix mustard and salt with the cider and lemon juice or vinegar and add slowly to heated cream and sugar. Beat egg yolks slightly. Add about 3 tablespoons of first mixture to eggs. Mix well, then add eggs to other mixture, stirring. Cook until sauce starts to thicken, about 3 minutes. Cool. Whip the remaining cream and stir it in. Serve at room temperature. Makes about 3 cups.

Serve with ham or pork.

HERB MUSTARD

HARVARD SHAKER VILLAGE

4 tablespoons brown sugar
3 tablespoons dry mustard
1 tablespoon tarragon or other
    herb vinegar

Reserve ½ teaspoon finely chopped
    dried tarragon, or 1 teaspoon
    fresh tarragon or other herb

([Blend sugar and mustard. Bring vinegar to boil. Add just enough to make a smooth paste. Put into a sterilized jar and seal while hot. Put away for two weeks. When it is ready to use mix in fresh tarragon before serving. If fresh tarragon is not going to be available, the dried herb can be mixed with mustard and will keep during the blending period.

The blending period for cooked mustards is very important to improve the taste of this prepared sauce. Makes ½ cup mustard.

COOKED HERB MUSTARD FOR MEATS

HARVARD SHAKER VILLAGE

3 tablespoons dry mustard
2 tablespoons brown sugar
1 cup vinegar (herb vinegar)
1 egg, beaten

2 tablespoons butter
½ teaspoon dried herb
or
1 tablespoon chopped fresh herb

❨Combine mustard, sugar, vinegar, and egg. Cook in double boiler over boiling water until thickened. Stir in butter and remove from heat. Add herb. Keep in refrigerator. Makes ⅔ cup.

NORTH UNION SAUCE

NORTH UNION SHAKER VILLAGE, OHIO

2 tablespoons butter
2 tablespoons flour
2 cups milk, rich and warm
Salt and pepper to taste

3 tablespoons freshly grated
  horse-radish
1 teaspoon sugar
2 tablespoons vinegar
½ teaspoon dry mustard

❨Make a white sauce by melting butter and blending in flour. Simmer over low heat, add warm milk gradually and salt and pepper. Cook gently 5 minutes, stirring to keep smooth.

Mix remaining ingredients together and add to the white sauce. Simmer but do not boil. Serve hot with fish or meat. Particularly nice with poached white fish, and boiled beef. Makes 2 cups.

ORANGE SAUCE #1

WATERVLIET SHAKER VILLAGE, NEW YORK

6 oranges
3 tablespoons sugar
1 tablespoon lemon juice

1 tablespoon rum
2 tablespoons butter

❨Peel and seed 6 oranges, remove membrane, and dice the flesh. Reserve juices. Combine orange meat and juice with sugar and bring to a boil. Stir in lemon juice, rum, and butter. Cook 2 minutes. Chill before serving. Makes about 3 cups.

ORANGE SAUCE #2

MT. LEBANON SHAKER VILLAGE

Grated rind and juice ½ lemon
½ cup orange juice
⅓ cup sugar
¼ teaspoon salt

2 egg yolks, slightly beaten
2 egg whites, stiffly beaten
1 teaspoon vanilla

❡Mix grated rind, fruit juices, sugar, salt, and egg yolks. Put on range and stir constantly until mixture thickens. Add gradually, while beating constantly, to stiffly beaten egg whites. Cool and add vanilla. Makes 1 cup.

"OUDE" (OLD) SAUCE

MT. LEBANON SHAKER VILLAGE

❡Chop all together 2 cups green tomatoes, 6 peppers (not large), 4 onions. Add 1 cup salt, and let stand overnight; in the morning drain off the water; add 1 cup sugar, 1 cup horse-radish, 1 tablespoon ground cloves, 1 tablespoon cinnamon. Cover with 1 cup vinegar and stew gently all day. Makes 4 cups of "Oude" or Old Sauce.

OYSTER SAUCE
(For Boiled Fowl)

WATERVLIET SHAKER VILLAGE, NEW YORK

1 quart oysters and liquor
3 tablespoons butter
3 tablespoons flour
1 cup heavy cream

1 teaspoon salt
½ teaspoon pepper
1 wineglass dry sherry

❡Heat oysters in their own liquid for 2 minutes until they plump up. Melt butter, add flour, and stir to make smooth. Add cream and seasonings and beat to a smooth consistency. Combine with oysters and their liquor, remove from heat, and stir in sherry. Makes 1½ quarts.

Nice to use also with boiled fish.

PARSLEY SAUCE

SHIRLEY SHAKER VILLAGE

2 tablespoons finely chopped parsley
2 tablespoons butter
2 tablespoons flour

6 tablespoons hot heavy cream
1 teaspoon salt
½ teaspoon pepper

⟨Rub finely chopped parsley with butter and flour. Add hot cream, add salt and pepper. Simmer to blend all ingredients and serve hot on broiled fish. Makes 1 cup.

RAISIN SAUCE #1
(To Use with Ham)
SHIRLEY SHAKER VILLAGE

3 tablespoons butter
4 tablespoons flour
½ teaspoon salt
¼ teaspoon pepper

2 cups ham liquor
4 tablespoons cider (fresh or hard)
1 cup chopped seeded raisins

⟨Melt butter, add flour, salt and pepper. Pour on hot ham liquor, stirring constantly. Add cider and raisins. Makes 3 cups.

RAISIN SAUCE #2
HARVARD SHAKER VILLAGE

2 tablespoons butter
2 tablespoons flour
1½ cups hot water
½ teaspoon salt
¼ teaspoon pepper
1 tablespoon brown sugar

½ cup chopped seeded raisins
½ cup chopped walnuts or almonds
2 tablespoons grated horse-radish
¼ cup fine bread crumbs
3 tablespoons lemon juice

⟨Melt butter and add flour. Cook 2 minutes. Add hot water gradually, stirring to make smooth. Add salt, pepper, and brown sugar. Beat out any lumps. Add raisins, nut meats, horse-radish, breadcrumbs, and lemon juice. If sauce is too thick, add additional hot water. Makes 2½ cups.

RAISIN SAUCE #3
HANCOCK SHAKER VILLAGE

2 tablespoons butter
2 tablespoons flour
1 cup hot chicken stock
¼ teaspoon salt
⅛ teaspoon pepper

½ cup grated cheese
¼ cup chopped seeded raisins
A few drops of saffron or yellow
    food coloring

⟨Melt butter, add flour, and simmer 2 minutes. Add stock gradually, stirring to make smooth. Stir in salt, pepper, and cheese and cook until cheese is melted. Add raisins and saffron or coloring. Makes 2 cups.

RASPBERRY (OR BLACKBERRY) SAUCE
HARVARD SHAKER VILLAGE

1 pint raspberries (or blackberries)
2 cups sugar
1 cup water

3 tablespoons raspberry (or blackberry) brandy
or
3 tablespoons hard cider

¶Crush berries, add sugar and water. Bring mixture to the boil and simmer, stirring constantly 15 minutes. It should be thick. Rub through a sieve. To the pulp add brandy or cider. Simmer 5 minutes. Serve with puddings. Makes 1 cup.

RED CHERRY SAUCE
WATERVLIET SHAKER VILLAGE, NEW YORK

½ cup sugar
½ cup water
2 cups pitted sour cherries

1 tablespoon cornstarch
3 tablespoons cherry brandy

¶Combine sugar and water and boil 5 minutes. Add cherries and cook 10 minutes. Stir cornstarch and 1 tablespoon water together and add to cherry mixture. Cook until it is slightly thickened. Remove from heat and add brandy. Makes 2½ cups.

ROSE WATER CREAM
HANCOCK SHAKER VILLAGE

3 cups heavy cream
3 teaspoons rose water

½ cup white sugar

¶Mix ingredients together. Chill. Makes 3 cups.

MARY WHITCHER'S RUM SAUCE
MARY WHITCHER'S SHAKER HOUSEKEEPER

¶Combine 1 whole egg and 2 yolks well whipped together, ¼ pound sugar, juice of 1 lemon, 1 cup of rum. Boil these all together, stirring all the time. Serve cool, at room temperature. Makes 1 cup.

AN EXCELLENT TABLE SAUCE
HARVARD SHAKER VILLAGE

❮The foundation of this sauce is any vinegar left in jars of pickles. Collect all such in a bottle until you have 1 quart. For this quantity allow 1 large onion, peeled and sliced; 3 apples with the skin, sliced; 3 large tomatoes. Boil all together 1 hour. Now put through a sieve.

Should the pulp be too thick, add a little new vinegar, return to saucepan, add a little sugar and simmer 5 minutes. Put in sterilized jars and seal. Makes 1½ pints.

TARRAGON SAUCE
HARVARD SHAKER VILLAGE

To serve with roast meats—best with lamb or chicken.

½ cup chicken stock
½ cup fat-free juices from lamb
    roast or chicken
2 tablespoons very finely chopped
    onion
Leaves from 2 branches or stalks
    of tarragon, chopped
        or
1 tablespoon dried tarragon

1 tablespoon chopped fresh chives
    or
1 teaspoon dried chives
3 tablespoons butter, melted
2 tablespoons flour
2 teaspoons brown sugar
4 egg yolks
⅓ cup tarragon vinegar
Salt and pepper to taste

❮Blend stock and meat juices. Add onion and simmer 3 minutes and strain. Add tarragon and chives and simmer 3 minutes. Blend butter, flour, and brown sugar and add seasoned stock a little at a time, stirring until it thickens. Simmer 3 minutes. Beat egg yolks and vinegar together and add to above mixture. Keep heat low, and stir constantly. When sauce is smooth and thick, strain and put in top of double boiler over boiling water. Season and cook to thicken. Makes 2 cups.

HOT TARTAR SAUCE #1
HANCOCK SHAKER VILLAGE

Make a white sauce as follows:

2 tablespoons butter
2 tablespoons flour

¼ teaspoon salt
1 cup milk

([Melt butter, add flour and salt. Stir until well blended. Pour on milk gradually while stirring constantly. Bring to a boil, boil 2 minutes. Do not bring to a boil again. Remove from stove and while still warm add following ingredients in this order:

⅔ cup mayonnaise
1 tablespoon finely chopped onion
1 teaspoon tarragon vinegar

1 tablespoon each of the following all finely chopped:
   pickles, olives, parsley, tarragon
1 tablespoon capers

([Mix together well.

. .

It's perfectly easy to make tartar sauce at home using remains of pickles in jars. Shakers loved buying olives. This is a later recipe, 1900, but much used. Makes 2 cups.

HOT TARTAR SAUCE #2
HANCOCK SHAKER VILLAGE

([To 1 cup of slightly heated mayonnaise, add 1 teaspoon each of chopped fresh chervil, dill, parsley, and chives—and 1 tablespoon each drained chopped capers and chopped pickle. Mix well. Add 2 tablespoons sour cream. Taste for seasoning and add salt and pepper to taste. Makes 1 cup.

TOMATO SAUCE
HANCOCK SHAKER VILLAGE

8 medium-sized tomatoes
4 cloves
1 tablespoon minced onion
2 tablespoons butter
2 tablespoons flour

Salt, pepper, sugar to taste
Dash cayenne pepper
Minced parsley (or basil, tarragon, summer savory, or thyme)

([Cut tomatoes in quarters, mash; put in saucepan and add cloves and onion. Cook slowly for 10 minutes, being careful not to burn. Strain through a sieve. Blend together butter and flour and stir into tomatoes. Add salt, pepper, and sugar to taste and dash of cayenne. Sprinkle with parsley. Makes 5 cups sauce.

Other freshly chopped herbs may be used in this sauce—summer savory or thyme or tarragon or basil. In the early Shaker herb gardens savory and thyme were grown but until the end of the nineteenth century not the tarragon or basil.

Note: To make Cold Tomato Sauce for fish, add 1 cup of heavy cream after tomato mixture has been cooled. Mix well, add herbs and chill.

SPICY TOMATO SAUCE
SHIRLEY SHAKER VILLAGE

6 large ripe tomatoes
3 cups water (less if tomatoes are very juicy)
2 cups catsup
2 tablespoons sugar

1 teaspoon salt
1 tablespoon lemon juice
1 tablespoon grated horse-radish
1 tablespoon finely chopped basil

⟨Peel tomatoes and remove hard core. Put in kettle, mash, cover with water, and simmer stirring often until reduced to a thick pulp. Add catsup, sugar, and salt, horse-radish, and basil. Cook a few minutes more.

Makes about 5 cups if not strained. If pulp is put through coarse strainer to make a smoother sauce, only 3 cups.

TOMATO SAUCE FOR STORING
HARVARD SHAKER VILLAGE

4 pounds tomatoes, sliced
2 large onions, sliced
1 pound sugar
¼ pound salt

2 tablespoons peppercorns
1 ounce cloves
6 ounces allspice
1 pint vinegar

⟨Combine tomatoes and onions, add other ingredients and pour vinegar over all. Let boil gently for 2 hours, stirring to prevent burning. Tomatoes burn easily. Rub through a fine sieve and when cold, bottle, seal, and keep in a cool dry place.

VEGETABLE SAUCE FOR HAM OR PORK
HANCOCK SHAKER VILLAGE

2 tablespoons chopped onions
2 tablespoons butter
1 cup peeled seeded tomatoes
1 tablespoon brown sugar
1 tablespoon capers

1 tablespoon lemon juice
1 tablespoon cornstarch
1 cup cider (or less depending on thickness desired)

⟨Sauté the onions in the butter, cook until soft. Add tomatoes, sugar, and capers and simmer. When well blended add lemon juice and cornstarch; cook until thickened. Add cider, bring to a boil, stirring to make smooth. About 1½ cups.

VENISON SAUCE #1

NORTH UNION SHAKER VILLAGE, OHIO

1 pound brown sugar
1½ pints currant jelly
1 pint claret wine
or

2 cups tomato catsup
1 tablespoon ground mace
1 tablespoon ground cinnamon
1 pound butter

⟨[Mix all ingredients together in order given. Bring to a boil and simmer 5 minutes. Makes 8–9 cups.

VENISON SAUCE #2

WATERVLIET SHAKER VILLAGE, NEW YORK

1½ cups butter
3 cups any tart jelly
3 tablespoons brown sugar

1½ tablespoons ground allspice
4 cups port wine

⟨[Combine ingredients in order given. Bring to a boil and simmer until sauce thickens to your liking. Makes about 2½ cups.

WHITE SAUCE #1—Thin

HANCOCK SHAKER VILLAGE

1 tablespoon butter
1 tablespoon flour

1 cup milk
Salt and pepper to taste

⟨[Melt butter, add flour, and cook 2 minutes over low heat. Add milk gradually. Season and cook 5 minutes, stirring all the while. Makes 1 cup.

Variation #1: Cream or half cream and half milk may be substituted for milk.

Variation #2: Beef, chicken, or fish stock may be substituted for milk.

WHITE SAUCE #2—Medium

HANCOCK SHAKER VILLAGE

2 tablespoons butter
2 tablespoons flour

1 cup warm milk
Salt and pepper

⟨[Melt butter, add flour, and cook 2 minutes over low heat. Add milk gradually. Season and cook 5 minutes, stirring all the while. Makes 1 cup.

WHITE SAUCE #3—Medium and Rich

½ cup butter
½ cup flour

2 cups chicken stock

〖Melt butter and gradually stir in flour. Cook 3 minutes. Add chicken stock and stir constantly until thickened. Makes 3 cups.

WHITE SAUCE #4—Rich
HANCOCK SHAKER VILLAGE

2 tablespoons butter
2 tablespoons flour
1½ cups heavy cream

1 egg
Salt and pepper

〖Melt butter, add flour, and cook 5 minutes. Slowly add cream, stir vigorously on heat for 5 to 6 minutes and remove. Be sure there are no lumps. Add egg and seasonings. Makes 1 cup.

CIDER DRESSING
HANCOCK SHAKER VILLAGE

This is nice to use with fruit salad.

⅔ cup of our own Sauce
   Mayonnaise*

3 tablespoons apple cider
1 teaspoon lemon juice

〖Combine ingredients and chill. Makes ⅔ cup.

HERB SALAD DRESSING
HANCOCK SHAKER VILLAGE

〖In a small bowl put a pinch of salt, a pinch of sugar, and a pinch of dry mustard. Whip in 3 tablespoons of salad oil. Stir in 1 tablespoon herb vinegar and 1 teaspoon each of very finely chopped fresh chives, tarragon, and basil. Put in bottle or jar and shake well. Refrigerate. Dried herbs may be used and, if so, use only half the amount. Makes about ½ cup.

TARRAGON SALAD DRESSING

SHIRLEY SHAKER VILLAGE

⅔ cup sugar (a little less)
1½ cups salad oil
1 cup lemon juice
  or
¼ cup lemon juice and ½ cup
  tarragon vinegar mixed
1 teaspoon Worcestershire sauce
1 teaspoon dry mustard
1 teaspoon salt

2 tablespoons catsup (homemade if
  possible)
2 whole cloves
A little grated onion
  or
1 teaspoon chopped chives
1 tablespoon finely chopped
  tarragon leaves

⟨[Mix all ingredients in order given. Beat well for 2 minutes. Put in bottle and refrigerate. Should stand overnight. Shake well before using. May be strained before using. Makes about 2½ cups.

PARSLEY DRESSING FOR POTATO SALAD

HANCOCK SHAKER VILLAGE

¾ cup salad oil
1 tablespoon lemon juice
2 tablespoons chopped parsley
½ teaspoon mustard seed
¼ teaspoon thyme
1 tablespoon vinegar

2 tablespoons grated onion
½ teaspoon or more salt
½ teaspoon celery seeds
¼ cup chilled undiluted evaporated
  milk

⟨[Combine all the ingredients except the evaporated milk. Mix well. Whip the milk. Gradually beat in the first mixture. Chill. Do not combine with salad until ready to serve. Makes about 1¼ cups.

SALAD DRESSING (Mayonnaise)[1]

FRANCES HALL, HANCOCK SHAKER VILLAGE

⟨[Combine yolks of 2 eggs, 1 tablespoon mustard, 1 teaspoon salt, a little red pepper, and oil (approximately 1 cup) to make it thick. Add 1 tablespoon vinegar or lemon last. Beat all together until thick. Makes about 1 cup.

---

[1]Also see Sauce Mayonnaise.*

HERB VINEGAR
SHIRLEY AND HARVARD SHAKER VILLAGES

[Cider vinegar is preferred as a base for herb vinegar. To 1 quart cider vinegar, add ½ cup fresh chopped herb leaves or green-dried (freshly dried) leaves. The method is to put the herb in a wide-mouth sterilized jar. Heat the vinegar but do not boil. Fill to neck of the jar. Seal tightly and allow to stand for 2 weeks. Press liquid from the herb leaves. Strain and bottle. Cork.

Tarragon Vinegar:
Add rind of ½ lemon or 2 or 3 cloves and use tarragon leaves as herb leaves.

Rosemary Vinegar:
Add rind of ½ orange, 2 or 3 cloves, and rosemary leaves.

Basil Vinegar:
Add rind of ½ lemon and basil leaves.

Thyme Vinegar:
Add rind of ½ lemon and thyme leaves.

Lemon Vinegar:
Lemon verbena and lemon balm make a nice vinegar. Add 1 teaspoon brown sugar.

Mint Vinegar:
Use white distilled vinegar. Add white sugar to taste with mint leaves— not very much sugar is required.

Sage Vinegar:
Use white distilled vinegar. Add celery seeds and fresh sage.

Spiced Vinegar:
To 1 quart of cider vinegar, add 4 tablespoons crushed whole black pepper, 2 tablespoons powdered ginger, 2 tablespoons allspice, 2 tablespoons salt, 2 tablespoons sugar. Mix with cider vinegar and simmer. Strain and bottle.

Dill Vinegar:
Add dillweed and dill seed as herbs to cider vinegar.

APPLE BUTTER MADE WITH BOILED CIDER*

HANCOCK SHAKER VILLAGE

5 pounds cooking apples, cut up but not peeled or cored

½ gallon Boiled Cider,* boiled down from 1 gallon fresh cider
1 tablespoon allspice

([Bring apples, covered with boiled cider, to a boil, then reduce heat and let simmer, stirring frequently to avoid burning on bottom of kettle. Remove from fire. Strain as much of pulp through a colander as possible.

Cook further to desired consistency. Add allspice.

Butter should be thick and dark. If butter is to be kept for any length of time, pour into sterilized jars with tight lids and seal. Makes 1 quart.

LEMON OR ORANGE BUTTER

THE MANIFESTO, 1878

([Take 1 lemon, grate the rind, add all the juice, 2 well-beaten eggs, and 1 cup sugar. Cook slowly over low heat until it thickens. Mix well and use as accompaniment to bread and butter or separately as a preserve. For orange butter, use rind and juice of 1 orange. Makes about 1 cup.

HERB BUTTERS

NORTH UNION SHAKER VILLAGE, OHIO

When the fresh herbs were in season the Shaker cooks at North Union, Ohio, kept an assortment of herb butters on hand. These were made by adding 4 tablespoons of minced herbs to ½ pound of fresh sweet butter. These delicious spreads were used on fresh homemade bread for their picnics and suppers, and were also used in flavoring vegetables or in giving that special touch to roasts and chops. Eggs and omelets cooked in these herb butters are delicious!

It is best to use sweet butter in making this delicacy, for salt draws the oils from the herbs and keeps them from forming a smooth mixture. Keep in small jars, refrigerated. North Union Shakers made them in pound lots and kept them in the springhouse.

From North Union we learn "Basil blesses all food that it touches—it is good from earliest spring to late fall. It is good in soups, salads, fruit drinks, cheeses, and egg dishes. Or put on boiled vegetables. Basil is one of the fine herbs which are so distinct in flavor that often they have to be toned down or blended. The others are thyme, marjoram, chervil, and chives. They all make excellent herb butters and vinegars."

HERB SALT #1
NORTH UNION SHAKER VILLAGE, OHIO

⟨Spiced salt should always be kept on hand. Mix 1½ teaspoons each of powdered thyme, bay leaf, black pepper, and nutmeg with ¾ teaspoon of cayenne pepper and marjoram and 3 teaspoons powdered cloves. Sift together and put in a tightly closed canister with 3 teaspoons salt. Use for seasoning soups, dressings, and meats.

HERB SALT #2
HARVARD SHAKER VILLAGE

⟨To ½ cup table salt add 2 teaspoons each of powdered thyme, sage, black pepper, nutmeg, and 3 teaspoons cloves and ¾ teaspoon ginger. Put through a sieve before adding to salt. Put in airtight canister and keep closed.

CURRY POWDER
MT. LEBANON SHAKER VILLAGE

⟨Mix 1 ounce each ginger, mustard, black pepper, 3 ounces of coriander seed, 3 ounces of turmeric, ¼ ounce of cayenne pepper, and ½ ounce each cardamom, cumin seed, and cinnamon. Pound the whole very fine. Sift and keep in bottle corked tight. Use to season gravies.

VEGETABLE STUFFINGS
ELDER FREDERICK W. EVANS
MT. LEBANON SHAKER VILLAGE

Used for cabbage, squash, tomatoes, eggplants, onions. These came from Frederick Evans after he went to a vegetarian restaurant in London.

APPLE AND PRUNE STUFFING

⟨Soak 6 whole prunes in boiling water 5 minutes. Drain and pit. Chop and mix with equal amount of peeled, chopped apple; add 2 tablespoons cracker crumbs, 2 tablespoons butter, salt, and pepper. Mix all together and use for onions, squash, or cabbage. Fill cavities and top with cream or broth if needed. One tablespoon sugar and 1 beaten egg may be added to mixture. Yields 1½ cups.

POTATO STUFFING

❡Mix together 2 cups dried breadcrumbs, ⅔ cup potatoes boiled and mashed, ½ cup melted butter, 1 egg, 1½ teaspoons salt, 1 teaspoon pepper, 1 teaspoon sage, 1 finely chopped small onion. Use to stuff or dress tomatoes and cabbage. Yields 3 cups.

RAISIN AND NUT STUFFING

❡Mix together 2 cups dried breadcrumbs, ⅔ cup melted butter, ½ cup cut up seeded raisins, 1 teaspoon salt, ½ teaspoon sage, ⅛ teaspoon pepper, ½ cup broken up walnut meats. Use to stuff onions, tomatoes, cabbage, squash, or apples. Yields 3 cups.

STUFFING FOR CHICKEN
FOR WORLD'S PEOPLE'S DINNERS
HANCOCK SHAKER VILLAGE

3 tablespoons butter
2 medium onions, minced
3 cups dried breadcrumbs
1 tablespoon finely chopped basil
1 teaspoon finely chopped fresh thyme
1 teaspoon finely chopped fresh rosemary

½ teaspoon salt, pepper, and sugar
½ teaspoon curry powder (optional)
2 cups seedless white grapes
½ cup hot water
3 tablespoons butter

❡Melt 3 tablespoons butter and sauté onion until light brown. Add to breadcrumbs. Add herbs, salt, pepper, sugar, curry powder and grapes. Heat water; add butter and mix well. Stuff chicken and truss well. Rub the skin with extra soft butter and dust with salt.

This recipe is sufficient for a 3 pound chicken (roasting).

Variation: Use 2 cups of crumbled cornbread and 1 cup of fine breadcrumbs.

Beverages

THERE ARE MANY accounts in the *Manifestos* of the changes in eating and drinking habits of the Shakers. Unless they were certain of the purity of the drinking water, they drank their cider—and later the wine or ginger beer made by their own members. When pure water was attainable they praised it as the most beneficial of all liquids.

Before 1841 tea and coffee were freely used, and at noon there was a liberal supply of good cider. But with the ban on meat, "the use of foreign tea and coffee as well as cider was dismissed several times." Ardent spirits were forbidden, unless recommended for medicinal purposes by the physician attached to each Society. The Harvard Shakers picked a wild tea herb (not identified) which they harvested in August as a substitute, and other families made out as best they could during the period of the ban. But says *The Manifesto*, "after an interval of but a few months the use of foreign tea and coffee has returned in all its freshness to its former place on the table."

Many visitors have noted the excellence of Shaker wines, and more than one the superiority of Shaker cider both in taste and strength.

Recipes for "a refreshing drink for a sore throat" or "la Grippe" appeared frequently in *The Manifesto* or were exchanged between Societies. An overseer of barns and stock wrote in praise of the commodity which most concerned him: "When overcome by bodily fatigue or exhausted by brain labor no stimulant, so-called, serves so well the purpose of refreshment and rest both bodily and mentally as milk. When heated as hot as one can readily take it, it may be sipped slowly from a tumbler and as it is easily digested one feels very soon its beneficial effect. Few persons realize the stimulating qualities of this simple, pure beverage."

Members were urged to grow lemon trees "within doors, as it is much easier than it would seem to be and the fruit can be used for most refreshing beverages."

BARLEY CREAM FOR THE INVALID

SHIRLEY SHAKER VILLAGE

2 pounds veal
¼ pound pearl barley
Salt to taste

Sugar to taste
1 cup milk

⟨[Boil together the veal and barley, covered, until soft enough to go through a very fine sieve like a thick cream. Add seasonings and milk to the desired consistency.

Excellent drink for invalids who cannot manage a spoon. Makes about 1 cup.

BARLEY WATER

NORTH UNION SHAKER VILLAGE, OHIO

⟨[Combine a heaping tablespoon of pearl barley (which has been washed in several waters), the rind of ½ lemon cut very fine, the juice of a whole lemon, and 4 large lumps of loaf sugar. Pour on 6 cups of boiling water. Set to let it clear (approximately 20–25 minutes). Strain. Chill. Refreshing and nutritious for invalids and the elderly. Makes 6 cups.

Use these larger amounts to make 12 cups. Follow same directions.

Rind 6 lemons and juice 2 lemons
½ cup pearl barley

½ cup loaf sugar
12 cups boiling water

BLACKBERRY CORDIAL

MANUSCRIPT FROM SHAKER MUSEUM
OLD CHATHAM, NEW YORK

½ bushel backberries, well mashed
1 cup ground allspice
2 teaspoons ground cloves

2 cups white sugar
1 quart best brandy

⟨[Mix berries, allspice, and cloves and boil slowly until berries are thoroughly cooked and soft. Then strain through flannels and add 2 cups white sugar to each 2 cups of juice. Boil again and when cool add 1 quart of best brandy. Good for diarrhea or dysentery. Makes 2 quarts.

Take 1 teaspoon or more in water, according to age.

BLACKBERRY JELLY FOR SICKNESS
(Blackberry Brandy)
HANCOCK SHAKER VILLAGE

½ ounce nutmeg
½ ounce cloves
½ ounce cinnamon
½ ounce allspice

2 quarts blackberry juice
1 pound loaf sugar
1 pint brandy

([Pulverize the spices, if whole. Boil all 15 to 20 minutes. When completely cold, add 1 pint of brandy. Makes 2½ quarts. This brandy was used for diarrhea. It makes a nice drink to sip.

BLACKBERRY SYRUP
THE MANIFESTO, 1874

([To 2 cups of blackberry juice, add 2 cups of white sugar, 1 teaspoon of powdered cinnamon, ½ teaspoon mace, and 2 teaspoons cloves; boil all together for a quarter of an hour, then strain the syrup, and add to each pint 6 ounces of (French) brandy.

A comforting mixture for the sick and elderly. Makes about 1 pint.

DRINKING CHOCOLATE
NORTH UNION SHAKER VILLAGE, OHIO

([Take ¾ pound of the best chocolate, melt in ½ cup of spring water in a pan, boil. Pour in ½ cup milk; wait till it boils and repeat process 4 times, using 3 cups of milk. Simmer for quarter of an hour. Makes 4 cups.

A CHOCOLATE DRINK
SHIRLEY SHAKER VILLAGE

([Allow a heaping tablespoon of grated or pulverized chocolate (made into a paste with a little water) to 1 pint fresh milk; let it come to a boil and sweeten to taste. Flavor with cinnamon or nutmeg. Serve hot. Makes 2 cups.

COLD CHOCOLATE
SHIRLEY SHAKER VILLAGE

⟨[Follow the recipe for A Chocolate Drink;* flavor and chill. When ready to use put ¼ cup heavy cream in a large glass bottle; add 5 large mint leaves crushed, 1 cup chopped ice. Fill bottle with chocolate mixture and shake well. Drain into pretty glasses and serve at once. Serves 2–3.

SHAKER APPLE DULCET
SOUTH UNION SHAKER VILLAGE, KENTUCKY

2 eight ounce jelly glasses apple jelly	1 nutmeg, grated
	6 egg whites
4 cups boiling water	Sugar
2 quarts best Shaker cider	8 sprigs mint

⟨[Whip the jelly to a froth by gradually beating in the boiling water. Cool and add cider; powder with nutmeg. Chill well. Pour into tall mugs or glasses and top generously with slightly sweetened beaten egg whites. Insert a sprig of mint into each mug. Spearmint or peppermint will do, but apple mint gives it just the right flavor. SERVES 8.

BRETHREN'S CIDER
SHAKER ALMANAC

⟨[One-quarter cup of apple brandy was added to 1¼ cups of very cold hard cider—flavored with lemon peel. Makes 2 cups (for one Brethren or two nowadays).

CIDER FLAP
HANCOCK SHAKER VILLAGE

2 cups fresh cider	1 cup grated peeled apple
1 cup orange juice	1 package standard lemon gelatin

⟨[Mix all ingredients and freeze to mush. Serve in frappé glasses with meat course. SERVES 4.

ICED COFFEE
NORTH UNION SHAKER VILLAGE, OHIO

⟨[To 4 cups of strong coffee add 1 cup of cream, 2 cups of milk, and ¼ cup granulated sugar. Stand in a wooden bucket half filled with finely broken ice and salt. Rotate the bucket in the ice for about 10 minutes and leave it in the ice for about an hour. Keep the coffee well stirred to prevent it getting lumpy. Very refreshing. SERVES 6.

CREAMY EGG NOG
ENFIELD SHAKER VILLAGE, NEW HAMPSHIRE

1 egg to each person	Beat whites and yolks separately

Add to each yolk:

1 tablespoon unrefined white sugar	
1 tablespoon whisky (or brandy)	1 tablespoon rum

⟨Work in the sugar first, then add whisky and the rum. Let it stand 15 or 20 minutes.

2 quarts heavy cream	grated nutmeg

⟨Add 2 quarts of heavy cream to each dozen eggs, stirring slowly, and fold in the stiffly beaten whites. Flavor with grated nutmeg. SERVES 12–18 for every dozen eggs.

LEMON BUTTERMILK EGG NOG
SHIRLEY SHAKER VILLAGE

1 egg, separated	1 tablespoon sugar (optional)
2 tablespoons sugar	Buttermilk
1 small or ½ large lemon	Grated lemon rind or nutmeg

⟨Beat egg white to a stiff meringue with 1 tablespoon sugar. Beat egg yolk, juice of lemon, and 1 more tablespoon sugar until thoroughly mixed and thick. Pour egg yolk mixture into a large glass and fill almost to the top with very cold buttermilk. Stir well with a spoon and add third tablespoon of sugar—or a part of it if thought necessary. Top with meringue. Grate a bit of lemon rind or nutmeg over it. Serve at once. SERVES 1.

Variation: Sweet, rich milk can be substituted for the buttermilk, but the consistency is not as agreeable.

This is a tart drink and it is especially recommended for the invalid to encourage his appetite.

SHAKER GRAPE JUICE
ELDRESS CLYMENA MINER
NORTH UNION SHAKER VILLAGE, OHIO

2 cups stemmed grapes   Boiling water
½ cup sugar

Put grapes in quart jar. Add sugar, fill jar with boiling water, and seal. Strain off juice when needed. SERVES 4.

OHIO SHAKERS' GRAPE JUICE
NORTH UNION SHAKER VILLAGE, OHIO

20 cups stemmed grapes—blue   1 cup water
   Concords or white native grapes   6 cups sugar

([Put grapes and water in enamel saucepan. Heat until seeds fall to bottom and pulp rises—about 30 minutes. Strain through linen bag as for jelly. Add sugar, heat to boiling, and bottle. Makes 1 gallon.

When serving, dilute this juice with cold water, half and half.

OHIO SHAKERS' SPICED GRAPE JUICE
NORTH UNION SHAKER VILLAGE, OHIO

1 quart grape juice   2 short pieces cinnamon
¼ cup sugar   2 tablespoons allspice
6 whole cloves

([Heat all together in a double boiler or over a slow fire. Do not boil. Strain out the spice. Serve hot in sherbet or tea cups, or cool well and serve in tall clear glasses over chopped ice—in this case serve a thin slice of lemon in each glass. SERVES 4.

SHAKER HAYING WATER OR SWITCHEL
NORTH UNION SHAKER VILLAGE, OHIO

4 cups sugar   2 cups molasses
    or   2 teaspoons powdered ginger
3 cups maple syrup   2 gallons cold water

([Put all ingredients together and stir until thoroughly blended. Pour into large jug, and chill. SERVES 30.

∴

In haying season, or when the Brethren were working on the roads, where they spent double the allotted time in working out the road tax in order to be exempt from military service, gallons of this thirst-quenching drink, switchel, were carried to them at regular intervals. Before the Shakers at North Union had icehouses, they made up gallons of switchel daily during the hot weather, and in order to cool it, they either kept it in their springhouses or hung the great jugs filled with the beverage down in the wells.

HAYMAKERS' SWITCHEL
HANCOCK SHAKER VILLAGE

Never in New England was there a haying without quantities of cold switchel at hand. Men working in the fields could drink any amount of it without cloying the taste or destroying the appetite. Even if it became tepid, it was still refreshing.

1 cup brown sugar	¾ cup vinegar
2 quarts water	½ teaspoon ginger
½ cup molasses	

❰Just stir up the ingredients and cool. SERVES 5 cups.

HERBADE #1
HARVARD SHAKER VILLAGE

½ cup chopped mint	(sugar syrup is made by boiling
½ cup chopped lemon balm	together 2 parts water with 1 part
(similar to mint, lemon-scented)	sugar for 5 minutes)
½ cup sugar syrup (or white crème	¼ cup lemon juice
de menthe)	½ cup orange juice

❰Combine all ingredients and let stand for 1 hour or more. If lemon balm is not available, use all mint.

When ready to serve, strain and add 4 quarts of dry ginger ale. SERVES 16.

HERBADE #2
HANCOCK SHAKER VILLAGE

1½ quarts boiling water
1 cup lemon balm
2 cups borage
1 cup mint
Juice 6 lemons, 2 oranges

1 cup pineapple juice
1 quart strong tea
Syrup made of 1 cup sugar boiled
   with 1 cup water
3 quarts ginger ale

⟪Pour 1½ quarts boiling water over lemon balm. Steep 20 minutes. Strain onto borage and mint leaves. Add fruit juices, tea, and syrup. Let stand overnight or at least 8 hours. Strain, add ice and ginger ale and fresh mint leaves at last moment. SERVES 12.

SHAKER GINGERADE
NORTH UNION SHAKER VILLAGE, OHIO

4 ounces ginger root
       or
3 ounces powdered ginger

4 lemons
2 quarts boiling water
Sugar syrup to taste

⟪If ginger root is used, cut into small pieces. Cut the lemon rinds into paper-thin strips and add to the ginger root or powdered ginger. Pour boiling water over this mixture and let steep for 5 minutes. Strain and when perfectly cold, add two cups lemon juice and sugar syrup to suit taste; some like it sweet and some like the tang of the lemon. Dilute with very cold water and chips of ice. In hot weather, sprigs of mint inserted in glasses add interest to this beverage. SERVES 8.

LEMON SYRUP #1
(Used To Make Lemonade)
MT. LEBANON SHAKER VILLAGE

2 cups white sugar
1 cup water
Rind 2 lemons, cut into thin strips

⅛ teaspoon salt
Juice 6 lemons
Mint (optional)

⟪Dissolve sugar in water, add lemon rinds and salt. Bring to a boil and simmer 5 minutes. When syrup is cool, add lemon juice. Mint can be added here or later. This makes about 4 cups syrup.

    When combining with water, use about 1 tablespoon syrup per cup of cold water; 2 tablespoons syrup per cup if chopped ice will be used. Decorate with mint.

LEMON SYRUP #2
HANCOCK SHAKER VILLAGE

⟨[Pare off the yellow rind of the lemon, slice the lemon, and put a layer of lemon and a thick layer of sugar in a deep plate. Cover closely with a saucer and set in a warm place. This is an excellent remedy for a cold. This is taken by spoonfuls for a cold in the throat. Makes ½ cup.

CARBONATED SYRUP WATER
LUCY A. SHEPARD, NEW LEBANON SHAKER VILLAGE, 1860

⟨[Put into a tumbler lemon, raspberry, strawberry, black currant, pineapple, orange, or other acid syrup,* sufficient in quantity to flavor the beverage very lightly. Then pour in very cold ice water till the glass is half full. Add half a teaspoon of bicarbonate of soda (to be obtained at the druggist's) and stir it well in with a teaspoon.

It will foam up to the top immediately and must be drunk during that effervescence. By keeping the syrup and the bicarbonate of soda in the house and mixing them as above with ice water, you can at any time have a glass of this very pleasant drink, precisely similar to that which you get at the shops. The cost will be infinitely less.

LEMONADE WITH EGG
MT. LEBANON SHAKER VILLAGE

⟨[Beat 1 egg with 2 teaspoons of sugar until very light—then stir in 3 teaspoons of cold water and the juice of a small lemon. Fill the glass with pounded ice and drink through a straw. Makes 1 serving.

MILK LEMONADE
SHAKER ALMANAC

⟨[Peel 2 lemons very thinly; squeeze the juice over the peel and let it sit all night. In the morning add to it 4 cups of powdered sugar, 4 cups of white wine, 3 quarts of fresh milk boiled hot. Strain it through a jelly bag till perfectly clear. Let it stand till quite cold, and you will find it a delicious summer beverage. SERVES 12–16.

PICNIC LEMONADE
MT. LEBANON SHAKER VILLAGE

12 lemons
1¼ cups sugar

3 quarts spring water
Mint sprigs

⟨Lemons should be at room temperature. Roll to soften. Squeeze and remove pips but not meats, fruit pieces. Add sugar and water. Stir well to dissolve. Taste and add more sugar if need be. Chill well.

Carry additional ice in blocks to the picnic. Pour lemonade from canteen, add mint sprigs. Stir well and ladle into little tin cups. SERVES 16.

SHAKER MINT CUP
MAY CASS, WHITEWATER SHAKER VILLAGE

2 cups sugar
2 cups water
Dash salt

2 cups finely cut tender mint leaves
2 quarts ginger ale (or Shaker Gingerade*)

⟨Make a simple syrup by boiling the sugar and water 3 minutes. Add salt. Pour boiling syrup over the leaves. Let stand about 5 minutes, strain. Then add ginger ale or Gingerade. You will find the salt will help draw out the mint flavor from the leaves. Serve very cold. A sprig of mint helps pretty up this good drink. SERVES 8.

MINT DRINK
WATERVLIET SHAKER VILLAGE, NEW YORK

1¾ cups sugar
3½ cups boiling water
1 large handful fresh mint leaves
     or

2 cups well-packed mint leaves
Juice 6 lemons
Juice 3 oranges

⟨Put sugar in mixing bowl; stir in water. Stir in mint and fruit juices. Cover—let stand for 2 hours. Press out mint. Strain. Pour over cracked ice in tall glasses. Makes about 2 quarts.

MOCHA PUNCH
MARY DAHM, HANCOCK SHAKER VILLAGE

½ cup instant coffee powder
2 cups hot water
1 cup sugar

1 gallon milk
½ gallon chocolate ice cream
½ gallon vanilla ice cream

❴In a saucepan combine coffee, water, and sugar. Bring to a boil over medium heat, stirring frequently. Remove from heat, cool.

Pour in large bowl (punch bowl). Stir in milk, add ice creams. Stir until smooth. SERVES ABOUT 18.

PEPPERMINT CORDIAL
MANUSCRIPT FROM SHAKER MUSEUM
OLD CHATHAM, NEW YORK

❴Take 60 drops of the oil of peppermint, 1 cup sugar, and 1 cup brandy. Put all together into a marble mortar and work them well. Then add 8 quarts of water and add more brandy and sugar till it becomes a pleasant cordial. Observe that the oil of peppermint will not mix with water without some kind of spirits. This is a pleasant and wholesome cordial. SERVES 24.

RASPBERRY SHRUB
HANCOCK SHAKER VILLAGE

5 quarts red raspberries   Sugar
1 quart very mild vinegar

❴Crush berries, add vinegar, let stand 24 hours, then strain. Add ½ pound white sugar to each quart of juice. Let come to boiling point and put in jars. Makes 2 quarts. To serve, dilute with 3 parts cold water to 1 part juice and pour over crushed ice in tall glasses.

Variation: A currant shrub may be made this way.

CURRANT SHRUB
LUCY A. SHEPARD, 1860
MANUSCRIPT FROM SHAKER MUSEUM
OLD CHATHAM, NEW YORK

❴Boil a sufficient quantity of currant juice 5 minutes with loaf or crushed sugar, 2 cups of sugar to 2 cups of juice. Stir it constantly while cooling. When cold, bottle it. A spoonful or two in a glass of very cold spring water is a very refreshing beverage. Makes 3–4 cups.

RASPBERRY VINEGAR
MT. LEBANON SHAKER VILLAGE

⟨To 4 quarts of red raspberries, put enough vinegar to cover, and let them stand 24 hours; scald and strain it. Add a pound of sugar to 1 pint of juice, boil it 20 minutes and bottle. It is then ready to use and will keep years. To 1 glass of very cold water add a great spoonful. It is much relished by the sick and elderly. Very nice. Makes 2 pints.

Blackberries may be used in place of raspberries.

ANOTHER RASPBERRY VINEGAR
HANCOCK SHAKER VILLAGE

⟨Cover raspberries with the best vinegar. Let them stand a day and strain through a flannel bag. Then make a syrup that will feather (using equal amounts of sugar and water) by cooking to the thread stage and boil an equal quantity of it and the raspberry juice for 10 minutes. Strain and bottle. This makes a delicious drink by adding cold water and ice. Two to 3 quarts raspberries yield 1 quart.

Note: Strawberry Acid may be made the same way.

MARY WHITCHER'S RASPBERRY VINEGAR
MARY WHITCHER'S SHAKER HOUSEKEEPER

⟨Put 1 quart raspberries into a quart of best vinegar. Let stand a week, stirring occasionally. Add 1 pound of loaf sugar, boil slowly 20 minutes, strain and bottle. Makes 1½ quarts. Serve diluted with water and over ice.

SHAKER COLD TEA
SISTER AMELIA'S SHAKER RECEIPTS

⟨Use 1 teaspoon of good imported tea to a large tumbler of cold water. Use only glass or porcelain container, and let stand for 12 hours. Strain and add ice. Sweeten to taste.

Tea made by this method will never "cloud," because the tannin is now drawn from the leaves. Made thus it has a delightful bouquet and the same stimulating effect as hot tea.

.·.

When the Shakers went "a-picnicking" at the Valley of God's Pleasure (North Union) they often took great crocks of this cold tea (made by the above method) and it was considered a delightful beverage by all.

When we learn that the tea plant belongs to the camellia family, we love its delicate taste and fragrance all the more. Historically, tea has played an important role in America. When in 1764 Queen Charlotte of England was presented with a gift of tea by the East India Company, she was so delighted with the beverage that it soon became a fashionable drink throughout the British Isles, and with increasing emigration, this British taste soon invaded our Colonies. It might have become our national beverage except for the tax placed on it, which resulted in the Boston Tea Party and led to the American Revolution.

COLD RHUBARB TEA
HANCOCK SHAKER VILLAGE

4 cups diced unpeeled rhubarb   Grated rind 1 lemon or orange
   (use rhubarb with red skin)   ¾ to 1 cup sugar
4 cups water

⟨Simmer rhubarb in water until very tender, about 20 to 25 minutes. Strain, add grated lemon or orange rind and sugar. Stir until sugar has dissolved. Cool well and serve over ice in tall clear glasses. SERVES 4.

HOT TODDY
(For Winter)
NORTH UNION SHAKER VILLAGE, OHIO

⟨Mix 6 eggs with 8 teaspoons of white sugar and beat well. Add ½ cup rum, ½ cup brandy, and 3 cups of boiling water. Serve hot in earthenware mugs. Sprinkle with nutmeg. SERVES 6.

WINES
MANUSCRIPT FROM SHAKER MUSEUM
OLD CHATHAM, NEW YORK

"Be sure to get perfectly ripe fruit for making wine, but do not gather it immediately after rain as it is watery then and less sweet than usual. Be careful to strop [cork] the wine securely as soon as fermentation ceases as otherwise it will lose its strength and flavor."

"Remember if water source is doubtful, drink the wine."

"Strawberry wine makes a delicious flavoring for syllabub, cake, jelly, etc., and so does gooseberry wine."

"Dewberries make a prettier and better wine than blackberries, and have all the medicinal virtues of the latter. The following process will make wine perfectly clear: to half a gallon of wine put 2 wineglasses of sweet milk. Stir it into the wine and pour it all into a transparent half-gallon bottle. Stop it and set it by [aside] for 24 hours, at the end of which time the wine will be beautifully clear, the sediment settling with the milk at the bottom. Pour off the wine into another bottle, not allowing any of the sediment or milk to get into the fresh bottle. The same directions apply to vinegar."

FRUIT WINE
(Such as Cherry, Plum, Elderberry, Blackberry, and Red Currant)
MT. LEBANON SHAKER VILLAGE

❲To each gallon of fruit allow 2 gallons boiling water poured on the fruit in a large pan. Let stand for 1 week (cover with muslin cloth), stirring every day. Then strain once through a sieve, then through muslin. Measure and add 3 pounds sugar to each gallon of liquid and ½ pound whole ginger, bruised (and 1 ounce cloves, if for elderberry), to every 4½ gallons. Take a little of the liquid and boil with the bruised ginger and cloves, if used, for 20 minutes. Then strain and add to the bulk. When sugar has thoroughly melted put in a cask or stone bottles, quite full. Do not cork down until fermentation has ceased. The wine should be quite clear and ready to drink in three months. If it becomes a little sharp add some sugar candy, crushed, to feed it. One gallon fruit plus 2 gallons water, etc., yields 2 gallons wine.

BLACKBERRY WINE #1

E. ALLARD, ENFIELD SHAKER VILLAGE, NEW HAMPSHIRE

⟨To a bushel of blackberries put in pure water enough to be just even with the berries. Put this through rollers. Strain, then add water to the berries again, to get out all of the goodness. Use same water. Do not add clear water. Use more berries than the water. Let it stand 2 weeks open in tubs, then skim the top regularly every other day. Put it in barrel or keg, bunging up tight. Let it stand 6 months. Then rack it off. Poor berries need more sugar than good ones. Sugar should be dry and white or very light. Never put over 3 pounds of sugar to a gallon of juice; 2 pounds is the rule. Wine should never be moved or jostled about, as it is liable to ferment by such treatment.

BLACKBERRY WINE #2

MANUSCRIPT FROM SHAKER MUSEUM
OLD CHATHAM, NEW YORK

⟨Bruise the berries thoroughly and add to each gallon of berries 2 quarts of hot water. Let this sit all night, then strain off the juice; add 1½ pounds of sugar, and put in a loosely corked vessel to ferment. This takes several days.

After fermentation it must be corked tightly. Some people put in powdered charcoal tied in a cloth to purify it. One gallon of berries yields 3 quarts wine.

CIDER WINE

MANUSCRIPT FROM SHAKER MUSEUM
OLD CHATHAM, NEW YORK

⟨To 1 gallon of cider, add 1 pound of sugar. Scald it thoroughly. When cold put into jugs or barrels and bung it up for about a year. Makes 1 gallon.

COWSLIP WINE
MT. LEBANON SHAKER VILLAGE

⟨[Boil 3 pounds of white sugar in a gallon of water for half an hour, removing scum as it rises.

Pour into a pan to cool, adding finely grated rind of a lemon. When cold, add 2 quarts of cowslip flowers with the juice of the lemon. Stir frequently for 2 days. Strain and pour into a cask and leave standing for a month. One cup of brandy can be added here. Bottle off, placing a piece of loaf sugar in each bottle. Yields 1 gallon.

CURRANT WINE
ENFIELD SHAKER VILLAGE, NEW HAMPSHIRE

⟨[Combine 1 quart of currant juice, 2 quarts water, 3 pounds brown sugar. Mix well until sugar is all dissolved. Pour it into a keg and let it stand undisturbed in your cellar with the bung out for several days until it has stopped fermenting. Then put in the bung and it will be fit for use in 2 months. Yields 3 quarts.

DANDELION WINE
MT. LEBANON SHAKER VILLAGE

⟨[Take 4½ gallons water to about 30 pounds dandelion flowers. Mix and boil about 20 minutes, then strain through a hair sieve, and boil again with 3½ pounds sugar, 2 oranges, 1 lemon, and 1 ounce brown lump ginger to the gallon. Boil about 20 minutes again. Strain and leave to cool before bottling. Do not cork down until fermenting has finished, 2 to 4 days. It will be ready to use in 3 months. If it is to be kept, put in a handful of wheat or sugar candy for each gallon. Makes 5 gallons.

ELDERBERRY WINE
HANCOCK SHAKER VILLAGE

⟨[To 3 gallons of water allow a peck of elderberries. Cut off the stalks. Bring the water to a boil and pour over the berries. Stand for 24 hours, then strain. To each gallon of juice allow 3 pounds of sugar, 1 tablespoon ground ginger, 6 or more cloves. Boil until sugar is dissolved. Cool. Let stand 10 days, then bottle. This will be ready to use in 6 months. Makes 3 gallons.

GRAPE WINE
MT. LEBANON SHAKER VILLAGE

⟪Bruise the grapes, which should be ripe. To each gallon of grapes add a gallon of spring water and let the whole remain a week without stirring. Then draw off juice and to each gallon add 3 pounds of white sugar. Let it ferment in a warm place for a few days. When fermented stop it up tight. In the course of 5 months it will be fit to bottle.

This is a first-rate recipe and also answers the purpose for currant and blackberry wines. One gallon of fruit and 1 gallon of water yields about 1 gallon wine.

RASPBERRY WINE
MANUSCRIPT FROM SHAKER MUSEUM
OLD CHATHAM, NEW YORK

⟪To 1 quart of well-bruised raspberries add 1 quart of spring water, and let them stand 4 hours. Strain off the juice (do not press the fruit), and for every gallon of juice add 3 pounds of white sugar—let it work, then skim and bottle it. Makes about 2 quarts.

RHUBARB WINE
(An Old Recipe)
SHIRLEY SHAKER VILLAGE

⟪To every gallon of cold water add 5 pounds of well-bruised juicy rhubarb. Let it stand for 5 days, stirring it every night and morning. Then strain off the liquor, add 4 pounds of Demerara sugar, the thinly pared rind of a lemon, and ½ ounce of isinglass to each gallon of liquor. Again let stand for 5 days. Skim off the crust very carefully and put in a cask, not fastening it down completely, for 14 days. Bottle in 6 months and wire the corks to keep tightly closed. One gallon water and 5 pounds fruit yields 2 gallons wine.

TOMATO WINE

MANUSCRIPT FROM SHAKER MUSEUM
OLD CHATHAM, NEW YORK

❴Take small ripe tomatoes. Pick off the stems and wash clean. Mash and strain through a linen bag. A bushel will make 5 gallons. Then add 3 pounds of sugar to each gallon, put into a cask, and ferment 36 hours.

Picnics

THE SHAKERS LOVED to take trips and go on picnics. They enjoyed and appreciated the beauty of nature and created choice little picnic parks and recreation places in their communities. In journals and diaries of Hancock Shakers there are frequent references to trips to the Canaan, New York, Family for a picnic, from Hancock, and letters tell of taking the children for a day of fun which ended in a picnic and games, wading in a brook, and fishing.

In the travel journal of Hiram Rule of New Lebanon, we are given a glimpse of the Hemlock Grove as he saw it in 1854. Eldress Prudence, who was in charge of the small children, often entertained them in this beautiful spot of native hemlock. The same journal gives us a delightful description of a picnic party planned for a beloved visiting sister.

> Her old friends wished to take Eldress Hannah back to her childhood play places (in Watervliet, Ohio). . . . The little band of sisters left their dwellings and crossed the fields singing like a flock of young blackbirds on a bright morning. Some aged sisters lingering behind placed great hampers of food in the wagon drawn by Old Bally. They now followed slowly along the roadway to the playgrounds. . . . They swing on tangled ropes of grapevines, gather wild dew-berries and wintergreens, and the younger group rides bareback on the old horse.
>
> The older sisters now spread their humble feast under a blooming red-bud tree. It is more than a feast—songs, mirth, good fellowship, and ample spread combined! . . . a spotless white cloth is spread on the green turf; great loaves of fresh-baked bread, plump rolls of golden butter, eggs, delicate cakes, and crusty cookies with fruit shrub and creamy milk emerge in abundance from the wide hampers.

Picnic food was chosen with thought so it would travel well and be acceptable—little mutton pies are mentioned frequently as picnic food by Harvard sisters.

[423]

There was a great deal of coming and going in Shaker villages. It was the habit of the Ministry of each Society to visit all the others once during the year and as a result the journals are full of entries such as "a load of visitors arrive from Hancock" or "our Ministry have started for Canterbury," and "the sisters packed a delicious lunch for our pleasure on the way to Harvard."

Traveling food and picnic food was studied and produced with the same energy and imagination as other edibles.

PICNIC FOOD
FROM A TRAVEL JOURNAL

Hot meat pies
Cold sausage rolls
Boiled or broiled chicken
Fried ham between split scones or
    biscuits
Sliced egg sandwiches, done up in
    muslin

Sliced pickles
A whole pound cake
Cookies
1 bottle cider (sparkling)
1 bottle coffee

ORANGE BREAD
HANCOCK SHAKER VILLAGE

1 cup small pieces orange peel
Water
1¾ cups white sugar
3 tablespoons butter
1 egg

2 cups milk
4 cups flour
4 teaspoons baking powder
⅛ teaspoons salt

[Cover orange peel with water, cook until tender about 15 minutes. Add 1 cup sugar and boil to syrup. Cream butter, add remaining sugar, egg, milk. Mix flour with baking powder and salt. Add to other ingredients and beat well. Add orange peel. Put in 2 buttered bread pans. Let stand 20 minutes. Bake 40 minutes in moderately slow 325° F. oven. Makes 2 loaves. Keeps moist and is nice to take along.

CHILDREN'S DELIGHT
THE MANIFESTO, NOVEMBER 1881

❲Take enough white bread dough to make a small loaf. Knead into it a tablespoon of butter, 2 tablespoons English currants, 2 tablespoons sugar. Let it rise until it is very light, then bake in a round pound tin in a moderately hot 325° F. oven. If you have any of the tin cans in which tomatoes are put up, use one of them for a baking tin, and bake the cake in it. You will have a pretty round loaf, and the size and appearance of the slices are also pleasing. Graham bread seems actually to taste better if baked in one of these tins. Send out on a picnic. Makes 1 loaf.

CHERRY SANDWICHES
MANUSCRIPT FROM SHAKER MUSEUM
OLD CHATHAM, NEW YORK

1 cup pitted cherries	½ cup sugar
¼ cup finely chopped blanched almonds	Bread slices
	Sweet butter
1 tablespoon lemon juice	

❲Crush and drain the cherries. Add the finely chopped blanched almonds, lemon juice, and sugar to make very sweet. Cut crusts from fresh white bread. Spread thin slices with sweet butter, cover with cherry filling and buttered upper slice. Cut across on the diagonal and wrap in waxed paper for a picnic—or in a damp cloth in a cool place for supper.

BACON PIE
SHIRLEY SHAKER VILLAGE

❲Cut rounds of pastry to fit a saucer, put in a slice of fried bacon crumbled, break an egg on top, cover with a round of pastry, crimp all around the edges to hold. Cook at 400° F. in the oven till the pastry is cooked, about 15 to 2 minutes. To be eaten cold at picnics. Take along a little mustard pickle.

COLD BACON AND EGG PIE
SHIRLEY SHAKER VILLAGE

"Taken with brethren when farming at a distance. We send good sharp, cold cider with this and whole tomatoes and a pound cake or two."

Pastry* for one crust 9 inch pie pan
6 slices bacon
5 eggs, unbeaten
2 eggs, beaten
1 cup light cream
1 teaspoon nutmeg
1 tablespoon flour
½ teaspoon salt
½ teaspoon pepper

⟨Line pie pan with pastry. Fry bacon until crisp. Drain, crumble over bottom of pie shell. Drop 5 eggs on top, keeping them whole. Beat 2 eggs with cream and remaining ingredients. Pour into shell. Bake at 400° F. for 15 minutes. Reduce heat to 325° F. and bake 30 minutes longer until knife inserted carefully in center comes out clean. Cut into wedges. SERVES 5.

FAVORITE LITTLE MUTTON PIES
HARVARD SHAKER VILLAGE

⟨Cut up into squares some lean cooked mutton and cold potatoes. Chop in some onions, a little parsley, and some thyme. Add a few chopped raisins and some nuts. Moisten with some sharp cider and some good stock. Add salt and pepper. Mix all well. Make a good pastry* crust and line some deep small cake tins with it. Fill with the mixture, put on the crust, and pinch well down all around. Brush over with egg white and bake about half an hour (350° F.). These are fine hot and very good as a traveling lunch.

Lamb can be substituted.

PICNIC PIE (Cherry)
MT. LEBANON SHAKER VILLAGE

1 quart (4 cups) sour cherries
½ cup white sugar plus 1 teaspoon brown sugar
1 tablespoon cornstarch
1 teaspoon rose water
Pastry* for 2 nine inch piecrusts
1 teaspoon butter

❰Pit and drain cherries. Mash slightly. Place juice in a saucepan, add sugar and cornstarch, and bring to a boil. Cook until thickened. Add cherries and let them cool, add rose water.

Line 9 inch pie pan with pie pastry. Fill with fruit and put butter in exact center. Top with upper pastry crust. Bake in a moderate 350° F. oven for 45 minutes, or until pie is golden brown. SERVES 6–8.

COLD PORK PIE OR PICNIC PIE
MARY WHITCHER'S SHAKER HOUSEKEEPER

2½ pounds pork—free of gristle and bone (2 parts lean meat to 1 part fat)	Salt and pepper to taste
	1 cup lard
	1¾ cups water
½ cup cubed lean salt pork	4 cups flour
Cold water	1 teaspoon salt
½ teaspoon black peppercorns	1 egg, beaten
2 teaspoons dried rosemary	2 tablespoons unflavored gelatin
1 cup minced onion	2 tablespoons apple brandy

❰Into a deep saucepan put pork and salt pork with water to cover. Add peppercorns, rosemary, onion, and salt and pepper to taste. Simmer, covered, for about 3 hours. Meat should be tender. Drain meat and reserve stock.

To make hot water pastry: Bring lard and water to a boil. Sift flour and salt together. Stir into lard mixture. When cool knead well. Put mixture into a basin and keep warm. If it gets cold it will become unmanageable. Reserve one-fourth of the pastry for the lid of the pie. Use a deep 2 quart pie pan. Line the bottom and sides with pastry by patting it into place.

Fill lined pan with pork mixture. Roll out lid and cover pie. Crimp edges together. Cut hole 1 inch in diameter in center. Brush with beaten egg.

Preheat oven to 400° F. Place pie in center of oven. Bake 30 to 40 minutes. Reduce to 350° F. and bake until total baking time is 2¼ to 2½ hours. Pastry should be golden but not brown. A piece of moistened muslin over top will control this. Remove pie from oven.

While pie is baking, take stock in which pork was cooked (there should be 2 cups) and strain; add a little of this to 2 tablespoons of unflavored gelatin. When dissolved, return to stock and add 2 tablespoons apple brandy.

When pie has properly baked, add as much stock as it will hold by pouring it via a funnel through the hole in top of lid.

Cool pie in a really cold pantry. On a picnic this should be served from the pastry dish and accompanied with a homemade catsup, unstrained. SERVES 6.

PORK AND SAGE HAND PIES WITH APPLES
MT. LEBANON SHAKER VILLAGE

½ cup peeled and chopped raw apples
1 cup chopped cooked pork
½ cup chopped cooked potato
1 tablespoon butter
1 tablespoon chopped onion
1 tablespoon flour

1 teaspoon salt
1 teaspoon pepper
1 tablespoon crushed sage
1 tablespoon Boiled Cider* (if cider is not available, add 1 tablespoon brown sugar to apples)
1 cup heavy cream

⟮Make a nice pastry* for a 2 crust pie to fit a 7 inch tin.

Line tin with pastry. Combine apples (and brown sugar if cider is not available), pork, and potatoes and fill tin. In a saucepan melt butter, sauté onions until tender but not brown. Add flour, cook 1 minute, add seasonings, sage, cider, and cream and simmer very slowly. Pour over mixture in pie dish. Cover with pastry lid. Prick. Bake in moderate 350° F. oven for 1 hour. "Makes several of these to go along with a picnic party." SERVES 4–6.

LITTLE FRIED PIES
CANTERBURY SHAKER VILLAGE

Pastry* enough for a 2 crust 8 inch pie
2 cups drained cooked apricots or apples

½ cup granulated sugar
½ pound fat for deep frying
Confectioners' sugar

⟮Roll out pastry ⅛ inch thick on lightly floured board. Cut into circles about 5 inches in diameter. Combine fruit and granulated sugar. Place 1½ tablespoons on one side of each round. Moisten edges with water; fold into semicircle, enclosing filling. Press edges with fork to seal.

Heat fat in deep skillet to 365° F. Fry pies for 3 to 4 minutes or until golden brown. Drain on absorbent paper. Sprinkle with confectioners' sugar. Makes 12. Good picnic pies.

PICKLED OYSTERS
THE MANIFESTO

1 teaspoon allspice
1 teaspoon cloves
1 teaspoon mace
½ teaspoon cinnamon

½ teaspoon sugar
2 cups mild vinegar
1 quart large oysters

❰Mix spices and sugar together and add to vinegar. Bring to a boil. When cold pour over oysters and let stand overnight. Next day boil the whole mixture for 1 minute. Chill well. SERVES 4–6. These are nice for your picnic.

PRUNE LOAF
SHIRLEY SHAKER VILLAGE

1¼ cups white flour
1 cup sugar
½ teaspoon salt
1 teaspoon baking powder
1 teaspoon baking soda
1 cup graham flour
1 cup chopped nut meats (optional)

1 large egg
1 cup sour cream
½ cup thick prune juice
2 tablespoons melted butter
½ cup chopped cooked prunes (or 1 cup if nuts not used)
1 tablespoon grated orange rind

❰Sift flour, sugar, salt, baking powder, and soda into a large bowl. Add graham flour and nuts. Blend. Beat egg with sour cream and add remaining ingredients. Stir this mixture into dry ingredients and blend thoroughly. Pour into a well-buttered loaf pan and bake in a 350° F. oven 50 to 60 minutes or until bread tests done. Always in our picnic basket. Makes 1 loaf.

CELERY WITH MAYONNAISE SALAD
NORTH UNION SHAKER VILLAGE, OHIO

4 cups chopped celery
1 cup chopped cucumber
1 small onion, grated
1 teaspoon salt
½ teaspoon pepper

½ teaspoon dry mustard
1 cup mayonnaise
or
1 cup boiled dressing
Lettuce

❰Cook celery in water until tender. Cool. Chop cucumbers and drain well. Add onion to cucumbers and let stand 10 minutes. Drain again. Combine drained celery, cucumbers, onions, and all seasonings. Mix well with mayonnaise. Serve on a platter of lettuce leaves. Or take on a picnic. SERVES 8–10.

POTATO SALAD

HANCOCK SHAKER VILLAGE

The Shakers had picnics and like everyone else took potato salad along. A little Shaker sister wrote about the potato salad: "We got set for the picnic, but couldn't find the pail to carry the potato salad"; later on in her letter she said, "I guess the little boy hid the pail because he liked to keep his marbles in it."

1 quart thinly sliced boiled potatoes	Salt and pepper
1 medium onion, chopped fine	2 hard-boiled eggs, shelled, sliced
1 tablespoon chopped chives	thin
½ cup chopped celery	Sliced pickle
1 cup our own Sauce Mayonnaise*	Nice crisp lettuce
6 radishes, sliced very thin	

⟨Mix together all ingredients except eggs and pickle and lettuce. Chill. When ready to serve decorate with sliced eggs, sliced sweet pickle and lettuce. Makes 6 servings.

Substitute Frances Hall's Cream Dressing for mayonnaise if this suits your taste.

CREAM DRESSING

FRANCES HALL, HANCOCK SHAKER VILLAGE, 1906

½ teaspoon salt	2 tablespoons butter
1 teaspoon flour	2 egg yolks
1 teaspoon dry mustard	¾ cup sweet cream
2 teaspoons sugar	¼ cup vinegar

⟨Mix the dry ingredients with the butter. Add egg yolks, then cream, and lastly the vinegar. Cook over hot water until it thickens. Strain if necessary and chill. Do not boil. Makes 1 cup.

CHICKEN CHEESE

ENFIELD SHAKER VILLAGE, NEW HAMPSHIRE

2 chickens, 2–2½ pounds each, quartered	1 teaspoon salt
4 cups boiling water	1 teaspoon pepper
4 tablespoons butter	1 teaspoon nutmeg

⟪Boil the chickens in the water until tender. Remove the bones and the skins and chop the meat fine. Add butter to stock and reserve. Season to your taste with salt, pepper, and nutmeg. Put into a mold. Pour in enough of the chicken liquor to make it moist. Chill well and let stand overnight. When cold (it will be jellied) turn out and slice. SERVES 6–8. Take to a picnic and slice just before serving.

JELLIED VEAL
CANTERBURY SHAKER VILLAGE

4 veal shanks, split
2 quarts water
⅛ teaspoon pepper
1 teaspoon salt
1 bay leaf
1 blade mace

2 stalks celery, minced and cooked
8 sprigs parsley, minced and cooked
1 carrot, minced and cooked
1 tablespoon minced cooked green pepper
1 teaspoon chopped chervil

⟪Boil the veal shanks in the water with the seasoning slowly for 3 hours. Separate the meat and shred. Put in a mold with vegetables and chervil. When the pot liquor is cold, strain until clear and pour over meat and vegetables in mold. Chill until it jells. This can be cut into slices and served on lettuce as a salad or as a cold meat. It is a very nourishing dish and travels well to a picnic if not cut until just before serving. SERVES 4–6.

An interesting Bill of Fare—not a picnic exactly; except for Mr. Skinner.

Among the Shakers

.·.

On a recent tramp through the Berkshire Hills I veered out of my track for fifteen or twenty miles to call on the Shakers at New Lebanon, New York, the headquarters of the sect. It was a bright, cool autumn morning when I strode out of Lee, and the church bells were ringing as I passed through Lenox. Dudes with English clothes and single barreled eyeglasses were dawdling through the streets, and important looking persons were speeding down the elm shaded avenues in glittering coupés, driven by coachmen in livery. People go to the country to cut that sort of figure! An easy walk across the mountains, rich in panoply of gold and crimson, took me to the *village of Hancock,* which is occupied almost entirely by Shakers, and there I paused for lunch. What was set before me is here set down:

Cold beef,	Potato cake,
White bread,	Apple pie,
Brown bread,	Milk,
Butter,	Pickles,
Boiled rice,	Cream cheese,
Baked beans,	Cottage cheese,
Blackberry jam,	Cake,
Blackberry pie,	Doughnuts,

And the bill was twenty-five cents! I reproduce this bill of fare because it is characteristic of the Shaker cuisine. The cooking is worthy of Delmonico's though the habitués of that restaurant might regard it as limited in scope. For breakfast and dinner, however, eggs, tea, coffee, and all the fruits and vegetables of the season are added.

—Charles M. Skinner,
Uncle of Cornelia Otis Skinner
The Manifesto, 1886, Article Signed C.M.S.

Shaker Herbs

·: HERBS :·

"stimulate appetite,
give character to food, and
add charm and variety to ordinary dishes."
—Shaker *Manifesto*

COMMENT ON KITCHEN EDUCATION

EXCERPT FROM THE SHAKER MANIFESTO
SEPTEMBER 1883

The origin of many of the troubles which afflict mankind may be traced to a disordered stomach. No doubt but some of our bad legislation may be attributed to indigestible hotel breakfasts, and the burdens of sorrow produced by social disturbances have no more prolific contributor than the disordered stomach which produces disordered minds. Give the stomach good, wholesome food, and it will fill your veins with pure blood; which in turn will give you a healthy brain and drive away the whole brood of manufactured troubles.

We Shakers have followed this philosophy throughout our existence.

NOTE ON SHAKER COOKING

Shaker cooking is not a collection of recipes but rather an attitude toward food and its preparation. In Shaker kitchens meals were planned and cooked to satisfy both bodily and, in a sense, spiritual hunger. The Sisters prepared food as efficiently, nutritiously, and tastily as possible. They steamed vegetables to retain nutrients and saved parings and leftovers for their "pot licker" soups. They knew, too, that meals must "create contentment, joy and satisfaction in those who partake of them." In this respect, herbs became almost a necessity to the Shakers' simple fare because they were a means of making each dish "a fascinating, outstanding viand."

GENERAL RULES OF THUMB

1 teaspoon dried herb is approximately equivalent to 1 tablespoon fresh
chopped herb.

Never cook your minced herbs longer than 10 minutes; they lose their
flavor and aroma.

—Shaker Housekeeping Journal

THE RHYTHM AND VALUES OF SHAKER LIFE

For a period of 10 to 50 years, "the bloodless diet" was followed at Mount
Lebanon and many other Shaker communities. This has been mentioned
elsewhere in *The Best of Shaker Cooking* (see p. 111), but in reading
again an account of the regimen, we are interested in the sophisticated
approach and to the good and delicious food served.

PEA SOUP
NORTH UNION

2 pints shelled peas (2 pounds
    unshelled, or 4 cups)
3 pounds chicken, without skin
8 cups water
½ cup thyme
½ cup parsley

1 teaspoon salt
½ teaspoon pepper
1 tablespoon sugar
¼ pound butter
Flour

In a large pot, boil peas and chicken in water and add thyme and
parsley. When chicken leaves the bones and peas are soft, remove both
chicken and peas. Mash peas, cut up chicken and return both to the pot
liquor. Cut butter into pieces and roll in flour. Stir into soup before
sending to the table. SERVES 6.

TOMATO SOUP TO EAT AND TO CAN
HANCOCK SHAKER VILLAGE

1 peck tomatoes, very ripe (about
    8 quarts
1 head celery (bunch), without
    leaves, cut in 2-inch lengths
4 large onions, sliced
Handful basil, without stems
½ teaspoon baking soda

¼ cup salt
½ cup sugar
½ cup flour
½ cup cold water
½ cup butter
5–6 whole peppercorns
1 clove garlic, diced

《Cut tomatoes in quarters. Add celery, sliced onions, basil, and baking soda. Cook over low heat, to avoid boiling over, for 2 hours. Strain. Mix salt, sugar, and flour with the water to form a smooth paste, and add to tomato mixture. Add butter, peppercorns, and garlic. Boil hard for 5 minutes, stirring to avoid burning. Remove peppercorns and garlic. Can in sterilized jars[1] or serve at once with chopped fresh basil to garnish. Makes 6 quarts = 24 cups (lose some in boiling).

POTATO SOUP
SOUTH UNION SHAKER VILLAGE, KENTUCKY

4 cups potatoes, peeled and diced
2 tablespoons butter, melted
1 teaspoon salt
1½ teaspoons pepper
4 cups milk

4 eggs, beaten
1 bunch parsley, chopped, free
of stems
½ cup chopped chives

《Boil the potatoes until soft, then beat them with a little boiling water until a thin batter forms. Stir the butter, salt and pepper into the milk and bring to a boil. Add the eggs to potatoes, immediately add the boiled milk to potatoes, beat and remove from the heat. Do not return to the stove. Add parsley and chives before serving. SERVES 4–6.

CHESTNUT SOUP
UNION VILLAGE, OHIO

2 quarts chestnuts, in the shell
2 quarts rich chicken stock
Salt and pepper to taste

1 tablespoon chopped tarragon
Nutmeg to taste
1 pint cream

《Shell the chestnuts, put them in a pan and cover with cold water. Let them scald until the inner skin can be removed, about 30 minutes. Drain. Pour cold water over nuts and remove skin by hand. When skinned, put in saucepan with chicken stock. Let simmer until perfectly tender, about 30 minutes. Mash through sieve and place back into stock. Add seasonings. Put in double boiler, stirring all the time until the soup simmers, about 20 minutes. Add cream and stir for 5 minutes over medium heat. Remove and serve. SERVES 6–8.

---

[1] Fill sterilized jars, seal and process in water bath 1 hour.

APPLE SOUP

2 cups beef consommé
1 tart apple, quartered and
   cored, unpeeled
1 onion, quartered

1½ teaspoons herb mix,*
   cinnamon, or favorite spice
4 tablespoons apple cider
1 cup light cream or half and half

❨Combine consommé, apple, onion, and seasonings in top of double boiler. Cover tightly and cook at 350° for 2 minutes until apple is soft. Strain, discard pulp, and return to double boiler.

When ready to serve, add cider and cream. Serve hot. SERVES 4.

HERB SOUP
HANCOCK SHAKER VILLAGE

½ cup sorrel, chopped
¼ cup shallots, chopped
½ cup chervil
¼ cup mint

¼ cup parsley
1½ pint milk, or to cover
4 slices bread, toasted and buttered

❨Boil first 5 ingredients together in milk, add butter to one's choice and salt to season. Pour over squares of toasted bread in soup tureen. SERVES 4.

Note: This can be pureed for a thinner soup.

MEAT CAKES OR BEEF CAKES WITH MARJORAM
WATERVLIET SHAKER VILLAGE

1 slice bread, 1½ inches thick
1 pound ground beef
⅓ cup chopped onion
1 teaspoon minced fresh marjoram

¾ teaspoon salt
¼ teaspoon paprika
1–2 tablespoons butter

❨Preheat oven to 300° F.

Soak the bread in water to cover; wring out the water. Combine bread with the rest of the ingredients except butter, mixing lightly with the hands until well blended. Shape into cakes. Brown lightly in butter.

Transfer to 1-quart greased casserole; add sauce.[1] Bake covered or uncovered, depending on the consistency of sauce, at 300° F. for 30 minutes. SERVES 4.

---

[1] Serve with tomato sauce from Canterbury.

TOMATO SAUCE FROM CANTERBURY

1 quart fresh tomatoes, skins
   removed, cut up
2 cups water

1 tablespoon chopped basil
2 tablespoons butter

⟨[Simmer slowly and reduce to 2 cups.

BEEF STEAK STEW
HARVARD SHAKER VILLAGE

4 tablespoons butter
2 medium carrots, chopped
2 medium onions, chopped
1 cup water to cover
1 tablespoon dried herb mix
     or
½ teaspoon each fresh summer
   savory, basil, thyme, marjoram,
   and parsley

2 cups diced rare cooked beef
1 small apple, peeled, cored, and
   chopped
Salt and pepper to taste
1 cup very fine bread crumbs
1 cup sour cream

⟨[Melt butter and sauté carrots and onions briefly, add water to cover and cook until soft. Add herbs, the diced beef and chopped apple. Add ½ cup of water and simmer, covered, for 10 minutes. Add salt and pepper. Add bread crumbs. Remove from stove and add sour cream. Mix well. SERVES 4.

CHICKEN FRICASSEE
HARVARD SHAKER VILLAGE

1 5 pound chicken, cut into pieces
6 tablespoons butter
4 tablespoons flour
2 cups water
6 small onions
2 egg yolks

1½ cups raw rice
herb bag, composed of 2 branches
   of tarragon, 2 branches of
   parsley, 2 branches each of
   summer savory, marjoram,
   chervil, thyme

⟨[Roll pieces of chicken in flour and brown in butter. Blend 2 tablespoons butter with 2 tablespoons flour and make a sauce with 2 cups water. Lay the chicken in a deep skillet, pour the sauce over it, add onions and drop fresh herbs or an herb bag into the liquid.

Cook until chicken is tender, adding enough hot water to produce about 2 cups liquid for gravy at the end of cooking. Remove chicken to a hot platter.

Make gravy by heating 3 tablespoons of the liquid in the skillet with the yolks of 2 beaten eggs, stirring back into the remaining liquid and boiling for 5 minutes. Remove herbs. Pile on the hot platter a mound of flaky boiled rice and arrange chicken around it. Serve gravy in a bowl. SERVES 6.

KENTUCKY MEAT LOAF
PLEASANT HILL SHAKER VILLAGE

Originally this recipe was made with leftover fresh vegetable soup, but we've adapted it here for you.

1 large onion, minced	1 cup fresh corn scraped from
3 tablespoons melted bacon fat	cob (not whole kernels)
1 pound round steak, ground	1 green pepper, diced
½ teaspoon each basil, marjoram,	1 cup bread broken into coarse
summer savory, thyme, and parsley	crumbs
1 egg, slightly beaten	1 can vegetable soup
1½ teaspoon salt	1 cup hot water
¼ teaspoon pepper	½ teaspoon Worcestershire sauce

《Preheat oven to 350° F.

Fry onion in 1 tablespoon bacon fat. Mix all ingredients except soup and hot water. Form into a loaf and place in a one-quart baking dish in which the remaining fat has been melted. Add 1 cup hot water. Bake for 30 minutes.

Pour the vegetable soup into a skillet. Thin with hot water and add ½ teaspoon Worcestershire sauce. Bring to a boil and baste loaf frequently by the continual addition of the soup until the end of cooking. By the time the loaf is cooked, a delicious rich gravy will have been formed in the baking dish. Serve in the baking dish. SERVES 4–6.

CREAMED OYSTERS
(or White Fish such as Cod or Haddock)

HANCOCK SHAKER VILLAGE

4 tablespoons butter	½ teaspoon Worcestershire sauce
4 tablespoons flour	½ teaspoon salt
1½ cups milk	Pinch each of marjoram, basil,
½ cup cream	and chervil
2 egg yolks	½ cup mayonnaise
2 cups raw oysters (or cooked	
cod or haddock)	

❨Melt butter; add flour and stir to a smooth paste. Add milk and then cream gradually, stirring constantly. Beat egg yolks and mix with some of the sauce, then remove sauce from the heat and add yolks. Continue cooking over low heat, stirring. Add oysters or fish, Worcestershire sauce, salt, and herbs. Raise heat and cook for 1 minute. Oysters should not curl.

Remove from heat; fold in mayonnaise; serve at once. SERVES 4.

FISH POACHED WITH CHAMOMILE LEAVES

Chamomile is listed by the Shakers in their Herb Catalogs from 1847 to 1874. Its uses include medicinal (weak stomach, typhus, fever, hysteria and nervousness); culinary (for tea, for cooking fish); and domestic (to refresh ladies' hair after a sickness, applied as a cold hair rinse).

2 pounds haddock or cod   ½ cup chamomile leaves
Salt and lemon juice, to taste

❨Wrap fish in cheesecloth to keep flesh firm and intact, and place it in boiling water to cover. Add salt and lemon juice to keep flesh white and tender, along with chamomile leaves. Boil or steam for about 20 to 30 minutes, depending on size. Check after 20 minutes; fish is done when flesh leaves the bones. Lift out of pan and arrange on platter. Dress with sauce or pass sauce in sauce boat. SERVES 4.

CHAMOMILE SAUCE

2 tablespoons butter   2 tablespoons chamomile leaves
2 tablespoons flour   (which are feathery)
1 cup chicken stock   Salt and pepper to taste
2 tablespoons chopped parsley

❨Melt butter, add flour, and cook over low heat. Add stock gradually and stir until sauce is smooth. Add parsley and chamomile and cook for 1 minute. Add salt and pepper to taste. Add ½ cup cream if thinner sauce is desired. Makes 1½ cups.

CREAMED OYSTERS

HANCOCK SHAKER VILLAGE

1 quart cream
½ dozen medium-large crackers,
   broken up fine, or ¾ cup
   cracker meal
1½ tablespoons butter
Salt and pepper to taste
1 tablespoon chervil
     or
1 tablespoon thyme (leaves only),
   or both

1 quart oysters, just shelled, at
   room temperature
6 slices buttered toast

❮[Boil cream, thicken with crackers, add butter, salt and pepper, chervil or thyme, or both. Add oysters and cook for 3 minutes. Serve hot with buttered toast. SERVES 6.

Note: If cooked too long, oysters become tough.

VEAL AND OYSTERS, SCALLOPED

HANCOCK SHAKER VILLAGE

2 pounds tender cooked veal, cut
   in small thin pieces
2 cups cream
2 tablespoons butter
1 tablespoon cornstarch

Mace, salt and pepper to taste
1 quart oysters
1 tablespoon chopped tarragon
   leaves
1 cup bread crumbs, buttered

❮[Preheat oven to 400° F.

Add veal to cream and bring to a boil. Add butter, cornstarch and seasonings. Stir well. Add oysters and tarragon. Pour into greased 3-quart baking dish and sprinkle with bread crumbs. Bake for 10 minutes. SERVES 8–10.

OYSTER STUFFING

HANCOCK SHAKER VILLAGE

25 large oysters
4 cups coarse bread crumbs
1 tablespoon chopped celery
¼ cup cream

Salt and pepper to taste
1 teaspoon summer savory
1 tablespoon chopped parsley
1 egg yolk

❮[Chop oysters fine, mix with bread crumbs, celery and cream. Add seasonings and at last the egg yolk. Mix well and stuff the turkey. Enough for a 10-pound turkey.

FINNAN HADDIE

HANCOCK SHAKER VILLAGE

Note: Haddock is in season throughout the year. When dried, smoked and salted, it is known as finnan haddie.

3 pounds finnan haddie	1 teaspoon pepper
½ tablespoon finely chopped shallots	1 tablespoon dried crumbled rosemary
½ tablespoon chopped onions	4 tablespoons flour
1 tablespoon finely chopped green pepper	1 cup cream
½ cup butter	1 cup milk
1 teaspoon salt	2 cups bread crumbs

❧[Soak finnan haddie in milk to cover for one hour. Preheat oven to 350° F. Bake in oven for 30 minutes and separate into flakes. There should be at least 2 cups. Cook shallots, onion and pepper in butter, stirring constantly, for 5 minutes. Add seasonings and flour, stir and blend. Pour on the cream and milk gradually, stirring all the time. Bring to a boil and add the finnan haddie. Turn into a 2-quart buttered baking dish, cover with buttered bread crumbs or cracker crumbs and bake until crumbs are brown. SERVES 6.

SCALLOPED COD

HANCOCK SHAKER VILLAGE

2 tablespoons butter	2 tablespoons chives
3 cups cod, cooked	1 teaspoon black pepper
1 cup onions, chopped fine	1 cup cream

❧[Preheat oven to 350° F.

Butter a 10-inch baking dish and line it with cold cooked cod, flaked but no salt added. Sprinkle with finely chopped onion, chives, spices, and black pepper. Add medium thick cream to cover (barely). Cook in oven at 350° F. for 40 minutes.

Serve with either Sweet Mustard Sauce, Dill Sauce, or Dill Sour Cream Sauce on page 374. A variation of this dish is to add 2 cups of sliced cooked potatoes to the cod before adding the cream. In this case, potatoes should be sprinkled with salt. SERVES 4.

SWEET MUSTARD SAUCE

2 tablespoons butter
2 tablespoons flour, sifted
2 tablespoons prepared sweet
mustard
2 tablespoons sautéed chopped
onions (cooked in water, not
butter)

1 cup milk (or more, depending
on consistency desired)
1 tablespoon dried mixed herbs

([Melt butter, add flour, and cook on low heat. Add mustard, onions and herbs, and thin with milk. Makes 1 cup.

DILL SAUCE

2 tablespoons butter
2 tablespoons flour
1 cup milk

2 tablespoons dill weed (not
seed), chopped fine

([Melt butter, and add flour. When blended, add milk and stir until smooth. Add dill. Makes 1 cup.

LAST EARS OF CORN, OR CORN PIE
HANCOCK SHAKER VILLAGE

2 cups corn scraped from the cob
2 tablespoons herb vinegar
1 large egg

1 cup cream
1 tablespoon chives

([Preheat oven to 350° F.

In a buttered 8-inch pie plate put a 2-inch layer of raw scraped corn. Sprinkle the herb vinegar over it. Beat a large egg with the cream, and add chives to flavor. Pour over the corn. Bake for 15 minutes. SERVES 6.

DILLED EGGPLANT CASSEROLE
HANCOCK SHAKER VILLAGE

2 large ripe eggplants, peeled,
cut in 1-inch cubes
6 medium zucchini, peeled, cut in
¼-inch slices
6 medium onions, peeled and sliced
6 green peppers, cut in 1-inch
pieces, without seeds
2 cloves garlic, minced

3 sprigs fresh dill
6 sprigs fresh parsley
1 tablespoon fresh or 2 teaspoons
dried oregano
1 large (28-ounce) can peeled
tomatoes
½ teaspoon black pepper
¼ cup salad oil

¶[Preheat oven to 300° F.

Combine all ingredients in a large casserole. Cover and bake at 300° F. for 2½ hours, stirring occasionally. Or cook on top of the stove on medium heat, covered for 1½ hours and uncovered for an additional hour. Can be served hot or cold; can be frozen and reheated. SERVES 8–12.

DANDELION MIXTURE
SHIRLEY, MASSACHUSETTS

2 cups dandelion leaves
2 egg yolks
½ cup cream, salt, pepper, herbs
   of your choice, to taste
2 slices stale bread

1 tablespoon butter, for frying
2 hard-boiled eggs, chopped
Oil, vinegar, chopped parsley,
   to taste

¶[Wash young dandelion leaves thoroughly, and simmer in salted water until tender. Drain and press to extract all moisture. Place in saucepan with egg yolks, cream, and salt and pepper, as well as any herbs desired. (Mint is suggested, as is lemon geranium.) Heat through, spread the mixture on slices of stale bread and fry quickly in hot butter or drippings. Garnish with chopped hard-boiled eggs. Season with oil, vinegar, salt and pepper and finely chopped parsley. SERVES 2.

ASPARAGUS, SHAKER STYLE

The Shakers at Hancock grew asparagus in a large bed west of the Meetinghouse. The Lenox "cottagers" bought it with great enthusiasm and loyalty. They said "it had very straight stems and was sweet and kept its color." They also thought it expensive.

The Shakers in cooking for their family bundled the asparagus in lots of twenty-five stems or, if the stems were very fat, in smaller bundles of twelve or fifteen, tied in even lengths. They cooked it quickly in 2 quarts of boiling water to which some salt had been added. It was served on toast with sweet butter poured over—or the following sauce.

SAUCE FOR ASPARAGUS ON TOAST
HANCOCK SHAKER VILLAGE

4 tablespoons butter, melted
4 egg yolks
½ teaspoon salt
Juice of ½ lemon

Pinch cayenne
Hot water
1 tablespoon chopped parsley

¶[Add the egg yolks to the melted butter. Beat well together and add salt, lemon juice, cayenne, and some hot water (½ to 1 cup, depending on size of yolks and how thick a sauce is desired). Stir in top of double boiler until thickness desired. Do not boil or it will curdle. Add 1 tablespoon chopped parsley before serving. Makes 1 cup.

ASPARAGUS
HANCOCK SHAKER VILLAGE

3 tablespoons butter
2 tablespoons flour
1 cup cream or milk

Salt and pepper
1 tablespoon vinegar or lemon
  juice

⟨Cut off tips of asparagus to make 4 cups. Wash well and cook for 10 minutes in boiling salted water. Drain. To make sauce, mix 2 tablespoons butter, flour, cream or milk, salt and pepper in a saucepan and cook for 3 minutes or until it is smooth and does not taste of flour. Flavor with vinegar or lemon juice and 1 tablespoon butter when removing from heat. Add asparagus to sauce and serve. SERVES 4.

Note: Instead of lemon juice or vinegar, you may add 2 tablespoons grated cheese, 1 tablespoon chopped chervil and 1 tablespoon chopped parsley. In this case, fry pieces of bread and, after arranging asparagus on platter, cover with sauce and surround with fried bread.

ANOTHER SAUCE FOR WARM ASPARAGUS
HANCOCK SHAKER VILLAGE

2 tablespoons vinegar
1 tablespoon butter

Salt and pepper
1 egg yolk, beaten well

⟨Bring to the boil vinegar, butter, salt and pepper. When boiling, remove from heat and add beaten egg yolk, salt and pepper. Pour over asparagus. SERVES 2.

ASPARAGUS OMELET
HANCOCK SHAKER VILLAGE

6 eggs, separated
3 tablespoons cream or milk
36 asparagus spears, cooked in
  boiling water for 5 minutes

1 tablespoon sharp cheese, grated
Salt and pepper
1 tablespoon butter

⟨Beat egg whites and yolks separately. Add cream or milk to egg yolks, fold in beaten whites. Cut the green part of asparagus into small pieces.

Mix with eggs, add a spoonful of grated cheese, salt and pepper. Cook in an omelet pan in which 1 tablespoon butter has been melted. SERVES 6.

ASPARAGUS MOLD
HANCOCK SHAKER VILLAGE

1 pound slightly cooked asparagus, cut up
2 cups slightly cooked peas
2 hard-boiled eggs, sliced
3 eggs
2 tablespoons flour

1 tablespoon melted butter
1 cup milk
Salt and pepper to taste
White Sauce #3*
or
White Sauce #4*

([Butter a 6-cup pudding mold. Put in layer of asparagus, a layer of peas and the two hard-boiled eggs. Beat the 3 eggs, and stir in flour and butter. Add milk, salt and pepper. Cook until smooth. Pour mixture over vegetables in mold. Cover with buttered paper and steam for 2 hours. Turn out onto a hot dish. Serve with white sauce.

ASPARAGUS BAKED WITH CHEESE
HANCOCK SHAKER VILLAGE

12–14 stalks of asparagus
3 tablespoons butter
3 tablespoons flour
1 cup water
½ cup cream

3 egg yolks, beaten
2 tablespoons grated cheddar cheese
1 cup fine bread crumbs
1 cup diced cheddar cheese

([Boil asparagus for 5 minutes. Make a sauce of the butter, flour, water, and cream. Boil for 3 minutes. Add egg yolks and grated cheese. Heat thoroughly but do not boil.

Preheat oven to 350° F. Lay asparagus full-length in a buttered oval baking dish, cover with sauce and sprinkle with grated cheese. Repeat until dish is full. Sprinkle with bread crumbs and diced cheese; dot with butter. Bake for 30 minutes. SERVES 5–6.

ASPARAGUS BAKED WITH CHEESE: Variation
HANCOCK SHAKER VILLAGE

1 pound bunch asparagus, slightly parboiled
1 cup White Sauce #3*
1 tablespoon tarragon
1 tablespoon parsley

1 teaspoon nutmeg
Salt and pepper to taste
1 cup grated sharp cheese
1 cup fine bread crumbs
4 tablespoons butter

◖Put asparagus in layers in baking dish. Cover layers with white sauce in which sharp cheese has been melted and flavored with tarragon, parsley and nutmeg. Add salt and pepper. Pour white sauce on top and sprinkle with bread crumbs and cheese, dot with butter. Bake for 30 minutes at 350° F.

Another variation: Put asparagus in layers in baking dish. Cover each layer with cream sauce in which 1 cup sharp cheese has been melted. Flavor with nutmeg, tarragon, parsley, salt and pepper. Have cream sauce layer on the top. Sprinkle with bread crumbs, cheese, dot with butter. Bake for 30 minutes at 350° F.

PARSLEY SAUCE
HANCOCK SHAKER VILLAGE

1 bunch parsley	1 cup cream
1 tablespoon butter	Salt and pepper
1 tablespoon flour	½ tablespoon dry mustard

◖Pick and wash a good bunch of parsley, dip into boiling water for 1 minute. Place in towel and wring out, then chop fine. Make a white sauce by melting the butter, adding flour and, over low heat, adding cream, salt and pepper to taste. Stir until smooth and thickened. Add dry mustard and parsley. Stir and serve over boiled potatoes or green beans. Makes 1 cup.

Variation: For a sauce for cooked beets, hot or cold, add 1 teaspoon caraway seeds, some cream, off the heat. Add 1 tablespoon prepared horseradish, if desired. Yields 1 cup.

STEWED CARROTS
HANCOCK SHAKER VILLAGE

2 dozen small carrots	3–4 tablespoons vegetable broth
1 tablespoon white sugar	3 tablespoons heavy cream
2 medium onions, diced	2 tablespoons chopped chives
1 teaspoon chervil	1 tablespoon brown sugar
2 teaspoons parsley	

◖Wash and scrape the carrots. Put them in a large saucepan with the white sugar, onions, a bunch of sweet herbs (chervil, parsley), and a bay leaf. Add a few spoons of vegetable broth and stew carrots until tender. Remove carrots. Strain stock and add to it the heavy cream, chopped chives, and brown sugar. Stir and pour over carrots. SERVES 6.

SUMMER SQUASH WITH CHIVES
MT. LEBANON SHAKER VILLAGE

4 summer squashes
1 cup sour cream
2 tablespoons chives, chopped

2 tablespoons butter
2 cups bread crumbs, buttered

(Preheat oven to 350° F.

Pick small squash in which seeds have not matured. Scrape, but do not peel. Chop fine. Steam or cook in small amount of slightly salted water for 15 minutes or until soft. Drain well. Mash and beat well. Add sour cream to achieve a good consistency and chopped chives and butter to taste. Put in 1-quart greased casserole, cover with buttered bread crumbs, bake 30 minutes. SERVES 4–6.

CARROT RING MOLD
MT. LEBANON SHAKER VILLAGE

Use new carrots, not too big.

2 cups cooked carrots, diced
1 teaspoon salt
¼ teaspoon black pepper
1 tablespoon herb mixture,
   crumbled (p. 464)

1 teaspoon chopped fresh chives
   or onion
3 slightly beaten eggs
1 cup milk
2 tablespoons melted butter

(Preheat oven to 375° F.

Mix all ingredients well and pour into well-greased 4-cup ring mold. Set mold in a pan of warm water, and bake for 35 minutes. Unmold and fill center with cooked buttered peas. SERVES 4.

HEAVENLY SQUASH
HANCOCK SHAKER VILLAGE

3 pounds yellow squash or white
   button summer squash without
   seeds, or zucchini
2 cups cooked corn scraped from
   the cob
1 cup grated cheddar cheese

3 eggs, beaten
1 clove garlic, finely chopped
½ cup oil
Salt and pepper to taste
1 tablespoon mixed dried herbs

¶Preheat oven to 325° F.

Mix all ingredients and pour into oiled 1½-quart casserole. Bake for about 1 hour, until knife comes out clean. SERVES 6–8.

Note: Heavenly Squash was also made by the Shakers using winter squash that they precooked somewhat, peeled and sliced. I believe this recipe is best now when made with zucchini.

CORN PUDDING
HANCOCK SHAKER VILLAGE

2 cups corn scraped from cob, milk removed	1 teaspoon sugar
2 eggs, beaten	1 teaspoon salt
½ cup finely chopped onion	2 cups milk or cream
or	1 tablespoon butter
1 tablespoon chopped chives	6 saltine crackers, crumbled
	Herb or herb mix to taste (p. 464)

¶Preheat oven to 350° F.

Mix all ingredients together. Pour into greased 1½-quart baking dish and bake for 1 hour. SERVES 6.

RICED SQUASH, A VARIATION OF HEAVENLY SQUASH
HANCOCK SHAKER VILLAGE

8 cups winter squash, peeled and cut up	Chopped walnuts
Salt and pepper to taste	Fresh tarragon and chives, chopped, to taste
6 teaspoons butter, melted	

¶Good for a large family. Cook winter squash in a steamer for 10 minutes until tender. Drain. Run through a ricer into serving dish, or mash by hand. Add salt, pepper, and butter. Sprinkle with chopped nuts, tarragon, and chives. Serve at once, while hot. SERVES 8.

RED CABBAGE AND APPLES
STEAMED IN ARCH KETTLE CIRCA 1830 AT HANCOCK SHAKER VILLAGE

1 head red cabbage, shredded fine	2 tablespoons sugar
2 tablespoons butter	2 tablespoons vinegar
3 tart apples, peeled, cored, and diced	1 teaspoon each salt and pepper
	1 teaspoon caraway seed

¶Put shredded cabbage into 2-quart covered kettle with a scant cup of water. Add butter and steam over low heat for 30 minutes. Add apples and other ingredients. Cook for another hour on low heat. SERVES 6.

COOK'S CHOICE (During the Meatless Diet)
HANCOCK SHAKER VILLAGE

The meatless diet, deemed to be a healthy regime, was in force for about 10 years in all Shaker communities. Many interesting vegetarian recipes resulted from this enforced diet which, according to contemporary accounts of non-Shakers, produced abundant and delicious dishes.

1 large onion, chopped	½ teaspoon pepper
2 tablespoons butter	1 large egg, beaten
1 pound sharp cheese, diced	½ cup basil leaves, chopped
1 quart ripe tomatoes, diced	very fine
1 tablespoon Worcestershire sauce	1 tablespoon finely chopped sage
1 teaspoon salt	

❮Fry onion in butter. Add cheese, tomatoes and Worestershire sauce. Simmer on low heat until thick and smooth. Add salt and pepper. Add beaten egg and basil. Simmer 5–10 minutes. Serve hot over rice or on crustless toast. SERVES 6.

Note: Although Shaker-made bread did not mildew, Shakers felt it prudent to remove crusts from bread made in other ovens, since it was the crust that "turned first because it was buttered before baking."

SHAKER STRING BEANS
HANCOCK SHAKER VILLAGE

1 pound string beans	Butter to taste
1 tablespoon summer savory	Salt and pepper to taste
1 tablespoon marjoram	

❮Select fresh string beans that are small in size. Add water only to cover. Add fresh summer savory and marjoram. Bring to a boil and remove from stove. Drain. Add butter, salt and pepper. SERVES 4.

SHAKER SWEET GARDEN PEAS
MT. LEBANON SHAKER VILLAGE

2 cups tender peas (very fresh), shelled	1 teaspoon dried rosemary
1 teaspoon dried basil	2 tablespoons butter
	1 teaspoon sugar

¶Cook shelled peas in boiling water to cover. Reduce heat at once, cook 5 minutes, remove from stove and drain. Add basil and rosemary, butter and sugar. Toss. SERVES 2.

Note: If fresh basil and rosemary are available increase amounts to 2 teaspoons each.

CREAMED MUSHROOMS
HANCOCK SHAKER VILLAGE

Soup herbs are basil, marjoram, summer savory, and parsley. They add depth to almost any dish.

1 pound mushrooms, medium sized	2 tablespoons flour
1 tablespoon soup herbs, finely cut if fresh, pulverized if dried	½ teaspoon salt
2 thick slices lemon	2 cups heavy cream
2 tablespoons butter	4 toast slices

¶Wipe mushroom caps and cut up stems. Put into kettle with water to cover, plus a little more. Add a bag of soup herbs plus lemon slices. Cook until mushrooms are tender and liquid is reduced to about ½ cup—about 20 minutes. Remove soup bag and lemon, strain and save liquid. Blend butter, flour, and salt in a pan on top of stove. Mix mushroom stock and cream to make a medium thick sauce. Stir in mushrooms. Cook 5 minutes and serve on toast. SERVES 4.

GLAZED CARROTS WITH HERBS
HANCOCK SHAKER VILLAGE

6 large carrots	Butter
2 tablespoons mixed herbs (basil, marjoram, summer savory and parsley)	1–2 tablespoons brown sugar
	½ cup water

¶Preheat oven to 350° F.

Split carrots in half lengthwise. Cover with hot water and cook for 5 to 8 minutes or until tender. Butter a shallow glass 2-quart casserole that can be served from at the table. Spread half the mixed herbs evenly over bottom of casserole. Lay carrots flat side down on herbs. Sprinkle remaining herb mixture evenly over top of carrots. Dot generously with butter. Sprinkle brown sugar over all. Pour water into casserole carefully and cook in oven at 350° F. for about 15 minutes or until carrots are tender. Test for doneness with fork. SERVES 4.

LEMON TOAST
WATERVLIET, NEW YORK

3 eggs, beaten
1 tablespoon finely chopped lemon
  balm
½ teaspoon salt

2 tablespoons sugar
6 slices day-old bread
1 cup milk
4 tablespoons butter, melted

⟪Mix eggs, lemon balm, salt, sugar, and milk in shallow dish or pie pan. Soak bread in mixture, turning once. Cook on a hot, well-greased frying pan, turning once to brown each side. SERVES 6.

PARSNIP FRITTERS
HANCOCK SHAKER VILLAGE

1 pound parsnips
½ teaspoon salt
4 tablespoons butter, melted

½ teaspoon black pepper
2 tablespoons flour

⟪Scrape but do not pare parsnips. Cut up and cook until tender in slightly salted boiling water—about 15 minutes. Mash with 2 tablespoons melted butter, salt and pepper. Form into small flat cakes, roll in flour, and sauté in remaining 2 tablespoons butter until brown on both sides. Drain thoroughly on paper towels. Serve with Herbed Mayonnaise Sauce. SERVES 4.

HERBED MAYONNAISE SAUCE
HANCOCK SHAKER VILLAGE

1 cup tart mayonnaise
Lemon juice, to taste

1 tablespoon chopped fresh parsley
1 tablespoon dried herbs (p. 464)

⟪Combine mayonnaise, lemon juice, parsley, and dried herbs. Mix well and refrigerate. SERVES 4.

PEA ROAST
HARVARD SHAKER VILLAGE

Although the "meatless diet" only lasted ten years (1837–1847), it was observed in most communities, but not strictly enforced.

1½ cups fine dry bread crumbs
1 cup peas
1½ tablespoons sugar
½ cup English walnut meats, chopped fine
2 eggs, slightly beaten
1 teaspoon chopped parsley
1 tablespoon chopped chives

1½ teaspoons salt
¼ teaspoon pepper
½ cup butter, melted
1½ cups milk
1 tablespoon mixed herbs (see p. 464)
1 tablespoon powdered sage

⟨[Preheat oven to 350° F.

Cook peas in water to cover and boil 3 minutes. Drain and puree in blender, sieve, or processor. Add bread crumbs, sugar, nut meats, seasonings, butter, and milk. Mix well. Line a bread pan with wax paper, fill with the mixture and let stand for 15 minutes. Cover with foil and bake for 40 minutes. Serve with Cheese Sauce (p. 120), adding 1 tablespoon powdered sage. SERVES 4.

SAVORY SALT

Make up a quantity of this salt and use to flavor meats, fish and sauces with cheese or plain white sauce.

2 large onions
2 tablespoons salt

1 tablespoon dried chives
1 tablespoon black pepper

⟨[Preheat oven to 350° F.

Cut onions in fine pieces and dry for 15 minutes in the oven. When onions are dry enough to flake or crumble, add salt, chives, and black pepper. Mix well. Put back in warm oven for 10 minutes to deepen seasoning. Makes 3 tablespoons.

SISTER MIRIAM WALL'S SUMMER MENU
CANTERBURY SHAKER VILLAGE

⟨[Sister Miriam loved to cook. One day she gave Gene Dodd, curator at Hancock Shaker Village, and me a delicious lunch. First we had some spicy ice cold lemonade. She teased us to guess the secret ingredient. It was lemon verbena or rose geranium, or both. She had heated some lemon juice, added the verbena or rose geranium, let it wilt, then drained and cooled it. The juice was poured over ice and some good pure Shaker water added. Then we had a perfectly ripe large tomato, peeled, cut in eighths, but not all the way through, served on garden lettuce. It was filled with homemade mayonnaise with a little lemon zest in it. Sister Miriam gave us sour cream biscuits with this. I asked, "From scratch?" And she said, "No, biscuit out of the box and sour cream. The biscuit is pure, just quick." Our dessert was very ripe cut up peaches and her elegant sugar cookies.

To bake Sister Miriam's Butter and Sugar Cookies, see p. 458.

VEGETABLE CHUTNEY
HANCOCK SHAKER VILLAGE

2 dozen ripe tomatoes, chopped
6 medium onions, chopped
3 red peppers (without seeds), chopped
1 dozen tart apples, peeled and seeded

1 pound seedless raisins
1 cup diced celery
1 quart vinegar
3 cups brown sugar
1 cup chopped basil, without stems
½ cup salt

❪[Combine ingredients and cook on low heat until chutney is thick and clear—about 2 hours. This must be watched, as tomatoes burn. Put into hot, sterile jars and seal. Process 1 hour in water bath. Makes about 5 quarts.

MUSH

Mush is any of a variety of cereal preparations cooked over hot water. The recipe may be increased to serve any number.

1 cup oatmeal, rice, fine hominy, cornmeal (white and yellow), or rye meal

1 teaspoon salt
1¾ cups water

❪[Cook cereal over hot water in double boiler, stirring and checking until all lumps are gone. SERVES 4.

OATMEAL MUSH WITH APPLES

6 apples
1 cup water
1 tablespoon chopped mint leaves

½ stick butter
1 cup heavy cream

⟨[Core and peel apples. Blend sugar, water, and mint to make syrup. Cook apples in syrup until soft but firm. Add butter to cooked mush, transfer to platter, and cover with cooked apples. Serve with heavy cream. SERVES 4.

FRIED MUSH

⟨[Cut leftover cornmeal mush into strips or squares and fry in butter. Cover with Spicy Tomato Sauce and sprinkle with grated cheese.

MUSH WITH MINT JELLY SAUCE WITH CURRANT JELLY
HANCOCK SHAKER VILLAGE

Another good use for leftover mush (see p. 455).

2 cups leftover cornmeal or oatmeal   4 tablespoons butter

⟨[Refrigerate any leftover cornmeal or oatmeal in flat pan. When firm, cut into strips or squares. Fry in melted butter. SERVES 4.

MINT JELLY SAUCE WITH CURRANT JELLY
HANCOCK SHAKER VILLAGE

1 cup mint jelly
1 cup currant jelly

½ cup heavy cream
mint, chopped, for garnish

⟨[Mix together well all ingredients except mint; add mint before serving. Makes 3 cups.

CHESTNUT STUFFING FOR A TURKEY
CANTERBURY SHAKER VILLAGE

1 cup boiled mashed chestnuts
1 cup mashed cooled sweet potato
1 tablespoon butter
2 tablespoons chopped cooked
  onion

1 cup cream
Salt and pepper to taste
1 teaspoon powdered summer
  savory
1 cup fine bread crumbs

❨Mix the chestnuts, sweet potato, butter, onion, and cream together. Add seasonings. When the turkey is half roasted, put in the stuffing and baste until well done. Makes 4 cups, enough for a 10–12-pound turkey.

TOMATOES AND SAUSAGE CAKES WITH HERBS
NORTH UNION SHAKER HEIGHTS, CLEVELAND

12 large tomatoes, peeled and quartered	12 sausage patties
3 cups coarse fresh bread crumbs	Dried mixed herbs

❨Preheat oven to 350° F.

Keeping ingredients separate, divide tomatoes, bread crumbs, and sausage patties into two equal portions. Layer one portion of tomatoes in a buttered baking dish, cover with 1½ cups bread crumbs, then with 6 sausage patties. Sprinkle this layer with dried herbs. Repeat once. Bake for 40 minutes, or until bread crumbs are browned. SERVES 8–10.

SUGGESTIONS FOR SALAD

Beets, cabbage, chard, chicory, endive, turnip leaves and all the wild greens such as dandelions, lamb's quarters, dock, and mustard are very succulent grub when properly combined and dressed. . . . Sour sorrel is another tasty plant one should not overlook for flavor in salads. . . . Borage—its tender leaves when added to salads awaken in one a new sense of joy. . . .

—*Gleanings from Shaker Accounts*

ICE CREAM CANDY
FRANCES HALL
HANCOCK SHAKER VILLAGE

3 cups sugar	Wintergreen mint, orange extract,
¼ teaspoon cream of tartar	oil of sassafras, or melted
½ cup boiling water	brown sugar
½ cup mint vinegar	

❨Mix first four ingredients together and bring to a boil without stirring. Flavor with wintergreen mint, orange extract, or oil of sassafras, or melted brown sugar. Drop a teaspoon of the mixture into a cup of cold water. This you may have to do several times until it turns out brittle. When it does, pour the whole batch onto a buttered platter to cool. When it can be handled, fold toward center as edges cool. Cut pieces and pull them out into small sticks. Makes 1½ to 2 pounds.

BUTTER TAFFY OR BROWN SUGAR TAFFY

FRANCES HALL
HANCOCK SHAKER VILLAGE

2 cups light brown sugar
¼ cup molasses
2 tablespoons mint vinegar
2 tablespoons water

Pinch salt
½ cup (4 ounces) butter
2 teaspoons vanilla

⟨Boil together sugar, molasses, vinegar, water, and salt. Try a drop in cold water. If it becomes brittle, remove from heat. Add butter and vanilla. Beat. Cool, mark into squares and cut. Makes 1 pound.

ROSEWATER ICE CREAM

HANCOCK SHAKER VILLAGE

1 tablespoon flour
1½ cups granulated sugar
1 teaspoon salt
2 egg yolks, slightly beaten

2 cups scalded milk
4 cups light cream
1 tablespoon rosewater

⟨Mix flour, sugar, and salt. Add egg yolks; stir until smooth. Add scalded milk slowly. Cook in top of double boiler until thick. When cool, add cream and rosewater. Pour into ice cream freezer and freeze according to manufacturer's directions. Makes 1 quart.

Variation: Beat 1 to 3 tablespoons rosewater into softened vanilla ice cream and refreeze.

SISTER MIRIAM'S BUTTER AND SUGAR COOKIES

CANTERBURY SHAKER VILLAGE

½ cup whipped butter
1 cup plus a little more
  confectioner's sugar, sifted

1 teaspoon vanilla
1¾ cup flour, sifted
½ cup milk

⟨Preheat oven to 350° F.

Beat butter and sugar until smooth. Add vanilla and flour. Beat thoroughly. Combine with milk.

Butter a 10″ x 12″ cookie sheet and spread with mixture. Sprinkle with sugar. Or drop by the teaspoon on the sheet. Bake for 8 to 10 minutes or until lightly browned. Cut into squares. Remove cookies quickly. Makes 40 cookies.

LOAF CAKES
MOUNT LEBANON

Cakes

Rub 6 pound of sugar, 2 pound of lard, 3 pound of butter into 12 pound of flour, add 18 eggs, 1 quart of milk, 2 ounces of cinnamon, 2 small nutmegs, a teacup of coriander seed, each pounded fine and sifted, add one pint of brandy, half a pint of wine, 6 pound of stoned raisins, 1 pint of emptins, first having dried your flour in the oven, dry and roll the sugar fine, rub your shortening and sugar half an hour, it will render the cake much whiter and lighter, heat the oven with dry wood, for 1 and a half hours, if large pans be used, it will then require 2 hours baking, and in proportion for smaller loaves. To frost it. Whip 6 whites, during the baking, add 3 pound of sifted loaf sugar and put on thick, as it comes hot from the oven. Some return the frosted loaf into the oven, it injures and yellows it, if the frosting be put on immediately it does best without being returned into the oven.

MIXED FRUIT DESSERT
WATERVLIET SHAKER VILLAGE

2 cups cantaloupe
2 cups honeydew
2 cups watermelon
2 cups pineapple, diced
1 cup sugar, more or less, to taste
1 cup finely chopped leaves applemint
1 cup finely chopped leaves orange mint
1 cup finely chopped leaves peppermint
1 cup finely chopped leaves spearmint
1 cup candied angelica cut up for garnish

⟨With sharp knife or small scoop, make small balls of the cantaloupe, honeydew melon and watermelon. Add diced pineapple. Put fruit in large bowl and pour sugar over, adjusting amount according to taste, but mixture should be tart. Add equal proportions of finely chopped leaves of applemint, orange mint, peppermint, and garden mint (probably spearmint), about a large tablespoon to a quart of cut-up fruit. Reserve some of the mint to be used later.

Let the mixture stand for 2 or 3 hours in the refrigerator. Just before serving, pile the fruit into serving glasses or bowls and scatter over the top a bit of the mint and a few shavings of candied angelica. SERVES 10.

SWEET POTATO CUSTARD PIE
"HOME TOPICS," APRIL 1878 MANIFESTO,

*Take good-sized sweet potatoe (either sweet or white)—boil, and as soon
as done—remove the skins and rub through a sieve. Add one-half dozen
eggs, two teacups sugar, beat well and add 1 quart sweet milk, and flavor
with lemon. This makes six pies. Before custard sets, sprinkle with lemon
mint. 1 large sweet potatoe is allowed to each pie. (Note—These must
be individual pies)*

Today's cook would translate this as follows:

2 cups boiled, mashed sweet potato
2 cups sugar
1 teaspoon salt
4 cups milk
6 eggs, beaten

1 tablespoon lemon juice
1 pastry shell, precooked
2 tablespoons finely diced lemon
mint

⟪Preheat oven to 350° F.

Combine mashed sweet potato, sugar, salt, and milk and beat until
smooth. Add beaten eggs and lemon juice and pour into precooked pastry
shell. Sprinkle with lemon mint.

Set filled pie shell in larger pan filled with ½-inch hot water. Bake for
35 minutes or until custard is barely set. Remove and cool. Refrigerate
for an hour before serving. SERVES 6.

DESSERT APPLES
WATERVLIET SHAKER VILLAGE

2 cups brown sugar
4 cups water
½ cup mint vinegar
½ stick cinnamon

6 cloves to taste
3 pounds apples
1 cup heavy cream

⟪Make a syrup as for canning peaches: drop in herb of your choice, mint
is best. Boil up and remove mint. Peel and cut the apples in fourths or
eighths, depending on size, and drop in. Boil until apples start to puff
like doughnuts. Remove with skimmer. Serve hot with heavy cream. Also
good using pears or crab apples. SERVES 6.

To make syrup: boil sugar, water, vinegar, cinnamon, cloves, and mint
together until sugar dissolves. Remove mint. Continue boiling for 10
minutes. Add apples and boil until apples puff. Remove with skimmer.
Serve with heavy cream. SERVES 6.

NUT GRAVY
FRANCES HALL
HANCOCK SHAKER VILLAGE

¾ cup cooked and mashed
  chestnuts or other nuts
1 tablespoon tarragon

½ cup heavy cream or broth
2 cups thin gravy

❮[Add to the gravy chestnuts or other nuts of your choice. Flavor with chopped tarragon. Thin as necessary with rich cream or broth. Serve over rice. Makes 2¼ cups.

HORSERADISH SAUCE
HANCOCK SHAKER VILLAGE

2 tablespoons butter
2 tablespoons flour
¾ cup milk or heavy cream
Salt and pepper to taste
2 egg yolks, beaten
2 tablespoons lemon juice
2 tablespoons tarragon vinegar

4 tablespoons grated horseradish
  root, juice and all (or bottled
  horseradish)
1 tablespoon finely chopped parsley
1 tablespoon finely chopped
  tarragon

❮[This sauce is best made in the top of a double boiler set over boiling water. Melt butter and add flour. Add milk or cream and stir until smooth. Add salt, pepper, egg yolks, lemon juice, and vinegar, cooking over a low boil. When mixture is smooth, add horseradish. Stir well and add parsley and tarragon. Makes 1½ cups.

Other uses:

To 1 cup mayonnaise add 2 tablespoons horseradish sauce. Blend ingredients together. Very good with potato salad.

To 4 cups apple sauce add 1 tablespoon horseradish sauce—or more to taste.

To 6 cups vegetable salad made with chopped carrots, chopped peas, chopped celery and 2 tablespoons chopped mixed herbs add 4 tablespoons horseradish mayonnaise.

HERB MUSTARD USING HONEY
HANCOCK SHAKER VILLAGE

3 tablespoons dry mustard
½ cup herb vinegar
1 tablespoon fresh chopped herb
  (basil or tarragon) or 1 teaspoon
  dried

1 tablespoon honey

([Combine mustard, vinegar, and herbs. Cook gently for 4 minutes, then add honey. Simmer. When reduced and thick, strain and put in jar and seal. Makes 1 cup.

Note: The recipe can easily be doubled. Use dark powdered mustard; it is milder than the french.

The thrifty Shaker Sisters pickled or preserved most anything to add relish and interest to food. Pickled nasturtium pods were used as capers are today.

PICKLED NASTURTIUM PODS
HANCOCK SHAKER VILLAGE

Flowers and leaves are often used in salads. The Shakers pickled nasturtium pods, picked as soon as the blossoms dropped, in vinegar.

1½ cups salt	6 cups nasturtium pods,
1 gallon water	homegrown
1 cup fresh herbs, any combination,	4 cups tarragon vinegar
basil, tarragon, chives, dill,	2 cups dry sherry
pounded	

([Make a 10-percent brine solution by mixing the salt and water; then add the fresh pounded herbs. Remove and soak the pods in this solution for 3 days. Drain, then drop the pods into boiling vinegar. Remove pods, place in small bottles, cover with sherry, and fill bottles to top. Add sherry or fresh tarragon vinegar. Makes 2 quarts.

SWEET MUSTARD
HANCOCK SHAKER VILLAGE

1 tablespoon ground yellow	1 tablespoon honey
mustard (from the seed)	½ teaspoon salt
2 tablespoons warm water	

([Grind about 2 tablespoons of mustard seed and sift so you get a smooth powder. Add 2 tablespoons warm water to make a paste. Add more powder, then gradually beat in teaspoon by teaspoon of honey, not making the mixture too stiff. Add some salt to taste. The mustard should be runny. Makes 6 ounces.

HONEY MUSTARD
HANCOCK SHAKER VILLAGE

3 tablespoons dry mustard
boiling water
½ teaspoon salt
1 tablespoon olive oil

1 tablespoon honey
1 egg yolk, well beaten
1 teaspoon vinegar (optional)

([Pour a little boiling water over 3 tablespoons of dry mustard. Add salt and olive oil. Stir in honey slowly. Add well-beaten egg yolk and cook over low heat until thickened. Add vinegar (white) if desired. Omit egg or add more honey to taste, if desired. Allow to sit for several days. Makes 6 ounces.

TANGY TOMATO JELLY
FROM THE GOOD ROOM
HANCOCK SHAKER VILLAGE

1¾ cups canned tomato juice
½ cup fresh lemon juice
2 teaspoons Tabasco sauce
4 cups sugar

1 package (3 ounces) liquid pectin (Certo)
½ cup finely chopped basil

([In a 6-quart pot, combine all ingredients except pectin. Stir over high heat until mixture comes to a full, rolling boil. Boil for 1 minute, stirring constantly. Remove from heat. Stir for 2 minutes while removing any foam (there will not be much). Add pectin. Pour immediately into hot sterilized glasses. Seal immediately with parafin. Makes 4 8-ounce jars.

Note: Adding about 1 teaspoon butter will cut down on foam, as will using a wooden spoon. Recipe can be doubled to make a worthwhile yield.

TOMATO JUICE
FROM THE GOOD ROOM
HANCOCK SHAKER VILLAGE

1 cup diced celery, plus a few leaves
4 tablespoons sugar
3 whole cloves
1 thick slice of onion, without outer skin

1 teaspoon salt
½ cup basil leaves
½ cup tarragon leaves
Lemon juice, to taste
1 quart tomato juice

([Mix all ingredients except lemon juice in a large pot. Let simmer 20 minutes over low heat. Cool, strain, add lemon juice to taste. SERVES 4.

HERB MIXES

Herbs go back in history hundreds of years—the Romans when they went to Britain took 400 different herbs with them, it is said, for both culinary and medical use. Among these are many we use today: parsley, onions, chives, lovage, sage, mint, chervil, basil, thyme, and many more.

The Shakers immigrating to America may have brought herbs with them, but once established they undoubtedly looked around for wild herbs; and as converts joined them in established Shaker communities, the growing of herbs for use in daily cooking and in a thriving medicinal herb industry became a source of considerable revenue.

The choice of ingredients and proportions are up to you! Simply mix, taste your concoction, adjust until you're satisfied, bottle and store. The herbs may be used whole leaf, sieved or ground, but they must be thoroughly mixed. A good method when using whole-leaf herbs is to measure them, mix well, and then rub through a sieve. Or teaspoons of the whole-leaf mix may be sewn into cheesecloth bags, which are used like a fresh bouquet.

These mixes have many wonderful uses. They provide quick and unique flavoring for (especially canned or frozen) soups, stews, vegetables and meats. They can also be used to flavor herb butter, herb croutons and the like.

HANCOCK SHAKER VILLAGE HERB MIX

This is a blend of the following herbs, dried and without stems or flowering portion: parsley, basil, marjoram, oregano, thyme, tarragon, sage, summer savory. Choice of proportions optional. Mix, adjust, taste, add, subtract. Use sparingly.

A good method when using leaf herbs is to measure them, mix well, and then rub through a sieve. Or teaspoons of the whole-leaf mix may be sewn into cheesecloth bags, which are used like a fresh bouquet. These mixes are especially good for flavoring stews, fine soups and the like.

The recipe for the *Herb Mix* prepared at Hancock Shaker Village is not available. It is a unique blend of parsley, basil, marjoram, oregano, thyme, tarragon, sage, and summer savory. It is sold only at the Hancock Shaker Village stores.

In making it, remember that equal quantities of all but sage and tarragon make a good mix. Amounts of these two stronger herbs should be reduced.

1 tablespoon dried parsley	1 tablespoon dried thyme
1 tablespoon dried basil	1 tablespoon dried summer savory
1 tablespoon dried marjoram	½ tablespoon dried tarragon
1 tablespoon dried oregano	½ tablespoon dried sage

The procedure depends on individual tastes for certain herbs.

Suggestions:

For ground beef: equal parts summer savory, basil, sweet marjoram, thyme, parsley, lovage, or celery

For lamb and veal: equal parts sweet marjoram, summer savory, rosemary

For fish: equal parts sweet marjoram, thyme, basil, sage, crushed fennel seeds

For egg and chicken: equal parts summer savory, tarragon, chervil, basil, chives

For pork: equal parts sage, basil, summer savory

For vegetables: equal parts summer savory, sweet marjoram, chervil, basil

For soups and stews: two parts parsley or marjoram and two parts celery or lovage leaves to one part each of sage, rosemary and dried ground lemon peel

(Lovage is a perennial, very hardy, not hard to grow, but seldom seen —except in specialty markets—taste resembles celery.)

General mix: One part each of marjoram, oregano, and thyme; two parts basil; three parts parsley; pinch of garlic or celery salt

The Shakers raised acres of sage as a money crop. It was probably the herb used in greatest quantity in the eighteenth and nineteenth centuries, as it was strong enough to mask the flavor of meats past their prime. It was also the primary flavor in sausage meat. Salt, vinegar, mustard and pepper seem to have been the other popular seasonings of the time. Shaker cooks didn't limit themselves to these few, however. They believed, so we understand, that herbs were beneficial to their health. This belief is supported by the appearance of medicinal herbs in Shaker catalogs as early as 1830, and before this, in journals written in the various communities.

One of the best professional accounts of the Shaker medicinal herb business was printed in *The Boston Medical & Surgical Journal* in September 1853:

> "Throughout New England, as well as other states of the Union, immense quantities of indigenous medicinal plants are on sale, in convenient forms, prepared by those conscientious, reliable people, known as Shakers. . . . They have no competitors of equal renown. In order to be able to speak understandingly in regard to the character of their medicines, we made a special visit to the Society at Harvard, Massachusetts, week before last. . . . With the knowledge thus acquired on the spot, in reference to this subject, we are prepared to encourage druggists and apothecaries throughout the country, to give their articles a preference over those from other sources. . . . Under the humble term of Shaker Herbs, the very best remedies in the vegetable kingdom are distributed extensively over the United States, and they deserve to be equally well patronized in Europe."

NOTE IN A SISTER'S "DAYBOOK"
HANCOCK SHAKER VILLAGE

Mint—Lamb
Fennel—Fish
Basil—Tomatoes
Savory—String beans

Caraway—Cookies and cabbage
Tarragon—Eggs
Thyme—Clam Chowder

SUGARED BUTTERNUTS THE SHAKER WAY
HANCOCK SHAKER VILLAGE

Shakers used butternuts from their forests. Walnuts can also be used.

2 cups brown sugar
½ cup water
2 cups butternuts, or walnuts

1 cup granulated sugar
1 cup confectioner's sugar

Boil brown sugar and water until a candy thermometer inserted in mixture reads 240° F. and it spins a dry thread; care should be taken not to overboil. Let cool a trifle. Place nuts in pie tin to cover bottom. Pour syrup on them, coating all sides of nuts. Then empty them into granulated sugar while still wet. Stir until well covered, then coat one or two at a time with confectioner's sugar. Stir well and place on plates to dry. This amount of syrup will coat 1 pound of nuts or perhaps more.

HERB CROUTONS

Croutons are the perfect garnish for soup, salads, and noodles, and are good snacks.

6 slices bread, fresh or stale
butter or oil, for frying

choose from:
fresh basil, chives, parsley, chopped
seeds of caraway, dill, fennel, anise
    (ground slightly)

⟪[*To prepare sautéed croutons:* Dice bread and sauté in butter or oil until evenly browned, about 5 minutes.

To prepare baked croutons: Butter the bread and dice it. Preheat oven to 375° F. and brown on cookie sheets for 10 minutes.

While they are still hot, drop sautéed or baked croutons into a paper bag containing salt, paprika, grated cheese, and/or finely minced fresh herbs. Close the bag and shake until croutons are evenly coated. Makes 1 quart croutons.

HERB BUTTER

1 stick (4 ounces) butter
2 tablespoons fresh or 1–3
    teaspoons dried herb

1 teaspoon lemon juice

⟪[Have butter at room temperature. Mince herbs with a sharp knife. Beat them, with lemon juice to moisten, thoroughly into butter. Put into custard cups or butter tubs for serving. Refrigerate or freeze. Makes ½ cup.

Suggestions:
   Use unsalted or lightly salted butter, adding garlic salt to round out the flavor
   Try herbs singly and in combination, such as thyme and summer savory; or basil, chives, tarragon, and thyme

HERB SALT

Perfect for soups, stews; to flavor meats and vegetables, such as corn on the cob.

Shaker Spiced Salt

1½ teaspoons each powdered thyme, bay leaf, black pepper and nutmeg	3 teaspoons powdered cloves
	3 teaspoons salt
¾ teaspoon each cayenne and marjoram	

❲*To prepare by hand:* Grind herbs to a powder, using a mortar and pestle. Sift together, and mix thoroughly with salt.

To prepare with a blender: Put herbs in blender and process at low speed. Makes ⅓ cup.

Choose from among these suggested combinations:

Garlic powder and celery salt are good basics

Paprika, red pepper, dry mustard add color as well as flavor

One part herbs to one part salt is a good rule for determining proportions

BASIC HERB RECIPES

❲*Herbs are an invitation to be creative.* Choose the ones you use and the proportions you use them in according to your own (good) taste. Experiment with different combinations and try them on a variety of foods.

Here are some ways for you to introduce herbs into familiar dishes by subtly altering standard ingredients.

HERB VINEGAR

Very good, particularly in salad dressings and sauces; wherever vinegar is called for.

Herbs of your choice (see suggestions below)	Vinegar, either cider or white

❲Put fresh herbs in wide-mouth sterilized jar, using about 2 tablespoons fresh chopped herb per cup of vinegar (or ½ cup per quart). Heat vinegar but do not boil. Pour over herb, filling to neck of jar. Seal tightly and allow to stand for 2 weeks. Decant, press liquid from herb leaves, strain and rebottle. Makes 1 quart.

Note: Cider vinegar is preferred for all but sage and mint, with which use white vinegar. Try tarragon, rosemary, basil (especially purple basil!), thyme, lemon balm or lemon verbene, mint, sage, or dill.

HERB SANDWICH FILLING
HANCOCK SHAKER VILLAGE

3 eggs, hard-boiled and chopped
8 ounces cream cheese, softened
1 stick (½ cup) butter, melted
8 stuffed green olives, chopped

Herbs to taste (1 tablespoon minced fresh basil or summer savory would be a good starter)

⟮Mix eggs with the cream cheese. Add butter, olives, and herbs. Fresh herbs should be finely chopped; if dried, pulverized. Spread on crackers, potato chips, or bread. Makes enough filling for 6 sandwiches.

POWDERED PARSLEY (OR OTHER HERBS)
HANCOCK SHAKER VILLAGE

A quick way to preserve the season's bounty.

1 bunch parsley leaves

⟮Preheat oven to 350° F.
   Pick leaves from the stems and plunge leaves into boiling salted water—enough to just cover the herb. Keep leaves in water only long enough to wilt—about 30 seconds. Drain. Spread leaves on a fine wire mesh laid on a flat pan. Put in oven until the leaves are dry and brittle, watching carefully to avoid burning. This will take 5 to 10 minutes. Rub the leaves through a fine sieve or strainer and store in bottle with tight cover. Makes 1 cup.

SYLLABUB FROM THE COW

⟮In *Listen for a Lonesome Drum*, Carl Carmer writes about the Shakers and in particular about one of his visits with the Shakers at Mount Lebanon, "The late-winter sun was promising the spring," and he spent the afternoon with the Neill sisters (blood sisters—Emma, age 92, and

Sadie, age 88). It was his first visit to a Shaker settlement, but like many visitors he benefitted from some straightforward talk from the aged Shakers: "He has come to talk with us about the Shakers, Sister Emma." . . . "I think he wants to write about us."

He also visited their shop and came away with the following recipes, which I've included in both original and updated versions:

To Make a Fine Syllabub from the Cow

Sweeten a quart of cyder with double refined sugar, grate nutmeg into it, then milk your cow into your liquor, when you have thus added what quantity of milk you think proper, pour half a pint or more, in proportion to the quantity of syllabub you make, of the sweetest cream you can get all over it.

Here's the modern version of the recipe:

Syllabub or Milk Punch   1 **quart milk**
1 **quart of apple cider**   1 **teaspoon powdered nutmeg**
½ **cup sugar**   1 **cup cream**

〔Blend cider, sugar, milk, and nutmeg until frothy. Add cream slowly, stirring constantly until smooth. Makes 8–9 cups.

·⁞ BIBLIOGRAPHY ⁞·

WE have consulted the following sources in studying the background of Shaker cooking.

〈The most important printed work has been the Shakers' own monthly periodical, successively entitled *The Shaker,* the *Shaker and Shakeress, The Shaker Manifesto,* and *The Manifesto,* published first at Watervliet, New York, and later at New Lebanon, New York, and Canterbury, New Hampshire, from 1871 through 1899. Recipes and household hints were included in great numbers in a column called "Home Topics," which also contained many items pertaining to diet and its relation to health.

Other printed works which we have found useful are the following:

Andrews, Edward D. *The Community Industries of the Shakers,* Albany, N. Y., 1933.

———. *The People Called Shakers,* New York, 1953.

Anon. *A Concise History of the Shakers and their Communal Homes,* 1899.

———. *Concise Statements Concerning the Life and Religious Views of the Shakers,* Mt. Lebanon, N. Y., 1899.

———. *Gentle Manners, A Guide to Good Morals.*

———. *Shaker Almanac,* New York, 1884, 1886.

Avery, Giles B. *Sketches of Shakers and Shakerism,* Albany, N. Y., 1883.

Evans, Frederick W. *Shakerism in London,* London, 1887.

———. *Shakers and Shakerism,* New York, 1858.

Holloway, Mark. *Heavens on Earth,* London, 1951.

Lamson, David. *Two Years' Experience among the Shakers* [at Hancock], West Boylston, Mass., 1848.

Melcher, Marguerite F. *The Shaker Adventure,* Princeton, N. J., 1941.

Neal, [Mary] Julia. *By Their Fruits,* Chapel Hill, N. C., 1947.

———(ed.). *The Journal of Eldress Nancy,* Nashville, Tenn., 1963.

Piercy, Caroline B. *The Valley of God's Pleasure,* New York, 1951.

Sears, Clara Endicott. *Gleanings from Old Shaker Journals,* Boston, 1916.

White, Anna, and Taylor, Leila. *Shakerism: Its Message and Meaning,* Columbus, Ohio, 1904.